The Personal Correspondence of Sam Houston

Volume II: 1846–1848

The Personal Correspondence of Sam Houston

of Sam Houston

Volume II: 1846–1848

edited by
Madge Thornall Roberts

University of North Texas Press ∽ Denton, Texas

Requests for permission to reproduce material from this work
should be sent to:

Permissions
University of North Texas Press
PO Box 311336
Denton TX 76203
940-565-2142

The paper used in this book meets the minimum requirements of the American
National Standard for Permanence of Paper for Printed
Library Materials, Z39.48.1984.

Library of Congress Cataloging-in-Publication Data

Houston, Sam, 1793–1863.
The personal correspondence of Sam Houston / edited by
Madge Thornall Roberts.
p.   cm.
Includes bibliographical references and index.
Contents: v. 2. 1846–1848—
ISBN 1-57441-031-8 (alk. paper)
1. Houston, Sam. 1793–1863—Correspondence. 2. Governors—Texas—
Correspondence. 3. Legislators—United States—Correspondence. 4. Texas—
Politics and government—To 1846. 5. Texas—Politics and government—1846–
1865. I. Roberts, Madge Thornall, 1929– . II. Title.

| F390.H833   1994 | 95-36738 |
| 976.4'04'092—dc20 | CIP |

Cover art by Dana Adams

TABLE OF CONTENTS

Preface

The editorial guidelines for Volume I have been continued in this work, with the exception of omitting the address at the end of Houston's letters. Because of poor quality of the paper and ink used in the letters from Volume I, they were very difficult to read. While it was possible to decipher most of the words, many punctuation marks were no doubt missed in the maze of spots and bleed-throughs from the opposite sides. Cross-writings also added to the problems.

In transcribing these later letters, which were written on a higher quality of paper and were much more legible, I became aware of Houston's unusual punctuation patterns. His use of commas followed no rules I had ever seen. It may be that he added them as he paused to replace his ink, or when his train of thought was interrupted. One can almost visualize his pausing at his desk in the Senate to listen to a speech, or his stopping to answer a question posed by a visitor in his rooms. The letters in this volume have been transcribed with the commas exactly as Houston placed them. For some of the letters, this meant examining them with a magnifying glass.

Adding to the problem of deciphering the letters in the current volume was the fact that for much of this time period Houston was suffering from the effects of a flair-up of an old shoulder wound from the War of 1812. Apparently, this caused his hand to shake, spattering ink spots onto the letters. There were times when I simply had to make an editorial decision as to whether a mark was an ink spatter or a comma.

As in the previous volume, word omissions or repetitions are usually found at the beginning of a new page. Often, Houston added a postscript explaining that he did not have time to re-read the letter to check for mistakes.

In this volume, Houston's personal correspondence begins when he leaves Texas in 1846 to travel to Washington, D.C., to take his place in Congress as a U.S. Senator. He was away from home for long periods of time. His letters reflect his opinions on national leaders, the Mexican War, and the problems facing Texas. They also express his mixed emotions about his position, as he longs to be with his family and begins to realize the sacrifice he (and they) must make in order for him to have a public service career.

Margaret's letters are filled with descriptions of the children and what she describes as "homely details," which she says would not bear repeating at a political gathering. However, she often expresses her opinion on political events. Her accounts of life on Raven Hill and in Huntsville paint an accurate picture of the problems faced by many of the women during this era of American History. Since mail went out only once a week, her letters were long and her handwriting small.

As with the previous volume, we are often left with puzzling allusions to events that happened when Sam and Margaret were together. No explanation has been located, for instance, for Margaret's "dream of the map" which so fascinated Houston, or for the exact reason of the estrangement of the Houston and Moore families.

New information to be found in these letters includes Houston's decision not to be a candidate for vice president, his views on the presidential election, his struggle over his religious faith, his anguish over his sister Mary's mysterious illness and Margaret's operation for a breast tumor, and physical information which includes Margaret's height and Houston's weight.

I am grateful to the Rhode Island Historical Society for allowing the use of the Houston correspondence from the Alva Woods Papers. I wish to thank Weldon Sneed and other descendants of Virginia Thorn for sharing their family documents with me. Only a small portion of this research has been used in the current volume, but much more of it will be utilized in Volume III of *The Personal Correspondence of Sam Houston.*

Madge Thornall Roberts
San Antonio, Texas

Chapter I

⤬

March 6, 1846 —August 10, 1846

April 29, 1846: Sam Houston to Margaret Houston
April 30, 1846: Sam Houston to Margaret Houston
May 1, 1846: Margaret Houston to Sam Houston
May 2, 1846: Sam Houston to Margaret Houston
May 4, 1846: Margaret Houston to Sam Houston
May 7, 1846: Sam Houston to Margaret Houston
May 10, 1846: Sam Houston to Margaret Houston
May 15, 1846: Sam Houston to Margaret Houston
May 15, 1846: Sam Houston to Margaret Houston
May 16, 1846: Margaret Houston to Sam Houston
May 20, 1846: Sam Houston to Margaret Houston
May 21, 1846: Sam Houston to Margaret Houston
May 25, 1846: Sam Houston to Margaret Houston
May 28, 1846: Margaret Houston to Sam Houston
May 29, 1846: Sam Houston to Margaret Houston
May 30, 1846: Sam Houston to Margaret Houston
June 1, [2], 1846: Sam Houston to Margaret Houston
June 1, 1846: Sam Houston to Margaret Houston
June 3, 1846: Sam Houston to Margaret Houston
June 4, 1846: Sam Houston to Margaret Houston
June 5, 1846: Sam Houston to Margaret Houston
June 7, 1846: Sam Houston to Margaret Houston
June 9, 1846: Sam Houston to Margaret Houston
June 10, 1846: Sam Houston to Margaret Houston
June 12, 1846: Margaret Houston to Almira Woods
June 12, 1846: Margaret Houston to Sam Houston
June 14, 1846: Sam Houston to Margaret Houston
June 16, 1846: Sam Houston to Margaret Houston
June 19, 1846: Sam Houston to Margaret Houston
June 19, 1846: Sam Houston to Margaret Houston
June 20, 1846: Margaret Houston to Sam Houston
(with note from Sam Houston, Jr.)
June 24, 1846: Sam Houston to Margaret Houston
June 25, 1846: Sam Houston to Margaret Houston
June 28, 1846: Sam Houston to Margaret Houston

Houston wrote the following letter to his brother-in-law on the eve of his departure to Washington, D.C., to serve as senator for the new state of Texas in the first session of the Twenty-ninth Congress.

[This letter is from the Atascosito Historical Society Collection, Sam Houston Library and Research Center, Liberty, Texas.]

To Maj. Vernal B Lea,[1] Grand Cane, Liberty County, Texas

Raven Hill[2]
6th March 1846

My Dear Vernal,

Tomorrow, at sun rise, I expect to set out by way of Houston for Washington City.[3] I was in hopes to have seen you here, previous to my setting out. It can't be the case now. I write by advisement of my dear Maggy. We are of opinion, that she can not go to Trinity,[4] by land at this time, at least if it would be possible to do so at a future day. Nor is there a much better chance by water. A buggy could not now go, and under existing circumstances, it would be neither proper, nor possible, as she thinks. Will it not be well, for Mother,[5] if possible to come, and stay with Margaret? If she can not, can not Sister,[6] and Sarah Ann,[7] one, or both? If possible I do hope some one, or more will come! Virginia[8] does not enter into this calculation at all!

I am called on suddenly to leave, and Mother so positively objected to Margaret's going on, that I am compelled to leave her unprepared. She has ample means to get anything that she may desire, or need. If Mr Moore[9] had arrived, I would be satisfied. I can only say that he has reached Galveston, or on the way. On the 15th of Feby, he was near the mouth of the Tennessee river, coming on well, but had set out in flat Boats. I hope he will soon be here. It may be that he will soon be here, and gratify my wishes. Taking every thing into view, I doubt much if it would not be best for Margaret to stay here during my absence. The time, trouble, and risk of removal, all regarded wou'd seem to decide in favor, of her stay here!

It seems that Nancy is not suited to us, and says she is sorry, that she had left her old mistress. Margaret, and myself have come to that conclusion, if you should think well of it all round, to let Vincy, and her two youngest children go, with your land, or the price of it, and take in exchange, Warner, and Betsy.[10] If you should not accept this proposition, why there is no harm done, (as the saying is.)

What the present, or probable advantages would be, you can judge as much about as we can. It may not be fair, but if in any respect, you should think it not a fair proposal, I really do not wish it accepted, and you know Margaret well enough to be assured, that the cause of it is a desire of convenience, and not a wish to make gain by traffic.[11]

If you chuse [sic], you can communicate it without further negotiation. I hope you will find time, to write to me often during my anxious, and painful absence.

We have not received a line from Grand Cane since you left us! Why has no one written? We hope to hear from you to night by the mail.

[no signature]

[1]Margaret's brother. Note: Relatives of Margaret and Sam Houston are listed in the appendix of Volume 1 of this series, pp. 372–375. Hereinafter these relatives will be identified for clarification only.
[2]The Houston's plantation home located fourteen miles from Huntsville, Texas.
[3]Washington, D.C.
[4]Grand Cane where Vernal Lea and their sister Antoinette Lea Bledsoe lived.
[5]Margaret's mother, Nancy Lea.
[6]Antoinette Lea Bledsoe.
[7]Sarah Ann Royston, Margaret's niece, nicknamed "Tose."
[8]Virginia Thorn. In 1842, Vernal Lea had been appointed the guardian of five-year-old Virginia in Galveston with the approval of her step-father, Dr. C. F. Worcester. Vernal then asked Nancy Lea to care for her. The Houstons later took Virginia into their household. Thorn-Gott family records furnished by their descendant, Tom Weldon Sneed, San Antonio.
[9]Samuel Moore, the husband of Houston's sister Eliza. The Moores were in the process of moving to Texas.
[10]Nancy, Vincy, Warner and Betsy were slaves belonging to the Houston family.
[11]Houston is referring to the practice Margaret had of selling the slaves with which she had problems.

5 : March 6, 1846—August 10, 1846

The following is the first letter Houston wrote to Margaret while on his journey to the nation's capital:

Huntsville, Texas
7th March, 1846

My Very Dear Margaret,

It is nine oclock, and I have just come from making a speech in the Academy.[1] I had no intention, nor expectation of speaking when I came here, nor <u>desire</u>. It is now over, and the folks appeared well pleased. I paid off some old scores, to my defamers, and I learned that even Mr. Stovall,[2] was quite delighted. I have not seen him, out of the house. Tomorrow, I hope to get off by nine oclock, and the citizens propose to give me an escort, but of what character, or size, I have not inquired. I will spend the night with Colonel McDonald.[3] Mrs Mc[4] was kind in her enquiries for you and Sam.[5] She says if you pass the summer at Raven Hill, she will visit you, as she is anxious to see you both. She looks quite <u>lean</u>, tho' Jimmy has been weaned, this six months.

I will now my dearest, speak of my departure from home to day. I had no forebodings of ill, and yet my heart was wrung, with extreme sorrow, and regret. No matter what may await me, in the character of success, or earthly fame, they will be poor requitals for what I felt. When I had rode four miles in comparative silence, I tried to sing "oft in the stilly night," as it was a sad air, and regret that I do not know the words of "Home Sweet Home," homely, as our home is, for surely it is, & will be the home of my affections. I feel truly sad, yet cheerful, that I left you in apparently better health, than usual, as I think.

I pray my dear, that you will indulge, as few regrets as possible. You can enjoy the consolation of a Saviors promises, of salvation. We are in his merciful, and beneficent care, and you will be constant, at the Throne of Grace! His ways, are wisdom, and past finding out. These are trials to us, which we have to endure, and had I sought for them, I would feel more unhappy than I now do. Had my present attitude been of my own choosing, or from feelings of selfishness, or ambition, my bitter feelings would weigh me down. I would believe that I was neglecting the best of wives, & the dearest of companions. Were you in all respects situated, as I could desire, and as I sincerely do desire, I wou'd feel more at ease than I now do. I hope however, that you will find in my relations, so soon as they arrive, that they entertain for you, all the affections, and consideration, that they could do for a sister, or aunt. I also hope that Mother can come up, and stay with you. This I desire may be done, as I think you cannot reach the Trinity, by any means, in safety. I have been interrupted by company since I began this letter, and it is now late. It was well that I came this rout [sic], for had I passed the lower rout, I could not have crossed the creeks. I hope you will get on well! Yes dearest, very well! You will please to kiss our dear Niece,[6] and Sam for me, and give them a hearty squeeze, each, for me, with a portion of my love. I was sorry that Sam, was in such a way, when I left home. He pointed at my cheek, and said, "Pappa what is that? Is it a tear??" I said "Yes my son," in hopes that he would sympathize with me, but I was <u>mistaken</u> in Sam, as <u>usual</u>. Dearest, I must close my epistle, with assurances, of my unceasing love for you, and prayers, for your health, and happiness.

Thy faithful & devoted husband
Houston

Dearest, write to me at Washington, often as you can!

[1]The Huntsville Academy, also known as the Brick Academy. Identified in Walter Prescott Webb, et. al., *Handbook of Texas* (Austin: Texas State Historical Association, 1952), vol. 1, 867. Hereinafter entries from this work will be identified as *Handbook of Texas*.
[2]The Reverend A. L. Stoval, a Baptist minister. Identified in Mabel Ponder Wilson, Dorothy Youngblood Woodyerd, and Rosa Lee Busby, compilers, *Some Early Alabama Churches* (Birmingham: Alabama Society of the Daughters of the American Revolution, 1973), 94.
[3]Alexander MacDonald. Identified in the vertical files of the Sam Houston Memorial Museum, Huntsville, Texas.
[4]Margaret Roberts MacDonald. Ibid.
[5]Sam Houston, Jr., now almost three years old.
[6]Elizabeth "Betty" Moore.

7 : March 6, 1846—August 10, 1846

Houston
10th March 1846

My very dear Wife,

To day about 1 oclock I came to Town. I ate dinner, seen [sic] to some matters, & by invitation, with several gentlemen, went to the arsenal, and received a salute of twenty-eight guns.[1] I there saw the U States flag, flying in the breeze. We do really form part, and parcel of the American Union. It may be that I will speak tomorrow at 12 oclock. I hope to be off by 3 oclock P.M. by the Boat. Mr Moore is at the Island, and all the family, but Houston[2] who has gone up the Trinity, with the baggage, and Negroes. Ire this, I hope you have seen him.

I have seen Jose,[3] and he says he will go up tomorrow, and I hope he will stay the summer. Mr Moore sent word, that he will await me, at the Island. I am anxious to see the family. If Mr Moore should wish to stay with you, until he can get his place in some kind of order, to go to, if it is agreeable to you, I wish it to be so. If he should go home, & Houston can stay with you, if Mother can come up, and stay with you, it may be best for you to spend your time, at Raven Hill. I will see Mr Moore, and talk to him about these matters. Your friends are all well, and make a thousand enquiries for you, Miss Betty & Sam. Mrs Nichols[4] has another fine son. The Col[5] looks very saucy! I understand that a boat will be in readiness at the Island, to sail for Orleans, when I reach there. Mr Ben Ellis is here, and Mr Worsham.[6] They start home early tomorrow. I send [sic] word to Mother, or some of the family, to go, and stay with you. I hope my dear, you will not be lonesome, while I am gone. I feel only concerned, for your happiness. I desire that you should want nothing, but that you should have every thing that you desire.

The braid is not in town. I will send it from Galveston, or Orleans. The silk I send you. By Sister Eliza I wish to send some things, if I can see any thing that I think will suit you. I send a horse, which I traded for. My paint became some what tired, and I swapped him off. The "Black Hawk," I am informed, is a fine harness, or work horse. This is well if true. Either Mr Moore, or me will need him, for the crop.

11 March

8 oclock P.M. The Boat did not arrive that was expected this morning, until this moment. If any news has been bro't by her, I am not apprised of it, but will be previous to sealing my letter. The speech went off to day at 4 oclock P.M.[7] If my vanity would have allow'd of it, I might have been flattered, for my opponents heretofore, as well as my friends were pleased, and praised the speech. Some rank Whigs from Virginia assured me, that they would be my friends in [the] future. Well! This was all well enough, but I solemnly declare, my Love, it did not compensate me, for my absence from you, and our dear Boy. My thoughts fly to, and embrace you, while sad, & painful reality, tells me that, I am distant, in sense, from all, that I most love on earth!

Had you been present, I might have said, and felt, that I was truly gratified, but as it was, all that I saw, and heard, left in my heart, the pang of absence.

Mr Miller[8] has not yet arrived, but I will expect him, either to come to night, or to join me soon at the city. You may rely upon it, that I will have him, if possible, with me.

What do you think? One of the faces which I recognized in the church, was your great friend Mrs Reily.[9] She has been home (& Donny) about two weeks, and is in daily expectation, of the Colonels arrival.[10] She has not seen him since he sailed for Europe.[11] I walked home with Madam from church to her gate, and she assured me that she would write to you to night, and send me the letter, that I may give it to Mr Roark,[12] for you in the morning. I will send it with pleasure, for I do really believe that she loves you, for your own sake. She had not heard that you were sick in Nashville, so I did not tell her the particulars, nor have I told her the reason of your not going on, with me. I informed her of the accession to your Library, and its character. It afforded her an opportunity, of paying you a pretty, and deserved compliment, by saying, that you were already, better informed upon Subjects of Theology, than any lady that she knew in Texas, (or I think "any lady").

This moment, I learn that letters have arrived from the Island for me, from our kindred, but the bearer has not handed over.

I send you some Figs, and candy, a pair of shoes for Sam, one pair for Billy,[13] and one for Mrs Palmer.[14] I went to Mr Milbys,[15] and he had sold all his, no less than a hundred pair. I then looked, and could get none of the kind, nor could I get a pair of 5's or 5/2s, so I send a pair of 6's which only cost $1.00. You will owe 25 cents to Mrs P. if they should suit her, and if they will not, they will do some of our Nieces, and you can pay her, $1.25 cents. Dearest, I will send you a few apples. The reasons that more are not sent, is, that I do not wish, to burden the animal. I sent two pounds of "all sorts" of candy, except Peppermint, and two pounds of Figs! I have been interrupted, and it has grown late, so that I must close for to night, as it may be that I will have to tell you some news, that may have come by the Boat. As yet I have lost no time, for the Galveston, instead of returning to New Orleans, went to Corpus Christi, & will not leave for Orleans, until tomorrow, or next day. The Alabama is expected on tomorrow, and if so, I hope to go over on her, as I abhor the <u>Wright</u>[16] <u>Concern</u>. Good night Love!!!

12th Mr Roark & Jose will set out, and the Boat is to be off at 10 oclock to day. You will detain Jose, if you think well of it, and I will arrange matters about his compensation. He will go to work on the farm, I expect. His compensation will be a mere trifle. You can then have the services of Maria,[17] I hope, as I think, it is only her care for him, that has caused her sickness.

I send you a bridle my Love.

Oh Dearest, you can have no idea, of my love, and my regrets, at leaving home. Press Sam & Betty to your bosom for me, and be assured of my unalterable, and devoted affection. Tell Mr Palmer[18] to do the best that he can. I intend to be satisfied.

Thy ever devoted Husband
Sam Houston

P.S. I am sorry the apples are so poor. They are pickled, and the best in the city.

Houston

[1]Texas was the twenty-eighth state in the Union.

[2]Houston's nephew, Houston Moore, the son of Eliza and Samuel A. Moore.

[3]A field hand hired by Houston. He is believed to have been the husband of Maria.

[4]Margaret "Mag" Stone Nichols. For a biography see Annie Doom Pickrell, *Pioneer Women of Texas* (Austin, Tex.: State House Press, 1991), 270–74.

[5]Ebenezer Nichols. Ibid.

[6]Archer B. Worsham. Both Ellis and Worsham are identified as neighbors of the Houstons in Grand Cane in J. H. H. Ellis, *Sam Houston and Related Spiritual Forces* (Houston, Tex.: Concord Press, 1945), 51.

[7]Houston spoke at the Methodist Church, giving his views on "Oregon and other questions," avowing his determination to sustain the policy of President Polk. Llerena Friend, *Sam Houston: The Great Designer* (Austin: University of Texas Press, 1954), 168. For a report of the speech see *Telegraph and Texas Register,* March 18, 1846.

[8]Washington D. Miller, who would serve as Houston's secretary. Identified in Sam Houston, *The Writings of Sam Houston*, ed. Amelia W. Williams and Eugene C. Barker (Austin: University of Texas Press, 1938–43), vol. 2, 389n. Hereinafter these works will be referred to as *Writings.*

[9]Ellen Hart (Mrs. James) Reily. Identified in Hugh Best, *Debrett's Texas Peerage* (New York: Coward-McCann, 1983), 334.

[10]Colonel James Reily. Ibid.

[11]Reily had served as U.S. Minister to Russia under President Buchanan. *Handbook of Texas*, vol. 2, 459.

[12]Reed W. Roark. Identified as a citizen of Walker County in Marion Day Mullins, compiler, *Republic of Texas Poll Lists for 1846* (Baltimore: Genealogical Publishing Company, 1982), 143. Hereinafter referred to as *Poll Lists*.

[13]A young Houston slave.

[14]Houston is probably referring to Rachel (Mrs. Thomas) Palmer, identified in *1850 Census of Texas*, V. K. Carpenter, transcriber, (Huntsville, Ark.: Century Enterprises, 1969), vol. 3, 1538. Hereinafter referred to as *1850 Census.*

[15]William Polk Milby. For a biography see *Handbook of Texas*, vol. 2, 193.

[16]Captain James Wright was the captain of the *Neptune*. He is identified in vol. 3 of the collection of Houston Materials in the Barker History Center, University of Texas, Austin.

[17]A servant, who was probably the wife of Jose.

[18]Thomas Palmer was helping Margaret oversee the farm at Raven Hill. Identified in *1850 Census,* vol. 3, 1528.

Galveston
14th March 1846

Dearest,

It is one o'clock, and at four, I have to start by the Alabama. I have seen our relations,[1] and only regret that I can not, with them, return to share your smiles. I need not tell you how the[y] look, and will only tell you they are all well. It was humbug, that Mr Wallace[2] told us of Isabella[3] etc. etc.

You can, when they get up, do as you may seem best about the present location of the family. I feel intensely for your happiness, and health. I can only say, that if you could read my heart, you would suppose, that all my thoughts, and cares embrace your happiness. You will find Sister a great solace, I hope, and therefore hope they may, at least for the present, locate at Raven Hill. Mr Thomas Palmer will go on with the farm. Mr Moore will let you have 300 lbs. of good bacon. One barrel of Pork, and other things were sent to Robinsons,[4] and there left. They will be sent up, and such others, as you need. You will, my dearest Love, I know, do what you deem best for us, and for Sam. The dear little fellow, how my bosom heaves for him, and his beloved Mother. Heaven, I trust my dearest, will again permit us to meet, and embrace each other. Dearest, the task which I have to perform, if spared, is a toil, or burden which bears heavily upon me. Cou'd I have realized, what I have done in my desire to return, I believe that I could not have consented to have left you & Sam. I write this in confusion, and many talking to me of other matters. Feel no pain, or anxiety, as to what I will think of matters, should I live to return. I intend to be satisfied, and you may rest <u>satisfied</u>, dearest, that the first moment in my control, will bring me again, to you, as the bright ray of existence, and affection. Sam, to be sure, is not forgotten, as the object of our care, and affection, but this is a matter of division. The Boat is to start in a few minutes.

I hope to write you from every point from this to the city,[5] and from there, occurrences of every day. I must close. My heart embraces you, Sam, & our dear Niece. I have not time to read this letter.

Thy ever devoted

Houston

[1]The Moore family.

[2]William Wallace, the husband of Houston's sister Mary.

[3]Houston's niece, the daughter of Eliza and Samuel Moore.

[4]The plantation of James B. Robinson was located on the Trinity River, 167 miles north of Galveston. Miriam Partlow, *Liberty County and the Atascocito District* (Austin: Jenkins Publishing Company, 1974), 66, 191.

[5]Washington, D.C.

∽

New Orleans

16th March 1846

My ever dearest

To day, after a trip of thirty six hours out, we arrived here. The voyage was pleasant. I depart to day at 5 oclock P.M. by the Prytonia, to Louisville. Genl Rusk[1] has not arrived, but may have gone on by another rout up the River. I could not obtain the trifles in Houston, or Galveston, but will try, and send them from here, so soon as I can close this letter. I am pulled, and hauled so that I have no peace. I will try, and write, as I go up the river from different places. All ask for you, and show every respect for you, and say why did not she come on with you General? My reply is, "She is not, or soon will not be, in first rate travelling trim," and "I regret the want of her society, but we do not quarrel about the course."[2] The excuse is received, "with pleasure," as our dear boy [Sam] would say.

My love, I leave all to your discretion in matters, without imposing any <u>responsibility,</u> upon you, for what you may do. I only hope that you will not allow yourself to be troubled, about our affairs.

Were I again at home, I could not consent to leave you, nor Sam. I declare to you my love, that I have no anticipations, of pleasure, or Glory, from what I may be, nor what I may do, in the Senate. My only delightful anticipations, arise from the hope, which I cherish of again meeting you, and Sam, with all our dear relations. These hopes are sustained, by my prayers to the Beneficent Author, of every good, and perfect gift, that God into whose wise, and eternal providence, I

13 : MARCH 6, 1846—AUGUST 10, 1846

can commend, all that is dear to me, on earth, or in Heaven. So far as God may enable me to do, I will not, in word, action, or thought, indulge in aught, that could, or would distress you, were you cognizant of my every emotion of heart. I will my ever Dearest, omit no opportunity, in contributing to your happiness, or amusement. I hope to see bro. William [Houston] at Memphis. It may be that I will write to you several times before I leave the Boat, if it should not prove too unsteady. To day, I am to take soup, with my friend Christy,[3] and then go on board. Mrs C's[4] health is restored. If I can, I will send you some extras, (I mean quilque-chose [sic][5]). If the Trinity is up, they will reach you. I will only be here a few hours.

My Dearest, my heart embraces you, with all the tenderness, of a devoted husband. Do hug, and kiss Sam, & Betty for me. I will write in my next about Sarah Ann & Mr., B. E.[6] Let matters go on there, as they may—Dont say a word!! I will write to bro Royston[7] so soon as I go aboard of the Boat. I will write all that you wish, and no more. I will not allude to S. A. & Mr E.

In great haste
Faithfully and truly ever thine
Houston

A thousand regards are sent to you by every body!!

Houston

[1]Thomas Jefferson Rusk, the other senator representing Texas. *New Handbook of Texas* (Austin: Texas State Historical Association, 1996), vol. 5, 722. Hereinafter referred to as *New Handbook of Texas*.
[2]Margaret was expecting their second child in September.
[3]William Christy. Identified in *Writings*, vol. 1, 388n.
[4]Katherine Krieder Baker Christy. Ibid.
[5]Probably "quelque chose," French for "something."
[6]Benjamin Ellis. Identified in Ellis, 51.
[7]Robertus Royston, the husband of Margaret's sister Varilla Lea, and father of Sarah Ann.

Ever dear husband,

Many a long, long mile will be between us when you read this letter, and it is with feelings the most painful that I think of it. But rest assured dearest, that ere it reaches you, many a prayer from your distant home will have arisen for your safety. We were very much cheered on wednesday after your departure by the arrival of Houston Moore. It was most opportune I assure you, for although my dear Betty was exerting herself greatly to cheer the anguish which I some-times felt to be insupportable, I knew that her own anxiety about the family was very great. She has been a blessing to me, and I can never cease to love her, almost as my own child. I find Houston quite a business fellow and very useful in preparing little household conve-niences. In matters of this kind his taste is exceedingly like yours.

All is peace and quiet on Raven hill. The balmy breeze murmurs so sweetly among the lofty pines, and the spring flowers look up so cheerfully that I sometimes almost forget my grief and fancy you are at my side. Betty, Houston, and Sam too, by thier merry peals of laughter cheat me out of many a sad moment for which I have no disposition to quarrel with them you may be sure. Soon after Houston's arrival Mr Palmer and his family returned to his own house, and he considered that we were no longer in need of his protection and we thought it best to prepare for the reception of Sister Eliza and the family. Mr Palmer evidently feels a great interest in your affairs here, and I think he has attended very faithfully to them. He and Jose have made one trip to the river in search of the cows, but saw only one and that was too poor to bring home, but I hope they will succeed better when they go out again.

I think Jose will remain with us, but he doesn't seem much in-clined to work. Billy is our house servant, at present, and gives me no trouble about any thing. He keeps everything in perfect order and is very active and efficient. Houston saw brother Vernal at his land-ing as he came up the river, and he told him that they were in daily expectation of us at Grand Cane. I can not tell how the mistake originated, unless Col. Palmer wrote to some of his acquaintances in that vicinity, that he was to accompany us down on his return from Austin. You will remember that he was very anxious to do so, when he left us, and I think he would be very likely to write such a letter. I would fain account thus for thier apparent neglect of me. I could not endure for a moment the thought that I had become an object of indifference to those whom my heart holds so dear. And I think too, that the mail between Swartout and Grand Cane has certainly stopped, or we would have had a letter from some of them.

I rec'd the letters by Mr Roark from yourself and Mrs Reily on last sabbath morning, and was much comforted I assure you, particularly by yours. Betty had the privilege of reading all but one page. The bundles also came to hand. I thank you for your <u>very careful attention</u> to my memorandum. I was delighted to hear of Major Nichols' new importation.[1] I did indeed rejoice with my friend M.[2] They seem to deal in the articles.[3] If yours should be a different class of goods, dearest, I hope you will not envy them!

We will soon be in constant expectation of Mr [Samuel] Moore's arrival. I do hope they will remain here until your return, for I am almost convinced that it will be impossible or at best imprudent for me to go to Grand Cane.

Friday 20th. I did not send my letter yesterday, in hopes of some news from Mother, but do not fear that I will despond. My health is excellent, and I am cheerful, and if you were with me I would be happy. Every thing grows finely that you planted. The grape vines, rose bushes, and bois-d-arcs have all put forth thier leaves and your favourite ash is covered with green leaves. Mr Palmer informed today that Jose seemed much more industrious and he thought would make a good hand. He is now assisting the well-digger who came the day before yesterday. They have only dug 8 feet. I do hope my dear husband, that you will not indulge any uneasiness about home, for I trust and believe that we will all do well. Yes, it is true, I was very gloomy during the last few days that you were with me, but I was merely in anticipation of the great trial which I had to endure of parting from you. I did feel at one time, as if I could not live through it, but my fortitude was greater than I supposed. My spirits are much better than I had any reason to hope they would be during your absence. I look forward to a great deal of consolation from your letters, but I am sure dearest you will need no hints on this subject. If you do not get letters from me regularly, you may charge it all to the irregularity of the mail from this place. Sam is still a very unmanageable fellow, but I will try to keep him as much within bounds as possible. His health is very fine and he grows rapidly. Betty sends much love to you. I am teaching her to play on the guitar, and I think she has a very good talent for music. She plays one tune very well, and I think she will perform it well before you get back. I did not suppose there was so much music in the family. I think from what Houston says that Isabella will get married soon. Kitty[4] is still my pupil but not a very promising one. I hope Mr. Miller is with you. Remember me kindly to him.

M. M. Houston

[In margin:] Poor Maurice died on the Monday after you left.

[1]The birth of a son. Houston to Margaret, March 10, 1846.
[2]Mag Stone Nichols.
[3]Margaret is referring to the fact that all the Nichols children were boys. Pickrell, 270–73.
[4]Kitty Hoffman, a ward whom the Houstons had brought from Nashville to educate. Identified in the Madge W. Hearne Collection of Houston materials in the possession of the editor, hereinafter referred to as M. W. Hearne Collection.

Mrs Margaret L Houston
Palmers P O
Montgomery City Texas
Mail

Louisville Ky
23 March 1846

My ever dear Wife,

We just reached here, at day light, and we will proceed on our way at 11 oclock A.M. I say we, because, we number eight Texians—

17 : MARCH 6, 1846—AUGUST 10, 1846

all for the city. We were seven days from Orleans. I called at Memphis, and saw William [Houston], Mary,[1] and two little ones. The two youngest.[2] The three eldest[3] being at school. I only spent ten minutes, & returned to the Boat. All the time, which I spent was occupied in enquiries about you, Master Sam, & the Kinfolk. William had given to Sister fine accounts of you, and Sam. As for you he could not well exaggerate, but of Sam he did, and said he was handsome.

I would have written to you a journal of the trip, but the Boat was in continual motion, so that I could not write, and now indeed it is difficult for me to write legibly. It seems to me, an age already since we parted. My anxiety to see you, and our dear Boy is inexpressible. What must it be, ire we meet? I will not write a love letter Dearest, but will write to <u>one</u> that I love!

I have so many things to write about, that I hardly know where, & how to begin. I have had the company up, of the great Baptist revivalist Preacher, of Kentucky, Rev'd Mr Fisher.[4] Some ten or 12 years since, he preached in Marion Ala, he says, and knew your family. On yesterday (sunday) he preached, and is certainty is [sic] one of the most able <u>divines</u>, that I have ever heard preach. He is as pleasant, as he is intelligent, and says he will visit Texas this fall. He is acquainted with Mr Stoval of Huntsville Texas, but does not admire him, so I opine. Mr S had parted from his wife, or she from him, for some alleged impropriety—or ties of conduct. This we can retain, so far as we are concerned, and let other people, do as they please about matters. I am writing in the cabbin [sic] of the Boat, and there is a large croud [sic] standing, and looking on, while I write.

I hope my Love, that you will have no trouble about our affairs, and I repeat, that if I find you, Sam, and our Kin in health, on my return, that I will be satisfied!! I hope it may be that a crop will be reared, but if it can not be, I will make no fuss. I will so economize, if spared, that we will have something to make up any deficiency, which may arise, from a want of management, at home, if such should be the case. You may be assured, that I will write whenever I can, no matter what the press of business, if I can only get in a situation sufficiently steady, to make straight marks.

Genl Rusk is two days ahead of me. I may over take him. I hope to do so. You would be surprized, could you be translated [sic] to this place from Texas. You would see no vegetation here. From the time we left New Orleans, it gradually disappeared, until there is none to be seen. I have not left the Boat, or been in the city, so intent was I, on writing, and dreading a crowd, that I have not been out. I may be out for a few moments ire we sail. To night we are to get to Cincinnati, and from thence, I intend to write again. Whenever we stop, if but for an hour, I will write, if only to say, that "I live, and love you dearly."

The Rev'd Mr Fisher has this moment bade me farewell, and desires me to present to you his warmest respects, and prayers for your health, and happiness, and said if all are spared, he will call on us, and spend some time. He has, in his ministry, immersed upwards of five thousand persons, and he is only thirty four years old. A married man, and may take his wife with him, as she is not very healthy.

In Orleans I had the pleasure to meet Mr Clay.[5] He came on board the Boat to see me. We were very cordial—Subrosa. There was a vast crowd to witness the meeting. You know my aversion to playing "the Lion." Were it not for that, I would be in the city, and not writing to my dearest wife, whose love and happiness I prefer, to all the shows on this Globe. You may be assured that I will avoid, so far as I can, all company, and display. If I can enjoy any respite from business, it will be employed in writing to you, if there should be nothing interesting to write, only that I love you, and our "Great big Boy."

My ever dearest I must close this Epistle, and hope when I next write, that I will enjoy a quiet place in which to write. Col Christy was to find the silk, and the braid, as I have not time, to get it, and put it in safe hands. He was to send it to Major Cocke.[6]

Do not permit yourself to want, or need any thing which money will obtain for you.

Press Sam close to your heart for me, and tell him, Papa will write him a letter. Give my love to all our relatives. And dearest be assured of my prayers, and my hopes, and my love for you, and you only.

Thy devoted
Husband
Houston

[1]Mary Ball (Mrs. William) Houston.
[2]Houston's nephews, Claude and Eugene Houston.
[3]Sallie, William, and Mary Houston.
[4]Reverend John D. Fisher. Identified in Wilson, Woodyerd, and Busby, 113.
[5]Houston is probably referring to Henry Clay who visited regularly in New Orleans. Rebecca Smith Lee, *Mary Austin Holley* (Austin: University of Texas Press, 1962), 359.
[6]James H. Cocke (also spelled Cooke) of Galveston. Identified in *Writings*, vol. 3, 70.

Raven hill March 27, 1846

My love,

Your letter by Col. Stubblefield[1] was rec'd with great pleasure but not until he had taken a good rest of five days at home with his cats and dogs. He then brought it to the barn and handed it to Houston, but immediately rode off in great trepidation. Wherefore—I do not say, but you, dearest, who have had so many hair-breadth escapes, who have so often faced the hostile army, may be able to assign a reason! To be frank, I was not in a good temper about the attention of the letter, and I am afraid—made some very ugly faces on the occasion—but n'importe—you could not see them.

On the night of the 25th we were delighted by the arrival of Mr. Moore Isabella, Mary, and Willie. The boat stopped at Galveston, and they came up on horseback. Sister Eliza will remain at Mr Bailey's[2] in that place until the return of the "Belle" next week, and then come up to Patrick's ferry.[3] I was much disappointed at not seeing her with the others, but I hope she will soon be with us. I regret to learn from the family that she will go immediately home. They think she will not be satisfied until she can see how they are going on. However, the girls and Houston will remain here, until you return, and I expect I shall see Sister Eliza almost every day. We all went over to look at Mr Moore's place yesterday, and enjoyed ourselves finely. The girls were delighted with everything they saw and if you had been with me, I should have pronounced it one of the happiest days of my life, but when you are away, dearest, there is always a blank for me, that nothing can fill.

As the family came up, they met Antoinette, Sarah Ann [Royston] and bro. Vernal, at the mouth of the Trinity, on thier way to Galveston. They came on board the "Belle," and had a few minutes conversation, said they were compelled to go to Galveston at that time, but so soon as they return would make us a visit.

I must not forget to tell you that Houston went out a few evenings ago, and killed two deer, the first in his life. He has never regained his composure since it happened, and he is hardly able to speak without a cough. Sam was the only member of the family who had not participated in his happiness. That gentleman presented a very dignified silence on the occasion, and seemed to look upon it as an exploit, to which he was fairly entitled himself. He is gone with Houston today to Mr. Roark's, and set off in high spirits. He asked me a few days ago, if he would pray to God, after he died and went to Heaven. I told him no, that he would not pray then, but always sing praises to God. "And won't they laugh at me then, Ma?" he then asked.

I fear dearest, it will be a great while before I receive a letter from you, as the mail contracts are all out this week. When is it to be done? I am sure my fortitude will not last three weeks without a letter from you, and it may be tried for a long period. When do you think you will be at home, Dearest? Oh how long the time will seem! But I will try to be cheerful. My duty to you requires me to be and I will yield to no unnecessary gloom. I think, Darling I shall send Kitty for 2 months to Mr Stovall provided Mrs S will keep her under her eye. She is so dull about her lessons that I can never teach her to read, and she is growing so rapidly, that I think it is my duty to have her taught immediately. The [Moore] girls will have something to say to you, and I will leave room for them. I wrote to you last week,

21 : MARCH 6, 1846—AUGUST 10, 1846

and will write whenever an opportunity presents itself. Farewell dearest husband.

Ever thine,
M. L. Houston

P.S. Dear Uncle,

As Aunt has left me a few lines I cannot let an opportunity pass without showing some of the gratitude to one I am so much indebted to. I have only been here two days, and so far as I have seen I am perfectly delighted. I think our house will be very pleasant and comfortable. Father is very much pleased and is preparing to take Mother home. Brother, my sisters and I will all remain with Aunt untill [sic] you return. She is quite cheerful and we will do all within our power to render happy one that is so dear to us all. Little Cousin is a very fine boy, and is very fond of Houston. Aunt M. is a lovely woman. I do not wonder you were loth to quit her society. I must leave room for sister Mary. Heaven bless and protect us all and bring you safe home to us is the sincer [sic] prayer of your devoted Neice, [sic] Isabella Moore

Dear Uncle,

Aunt and Sister have written all the news. I have not much to say to you only They are all here but Mother and if you and she were here our happiness would be complete. We will be happy when we all get settled. Sam is very much pleased with his cousins and is as fat and rosey as ever. I have learned to play one tune on the Guitar. Uncle do write soon and often. Father and Brother sent theirs to you. Yours truly, E. P. Moore

[In the margin:] N. B. Aunt Maria says tell Master she is getting well. E. P. M.

Dear Uncle, I am very well pleased with Texas and I think that the house we are going to is in a beautiful situation. I think that we will be very happy here but we would be much hapier [sic] if you were with us. I hope though that we will have many pleasant hours to spend together. Dear Uncle I am very well and I hope these lines will find you enjoying good health.

Your affectionate niece,
Mary W. Moore

[1]John Stubblefield. Identified as living close to the Wood family. *1850 Census*, vol. 4, 2025.
[2]Margaret is probably referring to Marcus Bailey, identified as a citizen of Galveston in *Poll Lists*, 7.
[3]Patrick's Ferry was on the Trinity River, 308 miles from Galveston and 2 miles from the Wood plantation. Partlow, 199.

Houston arrived in Washington D.C. on March 28, 1846, by train from Pittsburgh. His arrival and registration at Brown's Hotel was reported in the March 31 edition of the New York Tribune.[1] *On that same day Houston began his ritual of writing to report the news to Margaret.*

Washington
31st March 1846

My Dearest,

Three nights since, I arrived here. Sunday passed quietly, as I could make it. Tho' to be absolutely quiet was impossible. People would call, and did call. On Monday my colleague[2] (with whom, I am perfectly cordial) presented my credentials to the Senate, where I took the Oath, and my seat. So Texas is fully represented in the Senate, and persons say as <u>ably</u> as any State of the Union. Ably I say because, we are the tallest gentlemen from any State, and in all respects as sizeable [sic]. Already I wish to get home, and be my own "single side."

Were I pleased any where else than at home, I might be pleased here. Every person renders to me respect, so far as it is in their power, and nothing pleases me so much, as the enquiries which are made about you, and the character which they tell me, they have heard of you. This is done by old familiars, who more than rejoiced to see me. You have at least as much popularity, if not more than I have myself. Some wish me to tell them, just how you look. The ladies, what few I have seen have not failed to say "Genl is she pretty? But I know she is!" and many things of this sort, and my modesty permits me to say "I think so." To be thus writing, is to me very painful. If I could only be so blessed, as to be present with you, I would then be happy. My love, you can have no idea, of the pain which I endure, in absence from you, and our dear Boy. Of him too, I have much to answer, and it is done with the more pleasure, because, say what I may of him, I am compelled to blend a portion of it, with "his mother!" You will think this is a love letter my dear, unless I change my tone to narrative.

Well, To day we had a fine speech from General Cass,[3] and I will send you a copy, so soon as it is out in pamphlet. On the Oregon Subject, there is a pretty equal division, and it may be that the vote of the Texian Senators will decide the question in favor of the notice. This evening I was at the Drawing room of the President,[4] or as they are called, "Mrs Polks[5] drawing rooms." When I first came,[6] as well as to night, I was most kindly received, by both the President, and his Lady. She is quite what you would desire to see her, and does not appear to be older than twenty five, or eight years, tho' she must be forty five. She is not quite so tall as you are, but very much of your person, and of course, I think her very genteel. Not by any means flashy, tho' quite cheerful, & pleasant. The ladies, most of them, I was introduced to, or I might say (if you will pardon me) were introduced to me, as I asked no introduction. Now my dear, do not get angry—I really did not promenade with any one, nor did one of them touch my arm. You will be provoked at them, will you not for treating me with so much disrespect? If they do so again, I will not complain to you of their neglect. But should they do otherwise, I will tell you of it. Now I will assure you dearest, that my course is taken, and it will be, not to lose, one moment from business, that I can possibly avoid. We will have incessant labour to perform, and could I, when the toils of the day are over, only have the pleasure of sitting down with you, and Sam, and passing the evening, I would be in the enjoyment of earths greatest happiness. You will perceive that my hand write [sic] is still affected by my wound,[7] tho' I do not suffer, any pain from it. My health is good, and I was not fatigued by the journey. In passing the mountains I saw piles, or banks of snow several feet deep, and there was quite a fall of snow upon us. This to you would seem strange. I put on two pair of socks, lest I might be cold.

I came to this place in the <u>Cars</u>, and I assure you my love, in times past I have enjoyed, more pleasant rides, when my earthly all was mounted, or packed upon <u>Bruin</u>![8] I sigh for the return of those rural scenes, days of happiness which [I] declare, I would not exchange for the "White House," for life. You need entertain no fears, my dear that I will ever, desire to remain in public, and all the demonstrations which can be offered will never induce me, to desire a contrary course. If in the enjoyment of home, I cannot find happiness, then on earth, there is none for me. You dearest, are the sole repository of my love, and my hopes! You, and your love, are to me every thing, and without you earth would be cheerless. Your happiness, will be ever the choicest object of my care. To our dear Boy I must write, and he is to write me a letter on his slate, and read it to you.

My son! I am far from you. Days, and nights will come, & pass by before your poor Papa can see his son. Pa loves his dear boy (his great big boy) and hopes, that he is a good boy. Does his son say his prayers, and pray for his pa, & ma, and Grand ma? Does he obey his Ma, and not get mad? Does he love the Good Father, and his son Jesus Christ? My Dear Son, be a good boy, and make your dear Ma happy! You must write to pa and get Ma to send pa the letter. Pa will not forget the pretty dress for you. Pa loves his dear boy too much, to forget any thing, which he wants. Your Father loves you my dear Boy.

Sam Houston

Dearest, when you read Sam his letter, do pray describe to me, the influence which it has upon him. It is now one oclock at night, and an alarm of fire has just been sounded from a remote part of the

25 : MARCH 6, 1846—AUGUST 10, 1846

city. I have just learned that "Wisters Balsam of Wild Cherry" will cure the asthma, and if it is in the place, I will procure it tomorrow, and send it to Torrey,[9] and let him send it to you by express. There is a gentleman here, who assures me, that it has cured his wife, and she had no rest, but had to use Nitre as you do. Its effect is instantaneous! I will obtain the other medicine also. Command me as you will, for your spirit rules me here. Or rather, I will be, what you desire me to be!! Do give my love to all our dear relatives. My heart embraces you with unutterable affection.

Thine ever

Houston

[1]Friend, 168.
[2]Senator Thomas Jefferson Rusk.
[3]Lewis Cass, the senator from Michigan. Identified in *Biographical Directory of the United States Congress, 1774–1989* (Washington, D.C.: U. S. Government Printing Office, 1989), 139. Hereinafter it will be referred to as *Biographical Directory*. For information on Cass's speech, see Andrew C. McLaughlin, *Lewis Cass* (New York: Houghton, Mifflin, and Company, 1898): 226–27.
[4]James K. Polk.
[5]Sarah Childress Polk. For a portrait of Mrs. Polk at this time see Margaret C. S. Christman, *1846 Portrait of the Nation* (Washington, D.C.: Smithsonian Institution Press, 1996), 26.
[6]Of his meeting with Houston, Polk would write in his diary: "At 6 o'clock this evening Gen'l Sam Houston, late President of Texas and now a Senator in Congress, called. I was much pleased to see him, having been with him in Congress twenty years ago and always his friend. I found him thoroughly Democratic and fully determined to support my administration." James K. Polk, *The Diary of James K. Polk during His Presidency, 1845–1849*, edited by M. M. Quaife (Chicago: A. C. McClurg and Company, 1910), vol. 1, 309.
[7]Houston is referring to the shoulder wound which he received at the Battle of Horseshoe Bend during the War of 1812.
[8]Houston's mule.
[9]David K. Torrey, a merchant in Galveston. Identified in *Handbook of Texas,* vol. 2, 790.

∞

Washington City

4th April 1846

My Dearest,

　　This morning, before the house meets, I have time to say to you, that I am most miserably busy. I am busy, because I am in the senate each day from four to five hours. I am miserable, because when the day is over, I am confined to my rooms, and I have not you, and Sam to solace me, and make me happy. Without your presence, I do declare to you, if earth contains a joy, or happiness for me, I do [not] know it. Then the idea of being detained here, until July, is awful to me. How I can live without you, is to me an enigma.

If you are satisfied that you can travel without danger to your situation, and can come on with Mr Culp, and his lady[1] do not for once think of the expence [sic]! of the journey!! Do not let <u>my anxiety</u> <u>induce</u> you to <u>endanger</u> <u>your</u> <u>health,</u> <u>or</u> <u>your</u> <u>life,</u> attempting to come on. Your life is my life, and your health my happiness. Do as you think well. One thing my dear is certain, if I live to return to you, direct as the inducements are to my remaining in public life, I do most solemnly declare to you, that I will with pleasure resign them all, rather than ever be separated again from you, and our "Dear Big Boy."

It is true, that I have met with the most cordial greetings, that a man could do, but I would rather be in a situation, to endure a <u>frown</u> of yours, than to enjoy all the <u>smiles,</u> which I can receive, until we meet again!! My duties will be arduous, and weighty. I will get on with them if spared. I have sent to the care of Torrey's, medicine for you, and will direct him to send it, with a Book to you, by express.

I can tell nothing, to you of the fashions here, as I have not noticed them. I know you don't care for them, nor about them. I have not even seen in the Gallery of the Senate, nor bowed to a lady in the Capitol.

Dearest, I will try, and write you every day, if it is only a line. Embrace Sam for me, and all our dear relations. I will, if I can get time to write mother. I have seen Mr. Cobb[2] of Geo. He was particular in his enquiries about you, and sent his regards.

Thy ever devoted & faithful husband
Sam Houston

[1]Margaret's friend Betty Thilman had married Daniel D. Culp. Helen Smothers Swenson, *8800 Texas Marriages 1823–1850* (St. Louis, Missouri: Frances Terry Ingmire, 1981), 34.
[2]Howell Cobb, speaker of the House of Representatives. Identified in *Biographical Directory,* 138.

4th Apl 1846

Dearest,

I wrote to you this morning. I sent Anna's[1] poor sick brother five dollars, as he had long lain sick, and wrote to me for aid. On your account I sent him the small sum. I wrote to him, how much you, and Sam thought of Anna, and to let me know where she was.

You see <u>love</u>, that I retain every word of them.

My love dearest, I confide to you. Mr McDuffy[2] is speaking on the Oregon Question.

Thine ever
Houston

P.S. I may speak on the Oregon Question, but I am not determined.

H

[1]This may be Anna Coates, who was a governess working in Houston for Houston's friend, Archibald St. Clair Ruthven, in 1850. *1850 Census*, vol. 2, 931.
[2]Senator George McDuffie of South Carolina. *Biographical Directory*, 141.

5th April 1846

Ever Dearest,

This morning, before I go to church, I will devote a while to writing. I view my writing to you, a part [sic] from business, and in the line of duty. My heart is always with you, and Sam, when I have a moments leisure from the press of business, and I feel an irresistible inclination to be saying something, to you, or about you. You will be astonished to see my hand writing so bad. It is owing to my arm, and I think it was caused by the unusual use which I made of it, at home when I was there. I feel no pain, and in my life, my health has not been better, than at this time, with the exception of a cold. Colds are prevalent here.

On yesterday, when I wrote you the last note, Mr McDuffy was speaking. He finished, and on tomorrow Mr Webster[1] is to take the floor. My intention is to speak on the Oregon subject. This I will do, not to make a display, but to render the reasons, for the vote which I may give. It is as well to render my reasons, before in a speech, as it would be to render them in a hundred cases.

3 oclock P.M. I have just returned from hearing a fine sermon by a Presbeterian [sic] Divine. I paid unusual attention to the service, and if I am permitted by Divine Providence, I will attend church every sunday, that I may be detained here.

On yesterday I wrote to you to come on, if you could do so, with perfect safety. Nothing on earth could render me more happy, than to see you here, if it can be so, without risk of your <u>precious health,</u> and <u>safety</u>. If either is to be endangered, do not come, I beseech you! If you are at home, my heart will be with you, but this you cannot realise [sic]. If we live to meet again, I have no ulterior designs, out of Texas, or where I will be absent from you, for a single week. My presence here has dispelled all the clouds of calumny, which have been floating about the horizon of my character. I could desire, that my coming had produced less excitement, than it has done, and I fear is yet to do. To be with you, as I wish to be, and Master Sam, (as yet the sole objects of my care) is not consistent with public life, and therefore, I will cheerfully surrender all its charms, to those who are captivated by its influences. <u>I am not.</u> I long for the quiet of seclusion, domestic bliss, and the calm of private life. I know, and feel, that we will be more happy, and I trust that I can render to meditation, and to my family, and My God, the rest of my days. Should I live to return, I will try, and situate myself, in such a way as will relieve me of such cares, as only lead to irritation, without profit.

My love, my heart beats intensely when I think of home, of you, and the scenes of home. 'Tis the Lords day, and you, & others have returned from sunday school, and are reading holy books, in quiet, and tranquility. At sunset you will walk out, and look upon the flowers, and praise the author of our nature, the fountain of light, & life. I know well Dearest, that I will have a place, in each petition of yours to the Father of Mercies. You have each night in mine, and our dear Boy, with "all for whom, we should pray." Dearest, we are in the hands of the almighty, and this must reconcile me to my absence from you. In many parts of the city, it is not healthy, in summer. I will select the most healthy scite [sic] that I can find, and out from the dusty, and business part. I am invited to dine on Wednesday with the President, and with Genl Rusk, have accepted the invitation. Dining takes place at 5 1/2 oclock. This is nearly supper time in Texas.

Yesterday I sent you a Book by mail. It was Capt Fremonts tours.[2] I hope you will be pleased with it. I sent you a letter in relation to Anna, intending to act upon whatever orders you may give me, in relation to her. If you say so, I will direct her to join you in Texas, or if you come on, at this place, (if she should be disengaged soon.) In coming on by the usual mode of conveyance from Texas here, the travelling is bad so far as stages are concerned, as you are compelled to travel, day, and night, from the Ohio river, to the rail cars. You know how it was with us, on our journey.[3] There is no stopping the stage when it might be highly <u>necessary</u>. If you shou'd come on, (which I only desire, if it can be done without <u>any danger</u> to your situation) you must make Mr Culp, or whoever may come with you, make up a suitable company, and travel as it may best suit you. By the southern rout [sic] you can't come—it is too bad, as I am informed, and believe. You will, I hope write to me often.

Since I came from church, Genl Rusk presented me with a handsome family Bible. The General is perfectly steady, and extremely respectable. He bears himself well, in every respect. Texas is about as well represented, as any state in this Union.

When any thing of interest transpires, I will write to you, if I had only written an hour before. Not an hour passes, but what I think of you, and only love you more, each time that I think of you. You will believe me, for I speak only to Heaven, and you, as I am alone and the night far advanced.

When you see, or write to our Dear Mother, give her my love, as well as to all the family of Grand Cane.

To Mr Moore, Sister Eliza, and all the dear flock present my love. Kiss Sister & my nieces, for I hope they are all in your reach.

Dearest, I am nearly crazy to hear from you. I am so anxious that I search every mail, to see if I can hear from My Dear Margaret. Sometimes, I receive thirty letters in our mail. Don't suppose I will hurt myself writing, for I assure you I write to but few besides your dear self.

My whole heart is ever thine,

Houston

[1]Daniel Webster, senator from Massachusetts. *Biographical Directory*, 139.
[2]*Report of the Exploring Expedition to the Rocky Mountains 1843,* by John Charles Fremont.
[3]Houston is probably referring to the 1845 trip he, Margaret, and Sam made to Tennessee and Alabama.

Raven hill, April 6, 1846

My dear Love,

Mr Moore is about starting to the river for the negroes and frate [sic], and I have but a few minutes to write, but I must say a word or two to you. I did not know until this morning that he would go down before tomorrow, or I would have commenced writing sooner. Our dear sister Eliza arrived on yesterday a little past noon, and I was delighted beyond description to see her. She looks much better than when we saw her in Tenn. She is in fine spirits, and I think she will be quite happy in Texas. Every line of her expressive face is dear to me, because it reminds me of one—far, far away. Ah shall I ever look upon that dear one again! God grant it—and that we may spend years of happiness together. Yet, oh enable me to say "thy will be mine be done!"

My health continues to improve, and I trust I shall be supported through my trials. My fortitude is far greater than I expected it would be, and I will try to be patient until your return. My heart sometimes sinks within me, when I think of the long months that may intervene, and for a few moments—I feel as if my strength would yield, but the struggle soon passes and my "strength is renewed." I expect the latter part of this week, to make a trip to Huntsville with Isabella, Betty, and Houston, for the purpose of taking Kitty to school. Houston and I will go in the buggy, (and get out at all the bad places) the others on horseback. In another letter,[1] which I hope you have rec'd, I have given you my reasons for sending Kitty to school. In my present state of health, the charge of her was too much for me and she dislikes so much to study, that I can not compell [sic] her to learn. Sister Eliza will stay here, and keep Sam until we return. Dr. Mc clenny[2] has been down to see us, and examined my teeth, but only filled one with cement. He says when I go to Huntsville, he will plug it, and make a great tooth of it.

I recd a letter, a few days ago, from Antoinette which had been written some weeks before. She mentioned that Mother would come up by the first conveyance she could get. She said nothing about the marriage you alluded to, and I do not know what to think of it. I shall certainly take your advice about not interfering, and the fact is, if she is realy attached to him, I do not think we ought to say a word against it. This love you know "is a mighty thing!"

I am told that Mr Charles Power intends to court Antoinette, so soon as she lays off her mourning. I think it would be a useless attempt, if I know her disposition. At least I hope so—but I presume she has never recd an intimation of it yet. It came through Maj. Cocke to us. Mr Moore is in a great hurry, and I must say farewell. My dearest life—do come home—so soon as you can. But why should I ask such a thing? I know you will not delay a moment longer than you are necessarily detained. Our boy is well and growing rapidly.

Thy devoted wife,
M. L. Houston

[1]See Margaret to Houston, March 27, 1846.
[2]Stephen G. McClenny (also spelled McLenny) of Polk County. Identified in Swenson, 13 and *Writings*, vol. 5, 28n.

Washington
8th April 1846

My Dearest,

To Day as I wrote to you, I dined at the Presidents. The company was not numerous, but genteel and cheerful. I sat on the right hand of Madam President, after handing her to the Table. To be candid, my ever dear wife, I would rather have sat on your right hand in our Log Cabbin [sic], than to have been in the "White House." The Madam excused me from taking a Glass, of even "white wine." They all know what my imputed failing has been, and all ascribe my reformation to your benign influence, over me. This I do not disclaim. So you see my dear, the position which you occupy, in the esteem of the circles here. Were you here my dear, I doubt not but you would well maintain the high opinion, which is entertained of you. The Alabama delegation all claim my homage, or fealty to them on account of my obtaining you in that state. So you see my Love, I am agreeably taxed, on your account. It is a tax, which I pay, with the very greatest pleasure, and pride. Yes, I am proud, and happy, that I have such wife to talk, and think of, as my Dear Margaret. They claim Sam too, as a liege subject of the state, as some person has told them, he is very clever, and will be as smart as his Mother, or Father. The Oregon question is still on the tapis, and will be for some days, I presume. On this subject, I will feel no embarrassment. I will vote for the notice, to dissolve the joint occupancy Treaty, and then act, as we should do. By no means courting war, but conduct our affairs, without reference, to any principle, but justice, combined with sound policy, and if war should grow out of it, be prepared for its shock. This is all that we can do, to sustain the national rights, and national character. If I make a speech, it will be soon, and I will send you a copy. Dearest, as yet I have not heard a word from, or of you since I left home. Only Major Cocke wrote to me, that Bud, Antoinette, & Sarah Anne were at the Island, and that you were well, but not where you were at.

My Love, the clock has struck one past midnight. I must close, in the day my Labors are incessant.

Do embrace our dear "Great big boy," and love to all. I pray you dear to write me every week. I have the mails arranged for Raven Hill, & Grand Cane. I would write to our dear Big boy, were it not so late.

I have yet, my chapter to read, and my prayers to offer up to our Divine Father, ire I lay my head to rest.

May Heaven bless you, my dearest and only Love!

Thy devoted & faithful husband
Sam Houston

∽

Washington
9th April 1846

My dear,

At one this morning, I closed a letter to you. The day has passed, with another speech. Pretty dry, and on tomorrow Gov Bagby[1] is to make his speech. Whether I will speak on the subject, or when, I do not know.

I think so much about you, & home my dear, that I am fearful I will speak, of you, & Sam, but not of oregon. Raven Hill, or where ever you are, is my "Eldorado." If I could only transport myself as speedily as the "Telegraph" conveys intelligence, my arrival at home would surprize you, most suddenly. Each day if I am spared, (Sunday excepted) I will send you something, to let you know, that you are always present to my heart, and thoughts.

My hand write [sic] is returning to me, and I hope by use, it will be entirely restored. Mr Miller has not come on, and it is now, that I most want him. If I am compelled, to write you short letters, I pray you not to regard them, as any criterion of my affections.

34 : CHAPTER 1

It is not only the business of Texas, but from all parts of the US, that I have to attend to. Every day brings me one, or more applications for my autograph, and when it will end I can't say. You will wish to know how I dress, and I will tell you. A neat black hat, black vest, and cravat, Grey coat (frock) and pantaloons, with Boots. The very same round toes, which I brought from home. I have bought no new garments, only two plain linnens [sic]. So you see I am not fashionable. In the dress described I dined at the Presidents. So it will be consider'd fine enough, for any occasion.

My Love, it is twelve oclock midnight, and I must close this letter. May Heaven guard, and keep you, and our dear Boy!

Thy ever devoted Husband
Houston

[1]Arthur P. Bagby was the Democratic governor of Alabama, 1837–1841. Identified in Robert O'Brien and Harold H. Martin, eds., *The Encyclopedia of the South* (New York: Facts on File Publications, 1985), 497.

Washington
12th Apl 1846

My Ever Dearest,

The sabbath has passed, and it is now monday. The Senate has met and we are at business. Every thing here seems to move slowly, and this opinion may in part arise, from my intense anxiety to hear from you. No letter has yet reached me, and my heart is sad. In the absence of intelligence from you, and Sam, nothing can supply, the place, of the gratification, which I anticipate from you, of all that claims my devoted love! Dearest, to day I removed from the Hotel,[1] to a private House where Genl Rusk, and several friends constitute, or compose our mess.[2] The Landlady, reminds me some what of our dear Mother. It will be quiet, and retired, where I can attend to business. At the Hotel, I was never, an hour alone from the time I rose in the morning, until 12 Midnight. The idle are curious, and when they called to see me they forgot that I had any thing to do. Many called to see me, from good feeling, and many, very many from old acquaintances. I have called on, but one private family, and that was an old Lady,—the forever devoted friend of Mr Jackson.[3] She was once a resident of Tennessee. So you see my dear, that I have not become, the Gallant. On yesterday, I was at church, and heard an able sermon, and would have gone in the evening, only that it rained. So soon as I could be alone, in my room, I was engaged in reading my Bible, until one oclock this morning.

You see my dear, that I have not by any means, abandoned the habit which we kept up at home. In compliance with that custom, and duty, it seems to bring me in communion with you, and replaces me, in the associations of home. These are sacred, and pleasing reflections to me. They bring you my ever Dearest, near to my heart, or I might rather say, to my bosom, for you are always present, to my heart. Intending, as I do my dear to write often, I will not persecute you, with such long letters, as I have sometimes done, in days past. My hand writing is nearly restored, and I rejoice at the fact.

I have taken the floor, for wednesday, and will be employed, in reflecting upon the subject of Oregon. The boundary, I will say nothing about, but only confine myself to the Subject of the "notice to dissolve the joint occupancy of the Territory." We have a bill to regulate, and establish the mails of Texas, now before the Senate.

You will my ever dear wife, I hope write to me once, in each week, if your health will permit. If you only write, one sentence, to me in a letter, I will be happy. I do not know where to send my letters. If bro Vernal had written to me when he came to the Island,[4] I would have known where you were, and are! Where ever you are my heart, and thoughts must be.

Dearest embrace our dear Boy, and all our relations. Tell them to write to me. I will send you some pamphlets, (I think the Mothers Journal) sent for you, by some Lady. And with them her letter. I will send her the subscription, for one year. You will want them for the "Preacher."

Ever Dearest, my heart embraces you.

Thy Husband
Sam Houston

[1]Browns Hotel. Friend, 168.
[2]During this time many congressmen sharing the same views would live together in boarding houses called messes. No documentation could be found for Houston's residence, but it is possible that he is referring to the Atchison mess on F Street where many Southern Democrats boarded. William W. Freehling, *Secessionists at Bay 1776–1854*, vol. 1 of *The Road to Disunion* (New York: Oxford University Press, 1990), 550.
[3]Andrew Jackson.
[4]Galveston.

Raven hill April 14, 1846

My dearest love,

 If you have recd all the letters which I have written to you, since you left me I am sure you infer (and very correctly) that you are never absent from my thoughts. I begin this with the expectation of finishing it in Huntsville, hoping to find an opportunity of sending it from that place to Houston. Our trip to Huntsville, which I mentioned in two previous letters, has been postponed in consequence of bad weather. The citizens having learned that we contemplated a visit to the place, have made up a large party (but I think not a dance) for the occasion. You know my opinion of parties dearest, and I should not hesitate to decline it, but for the girls, who are perfectly enchanted at the prospect. They have attached my name to the tickets, which they designed as a compliment to the young ladies, and another evidence of thier affection for you. I have spent some pleasant hours with our dear sister Eliza, and my affection for her increases every day. She has removed to her own home, but the three girls and Houston remain with me. I hope you will not be surprised Love, to hear that the latter has taken charge of the farm. He is writing to you this evening, and will give you the particulars. I am satisfied that he will take a greater interest in your business, and is a more capable man-

37 : March 6, 1846—August 10, 1846

ager than Mr Palmer. Several of our cows have come in, and thus far, I am well pleased with them. In fact, I hope we will be agreeably disappointed in the stock. I have only had two brought from the river (very pretty cows—with young calves,) which I sent sister Eliza today. The others come in voluntarily. In a few days, I hope to send her two or three more. These are homely details—love for a senator at Washington, and would not bear repitition [sic] at a "President's" levee, but you must remember that our little world is a very contracted one, and we know little that is occurring beyond it.

We all enjoy fine health. Sam is the most robust fellow, I ever saw. When asked why his pa is gone to Washington for, he answers— "to get me a coat and Panteloons [sic]." He was wading in the water yesterday, after I had told him to keep out of it. When I called him, and asked him where he was, he answered, "no where, Ma!" I did not like the spirit he betrayed, but I thought it best to pass it over in silence, for it was too laughable a thing to lecture upon.

We expect to set off for Huntsville tomorrow, and I hope while there to complete my letter to you.

Huntsville, Thursday night—16th

My love,

We arrived here yesterday about 5 o'clock P.M. and stopped at Mr [Alexander] McDonald's, expecting to remain with Mrs M. but he was in Austin,[1] and she looked so shy that we thought it best to come to the hotel, but as the chance was, I have since learned that her manners were caused by embarrassment, and that she was deeply mortified at our leaving. I merely give you these details dearest, but you might hear of our stopping the hotel and feel somewhat astonished at it. The party is going on below, and is rather a brilliant thing for Huntsville. There is a room for dancing, and one for conversation. You will readily imagine where I held my levee.

The girls and Houston have occupied both by turns, and seem perfectly delighted. I have been introduced to a great many persons, and every one is exceedingly kind, but on hearing from Mr Gibbs[2] that he expected to leave in the morning for Galveston, I made my excuses and withdrew. We expect to leave for home tomorrow at daylight in order to avoid the heat of the day. I have found an agreeable associate here in Mrs Merritt,[3] who is boarding at the hotel. But I must tell you who Mrs Merit [sic] is. Do you remember Miss Morgan the tutoress at Galveston, who called on us at Mr Price's, and again at Mrs Maffit's?[4] Well she is happily married to an intelligent lawyer[5] of this place, and has really "made a merit of necessity!" I told her that I was writing to you and she begs to be kindly presented. Dr McLenny also sends his regards. Mr Merritt is to aid you in his suit,[6] and tells me there is a fine prospect of success.

Oh my little Sam, how I do want to see him.[7] Darling, how can you live without him? With me, it is the next thing to being without you. I have been much flattered about both you and me in this place, and I believe they are truly attached to you. This is a miserable scrawl love, but I know you will excuse it when you consider the circumstances under which it is written. I was terribly disappointed at not finding a letter from you here. The last I recd was the one written at New Orleans. Oh that I could hear from you! Farewell dearest.

Thy devoted wife.

M. L. Houston

[1]For an account of MacDonald's trip to Austin and his efforts to establish the penitentiary in Huntsville see Alexander MacDonald to Margaret MacDonald, April 3, 1846, in the Alexander MacDonald Papers in the vertical files of the Sam Houston Memorial Library, Huntsville, Texas.

[2]It is unclear as to whether Margaret is referring to Thomas or Sanford Gibbs. Both were friends of Houston. Identified in *Handbook of Texas*, vol. 3, 337.

[3]Louisa Morgan Merritt. Identified in Swenson, vol. 2, 5.

[4]Anne Carnic (Mrs. John Newland) Maffitt. Identified by Philip Graham, *The Life and Poems of Mirabeau Bonaparte Lamar* (Chapel Hill: University of North Carolina Press, 1938), 78.

[5]Louisa Morgan married Josiah Merritt on March 21, 1846. Swenson, vol. 2, 5.

[6]For an explanation of Dr. McClenny's lawsuit see *Writings*, vol. 5, 28n.

[7]Sam had been left with Eliza.

39 : MARCH 6, 1846—AUGUST 10, 1846

Washington
15th April 1846

Dearest,

To day I spoke, on the Oregon Subject,[1] and so soon, as it is published, I will send it to you. Had you been here, I would have done better. I had no one to please, and therefore, was rather tame, as I think. Rusk, and others say I did well, and was of use to the proposition, to "Give notice."[2] Be this as it may, the audience seemed contented, under the inflection, of a two hours speech. It was orthodox, in politicks, and will pass muster, with the Democracy. I said, what I believed, and felt, as I spoke. I commenced with an ague, on me, and I think my speech, was rather "<u>chilly</u>." I took a bath this morning, in hopes it would help me, but I think it was the reason, why, I was chilly. One thing was, that I had <u>men</u>, and only men, to address. Men, all men, are only mortals, and no more. I must confess, I would rather make a stump speech in Texas, than one in the U S Senate. There is a degree of show, and display unfavorable to new members.

You often heard me say, that I never would yet (as I then thought) speak from <u>notes</u>. I did to day, and I really think, for the last time. I did <u>not</u> try to please either party, but sustained the President, in his position, and the true principles of national honor, and of national Safety.

I must revise my speech, and therefore, I will write short!

My love, I embrace you, and beg you to give our dear boy a hearty squeeze.

Salute all our relations. I want you to say to Sam, that, I will write to him, so soon as he answers my letters! I am over my chill, and hope I will have no more!

Thy ever devoted Husband
Sam Houston

P.S. I think dear, my speech was well received, as to its import. I did not abuse England by any means.

Houston

[1]For the text of the speech see *Writings*, vol. 4, 451–71.

[2]The occasion for the speech was President Polk's request for authority to notify the British Government that the United States wished to withdraw from the agreement for the joint occupation of the Oregon Territory. *Writings*, vol. 4, 47n.

Washington City
17th Apl 1846

My ever dear Wife,

You can have no idea of the pleasure which I derived from the receipt of your favor of the 19th March. I had been desponding and was most melancholy, when it came to me. Its contents repaid me, for all that I had felt, and suffered. I caught that part which said you were "well" and "Sam robust, and growing fast" and I was happy. From the press of company, I was an hour prevented from reading the balance of its contents. They were not, any of them distressing, tho' I was sorry to hear that poor Morris, did not recover. This never cost me a pang, as he had so long suffered!

My duties, are beyond any thing, which you can conceive of, even from my past experience. My health is so good, that I can bear to be harrassed, to great extent. My correspondence, is the most distressing part of my duties. I will so long as I have the health to write you once a week, and if I have anything good to tell you, I will write you more frequently, or if I have anything to cheer you, or flatter your vanity, in a harmless way, I will write. Each day you know, I am to send you a paper, or something to let you know that you are always present to my heart, and mind. You will suppose me clownish when I assure you, that I have never been in the Galleries, nor to visit a lady of this city, tho' I have [a] hundred acquaintances. I am out of that line, and I declare to you, that I have not once retired before midnight since I came to this city. About that hour, I usually read my chapter, and after thanking our Heavenly Father for his mercies, thro' the day, as well as all his mercies, to us sent I invoke then his kind protection and mercies, and above all [t]his, that his grace, may be sufficient for us. You see my dearest, that your example has not, been

41 : MARCH 6, 1846—AUGUST 10, 1846

in vain, thus far with me. Perfectly devoted to you, I cherish every virtue, and every principle which can endear me to you! I trust too, that I am not all together, without a hope, that by adhering, to the course, which your example, enforced upon me, God in due time, may bring me into the fold, of those, who, by the blood of Christ, are washed white, and redeemed from sin, and death. Of ourselves!!

Sunday evening 19th

Dearest, tho' my letter was long enough, on yesterday, I was so busy, that I did not close it, but left it for this evening. I do not often violate the sabbath by writing on business. When writing to you, I do not consider it a breach of the day, but as communing with you, as tho' I were with you, and conversing on subjects which would become the day.

To day, I have not been out of the house, save to church, and my love, I must call your attention to one matter, of which we have often conversed. Would you believe it my Love, that tho' I have been to church every sabbath, since the first that I reached here, the "little Green bag," is invariable [sic] handed, or rather <u>pushed</u> <u>at</u> <u>me</u>. It is made fast to the end of a handsome stick, and gracefully, extended along each Pew, and as gracefully, drawn back again. Well, my Love, I think of you, and contribute my mite. I hope it is for good, for so, really I intend it to be. The church to which I go, has one of the most able Pastors, that I have heard in any church. I would, if it were as convenient, go to the Baptist Church, but it is not, and Mr Sproul[1] does not preach about doctrine, but the practical duties of man, as they relate, to his Maker, & fellow man. He took the 6th Commandment, on last sabbath for his text, from which he is to preach four sabbaths. To day was his second. The text is "Thou shall not kill."

My Dearest, as it may gratify you, a little, I send you from the Phila. Sentinel, a slip. I could send you slips from almost all the Democratic Papers, which have come here, since the public has heard of my speech. It is not yet out, for I have not received the notes of it, and I will correct it my love, tho' I do dislike to take the trouble. You would wish me to do it, and therefore, I will do it.

This moment my great friend Mr Wallach,[2] has just slipped into my room. He has a sweet little wife,[3] & one who is, by no means, in a situation to travel! Besides this, he has two little daughters, the youngest, about a year [and] a half old. The parents are a small couple, but both smart. This reminds me Dearest of the "importation" of which you speak, when you refer to your friend Mag Nichols! If I could, order my dear any class, of the article spoken of,[4] I would order it, according to your wishes. Not that I am indifferent, to the subject generally, for I assure [you], I feel, all that you could wish me to do. You have it to pay for my love, and I wish you to be pleased! My prayer only is for your safety. If ever anxiety was felt, by a husband, I feel that anxiety for you. I will not fail, to offer my earnest prayers, unworthy, as they may be, to our Maker, and Father, for blessings to you, and our dear Boy! How my affections glow for you all! You are always present to me, & I assure you, I will so act, as tho you had percieved [sic], and were present, at my every act or thought!

I will enclose you a letter from Young Royston. I have written to bro Royston, soon after I came here, but have not heard from him. I will write to "Tene"[5] soon. I told bro Royston, that I could not go by that rout home.

My friend [Washington D.] Miller never rec'd my letter, and did not come on as I hoped. I do wish he had done so.

I send you a card of mine,[6] tho' I have not had time to send out any. I go but little in society. The Presidents Levees are over, and were so before I came to this city. Twice a week, each Tuesday & friday, the House is open, and company received, but only a few, say fifty, or from that, to one hundred of a night visit there. I have been there often enough to let it be known, how I stand with the administration. Straws show, how wind blows. You may rely upon it Love, tho' I have no ulterior views, but to get to, and stay with you and Sam, that I will make no committals, but such as will sustain the President, in a proper course. You see my dear that I write with a steel pen! I have it to do, as I write so much. I will not say how many autographs I have had to send to different persons. I have received from two Democratic societies of the north "Honorary memberships" which I have to acknowledge. I have to visit Mrs Madison,[7] the Relict of the late President Madison. She expects it of all men, who <u>she thinks</u>, distinguished, and so my dearest, your husband will introduce you to her soon, by paying his personal respects. I have been so busy that, I have returned no visits as yet!

I send you a daisy, presented by Mrs Watson,[8] the old Lady, a friend of Mrs Jackson.[9] Could you, or will you believe me? I do not expect to be in the Gallery, among the ladies, this session, as I have not been. I am never out of place in the Senate. My associates, all treat me most kindly, and Genl Rusk, and myself are very friendly. He demeans himself remarkably well, and is much respected. He is a man of talents, and mind!

Now my Love, are you not weary? I was happy to hear, all that you had to write me about home—for home is a dear place to me. You did not say how Maria was. If she is well you will get on well, I hope.

You may rely my Love, that I will try, and save all the money that I can. Will you send me word, what kind a velvet dress you want, and let me know how <u>tall</u> you are. You need not make any guess about <u>thickness</u>, I will suppose that my dear. But you may send me a measure upon <u>calculation</u>, as to the size you would wish it to be. I hope dearest, you will write to me, for any thing, which you may desire, and I will try, and contrive it to you. If not, take it to you, if I live! You must say to Sister, and all our relations, that I can only write to you. Apologize to Sam, and tell him his pa must wait for his replies.

Give my love to all, kiss them, and press Sam, and Betty, to your heart for me! I soon may write to Miss "Tene" for you! I am thy faithful, and devoted husband,

Houston

[1]Thomas Sproull, a Presbyterian minister. Identified in *Dictionary of American Biography*, edited by Allen Johnson and Dumas Malone (New York: Charles Scribners, 1964), Part I, vol. 9, 485–86.
[2]William D. Wallach, the former editor of the Matagorda *Gazette and Advertiser*, was at this time a correspondent for the Richmond *Enquirer*. *Handbook of Texas*, vol. 2, 856.
[3]Margaret Newton Wallach. Ibid.
[4]Houston is referring to the baby Margaret was expecting.

[5]Margaret's niece, Serena Royston. She was the sister of Young Lea Royston.

[6]A calling card bearing the printed facsimile of Houston's signature is in the possession of the editor.

[7]Dolley Madison.

[8]Mrs. Elizabeth Watson. Robert V. Remini, *Andrew Jackson and the Course of American Freedom, 1822–1832* (New York: Harper & Row Publishers, 1977), 149. She was probably the wife of Thomas Watson, who was Jackson's partner in the mercantile business. Marquis James, *The Life of Andrew Jackson* (New York: Bobbs & Merrill, 1938), 99.

[9]Mrs. Andrew (Rachel Donelson) Jackson.

Washington
21st Apl 1846

Dearest,

Last night Maj Donelson[1] and family arrived. This morning I called to see them. They had a thousand things to ask, and say about you, and Sam. I presented them a large portion of your love! They were very happy, & said many fine things of you. Mary[2] is the same cheerful girl, and asked for Mr Miller. They will all go with the Major, on his mission.[3]

I send you a New York paper, which has been in the habit of abusing me. You can see its tone. I send you this nonsense, for such I look upon it. My purposes as professed to you my Love, I solemnly declare are not changed. Nor have I had any Agency in starting the matter. It is true my presence, has killed of[f] my enemies, as it would seem! I am attentive to my duties, but do not enter into any clubs, nor cabals!

My Dear, I have no news to tell you! My notes, of my speech have not yet been handed to me.

Embrace our dear relations all. Send love to Mother, & the family, if they are not with you. Tell Kitty to be a good girl, & give my compliments to Messors Palmers & famalies [sic].

Press Sam to your heart, more than ever, I am thy devoted husband!

Houston

[1]Andrew Jackson Donelson. For a biography see *Handbook of Texas*, vol. 1, 512–13.

45 : MARCH 6, 1846—AUGUST 10, 1846

[2]Mary Donelson, the major's daughter. Ibid.
[3]Donelson had been appointed to serve as U.S. Minister to Prussia. *New Handbook of Texas*, vol. 2, 676.

Washington City
23 April 1846

Dearest,

This moment the Senate has passed the Resolution of notice, to the British Government to abrogate, the Treaty of joint occupancy, of Oregon! It is an important move, and right to make it.

An old friend of mine, with whom I served 30 years ago,[1] has written me a letter, which I enclose to you! My speech is not yet out. A synopsis was published. I hope in a few days to get the notes, correct, and publish it.

I have no news since my last. Do you wish me to send you a small, or large locket with a Degareatype [sic] likeness. If you wish one dear, I will send, or take it to you!

My Dearest, my health is very fine, and I am fatter, than you have seen me. I must have gained some fifteen, or twenty pounds. I hope my dear, that you are <u>gaining</u> <u>Size</u>, as fast as I am. I wrote to you about a dress, which I wish to send you. <u>I will have it made, to your direction</u>. If you want any thing, write to me about it. I will always have time, and opportunity to comply with your requests. Until I had written the first page, I did not observe, that it was not a whole sheet.

My love to all! And embraces to our dear Boy. I will soon have to write him again.

Ever thy devoted husband
Houston

[1]Waddy Vine Cobbs. Houston to Cobbs, April 8, 1846, *Writings*, vol. 4, 349–50.

The following letter has the bottom of the pages torn off. Several sentences are missing from the bottom of all four pages.

Washington
25th April 1846

Dearest,

I sent you a paper to day, and as I have a moments leisure, I will write you a note, and send you a slip from the Richmond Enquirer, supposed to be written by Mr Ritchie[1] from this place to his son, the present Editor, of the Enquirer.[2] I send you these things, in hope that they will cheer you, by the assurance, that I behave myself well, which will be delightful to you. It is not done my dear, to induce you to change, or relax your determination that I must quit public life. No my love, there is no honor, nor vocation on earth, for which I would exchange, your invaluable society. For it, I find no recompense. My heart is even now with you, and at our peaceful fireside. You cannot fancy how vapid, and cold, are all things, which are presented to me here, compared to one smile of thine, and Sam (poor little fellow) . . . *[torn]* . . . without thinking of the trifling perplexities, which, were attendant, upon those happy hours, I only feel, and reflect upon, the realities of bliss. If once more, permitted to enjoy them, I hope to estimate them according to their value, which I now set, upon their absence. There is no sacrifice, which could in the nature of things, be required of me, that I would not, fondly make to enjoy those pleasures, (the pleasures of home) again. Were I not bound to duty here, I would freely start, in one hour, to meet, and embrace my dear, my beloved Wife, & boy. Without them my love, I assure [you], I cannot be happy, a single moment. If it were possible to love you in moderation, I might be more free, from the pains of absence! I hope after we meet again, never to feel, that pain, but to remain, as we ought to do, inseperable [sic].

Before I came here "Green,[3] the Book-maker," had fled. Moore the [torn] Commodore was here, and was . . . *[torn].* I have mentioned these facts, because I thought you might feel some anxiety about them, on account of previous threats made by them![4]

My presence, and conduct, has had the desired effect, and no one is heard, to say aught against me! If it is true, that the article, which I enclose, was written by the person supposed, you can judge of the standing, which I have, in the Metropolis! The old Lady of whom I have before written, and the one, who sent you the <u>daisy</u>, says she has a Religious Book to send you, by me!

It is now midnight my love, and I know you would advise me to retire. You would suppose my anxiety to be great, when I tell you, that I have not received but one letter from you, since I left home. You will please give my respects to Messers Palmers, and their families. Say to Mr Thomas Palmer, I know he will do the best he can, and so, I will be satisfied! *[torn]* . . . The people here never cease to ask me, "Why did you not bring Mrs. Houston??" My answer is different, to different people. To some, I am explicit, and to others less so. They never cease to ask of you, and about you. Some persons have been here, who represent you, as very clever, even more so, than my merits deserve! So those who think well of me, deem you <u>peerless</u>. If you do not come on this session, I cannot think myself, of coming again, without you. I have not heard from Anna, since I last wrote you, on that subject. In relation to her, I will expect your directions! I have not written, but now, and then, send Document, to Vernal and the family, to let them see, they are not forgotten.

Hug dear Sam, and tell him to write often! and to keep a letter ready to seal & send, by every opportunity! [Tell] Kitty to be a good girl and obey you . . .

[torn] [Hou]ston

---

[1]Thomas Ritchie, the editor of the *Union* and the Congressional Printer. Friend, 183.

[2]William F. Ritchie. Identified in Chaplain W. Morrison, *Democratic Politics and Sectionalism: The Wilmot Proviso Controversy* (Chapel Hill: University of North Carolina Press, 1967), 139.

[3]Houston is referring to Thomas Jefferson Green who wrote *Journal of the Texian Expedition Against Mier*. Friend, 83–84.

[4]Green and Commodore Edwin Moore were both enemies of Houston. Friend, 83–84.

Washington
27 April 1846

Dearest Love,

I was at church to day, and heard another fine sermon. It was the last of four, on the text, which I wrote to you of. Since I came home, I had the delightful satisfaction to receive yours of the 5th Inst, and one from Mr Palmer. (Thomas) He told me everything about the <u>Well</u>, etc. It can not be helped, and I blame no one! I hope, it is all for the best! I was happy to read the contents of your letter! so far as the[y] related to home, and home matters, but I was not happy, about the report of Sister Antoinette. It is all over now, I see by a letter from Major Cocke, which announced to me, that the wedding of Antoinette & Mr Power, would take place, on the 15th Inst. Well let it be so! I am sorry for one thing, and that is his friendship, and intimacy, with old <u>Monster Jones</u>.[1] I am sick at heart, and hourly pray, my Divine Master, to prepare me for his call. My Love, there is but one thing, which links me too fast to life! Yes, two things, You and Sam! Could it be his wealth? Did she, I wonder consult her relations? I see by the letter which, I enclosed to you from our friend, that Vernal had left there sometime since. Could she have not married at home? But my love these are matters, which we have little to do with. So soon to marry,[2] and from home too, distresses me! Lord, thy will be done!

You will have thought of these things, as I presume, or I would not have mentioned them! I fear, that Antoinette will receive but little aid from her companion, in affairs of religious character! I hope she may. If she, and the family are satisfied, we ought not to object, and further more, it is too late, to express regrets! We are all in the hand, of an almighty maker, and I pray that in his providence, we may meet again in health!

My whole heart is with you, and our boy, and relatives. I hope you had a pleasant, and safe trip to Huntsville, and I wish Kitty may do well, but I fear she will do no good at school. Do not my love, think that I disapprove of your decision, for, I <u>do not</u>.

I solemnly declare to you, My love, that I do not, hope to spend, one pleasant hour, until we meet. I would not leave my home, and my dear Wife, and kindred again, not for the honors of earth. If I am spared, there seems every probability, that I could command the confidence, of the American people, to the greatest extent, but this my Love, would only entail upon me misery! I am sated with public cares, for they cause me to contemplate public woes!! Yes my ever dear wife, and private woes also! My love, it may be, that Mr Power, and Antoinette may visit you, and if they should, treat them with all the kindness in your power! Forget all that has passed. She is our Sister!! I know your great affection for her, and that it would wring your heart, to say, or do anything, that would wound her feelings! I do not know how mother will like the match! I have not written to Sister Polly,[3] nor have I heard yet, particularly from them. My dear, when I reflect upon matters, it seems to me, that it will be best, to cast the affairs of others, upon their own hands, and the care, of Providence. To distress ourselves, would do no good, nor will it recall past. If you and I, can be reunited, I will be happy, and let the world move on, in the way of peace. I am so sorry, that you had so little time to write. I would like to hear more of Isabella's probable match.

I am very happy to hear that Sister Eliza, is a comfort to you! I pray, that you may be happy, and that your time will pass agreeably, and that a kind God, and Father, will sustain you, in your trials. I only wish that I could be with you, all the time of your sorrowing, and melancholy. Dearest, I know well, that you require soothing, and gentleness. All that our dear Sister, and the family can do, will be done, and if I live, and Congress should sit too long, I will leave here, and return to you!

I want you, to write to me particularly, and how you advance in health, and flesh.

I have been in my room all day, since I came from church, and part of the time reading my Bible. Not a night, do I retire to repose, until I have read a chapter, and invoked a blessing, from the most High, and if the prayers of the wicked are regarded, by the almighty, I hope to be answered, in the renewal of my heart, and in blessings upon you, and to our dear son, with all others, for whom we are duty bound to pray! To day I was reading in the 2nd kings, respecting the works of Elisha. Would it not interest Sam, to hear the history, of the narrations of the Shunamitish woman, and her Son? I feel a deep, and abiding interest in the course taken with him, and I feel that you will do everything, for him in your power. Don't whip him much my dear, as I hope he will harken to you without it. Consult with Sister. She will be for whipping enough I'm sure! Sam will be governed more by love than by fear. Don't you find it so? I am happy to hear that Sister will, as you think, be happy in Texas. I am also rejoiced that Mother will be with you. Were I in your place, I would not visit Trinity. You cannot do so, without danger to your situation. Indeed, I will fear some accident, on your trip to Huntsville, until I hear from you! I have written to you about coming on. This, you ought not to do, unless it can be done in safety, and in suitable company. The danger to you would be something, and you as well as I, are a <u>mark</u> for the arrows of malice, and detraction to be aimed at, without conscience, or remorse! I trust the baseness of the meanest heart, in the world may spare you! I defy all their shafts, while virtue, and integrity compose my shield!

Mr Palmer wrote to me about overflow. I am sorry for it! He also wrote to me about matters, of the farm. I am satisfied about all things, and know he will do the best he can!

You must embrace Sister Eliza for me, and all the family. Tell Mr Moore, I am sorry, his fence was not satisfied to remain with him!

Hug our dear boy, and William Louis.[4] Say to Houston, that I sometimes send him Documents, & papers. Tell the servants howda for me.

Thy ever devoted & faithful husband
Houston

Remember me to all the neighbours

---

[1]The friendship of Anson Jones and Houston had ended when Jones publicly claimed credit for the annexation of Texas and accused Houston of conniving with England and France to the prejudice of Texan interests. For more information on their feud see Friend, 191–92.
[2]Antoinette's first husband, William Bledsoe, had been dead less than a year.
[3]Houston's sister, Mary Houston Wallace.
[4]William Louis Moore, Houston's nephew.

51 : March 6, 1846—August 10, 1846

Washington
29th April 1846

My ever dear wife,

The Senate is in session, and members debating, all road bills. I cannot deny myself the pleasure of an effort to write you a few lines. You were right, (as I was informed) about Genl Henderson.[1] His appointment of Burnett[2] as Secy of State, seals his truth of opposition towards me—Let this be as it is!!! Last evening I received a letter, from a friend, who assured me, that Henderson, Burnett, Gov Runnels,[3] McKinney,[4] Williams,[5] Love[6] and their <u>retainers</u>, are to form a new party. *[An "X" is inserted here to correspond with the statement at the end of this letter.]* Well be it so. It will all be for good I hope! The person, or persons, who inform me, of these facts, are to be relied on. It excites me a little, and but a little! I have seen the announcement of Antoinettes marriage. A private letter advises me that, they have all gone to Caney to Mr [Charles] Powers plantation. They are to return to Galveston, and will, no doubt invite you there, on a visit. If they should, you can excuse yourself, from a compliance, and to be candid, I would be very sorry, that any one, whom I love, should be subject to association, with many of the friends of Mr Powers. He is a clever man, and one that I like, but his associations run into the circle, of those who would sacrifice me, if they could! With such you could not be happy, if you were safe! The object of my enemies, will now be, to assail me, in my domestic relations. They know that they are dearer to me, than all other things on earth! Their assaults will be, I apprehend, against the <u>females</u>, of my family. This they think would render me <u>desperate</u>, and thereby, they would gain the only advantage which they now hope to obtain.

Dearest, you can think of these things! For my own part, I will not lay myself liable, to any assault, from secrete [sic] enemies, if they were to know my most secret actions. My God who sees, and knows, my most secret acts will vindicate me, to <u>virtue</u>, and to <u>truth</u>!

My dear, Every day grows more and more irksome to me. I am as unhappy, as I can be, and will remain so, until I can embrace you & our dear boy, and meet all our kindred. No one can tell the extent of my affection for you. I thought it great, always, but now I realise more than I had before thought of. I only pray that we may again meet, and never again part, as we have done! To be seperated I can not endure! I was long since cured of my ambition, and now I am <u>doubly</u> cured! My friends, I learn have invited Genl Rusk and myself to New York, on the 12th of May. *[An "X" is inserted here to correspond to the one at the end of this letter.]* It is possible we may go, as that has been the point from where, so many slanders have issued against me. Dearest! Hug Sam, kiss Sister, and the Girls. Salute Mr Moore, and the Boys.

Thy ever doubly devoted Husband
Houston

[in the margin of the last page:] ^X We have not yet received the invitation, if it has been issued.

Houston

[in the margin of the first page:] ^X They say they "cant reach Houston, but they can kill off his Dogs." So says my friend—This is "declared publicly."

[1]James Pinckney Henderson, the first governor of Texas. Identified in Pickrell, 172.
[2]David G. Burnett, an old Houston enemy. *New Handbook of Texas*, vol. 1, 849.
[3]Hardin Runnels. *New Handbook of Texas*, vol. 5, 715.
[4]Thomas McKinney of Galveston. *New Handbook of Texas*, vol. 4, 420.
[5]Samuel Williams of Galveston. Ibid.
[6]James Love of Galveston. *New Handbook of Texas*, vol. 4, 305.

Washington
30th April 1846

My ever Dearest,

I have only time to say a word. Enclosed you will receive a letter from Mr C. Power.[1] I sent it so soon as perused. You will see its contents. It is all well enough. I will write a kind letter in return. I will not for the world do aught, that could mar your intercourse, with your Sister.

We have not too many kindred, that we need fall out, with any of them. Let us rather cultivate good will, and affection.

Tomorrow I hope to bring out my speech. To day, the senate adjourned over until the 4th of May. This is outrageous. They say it is to have the carpet taken up for summer! This is worse, than all! I hope my dear, that you will be well, and happy, until we meet. I sent you a paper to day merely to let you know, that I would keep my word even in trifles, by sending you something every day.

Embrace our dear kindred, with love to Mother & Vernal. Salute the neighbours. Tell the Servants to be faithful. Hug our dear boy. Your letters, are worth more to me, than Gold or diamonds.

Thy ever devoted Husband
Sam Houston

I send you my friend "Uncle Joe's alias," Col Eldridge's[2] compliments, and a squeeze to Sam, with a N. York Herald of the 29th. It contains news from England. I will by the first chance, send a locket to you, with a Dagueratype likeness of myself, and a place for one of yourself. Mr Heeley,[3] whom we saw at the Hermitage,[4] has me sitting at every leisure time, for him, to take a likeness of me, for Louis Phillippe. It will be a good one!

Devotedly
Houston

P. S. Dear, I have just thought of it! <u>We married, to please ourselves</u>, and Antoinette, and Mr Power, have only done the <u>same thing</u>! Just thought of it!!!

Houston

[1]This letter has not been located.
[2]Joseph Eldridge. Identified by Frank X. Tolbert, *An Informal History of Texas from Cabeza de Vaca to Temple Houston* (New York: Harper and Brothers, Publishers, 1951), 169.
[3]In May of 1845, George P. A. Healey, an American art student from Paris, had been com-

missioned by Louis Philippe, the Emperor of France, to paint a series of portraits of American statesmen to hang in the royal gallery in Versailles. George P. A. Healy, *Reminiscences of a Portrait Painter* (Chicago: A. C. McClurg and Company, 1894), 138. Among his portraits were Andrew Jackson, Henry Clay, Daniel Webster and John Quincy Adams. No information has been located to indicate what became of this portrait of Houston.

[4]Andrew Jackson's home in Nashville, Tennessee.

∞

Huntsville, May 1st, 1846

Ever dearest love,

No letter yet, since the one from Louisville.[1] My anxiety is almost more than I can bear, but it can not be interminable, and I have some fortitude with it, and a <u>little</u> <u>pateince</u> [sic], which I hope will not desert me at this trying season. I had calculated upon getting letters from you, by Mr William Palmer, who recently made a visit to Huntsville, but he returned on yesterday, with nothing from you, except a newspaper containing the intelligence of your arrival in Washington City.[2]

This was a sore disappointment, but it was immediately followed by another. Tonight I recd a book with your direction, entitled "Fremont's first and second expeditions," but no accompanying letter. I thank you Love, for the book, and for the "Balsam of wild cherry," which came with it, but oh how delighted I would have been by one of your sweet <u>love-letters</u>. Isabella and I went over this evening, to see sister Eliza, and as Houston was absent for the night, on some of your business, Mr Moore returned with us. As we passed Mr Palmer's, he came out, and informed us that a gentleman was spending the night at his house, on his way to Cincinnati Ohio, who was a resident of that city. I hastened home, for the purpose of beginning a letter to you, before night, but found it impossible to do so, and I am now writing to you at a late hour of the night, but am cheered by the soft breathings of our sleeping boy. He is truly a comfort to me, but my concern for his future well-fare is indescribable. I fear my affections are too much engrossed by earthly ties. Should the Lord call me away, they would cause me some sad struggles, but oh who can resist the fascination of those sweet words husband and child! I will try to prepare myself for any event, and if it should be his gracious will to call my spirit home, will endeavor to leave my dear ones entirely in his hands.

I wrote you a few days ago, in relation to Antoinette's marriage, but I was so excited about it at the time, that I hardly know what I said. I hope that she has married very well, but I can not imagine why she did not consult her relations about it. I should be gratified to know that you were pleased with her choice, though I know you would have preferred a postponement of the marriage.

How did you like Gen Rusk's escort to the Senate chamber? Not much, I opine. "A bad beginning," truly, but perhaps the old firedrake may hold good with him, and he may yet end well. Most earnestly do I desire it, for I know that much depends upon a unanimity between you. Did you observe the paragraph concerning him and yourself, in the 5th column of the 106th page of the "Weekly Herald," April 4th? If so, do you intend to let it pass? Will Gen. Rusk say nothing about it? I hope he will, for I should be sorry to think he had so little honesty as to wear the laurels, which another had won.

Col Stubblefield made his first appearance at Mr Moore's today. He came on the very unromantic business of having his horse shod, but found it convenient to go to the house to rest a few minutes and get dinner,—of course a very good one.

Mr Palmer tells me that Kitty has had one whipping, since she commenced going to scool [sic], but that she is learning very rapidly. It is a great relief to me, for in my present state of mind and constant suffering of some kind or the other, peculiar to my situation, I believe the care of her would distract me. I feel very reluctant dearest to take leave of you, but it is late, and I am feeble and nervous. I expect to have an opportunity of writing again on monday by the "Belle."

I have never suffered an opportunity to pass, of writing to you, when there was the slightest chance of conveying a letter to you, but I fear you have recd very few of my letters. Be that as it may, I intend still to write when ever I can do so. All send thier love to you. Mary says give my love to Uncle, and tell him I intend to write to him soon. Present me affectionately to our cousins and namesakes, and my compliments also to Col. Elridge who is with you I perceive by the paper.

Ever thy devoted wife,
M. L. Houston

[1]See Houston to Margaret, March 23, 1846.

[2]Margaret may be referring to the *New York Tribune* of March 31, 1846, whose Washington correspondent reported Houston's arrival from Pittsburgh and his registration at Brown's Hotel. Friend, 168.

Washington
2nd May 1846

Dearest,

All day, I have been engaged, in preparing my speech, for the Congress, and sitting an hour, to Mr Healy, the artist. Major Donelson, & family left yesterday, for the mission to Prussia. I only saw the family twice, but if I had known, that they would have been off so soon, I would have gone, and taken leave of them. The last time that I saw them, was in a small party at the Presidents. You, and Sam, were the themes of conversation. You with the Madame,[1] and you & Sam, with Mary.[2] Sam, tho' was the principal topic, as I had told Mary, that he yet loved, & spoke of her in Texas! This morning, I promised to spend with Mr Ritchie, of the "Union" in a family, & social way. I would if I could, be glad to forego my promise, but a month has passed, and I have not yet returned his visit.

My Dear, I feel sad, and melancholy. Sad, because I will be detained here, and melancholy, because you are far from me, and I can not see you every hour, or hear from you every day. I would say more, on this subject, only that I am fearful, you would suppose it an effort of mine to please you, and thereby, fail in the attempt.

To day I rec'd a letter from Major [James] Reily in New York. He is as kind as ever, and will be here in a few days. By him, I hope to send you some things—trifles of course.

My Love, I pray you to have no uneasiness, about my leaving you again. I assure you, that will depend entirely, upon yourself. As to me, I am more than satisfied with absence. It is doubly painful, to what ever was before. I have not enjoyed, an hours happiness since we parted! Nor do I, my love, anticipate one, until we meet. To this, I invoke my Creator as a witness. I am more change[d], in habits, and character of thought, than I before conceived it possible to be changed. I am not morose, nor selfish, but there is a seriousness of feeling, and an apprehension of ever indulging in too much levity, which, I never before experienced.

That you feel anxiety, my dear, I doubt not, but then you are at home, and Sam is with you. Poor little lad, how I would rejoice, to meet his greeting, and again hear [h]is noise, trying to drown, his mothers voice, that his might be the first, to claim response. Dearest, do you remember, once at Judge Lockharts[3] how deeply his feelings were wounded, because I passed by him on my return from town, and did not caress him! My heart—my entire affections, are with you, and with him. If Heaven, should kindly permit, us all to meet, I will then be able, I hope to appreciate properly, the kindness of our Almighty Father!

I do not know, what more to write! It seems to me, that I could write always, and yet wish for the capacity to write double. For sometime, I have not written, our dear Boy, a letter. The next time, that I attempt to write him, I think I must also embrace Cousin Betty. I would truly like to see how they come on, in the way of friendship! Sams friendship, I think, in some degree, depends on how much, he is affraid [sic]. I hope as he gets older, he will feel higher impulses, and nobler motives, for attachments. Caressed as he has been, it is natural, for him, to think that he alone, is an object of care, and preservation, and so conduct himself.

Sunday 3rd

My Very Dear Margaret,
I have just returned from church, and after dinner, I intend to return and witness the administration of the sacrament. It will take place at

4 oclock. To day a strange gentleman preached, and one of less ability than Mr Sproul. I have seen Maj Reily, since he arrived. He went with me to church, and will dine with me, to day. He will leave here on wednesday for Texas. By him I must try, and write! If I should keep on thro' this Session, writing, as I have done, you will think me quite a troublesome correspondent, I fear. Not as to matter, or quality, but quantity. Tomorrow, I hope to get through with my speech, and soon have it for you? To extremes—My dear, you have not said a word about the "Cat" & —. How many had she? What does poor Sam say, and do? that is smart? Does he talk of me? Is he amiable? What traits of character, does he disclose, that are desirable, and that will conduce to your happiness? Many I hope!!!! Is he yet truthful, & honest. Dearest, Don't whip him, if you can avoid it. I have since we parted, thought much, on that subject, and conclude that little whipping is best. Let it be if at all, for good cause. Dearest, when I begin to write about these things, it brings me, so near home, that I am almost maddened. My brain, and my heart, are almost on fire! The sun here, does <u>not</u> shine so bright, nor does the earth look lovely here, as it does in Texas. You my Love, are there! You lend, or impart to me, a cheerfulness, to every thing associated with you, or with which you are associated, in my memory!

Last night, until after 10 oclock, I passed at Mr Ritchies, and had as usual, to answer many questions, why you did not come! I told them, <u>Sam was near three years old, and that you could not well come</u>!

Dearest, I have again been to church, and witnessed the ceremony, of the Sacrament. It seemed to me, to partake of the fashions, of the city—cold, and no feeling. Indeed, my ever dear Wife, I love our homely scenes far more, than all, and every thing, which I here behold! The sun is setting, and if I could, only be at your side, or calmly walking, in the sweet evening, I would be, the most happy of mortals. We could talk of the present, and the past! But now I may breathe of it, think of it, and even speak of it, but there is no one to give a response. You alone can do that, and impart happiness.

Your voice, would assure me, that indeed, you were with me,

and, I could tell you, how much, how truly, how devotedly, and how faithfully, I do love you! And then Sam, with his "little words," and his gambols, would make us happy, truly happy! These are scenes, which I once possessed, and once enjoyed! I pray for their return, and with them, <u>additional</u> pleasures![4] It is to me most painful, that I cannot be alone, and uninterrupted, when writing to you. There is some excuse for one friend, calling on me, this evening. It was my friend Blair,[5] who gave me the "New Testament"[6] when I was in exile. Fourteen years I think, we had not seen each other. His heart is as warm, and devoted as it ever was! He has changed less than almost any one, with whom I have met! For fourteen years, he says he had not any children, but has renewed the good work, and as his first, are married off, he can provide for several. I do not know how many, but he has several Grandchildren! "'Tis *[blurred]*, is a mighty *[blurred]*." All day, I was in hopes, that I would get a letter, but none has come! I am fearful, that you have no mail, at Raven Hill, from what you wrote me! I must see to it on tomorrow! It is the only hope of pleasure, that I cherish, hearing from you often, and hearing that you are happy. That embraces every thing—You must be well, to be happy, and all that we most love must also be happy. It is now past eleven P.M. I must "read," and retire to rest.

Oh! do embrace our dear Boy, Kiss Sister, & the Girls, and my love to Mr Moore, & Sons.

Thy faithful & ever devoted Husband
Sam Houston

[1]Elizabeth Martin Randolph (Mrs. Andrew) Donelson. *Dictionary of American Biography*, v. 3, Part I, 363–64.
[2]Mary Donelson, Andrew's daughter. Ibid.
[3]Judge John Lockhart, with whom the Houstons stayed at Washington-on-the-Brazos. For more information see Johnnie Lockhart Wallis, *Sixty Years on the Brazos* (Austin: Texian Press, 1967), 24, 52.
[4]Houston is referring to the expected baby.
[5]Francis P. Blair was the editor of the *Washington Globe*. Friend, 34.
[6]This book is in the collection of Houston artifacts at the Sam Houston Memorial Museum, Huntsville, Texas.

The following letter written by Margaret is in the holdings of the Texas State Archives, Austin, Texas. Due to a large hole in the center of the letter, several words are missing, for which the editor has supplied possible interpretations in brackets.

Raven Hill May 4, 1846

My dear Husband,

If you [received] all the letters which I have written you, I am sure [they] consume [?] a great deal of time to read them. *[torn]* have no fear that it was bestowed grudgingly, for I must be[lieve] any news from home, however common place, will be [interesting] to you. Our life here, is so unvaried, that I have seldom ever any thing with which to entertain you, except the continuation of God's mercies to us, in the preservation of our lives and health, but this I am sure is more welcome, than any other intelligence I could give you. Our days pass along in one calm unruffled stream. We have few pleasures, but as few sorrows. The girls[1] sometimes become very low-spirited, on account of thier total seclusion from society, but I try to keep them alive by holding up bright pictures of the future, and assuming a cheerfulness, which does not belong to me. I fear I am a sad comforter, but it keeps my mind from dwelling too much upon the loss of your society, and perhaps is good for me in the end.

Houston says I must [tell you] that you must not calculate too much upon your crop, and then whatever the result may be, you will not be disappointed. I sincerely hope that it will turn out well, but it depends much you know, upon the seasons, and they are in the hands of our Heavenly Father, who will order everything aright. He has brought us safely thus far, through many trials and difficulties, and oh let us confide cheerfully in his goodness and mercy through the remainder of our lives! It will soon be the 6th anniversary of our marriage. How many thousands have been longer married, and have had less happiness and [more] sorrow than we have had! I love to

61 : MARCH 6, 1846—AUGUST 10, 1846

think of [the sweet] hours we have passed together, particularly those [*torn*] enlivened by the prattle and smiles of our dear [son.] There may be happier days than these in store for us [*torn*] smiles as bright may cheer our little [*torn*] but I must not indulge this sweet dream. [*torn*] must be prepared for the worst, for who can tell [what] the result will be!

I can scarcely write Love, for my [tea]rs. My feelings have been so long supprest, that I can scarcely restrain them longer. Oh that you were near me, that I might weep on your dear bosom, and tell you all my hopes and fears. I fear dearest my letters are very egotistical things, but I realy see so little to direct my mind from myself, and our own little circle, that I have nothing else to write about.

Sister Eliza came over and spent yesterday with us. The visit was realy cheering to me, for she has been confined so closely at home, by the protracted illness of one of her young servants, that we very rarely receive a visit from her. Our dear Betty's health is improving. She has spent several days at her Father's, and the use of the water, which is evidently mineral, has done a great deal for her. Mr Moore's health is not good. He suffers much from an affliction of the stomach, and sister Eliza seems quite unhappy about him. Have you ever written to any of our relations in Ala.? If you have not, I will not complain, for I know your time is much occupied.

I am in daily expectation of a letter from Antoinette, announcing her marriage. The cessation of the mails, accounts to me satisfactorily, for not rec[eiving] one before. I have heard, but I do not know with much truth, that they are living in Galveston [and] that it is reported in that place, that Sarah [Ann will] marry Thomas Power, a younger brother. I do[*torn*] how a cousin of our family with the John[*torn*] stock, will turn out these stormy times, but [God] grant that it may not prove a disunion of those who have been reared like twin flowers on the same branch! Do tell me what you think of it Love. Isabella says I must tell you, that she will not marry Gustavus, at least until your return. Dearest, do you intend to let Williams[2] palm his Mexican negotiation upon you. I hardly think you will, but he is making strong efforts to do it. I enclose a heart's ease which Sam and

I have kissed for you. You must take the kiss, and then present it to our interesting cousin Miss Houston,[3] of whom we have heard so much. I think she will prize it, on account of its having bloomed on Raven hill, but if you doubt it, do not give it to her.

Farewell my love
Thine devotedly
M. L. Houston

[1]The Moore nieces.
[2]Samuel Williams had been a Commissioner to Mexico during the Republic. Friend, 86.
[3]Mary Houston, the daughter of Houston's cousin John Houston.

Washington
7th May 1846

Dearest,

Two notes of yours came to hand last night. One of them was finished at Huntsville.[1] Oh they made me very happy, for I was depressed, and sad! (I was sorry for the little mistake, which you made with Mrs McDonald). You would have been welcome, and I regret, that she would be liable to be mortified. You must explain it delicately to her!

Houston wrote to me, but did not tell me why Mr Palmer gave up the farm. If it was for the reason of <u>expence</u> [sic], why that was not much. If Houston will do as well, and I hope he will, and Mr Palmer was not mortified, why I am glad of it. If Houston, does not understand matters, he can call on his father, or Mr William Palmer for advice, If any difficulty should arise, their advice may be useful. I am glad that you are pleased with the cows, and I like the Disposition which you have made of some of them. I am glad that Maria is getting well, and hope Billy will have some time, to work in the farm. You said nothing of Jose! I hope ire this time, the mails are running again in Texas, and will continue.

You have no idea of my happiness, on finding that your spirits are so good, and I sincerely hope, they may so remain. Last night, I dreamed that I was at home with you, and it was a pleasant night. I only dreamed of <u>you</u>, and no one else.

Your Dear story of Houston, & Sam, amused me! Sam must have had, some profound reflections, about future manhood and a <u>hunters triumph</u>! I rejoice, that he is so hearty, fat, and promising. Dear Boy, I hope he will be a blessing to his Parents! In my last I gave some advice about him. I hope it may please <u>you</u>, Love!

I will write to Houston so soon as I can get time. I thank my dear nieces, for their kind notes, of regard. They have time, and it would give them employment! They had better have me, to criticize their letters, than lovers, to whom, they may chance to write! I do not know what my friend Stubblefield, meant, by his conduct. I am happy to know, that Mr Moore, Sister, and the family are pleased with Texas, and that the Girls, & Houston will remain with you. They are most welcome, and by no one more than Sam, as I presume. Won't they, without any design, help to spoil him?

Do write me, about, his manners, and what he says, when a letter of mine, is received, and read! I wish you would have him measured, to see his hight [sic], at three years old. It will be half his hight, when he is grown. Let him know for what reason his measure is taken. I hope to take, or send some fine things to you, and him, <u>and some others</u>! What they will be, I dont pretend to say. Maj Reily has been sick here, for two days, with a chill, and Genl Rusk, has also been ill, with a bad cold![2]

I was unwell for a day or two, owing to a cold, and the dampness of the Senate chamber! I am now writing in the Chamber of the Senate, and speaking is going on! Not of as much interest to me as to think, and write about you, and those, that we love!

I have written you so many, and such ardent "love letters" that I am fearful, you will think, that I can not realise, that we are married, and that, I am now courting, and deem it necessary to flatter you, by constant professions! Don't it look very much like this, my dear? I certainly, do not love you less, than when I was your <u>professed lover</u>. No! I love you a thousand times more, than I ever did! I cannot for one hour, cease to think of you, and often, when Sam, does not enter into the picture of my thoughts! You are always present, and Sam often!

I think of all your cheerful group, and wish myself with you, every hour! The only solace, which I have, is to write to you, every moment, which I can spare. Tomorrow night, I intend to go with Col Reily, to the President's to a small "levee," [*in the margin:* the last this season, if I have not to go on account of some Texian!!] and I can assure you, that if I live I will think of you, and the "cows," and if I speak of them, I will let you know what I say. If it is not great, or smart, I will try, & make it genteel, and cheerful, if I can. You may say to Houston, that I will be satisfied, at what he may think best to do! Tell him to write to me, what he thinks, will be the number of acres, which he thinks will be in corn this year! Tell him to let the ground be planted when the Rye is cut. Such things as he may want, or need, for the use of the farm, he can get at Mr Hannays,[3] in Huntsville.

You must hug Sam. Give my love to all our kindred, compliments to the neighbours, and say to the servants, that I will rely upon them to be faithful!

Since I wrote to our relatives in Alabama, I have not heard from them. I will send you the letters, when I get them. If I should live, and return to the City, next fall, and you should wish, or cannot come all the way on, I will so arrange matters, that you can come as far as Alabama, if you shou'd wish to do so. I cannot bear, to be removed so far from you! About my returning to the Senate, will depend upon you. I am cured, of all love of office, or station, when it interferes, with my love of you, and the sweets of home! My hand writing, is now improving, owing to the condition of my wound. Rusk, and myself are invited, on the 12th Inst to New York, to a celebration of the Tamany Society (democratic).

Thy ever Devoted Houston

P.S. I do not know that, we will go there!

[1]See Margaret to Houston, April 14, 1846.
[2]Rusk was also suffering from chills, fever, and rheumatism. Mary Whatley Clarke, *Thomas J. Rusk: Soldier, Statesman, and Jurist* (Austin, Tx.: Jenkins Publishing Company,

1971), 165.
[3]Houston is probably referring to Robert Hannay, who had done business as a merchant in Galveston. Identified in Gifford White, *The First Settlers of Galveston County, Texas* (Nacogdoches, Tex.: Ericsons Books, 1985), 14.

Washington
10th May 1846

My ever Dear Wife,

Last night, about 12 oclock I returned from the Presidents, where I had been by request, to discourse about the unpleasant news from the Rio Grande.[1] On my return to my room I found my mail, which had been brot [sic] in, during my absence, when I had the inexpressible pleasure to find a letter from you, of the 19th. I read it with the greatest avidity possible. The contents of it made me truly happy— happy to hear that you had received my letter from Louisville, and that all the family were well. You certainly did right my Love, in placing Kitty at school, and you ought to keep her there until she gets a start, and learns to read. As to the other matters, of the letter, I will prat [sic] of them, in the sequel of my letter. For the present, I had intended to have ceased until I went to church, and returned, but a heavy rain commenced as I was ready to set out, and will prevent my going. I was there in the morning, and as usual, I "contributed," for some purpose, which was not announced by the minister. It was not the stated Preacher, but a stranger to me! If I am spared until next sabbath, I will try, and go to the Baptist Church. If I do contribute, my Love, I would rather do it to that church, because it may be a means, of enabling that society to send, a missionary to our neighbourhood, and add to your happiness! In looking out my window, I see the avenue deluged in water! and the rain continuing.

I was happy to hear all that you had written, and amused at some portions of your letter! You say my Love, if we should all live to meet, that Sam, <u>will be quite a companion for me</u>! and then you speak of "selfishness," and denying Sam, my companionship! I do assure you, my ever dear Wife, that tho' I love our boy dearly, yet I would think his society, a part from that of his <u>dear Mother</u>, as a poor requital, for the loss of hers! I am glad that you esteem him, absolutely, a <u>noble child</u>, and still think him <u>handsome</u>. It delights me to <u>hear</u> from you, what he says, and how he says things. I pray every night of my life, to our Gracious Father for blessings, upon you, and him, & that we may all meet again, and be happy, under our own Vine & Fig tree, and never again to be seperated, until He shall call us, to our everlasting home, and the bosom of our God, & our Saviour.

My love, you speak of my <u>taking care of your</u> interests, "in your absence," "or my absence from you!!?" Be <u>confident</u> my Love, that <u>they</u> <u>will</u> <u>not</u> <u>suffer</u>, or be disregarded, for just so far, as my hopes of Heaven extend, so far shall they be maintained inviolate, and inviolable!! To commit an act of deliberate perjury, no one would suspect me! And you my love, when we meet, at the Bar of our God, will find that my last assurance to you, has been, and will be kept <u>sacred</u>, and <u>inviolate</u>! This place has the character of immorality and impurity. It is so, no doubt, to a great extent, but fortunately, for me my associations, are not of a character, ever to expose me to temptation, & if they were, my love, for you, and for my conscience sake, would be enough, to <u>ensure my fidelity</u>! If I were <u>not pure</u> from principle, very fear, would make me so, lest, I should provoke the wrath, of the almighty, and He, should in anger destroy my domestic, and conjugal happiness. Enough of this my Love, for I am sure, you do not suppose, that I would either be ungrateful, or unkind to you, if I had no other risk of action! I thank you, for telling me of the wedding of my old friend Stedham![2] There is some romance truly in the matter, and the very <u>gist</u> of it is, that my "old Dentist fend," as Sam would call him, should object, to his Daughter marrying any person! I hope the new <u>pair</u>, will pair <u>well</u>, and <u>pairing</u>, make pairs!

My Love, By the bye, I hope, if I were to take Sam, from you occasionally, should we be so happy as to meet again, that you would not be alone, but even have <u>company</u>, in which, you would feel, at least, <u>equal</u>, if not <u>greater interest</u>? In your last two letters Dearest, you have made no allusion, to <u>this</u> subject! I hope <u>all</u> is going well, and that you will not suffer from the "lyp[*blurred*]" until by the blessing of Heaven, we may again, embrace each other.

Do you my Love recollect, a request of Sam's, made (a few days previous to my starting) of you, "to get a little sister for him?" Should Sam's wishes have been anticipated my dear, I will not be angry, if you are reconciled. At all events my Love, we are too far a part, to quarrel on this subject! I hope Dearest, we will sooner, (than we have anticipated) have an opportunity of settling all our differences, face to face, and not defer, their adjustment! "Adjustment!" You will see by my speech,[3] which I send by to days mail, that this is a favorite term with me, in preference to "compromise," and "temporize." You will find my speech in the daily Union. It is not a very fine one! The positions are all good, and tenable! Much as I was dissatisfied with it, at first, I concluded to publish it, and let it pass, for what it is worth. Truly, it is better in print, than I thought it would be. If it is not good, it is because you were not present. Had you been present, the speech would have been superior to what it is. Since I have read it, I think, you will be gratified with it, as it was my first Senatorial effort! Enough of this!

I am amused at what you write about our Nieces,[4] but will not express any opinion, as to propriety of disposing of them, on the terms, which you think may be proposed! This recals [sic] information, which I have about Sarah Ann! It is said in Galveston, that she is about to marry Mr Thomas Power, the brother of Charles.[5] I do not vouch for it! I learned that he is quite clever, and wealthy!

Young people will marry, and there is no way to prevent such things. Will she make him go to Alabama for her?[6] or marry at the Island? Our relations are more cheap, I fear, than when you would not marry, or come to Texas, but required me, to go after you to Alabama, and indeed, my Love, tho' six years have now passed, I think that I got a "good bargain," and tho' I might not be willing, to go as far again for any other Lady, I certainly would for you.[7] This is monday night 11th May. To day we had a smart debate on the affairs of the U States, and Mexico. I took some part in the discussion, but, as the main question did not come up, I said but little. So far as I did go, I sustained myself, well enough! It is past midnight, and I hope you, and the family, are all enjoying sweet, and healthy repose!

Major Reily left here, at a time when I had not finished a letter, and therefore, I did not send the Locket, nor a Breast Pin, which he presented to me for you.[8] It is made of Buckhorn. It is pretty, and when you see it, you can then judge of its merits. I will soon, I hope be able, to send it to the care of Major Cocke for you! or to Mr. Torrey.[9] All my old friends, Ladies, and Gentlemen, beg me to present them to you, when I write. They say, you must be most worthy, and the best evidence, of your worth is my reformation, and improvement. You can, from this infer, that my conduct is much approved, which is certainly true! I will hope for as many letters, as can be conveniently written my Love, for I do again declare to you, that the only thrill, of pleasure, which I have felt, since we parted, has arisen from your letters to me. I was happy to see Bro. Will, and his family, but even that was not like the pleasure, which I feel, when I can kiss a letter, of yours, ire I break the seal.

'Tis long past midnight, Love, and I must retire. Salute all, who are most dear to us. Press our dear Boy to your heart, for me. I will pray unceasingly, for your health, and happiness.
My ever dear Love,

Tomorrow, I think my dear, that the Senate, will pass an act or Bill, declaring <u>war against Mexico</u>. The House passed it *[X in margin here corresponds to note below]* to day? I hope, neither Mr Moore, nor Houston, will go out in the army, at this time. They are "new comers" to Texas!

Thy ever devoted and truly affectionate Husband
Sam Houston

[X]Appropriating 10,000,000$, and authorizing, the raising [of] 50,000 volunteers!

[1]According to Polk's diary, Houston approved administration policy and thought that the war should be prosecuted with vigor. James K. Polk, *The Diary of a President, 1846–1849*, ed. Allan Nevins (New York: Longmans, Green and Company, 1929), 84–86.
[2]Houston is probably referring to Zachariah Steadham, a resident of Houston County. Iden-

tified in *Poll Lists*, 160.

[3]Houston is referring to his speech on the Oregon Question given April 15, 1846. *Writings*, vol. 4, 451–71.

[4]Isabella, Mary, and Bettie Moore.

[5]The marriage took place on May 21, 1846 in Matagorda. Swenson, 28.

[6]Houston is referring to the fact that he had to return to Alabama in order to marry Margaret.

[7]Houston is referring to the fact that Margaret declined to marry him in Texas, but insisted that he return to Alabama for the wedding.

[8]This pin is now in the Sam Houston Memorial Museum, Huntsville, Texas.

[9]David K. Torrey, a merchant identified in *Handbook of Texas*, vol. 2, 790.

∽

Washington

15th May 1846

My Dear Love,

I know this will be one of the most agreeable communications, which I have made to you, since we parted. It encloses one, from your dear friend Mrs Woods,[1] late of Boston.

I went the other night to the Levee, to introduce some Texians, and had the happiness to meet her Ladyship, and at once we became friends. The moment that we "shook hands," (for you must know my dear, that the ladies claim the right) she told me who she was, and made tender enquiries, for you & Sam. There upon, I asked her to accept my arm, and was her Beau, for the evening. This was the first instance, of the kind which has taken place with me, and so I told her Ladyship. I presented her an ever green on your account. On last evening I took her a boquet, sent to me, by an old Lady, from Mount Vernon, but she was not in, so, as I was coming down stairs, who should I meet but Mrs [James H.] Cocke from Galveston, on her way to see her mother, about twenty miles from this place on the Potomac. After conversing some time with her, I left her, promising to see her this morning with her baggage to the Steam Boat, which I did.

Thus my dear, you see I am useful to your friends. Mrs Cocke, will remain sometime with her friends, unless her Mother will return with her. In that event, she will soon leave, for home. The Major had sent me a letter for her, which I had the pleasure to deliver early this morning.

I am in great haste, as the Senate will meet in a few moments, so I must close. To day, I send you one of my speeches in pamphlets!

I will see Mrs Woods, again if I can. I will write you more anon. On tomorrow she leaves town.

Hug our dear Boy, for me, and embrace all our dear kinsfolk. I will send a speech to Vernal & Mother.

I did not go to N York, as proposed. Business would not allow me.

Thy ever devoted and doating [sic] Husband
Sam Houston

[1]Almira Marshall Woods. Identified in Pauline Jones Ganrud, *Marriage, Death and Legal Notices from Early Alabama Newspapers 1819–1893* (Easley, S. C.: Southern Historical Press, 1981), 610.

Washington
15th May 1846

My Love,

Since I wrote to you this morning, I made a short speech in Senate, on some army matters,[1] while your friend, Mrs Woods, was in the Gallery. Another subject had been on tapis yesterday, and I intended to speak, and I told her so. She had attended, and I considered her as your proxy, so I made what Genl Rusk pronounced, one of the best efforts, that I ever made. So you see my love, that I can only make an effort, to please you! Not that you are so hard to please, but that I love you, so much that I only feel an interest in pleasing you.

I send you a slip from the "Kentucky Gazette," in which you will see a puff to me. I do not know the writer. He is a Democrat! I send you many things of this kind. They will do to amuse you.

You need have no uneasiness, about my going into the army! I have no intention of the kind my love. It will be some time, before laurels will be gathered in Mexico!!! I fear that mishaps, will have to teach the Generals, how to win success! I hope they will make short work of the war. They ought to do so! If they do not, they will learn

Mexico, how to defeat them!

I am tormented almost to death with company, and have to cut short this letter. Tomorrow I have to visit Baltimore, and return next day. I will write so soon as I come back. Two letters a day is rather too <u>digging</u>! Don't you think so Love?

Thy ever devoted Husband
Houston

[1]For the text of this speech see *Writings*, vol. 4, 430–31.

∽

The original of the following letter from Margaret is in the Houston Collection of materials in the Center for American Studies (formerly called the Barker History Center) at the University of Texas in Austin.

Raven hill May 16, 1846

My beloved husband,

I was made exceedingly happy, on last Monday, by the reception of several packages of letters from you. All that you have written since your arrival in Washington City, up to the 15th ult, were received at the same time. You can imagine my state of mind, for a few weeks past. It amounted almost to desperation, and I often longed "for the wings of a dove, that I might flee away and be at rest." I now mourn over the impatience and restlessness, which I then indulged, but alas, I can not recall the precious moments, I have wasted in useless melancholy. Never have I been so strongly tempted, to act in opposition to the dictates of my judgment, as by your proposal to join you in Washington. I felt willing at first, to risk my life, in the attempt, rather than be longer without you, but our dear sister Eliza's cooler judgment prevailed against it, and I agreed the more readily, to be governed by her, because I knew that with me, feeling had so much to do, in the matter, that it would realy be unwise to decide for myself. Sister E. came over on thursday morning, and in the evening, we had so violent a hailstorm, that she spent the night with us. We conversed much together, and I was much cheered by her visit. She says I must tell you, that she is as well satisfied, as she could be in Texas. We have great excitement throughout our county, about the war. A large number of volunteers are preparing to set off, and as usual on such occasions, a perfect mania is abroad, on the subject. Houston [Moore] is almost crazy to go, but I have no apprehension of his doing so, before your return. Nothing however, but the care of us, could keep him. Col Wood[1] expects to set off, with his company on thursday. He sent up today, to request my presence at his house on next monday, to direct the making of his flag. Perhaps he thinks my connection with you, may give it some charm. I think I will go and take the girls, as it will be a sort of recreation for them.

Sam was delighted with his letters,[2] and looked very important, but did not say any thing sufficiently smart for repitition [sic]. I wish you could have seen him this morning, in the yard, picking flowers, and arranging them in a boquet. I watched him, with a great deal of interest, for I knew its destination. At length, he brought it to me, and exclaimed "here ma is a boquet for you!?" I said "I thank you my son, you have made mother very happy!" "Now ma," he then asked "will you not tell pa that I treat you so good?" His great ambition seems to be, that I should make a good report of his conduct to you. He says I must write to pa, that he has put away some pretty wood for him to cut.[3] He is now quite familiar with many portions of bible history, and seems each day more interested in it, but I find it necessary to be very particular in selecting narratives for him, and delineating characters, for if he once receives a wrong impression, it is almost impossible to eradicate it. For instance he is horror-struck at Abraham's willingness to slay his son. I have endeavored to explain to him, in the simplest language, the faith and obedience of the venerable patriarch, and to fix his attention entirely upon those beautiful traits, in his character, but when I tell him, that after a while, Isaac himself, became the Father of two sons, he eagerly looks up, and asks if Abraham wanted to kill them too! But notwithstanding these little difficulties, I would not exchange the happiness, which I derive

73 : March 6, 1846—August 10, 1846

from instructing him, for all the wealth of the world.

Dearest I enclose you my letter to Mrs Allen,[4] which I wish you to read and forward to her, enclosing _if you please_ Love, one dollar for the year's subscription. It is a poor price for all the aid she will give me. A few lines from you, accompanying my letter, I know would be very gratifying and encouraging to her, but I do not require it of you darling, for I know you have few moments of your own, and I am almost selfish enough to claim them all. A thousand thanks for your willingness to pay my subscription to the A. F. B. society. I thought Mother had paid it, but she removed to Texas, so soon after it, that I suppose it escaped her memory. I would like very much to have the bibles, but be careful love to send the money, in such a way, that it will certainly be recd. I return the letter,[5] that you may see how to direct your answer, but I wish you to preserve it very carefully, as I place a high value upon the last page, on account of your allusion to an old acquaintance of mine! You say you were once prodigiously in love with her. Well darling, I know that she loved you devotedly, but oh her love does not deserve to be mentioned on the same day, with what I feel for you now. But why do I speak of my feelings at all! I can not describe them. Oh my Love, if you could only look into my heart this moment, I know you would never leave me again.

My love, I would be glad indeed to have Anna's services, if you think she would be satisfied with our rude fare. If I survive the ensuing autumn, I do not know any one that would suit me so well. But if there is any danger of her becoming dissatisfied, I would not like to risk it. If you ascertain, that it is her wish, to come, I would like to have her, as soon after Sept. as possible. I felt deeply your kindness to her brother. I fear from what Anna told me of him, that he is very dissipated. The girls[6] say, I must ask you to bring them a book entitled "The young lady's friend," by a lady.[7] Sam thinks now, he would rather have a green suit, than red. I recd a beautiful letter a few days ago from Mrs Merrit of Huntsville, (formerly Miss Morgan of Galveston). She expects to make us a visit shortly.

As ever thy devoted wife
M. L. Houston

17th I have just recd a very affectionate letter, from our new brother, Mr. Charles Power.[8] He and Antoinette are very much afraid that my feelings are hurt with them, and in truth, they were, at one time, but I am willing to forgive their youthful <u>indiscretion</u>, as he makes so many pretty promises to "<u>love, honour, and obey</u>," or that which amounts to the same, "to make her happiness his study." He writes that Antoinette and he, accompanied by Sarah Ann, are to visit Matagorda[9] shortly, and probably spend the summer there.

---

[1]George T. Wood. For a list of men in his company see Charles D. Spurlin, comp., *Texas Veterans in the Mexican War: Muster Rolls of Texas Military Units* (St. Louis: Ingmire, 1984), 34–39.

[2]See Houston to Sam Jr., March 31, 1846. Other letters have not been located.

[3]Margaret is referring to wood for Houston to whittle.

[4]Mrs. Eliza Allen, the editor of the *Mother's Journal*, not to be confused with Eliza Allen, Houston's first wife. William Seale, *Sam Houston's Wife: A Biography of Margaret Lea Houston* (Norman: University of Oklahoma Press, 1970), 111.

[5]It is unclear to which letter Margaret refers.

[6]The Moore nieces.

[7]During the nineteenth century, it was a common practice for women writers to use the phrase "by a lady" in order to remain anonymous.

[8]This letter has not been located.

[9]Charles Power had a plantation near Matagorda.

20th May [1846]

My Dearest,

I send you a paper, as I have not had time to write! To day, we had a joint Resolution passed about our mails. I hope they will now be more regular. I am as busy as it is possible for me to be. There is a general desire that I should go to the army with a <u>high command, but</u> I <u>decline</u> all offers and solicitations, and will not leave you my Love. I suffer enough, in my present situation. My absence is painful. I cannot see a Lady, but what I think of you, nor can I see, an urchin, or child, but what I think of our dear Boy.

You constitute my all on earth, and how could I leave you, for honors, or for <u>fame</u>, when it could not be united with your society. I would freely, defend our hearth, or our altars! That requirement, I hope, will never be made, by the necessities of our situation!

I hope soon to write you a long letter. I have not gone to repose, one night, since I came here, until midnight, and now I have more than fifty letters to answer. I cannot stand such labour, as my situation requires. My Love, I must say good night. I will retire, and think of you.

It was a family dinner that I ate with Mayor Davis [sic],[1] at Baltimore. I assure you my Love, that <u>wine</u> has not passed my lips, nor any thing else <u>since I kissed you.</u>

Embrace Sam, and all our kindred.

Thy Husband
Houston

[1]Jacob C. Davies, identified by J. Thomas Scharf, *History of Baltimore City and County* (Philadelphia: Louis H. Everts, 1881), 187.

Washington
21st May 1846

My Dear Love,

I wrote you a short note last evening, and as I have a moment at my Desk in the Senate, I will write again. To day, I have heard as news, that Louis Philippe,[1] is no more, and that France is in Revolution. The dangers apprehended, by our statesmen, of a coalition between England, and France, against the U. States are obviated, by this occurrence.

The Senate to day is not well attended. The <u>Races</u> are going on within two miles of the Capital. I do not attend Theatres, Races, or any places, which you would not approve were you here. I have had the pleasure to go to the Menagerie, and tho' they are not so good as they were once, I yet like them!

If you, and Sam could have been with me, I would have been happy! Yes Love, it seems to me, that I would be supremely happy if I cou'd again embrace you. Tomorrow a War Bill will be taken up, and as our committee reported the Bill, (the Military) we will have all to take part in the discussion. I may get some <u>raps</u> over the knuckles, and if I do, I can stand it very well.[2] My Love, there is not so much difference, in the capacity of great men, as we, at a distance, suppose.

I look on with critical observation, and will try and profit by the rule!

I wrote to you by last nights mail, and assured you that I would not consent to accept any Military, or civil appointment, unless by your <u>free</u>, and <u>voluntary</u> consent! I love you, and home, more than all the honors of this world. I say <u>home</u>, Sam is part of home, and therefore he is <u>homely</u>! Bless the Boy, I hope to see him in his "Red Coat & pantaloons," or if he would prefer, they shall be gray!

It may be, that you are on your way here, and if by chance it is so, I can tell you all when you come. If you are not, it will be too late when this reaches you, to come on this session!

I am crazy to see you, and every day increases my anxiety. Judge Toler,[3] will leave in a few days, for Houston, and by him, I hope to send some trifles. On Sams birth day, I hope to write him.

Render my affection to all our relatives. Embrace Sam & Betty.[4]

Thy devoted Husband
Sam Houston

[1]Healy reported that the portraits intended for Louis Philippe were either not finished or remained in the artist's hands. What became of Houston's portrait is unknown. Healy, 165–66.
[2]Several Army Generals, all members of the Whig party, were using their influence with members of Congress to prevent the passage of the bill which authorized the appointment of two additional major-generals and four brigadier-generals. Paul H. Bergeron, *The Presidency of James K. Polk* (Lawrence: University Press of Kansas, 1987), 79.
[3]Daniel J. Toler. For a biography see *Handbook of Texas*, vol. 2, 786.
[4]Elizabeth Moore.

Washington
25th May 1846

77 : MARCH 6, 1846—AUGUST 10, 1846

My Ever Dearest,

To night to my great joy, and delight, I rec'd your two last favors, with news of the Success, and Splendid triumphs of our arms.[1] I truly rejoice, as I believe, it will promote the cause of humanity.

If I could be with you but one hour, I could tell you strange things which would convince you, that I am not ambitious of Glory, or I could be in the field at once, and with high command. To all who speak to me, I reply, that "I will not again accept of any station, which will seperate me from my dear family." This much only, have I promised, that "I will write to Mrs Houston, and see if she will freely consent for me to take a command, or go to war." So you see my love, I will not commit myself, without your free consent. Dearest, I have no wish, but yours. And to see that you, in contemplation of the delicate, and irrepressibly interesting crisis, to which you are advancing, that you feel depressed, are unhappy, I would be the most unkind, and unnatural of beings, if I were not to sympathize, and remain with you! Distance, and time, only endears you to me! You may rely, upon my hope of Heaven, that not one unholy thought has estranged my heart, or my fidelity, from you, or my nuptial vow! Heaven has and will sustain me, in my integrity! Oh! how fondly, how devotedly, do I love thee, and our boy! Poor lad, I think, I can hear him demand, "bran for the hungry chickens"! Yes for "the poor little chickens." I am almost crazy to see him. (27th May) My Love, I really have been so pressed with my duties, that I have not had time, to finish my letter. Never have I retired to repose for one night until after midnight. I have so often written to you, that you will not stand in need of remembrances. You will suppose, how very happy, I will be to procure "to order" the "Squaw root," and the "N Glasses." I will do so, with the fervent prayer, that you will derive from them, every aid, & benefit, which you can desire, or that can arise from their use. The Glasses, I hope you will have use for, and I dont care how much, as it will be evidence of the excellence of your health! I am very, aye, truly happy, to hear that you, and Sam, are both "thriving," tho' from different causes. Has Sam, not observed your improvement, of condition? I think he will soon do so, as he is so observing! My Love, I am truly gratified to hear any, and every thing, about him! You say that I am not <u>candid about him</u>. My Love, I am truly candid, when I say to you, that I regard him, as a noble, sensible, and good looking "big boy." I love him much, and his dear Ma, no less, because he is her son! I think he is a blended likeness, and representative, of his Parents. I would be more happy, if he had less of my disposition. He has some of my characteristics to which [I] do not object, but they are also yours. His affections are warm, and by them, he can be controlled, but not by force! As to his intellect, I believe, and I hope, it partakes largely of yours in character. One thing in him, I do not condemn. He is not <u>jealous</u>, and his ma, & pa, are a little so! His conduct, with his Nurse, and the little Boy at Poor Bledsoes, proves him exempt from that infirmity. His dislike to ridicule, arises from both families. This quality will make him the more careful, in his conduct, thro' life.

You have written about our Niece![2] I will write, and direct Doct Fosgate,[3] and get him, to send you his opinion, & advice, with the necessary remedy. I have more confidence in him, than any one that I know here, or indeed any where else, where knowledge has the claim to superiority! I hope, my dear, you will approve the course suggested! I will do all in my power to procure her restoration to health. She is a dear Niece, and we ought to love her. I love her more, because she loves you, and Sam so much.

You write about our dear Sister Antoinette. I was distressed and some what irritated at first, but upon reflection I am perfectly satisfied, with the <u>match</u>. I hope they will do well, live long, and be happy! Dont think of it again. Be satisfied, and not distressed! We do not know, the reasons, or the motives, which caused her apparently hasty action!

I am happy, that Houston gets on well, and makes a good manager. I hope he will get on well! I was at Baltimore, and made a speech to the sovereigns, which went off well! I send you many news papers, with puffs in them, hoping they may gratify you. If you can send me, the piece to which you allude, about Rusk & myself, he will correct it, with much pleasure! Such things do not affect me, nor my reputation. Write to me my love about all that I touch on, in my letters! I hope my dear Love, you will get relief, from the "Wild cherry Balsam." I did all that I could, to send it to you. Any thing, which can be done, my Love, you have only to command me, and it shall be done!

I am invited to a marriage of a Genl Camerons,[4] a Senators Daughter in Harrisburgh Penn! It is the land of my forefathers, but I do not know, that I will go. I think I can not go, but if I do you will hear of the "doings." I will do nothing, that can delay my return, to the embraces of my Wife, Boy, & Kindred!

Salute affectionately all our family—all the Kin! Hug Sam & Cousin Betty! Salute the neighbours, all.

Thy faithful and devoted Husband
Sam Houston

[1]Houston is referring to Taylor's victories at Palo Alto and Resaca de la Palma. Odie B. Faulk and Joseph A. Stout, Jr., eds., *The Mexican War: Changing Interpretations* (Chicago: The Swallow Press, 1973), 4.
[2]Houston is referring to the illness of Bettie Moore.
[3]Dr. Walter Fosgate. Identified in Pat Ireland Nixon, *The Medical Story of Early Texas, 1528–1853* (San Antonio: Mollie Bennett Lupe Memorial Fund, 1946), 428–29.
[4]Senator Simon Cameron. Identified in *Biographical Directory*, 141.

Raven hill, May 28, 1846

Ever dear husband,

On last saturday, I received your second package, from Washington city, containing dates to the 23 of april. I was truly rejoiced to hear of your continued health, and to learn from the papers, your increasing popularity. By the same mail, I received a letter, from my friend Mrs Reily. She mentioned that she had just heard a letter read, which was recd from Washington, by a gentleman of Houston, stating that you were "winning golden opinions from all classes of persons by the strictness of your habits and the suavity of your manners." These things are very cheering to me, love, but not as you may suppose, on account of the bearing, which they may have upon your political advancement. Ah no, but that may have a slight influence with me, I admit, but the principal cause of my rejoicing, is the hope that it may be the "promise of better things, even things pertaining to life everlasting," and that the calmness and serenity, for which you are so much esteemed, may be the dawning of that change, which I have so earnestly sought for you, at the throne of grace. Oh, my husband, I have prayed for you, until it has become so habitual with me, that a day past, without bringing your cherished name, before my Father's throne, would seem like a day lost! When oh when shall I see the answer of my prayers! When shall I feel, that our hearts are indeed united in the love of God? I have many a hard battle with the enemy of souls, but thanks to my Heavenly master, I believe I am gaining the victory. Each day I can perceive within myself a greater desire for holiness, and less relish for all worldly enjoyments. It is true the little world around me, presents few temptations, which compared with those which many Christians have to resist, but if I have any desire to go beyond it, is that I may extend my sphere of usefulness, that I may have more to do for my Heavenly Father. Dearest, do not think me gloomy, for I can assure you that my spirits have never been better.

On the day previous to the reception of your last letters, brother Vernal arrived at Raven hill. This visit was a source of great happiness to me, as I have been very anxious about them, and he brought me the welcome intelligence of Mother's good health and thier general prosperity. He is not yet recovered from his depression of spirits. His grief has lost its violence, and seems to have mellowed into a sweet sadness, which never varies for a single instant. His greatest pleasure seemed when talking to me, of his lost Mary,[1] and of thier reunion in a better world. I never saw anyone, so completely wedded to the memory of the dead. It is melancholy to see one so young, thus yield himself entirely to grief, but there is something so holy, so unobtrusive in his sorrow, that I know not, how to reason with him about it. He only remained with us one day and a half, and then set off for Fort Houston.[2] He promised to write to you, as he past through Washington [on-the-Brazos], if he stopped long enough. He has been

81 : March 6, 1846—August 10, 1846

trying to come up, a great while, but his overseer had left him, and he was put to great inconvenience by the overflow of his farm. His reasons were entirely satisfactory to me. So soon as he returns, I expect Mother will come up, and stay with me during the summer. If you find her here on your return, My Love, I hope you will endeavor to yield as much as possible to her prejudices. She is high-spirited, and a <u>little</u> <u>overbearing</u> I admit, but she has one of the most gentle and affectionate hearts that ever beat, and the surest way of gaining her acquiescence in matters of importance, is by yielding to her in trifles. At all events darling, she has had much more experience than either of us, and as a daughter, I feel bound to respect her judgement [sic], when it does not conflict with yours.

Mr Benjamin Ellis came up with bro. Vernal, on his way to the army. You were mistaken in your suspicions of Sarah Ann being engaged to him. Bro. V. thinks she will either marry Thomas Power or Mr. Gerry. Bro. V. shewed [sic] me a letter he had recd from Antoinette since her marriage. She wrote as if she considered herself the happiest being on earth. I fear much that the inducements of wealth and fashion will engross all her time. I can only pray for her, with an humble trust that the Lord will protect her.

Mrs Reily writes to me, that she will try to visit me, in a few months, and asks <u>when</u> <u>she</u> <u>must</u> <u>come</u>! I have not yet answered her, but intend to do so, very soon. Betty is with me, at this time, and much improved in health. The other members of the family in good health. Sam continues to thrive, and <u>I think</u> he is a noble fellow, in every aspect. He dictated a letter to you, yesterday, of his own accord, and I thought I would give it to you verbatim, but it was so complicated, that I am almost afraid to undertake it. I will however give you the beginning, which was as follows—"My dear pa, I hope you will soon come home to your son. I would be very happy to see you, and please to bring my green breeches. I am a good boy. He! He!"

On the subject of the velvet dress,[3] dearest, I do not know what to say. If I thought your happiness at all concerned in it, I would wear it, to make your happy, but I know it is of no great consequence to you, and with me, it would be a sacrifice of matter of principle. If you are willing to postpone the discussion, I will give you my reasons, when I see you. My height is about 5 feet 7 inches, and if it would gratify you, to have a dress made for me, get some simple material neither showy nor very costly. To tell you the truth, I would rather pack [sic] you with a few books, which I could name, for instance "Law's serious call to a devout and holy life," Drillingcourt's christian's consolations against the fears of death, and a few numbers of Nelson's cause and cure of infidelity, all of which I suppose you can procure at Washington or on some place on your return, but do not, I implore you, give yourself any trouble about them.

I expect Jose will leave us this week. I will pay him, whatever Houston says his work is worth, as he is very importunate to get his wages, and return to Houston. He has never been contented here, since we detected Billy, in riding the horses at night, and bringing liquor to the place. Not a word was ever said to him on the subject, and Billy alone was punished, though we have every reason to believe that he and Maria were equally culpable. Do not, I entreat you, let him extract a cent from you, as you come through Houston, for I will pay him here.

I am sorry dearest that I am under the necessity of troubling you, with our homely details, but I merely did it to prevent your being taken in with Jose, as you come through Houston. Maria has been feigning herself helpless, for many months, that we might be induced to determine, she would be of no further use to us, and let her go to Houston with Jose, and set up shop for themselves. I have sent her to Dr Evans,[4] who will keep her, until you return. At present, I will not trouble you with further particulars, of this kind. I hope and believe that every thing will go well with us. I have never enjoyed better health and spirits, with the exception of a slight coughing spell, now and then. I have nearly finished the *[blurred]* bottle of the Balsam, and I am so much improved that I would like to have another supply. I thank you sincerely for the remedy. Sam measured on his 3rd birth-day, 3 feet 1 inch and a half.[5]

Thy devoted wife

83 : MARCH 6, 1846—AUGUST 10, 1846

[1]Vernal's first wife, who died a few months after their marriage in 1845.
[2]Fort Houston was in Anderson County, near the present day city of Palestine. Bob Bowman, *The 35 Best Ghost Towns in East Texas and 220 Other Towns We Left Behind* (n.p.: Best of East Texas Publishers, 1990), 163, 189.
[3]See Houston to Margaret, April 23, 1846.
[4]Dr. William Fitzpatrick Evans. Identified in Walker County Genealogical Society, *Walker County History* (Dallas: Curtis Media Corporation, 1986), 276.
[5]Houston believed that Sam's adult height would be twice what he was at three years. See Houston to Margaret May 7, 1846.

∞

Washington
29th May 1846

My Dearest Love,

I am in the committee Room, and no other member has yet come, so that I have a moment to write. Would that I had a day, I could well employ my time. I trust by this time you have received letters enough to convince you, that I am not forgetful of you, & Sam. My thoughts are of you, and with you every hour of my life. Not only waking, but sleeping. Home with you, log cabbin as it is, is endeared to me far beyond all the earth beside. In writing, I think of many things, which I could tell you of, were I with you, which I can not write, some political, and some personal, none of which I feel sure, would be distressing to you.

Calls are made upon me, or allusions every day to the subject of the next Presidency, and again I declare to you, if I could command the station, (if I know my own heart) I would not be willing to accept the Situation. Thus you see my dear, I am more in love, with your Dear Society, and presence, than with earthly honors. They have no charms for me, when they would call my time off, from you & Sam. The office of President, will be a thorny path, to those who are confined to it. I would deplore my absence, and distance from you, if it would do any good. I must, painful as it is, bide my time. There is at this time, a national fair, here for the purpose of exhibiting manufactures of various kinds.[1] They are beautiful, and I intend to get some of the most beautiful manufacturs [sic] for dresses. I mean such dresses, as Sam, would call "beautiful Ladies dresses." There have been at the fair, thousands, and tens of thousands of persons, from every state, and part of the Union!

Your regards were most kindly welcomed by our relatives, and returned, with devotion. My God Daughter,[2] pleases Col Eldridge very much. By the bye, Col E. has obtained a Clerkship, at the rate of $1,150 per year! You could not credit the number of applicants for clerkships. I have been assured, that there are no less than 3,000 applications. This does not auger [sic] well, for the condition of our country. You know that I regard industry as the foundation of national glory, as well as its duration. When people look to office, and to patronage of the Government, it augers a dependent, or idle condition of the masses. It leads to sycophancy, and deceit, as well as debasement of soul, & character. Industry in laudable pursuits, is all that will prevent these deplorable evils. I hope, and trust that no son, or kinsman of mine will ever become a resident of a city. I love the homely, honest, and virtuous life of the backwoods, where the sabbath is regarded, and when the evenings are passed in social converse, or in reading some useful Book.

I love the evening stroll, where souls breathe love, and peace, and where sweet content gives soundness to repose.

Business begins, and I must close. My love to all. Hug Sam & Betty, if not inconvenient.

Thy faithful and devoted Husband
Sam Houston

---

[1]The Manufacturers Fair was held in a building erected only for the occasion at a cost of six thousand dollars, and demolished immediately afterwards. For more information see Alfred Hoyt Bill, *Rehearsal for Conflict: The War with Mexico 1846–1848* (New York: Cooper Square Publishers, 1969), 111. President Polk wrote, "The manufacturers have spent many thousands of dollars in getting up this fair, with a view no doubt to operate upon members of Congress to prevent a reduction of the present rates of duty imposed by the oppressive protective tariff act of 1842." For his description of the fair see Polk, *Polk*, 102–103, and Christman, 44–48.

[2]Mary Houston.

The following letter from Houston has missing lines where the bottom of all four pages are torn off.

Washington
30th May 1846

My Dearest Love,

I wrote to you yesterday, and, as I have said, I could write always, when writing to you, I have fortunately, a few moments of my own. By way of news I can tell you, that to day, I have procured a midshipmans warrant for William Maffett.[1] This I did not do, for any expected return, or thanks, but because I choose to do it. In anticipation, the old Lady[2] complained that William was not preferred, to other boys, for whom I had previously applied, even before he became an applicant. So I must do what I deem right, regardless, of the old Lady's preference for Lamar,[3] and McCleod,[4] and others. I know her politicks, but not her principles. I also obtained one for Maj Allens brother in Law, young Brain [sic], a noble youth. Jno C. Watrous, Geo W. Brown, & major Jno M. Allen were appointed, Judge, District Atto, & Marshall. *[torn]* To day I made a call on the Mother of Col Daingerfield[5] by request. She is here on visit. She is very accomplished old Lady, and much like her son. She was greatly pleased with the visit, as she had heard him say, so much of you, & myself. She was sorry that she could not see you, and Sam. The Col is her youngest son, and child. Donelson[6] with his family have sailed. My friend Gov Yell[7] and Mr Howell Cobb are present, and desire to be presented, to you & Sam.

31st. Indeed all whom I see and become intimate with me express the greatest anxiety to see "Mrs Houston & Sam." They have heard, that you have done so much for me that they regard you, as a very extraordinary personage. To tame, and regulate a man, who has heretofore, been deemed, untamable, and now so sage, and regulated is rather novel. With all their anxiety, and curiosity, I can assure you my Love, there is no one, who can conceive my intense, and . . . *[torn]* clasp that heart, that beats for you, and you alone. Should kind Heaven, again permit us to meet, I have a funny conceit to tell you of! Or I may as well do it now! I would rather add to your happiness, that [sic] excite your curiosity. The matter is this, I can not forgive myself for not marrying you, when we were first acquainted, provided, you would have consented. Now—for certain reasons I think you would have done so. The reasons, I must tell you in person, as they will amuse you! While I am writing, I am almost tempted to fly to you, and leave the world here, behind me. Oh my Love, no fancy, nor all the touches of romance, can essay, to give, an idea, of my fond, and abiding devotion to you. My heart is desolate, and must remain so until we meet. To day at the Church, I met our relations the Houstons,[8] & presented your love to them. They were delighted, and return a thousand caresses to you, Sam, and all the family. I have only been to see them once, since my arrival in the city. They *[torn]* I must be more social, and kinlike. My Love, I have no time. I must cease writing soon or finish this epistle. In a half hour I must go again to church, as I regularly attend Divine worship, and my Dearest no matter, at what hour of night, I get thro my toils of business, I never lay my head on my pillow without reading a chapter, in the new Testament, and asking forgiveness, at a Throne of Grace, and imploring, a blessing of God, and our blessed Savior, on you, and our dear Boy, and our loved kindred. I feel that we are poor dependent worms, of the dust, and that we are less than nothing, compared to the least attribute of the Great Jesus! I pray to be good, and to do good, for I know my nature, that it is "enmity against God." He preserves me from temptation, and from stumbling, in forbidden paths, of <u>faithless</u> transgression!!

Your prayers, will be answered, and my resolution, will not give way, nor my feet <u>slip aside</u>! But few here, (I fear) will follow my example. I will close, and go to church. On my return, I will write, again.

Thy ever devoted,

87 : MARCH 6, 1846—AUGUST 10, 1846

[1] The son of John Howland Maffett of Galveston.
[2] Houston is referring to Anne Maffet, the mother of William.
[3] Mirabeau B. Lamar. He would later marry the Maffett daughter, Henrietta. Elizabeth Brooks, *Prominent Women of Texas* (Akron, Oh.: The Werner Company, 1896), 22.
[4] Hugh P. McLeod, Lamar's relative. Both Lamar and McLeod were enemies of Houston. *New Handbook of Texas*, vol. 4, 434.
[5] William Henry Daingerfield. For a biography see *New Handbook of Texas*, vol. 2, 472.
[6] Andrew Jackson Donelson had left for Prussia. *Handbook of Texas*, vol. 1, 512.
[7] Archibald Yell of Arkansas. Identified in O'Brien and Martin, 460.
[8] Houston is probably referring to his cousin John Houston and family who lived nearby.

∞

Houston dictated the following letter to Margaret. It is in the handwriting of his secretary, Washington D. Miller.

Washington City
June 1st, 1846

My dearest:

I know very well that you will, with pleasure excuse me, for employing Mr. Miller in writing this epistle. On yesterday, when I closed my letter, he had not arrived. But about 8 o'clock he gave me an agreeable surprise by presenting himself. His aid was as necessary as his arrival was agreeable.

I have given you repeated assurances, that I would take no course for my future action, incompatible with your voluntary and unconstrained wishes. Affairs here have been rather exciting and will continue to be so, unless Mexico sues immediately for peace. If that is done, matters will settle down, and a calm will ensue to the present agitated state of the public mind.

In contemplation of protracted war, or sufficiently so for the reduction of Mexico, there is, I believe, a very general feeling that I should control one of the armies of invasion. You will certainly suppose that in this matter, I had no agency. I was an advocate for war—

as it was necessary to the maintenance of our rights and the vindication of national honor. Such is the general appreciation of my motives, I believe, at this time.

Upon the subject of taking a part in the war, I am totally uncommitted; and though strongly urged, it has not changed my original resolve not to adopt any cause that can in the slightest degree violate my pledges to you. My desire still is, to return home, and to remain with you, as I have not and cannot adopt any step with reference to any ulterior projects without your advice. My heart abides with you, and our dear boy. Had my resolution not been immoveable [sic], I might have been induced to suggest some arguments in favor of my entering the service; because the service would be much more agreeable and profitable than that in which I have heretofore been engaged—agreeable, because I would have the resources of a nation to sustain me, and profitable because I would have a salary of upwards of six thousand dollars a year. I would be surrounded by the best blood and chivalry of the nation, and with means of enforcing subordination to my commands.

Now, my love, I beseech you to consider of the matter and make such a decision, as will be conformable to your happiness, and feelings, without regard to any desires which you might suppose me to entertain. Do not let your decision give you the least pain, for if you decide against my entering the service, you will not inflict upon me, the slightest pain, nor, under any circumstances, will you ever incur from me a single reproach; for I will only regard it as an evidence of strong affection. Should you decide in favor of it, I will see you and pass as much time with you as possible, previous to my entering upon the duties of the new station.

I have reluctantly written you this letter, because I have been fearful that it might cost you a moment's pain. Do not let it cost you one throb, nor cause you one anxious moment. I know the decision will be painful, whether you decide for or against it; but I conjure you, as your happiness is more to me than all my earthly desires, that you will decide without hesitancy, and by the express which will bear this to you, reply to me and regard this matter as a thing which has no existence. By this I mean, forget everything connected with this subject.

I send you a miniature and a pair of gold spectacles for sister Eliza; also, a breastpin which I intended to have sent by Maj. Reily, as he was so kind as to present it to you through me. But he went off in such haste that I did not send it. It is made of elk horn, and the emblems are characteristic. You will please, my dear, give Sam a Hearty hug, as well as his cousin Betty, and present my love to all relations.

[In Houston's handwriting:] Thy ever devoted Husband
Houston

[Written in the margin in Houston's handwriting:] All these matters my Love, will be regarded as rather <u>private</u>! I do not wish them to get out.

That same evening Houston added the following separate letter in his own handwriting

Washington
1st [2nd] June 1846

Dearest,

It is now past midnight and, as Mr Miller has retired to his own room, I can not, but write some myself, and of myself, as well as to my <u>better-self</u>.

One thing I could not allude to, in the letter written by him, and that was your <u>particular situation</u>.[1] No one can judge of that, and the feelings incident to it, but <u>yourself</u>. For this reason, I do most truly, desire you to consult your own wishes, for were I to be absent, and any thing were to befal [sic] you, unless by some unavoidable necessity, my cup of earthly <u>bliss, would be dashed forever</u>. It is true I might win Glory, & disappoint, as well as war, the plots of some of my enemies, who have been running riot, since I left home, but would this make you happy, and wou'd it be, worth your sacrifice of contentment? My station here is honorable, and some say <u>enviable</u>. Be that as it may, I say nothing. Only that my enemies are, as I think prostrated, and so far as I can judge, they have, all disappeared, and are silent. I feel assured, that you will know my unutterable devotion to you, and can appreciate my feelings, about entering the army. You will regard the whole matter, as placing your feelings, and happiness, and my love for you, above all, & every earthly consideration, and in view of these matters, you will decide. For myself, I do not think the war will last long, unless England sustains Mexico, and as yet, no one can decide here! I think it probable. If I were to enter the service I would not be subject to the orders, of any other General! I would only be subject, to the Sec'y of war. The truth is, my mind is suspended on the subject, and I only think of you, and Sam, any dear little visitors, which may <u>be</u>, to add to our family circle!!! I hope to get home by the 15th of August, or before. If I should join the Army, I will be home, by the 20th of July, and after a short stay, I would have to leave for the frontier!

You will please to return an answer, as I will be pressed, and as yet, I have given no encouragement, to solicitations from all quarters of the country. You will even see, that your friend Doct Woods,[2] wishes me to go to the war. My heart embraces, you with unerring affection.

Thine truly,
Houston

[in the margin:] My Love, what do your dreams indicate? You know they are famous, for making great men!

[1]Margaret's pregnancy.
[2]Dr. Alva Woods, who at one time was head of the University of Alabama. Ganrud, 610.

Washington
3rd June 1846

My Dearest,
I must write again as I have a moment, at my Desk. The Senate

has up a dry Land Bill for discussion & I take no part, and little interest in it. Enclosed you will receive a letter from my friend Donelson.[1] I send it to you, as I have so many papers to take care of, that I do not wish to accumulate their number. You can my Love, put it with Genl Jacksons letters.

Every day, which I pass here, only adds to anxiety to get home. Oh my love! I will become, a huge man in size, if I live. I now weigh 210 lbs. I have gained no less than (30) thirty pounds since I came here. I hope your appearance has changed quite as much as my own. I wish very much to be at home, and see how all look!!

I wrote to you on the 1st which you will receive, I hope, by express. Let not, the contents trouble you! Just do, and say, what you think proper. I entertain no wish, nor desire, but to be with you, and Sam, and our kindred. I have no news to write to you my Love.

I am as ever, thy faithful and devoted Husband.

Sam Houston

P.S. Write to me any of Sam's smart sayings!!!

Houston

[1]This letter has not been located.

∞

Washington
4th June

My Love,

I would have written you a long letter, had I known that I would be bored, by a long, and useless speech. There has been nothing new since I last wrote to you. I will in a day or two, send you letters from Henry,[1] and Young [Royston]. They are now at my room, and I am in the Senate Chamber.

As I have often stated to you my Love, I am more and more anxious to see you, and be with you, than ever. I would like to see Master Sam, our "Great Big Boy." But whatever I may think of the dear little fellow, it does not compare, to my desire to see his dear

Mother. I do not see a lady, but what you are brought to my heart, and there remain, while I am present. I reflect, where is my own dear wife. How is she, is she happy, or is she miserable? Is she in health, or is she in sickness? These reflections almost run me mad. Not a night do I retire to repose, without the most sincere prayers, for your health, and happiness here, and felicity hereafter. Our dear Boy too is embraced, with all a Fathers love, and hope, and joy! He is a noble boy, and indeed my dear, I think him likely, not <u>very</u> handsome! He is our son my dear, and we love him! This is sufficient, to make him very perfect, and very beautiful. I think him more lovely, than I otherwise would do, if I did not think, that he resembled his lovely Mother! I can only say this my Love, of our boy. I live to get home again, and embrace his dear Mother, with the boy of our heart, I will agree that he is one, of the finest lads, in the world! and very handsome. Now my Love, I hope you will be satisfied that I love our Boy much, but his dear Mother <u>more</u>! You may now my Dear tell me of any smart things, which Sam may say. This will enable you to indulge, a Mothers feelings, and gratify her heart.

To day I sent word to Doct Evans, to send to Houston for such medicine as he may need, or want this summer. I made the arrangement with Grosebeck,[2] before I left Houston for him to get such medicine as he might want, or need. But really the press was so great, that I did not advise him, as I ought to have done. Yet it seems to me that I did advise him either by message, or in writing.

I hope Love you will all be healthy, and not need a physician, but a cook! I will be unhappy until I can hear from you. But this, I do enjoin. At the first appearance of sickness send for Doct Evans.

It is only a few hours, since I put a letter in the mail for you.

This I will send by Major [John] Allen, and the news paper, from Marion.

Thy devoted & faithful Husband
Houston

[1]Henry Lea, Margaret's brother.
[2]John D. Groesbeck, a Houston druggist. Identified in *Handbook of Texas*, vol. 3, 360.

Washington
5th June 1846

My very dear Love,

Yesterday, I began a letter to you but did not finish it. Then I was in great hopes, that I would get a letter by last nights mail. The mail came but no letter. You can imagine my Love, how painful it was to me, and how agonized I was, not to hear from you, and home.

I do not my <u>own one</u>, attach any blame, for I know the condition of the mails in Texas. Mr Miller told me, that he sent you by Ralph, numerous letters etc, from Washington [on-the-Brazos], before he left home, which had then accumulated. So my love, I have no doubt but what many letters are on their way to me. I will hope that all are well, and happy, and that each day of anxiety, which I pass here, only brings me, one day nearer to my Margaret, my boy, and my home. I know too my dear, and often reflect on the fact, that it also brings me, one day nearer, to my home, beyond the sky.

My love, not one night passes, but what brings me, to the duty of reading a chapter, in the New Testament. I was much struck, by reading the 3rd & 4 chapter, of 1st Thessalonians. One I read, last night, and the others the night previous. The intensity of feeling, must have been great, which inspired St. Paul. He was the great agent of the almighty on earth, to carry out the plan of mans [sic] salvation. I endeavor to feel, while I read, and afterwards to reflect upon their substance. So far, as self denial, is concerned, I can comply with the requirements, but I can not command my thoughts, so as to bring my heart into spiritual conformity to the <u>spirituality</u> required, on part of those, who have felt the influences of Divine Grace. The subject of an adjournment, has not been disposed of, nor can I say when we will adjourn, and leave this miserable place. I have not enjoyed one hour of pleasure since I came here, only at the <u>Levee</u> with your friend Mrs Woods, and in her company to Baltimore. By last mail, I sent you a letter from the Doctor [Alva Woods]. To day, I will send you by Major [John M.] Allen, a news paper from Marion, and by mail, letters as I stated in my letter which I partly finished at my Desk yesterday. When I return to the Senate I will finish it. Mr and Mrs Culp[1] were here, in tolerable health. They will spend a few days, and then proceed to Virginia. I will pay all attention to them in my power. I wrote to you to come on to the city. The letter would not reach you in time to come on this summer. So I will write & keep writing, as tho' I had not sent you such word, or expressed you such a desire. Truly, I would be happy to see you, for then I would be "appie." I have written this letter in the committee room, while the committee is in session.

My Love, my heart embraces you, and pray Hug Sam, Cousin Betty, and render my love to all the rest.

Thy devoted Husband
Sam Houston

P.S. I hope we will adjourn on or before the 20th July.

Houston

[1]Daniel and Betty Culp.

⚭

Washington
7th June 1846

My very dear Love,

This is the sabbath day, and I have returned from church. I went to hear the Reverend Mr Richardson,[1] of Texas. He preached from the 3rd chap. of Timothy, and 16th verse. He preached a very good sermon to the people of Washington. If he had rendered it less showy, it would have been as well received. I had before met with him, and went to see the President with him, but we did not succeed in seeing him. He then concluded, (which was yesterday,) that he would remain in the city, until Tuesday next, at which time I am to take him again, as it is the evening, when the "White House," will be open to receive company. So you see my Love, that I am willing to submit myself to the scrutiny, of the Clergy. I would rather Love, that I were subject to your own dear scrutiny, and observation either here, or at home. No matter where Dearest, if I could only be with the object of my affections. I know well, that you think, I must sometimes be happy, while absent from you, and that my feelings, or thoughts, are for a while withdrawn from you, and that Sam, too, is forgotten, amidst the scenes, thro' which I pass! I voluntarily declare to you, that such is not the fact. I would sometimes forget Sam, I do think, if it were not, that you reproach me for every seeming neglect, or indifference towards the dear lad! For had he not one attraction, besides being <u>our</u> Boy, I would love him dearly! Dearly as I may love him, you Dearest, are dearer to me, being my better half, and I do declare again, and again, to you that every day, only endears you more, and more to my heart, and to my love! The past hours, of happiness with you, are all that I dwell on with pure, and unallayed delight! My anticipation, of joys to come, on earth, or in Heaven are blended with you, and inseparable from you! With such feelings, & such hopes, I am confident, my Love you will never <u>distrust</u> my <u>fidelity</u>, and <u>constancy</u>! Since I commenced writing this letter, I was called on to go, and see, an old friend of mine (a cherokee)[2] who was a friend of mine, in early life, and when I was in exile. He is the chief of those opposed to the Tyranny of the Ross[3] party. He has been here, and taken sick some time since. To day his life has been despaired of. He sent for me, and I immediately called to see him. In a firm an[d] fixed tone, he told me what he wished done, in the event of his death. Poor man, he was once the apollo of his Tribe, and his voice once swayed the councils, of his chiefs—Alas! frail mortality! He must soon go hence, the way of all living. If the aspiring, & vain of earthly Glory, could but look upon the poor cherokee, what an impressive lesson they might learn. Far from his Indian home, his wife and little ones, the glories of this metropolis, can not smooth his pillow, or impart solace to his departing spirit. I will try, and be with him in his last moments, and afford him the consolation of a friend.

My Love, I am sick of the vanities of this world. They cannot, nay, they will not give rest, in time, nor happiness in eternity! I will endeavor my Love, to renew, and increase my efforts, to live in such a way, as will deprive death of its terrors, and the grave, of its gloom! I will endeavor, to serve the Lord in such manner, as may propitiate His gracious favor. I will walk uprightly before Him, that through Christ Jesus, I may be saved, with all whom I love, on earth!

Time passes sadly with me here, because I have not your presence to be with me, in the calm of a Sabbath evening! I do not admit visitors, on this holy day, nor do I give myself up, to business. The Creator made but little requisition upon our time, tho' "our days are few."

No doubt my ever Dearest, but what you sometimes think on Sabbath evenings, "my Husband is far from me, and his thoughts, are on objects, with which he is surrounded!" Indeed my Love, it has not been so, nor can it ever be!

I do not look upon the writing of letters to you my dear, more harmful, than communion of thoughts, and expressions, were we present with each other. There is, my own <u>one</u>, a pleasure in thinking and speaking of you, and why not a duty, in writing to you. If I enjoy a scene of nature, I wish for your presence! If I walk in the public grounds, or ride by them, my thoughts are with you! Indeed, see what I may, and be where I may, you are present to my thoughts, and your <u>dear</u> <u>image</u> constantly impressed upon my heart! And ever, and anon, our chubby Boy, presents his face, either with the salutation of Ma, or Pa! I tried to fancy his dress, and how he looks, and after all, I have to dress him out in his Tartan Plaid bare footed, and bare head! Thus you see my Love, I am constantly dwelling on you, and those who are of you.

My fancy is not confined to Sam, and his appearance only, but I fancy a little about you my Love. I fancy, that you are just as I would <u>wish</u> to see you,—In good health, <u>sizeable</u> [sic], and ruddy cheeks. I <u>do</u> wish to see you, in the <u>fancied</u>, and <u>real</u> condition, which I have described. I am alarmed at my increased <u>size</u>. 'Tis true, I am not encumbered with flesh, & my complexion, is much better than you ever saw it!

Dearest, last evening I saw our God Daughter and gave her your present,[4] and Sam's, but not until I took both the kisses from it myself. I let her read the sentence in your letter. She was much pleased, and she and all the family sent to you and Sam, and the Kindred all, vast love. I have sent by this mail a letter from Bro. Henry & Young [Royston], one also! Their letters were so too much of a business cast to gratify me much! As you would have desired, I went forthwith and presented the affair of Genl King[5] to the President, and met Gov Bagby[6] there who united with me, and we urged his claims in good earnest! The General had written to me himself! All that could be done has been here done, in his favor.

I will write soon to the General, & I will make our regards in such terms, to himself, and Lady, as you would wish me to do!

Dearest, I must close my letter, tho' I could write another sheet, and still be inclined, to write more, if not very interesting.

My heart embraces you, my ever dear Love! Hug Sam, Kiss Betty. Love to all the rest. Salute the neighbours.

Thy faithful Husband
Houston

Tell the servants to be faithful!

[1]Chauncey Richardson, identified in *Handbook of Texas,* vol. 2, 469.
[2]John Rogers. For Houston's relationship with Rogers and his family see Jack Gregory and Rennard Strickland, *Sam Houston with the Cherokees, 1829–1833* (Norman: University of Oklahoma Press, 1996), 36–37.
[3]Cherokee chief John Ross. For information about his party see Christman, 41–44.
[4]The flower from Raven Hill which Margaret sent to Mary Houston, the daughter of his cousin John Houston. See Margaret to Houston, May 4, 1846.
[5]General Edwin Davis King of Alabama. Identified in Brewer, 495. Houston was hoping to secure an appointment in the army for his old friend.
[6]Arthur Bagby, governor of Alabama.

◯◯

In August of 1845, the United States War Department had ordered General Edmund P. Gaines to draw an auxiliary force from some of the United States and from Texas forces. Acting with good intentions, Gaines, without any specific authority, had called for a force of 12,000 men. On June 5, 1846, Senator Lewis Cass asked that President Polk inform the Senate if any officer of the army had called volunteers or the militia into service without legal authority. Houston wrote Margaret of his parts in the events.

Washington
9th June 1846

Dearest,

Yesterday, I did not write to you, because the Senate was very busy. There were matters of serious import laid before the Body. The correspondence of Genl Scott,[1] as well, as Genl Gaines[2] with the sec'y of war.[3] Poor Scott has killed himself off, and Gaines has been ordered here, and no doubt, has done very wrong, but with no bad intention. The other day I took his part in debate, upon resolutions affecting him, or his course.[4] I was sorry that I could not justify him, so all that I did was to excuse him.

At this time, congress is, rather in a calm, but I think is only preparing for a storm. I take no violent course, because I think peace is best, and no one has assailed me. I hope no one will deem it necessary to do so. My poor Indian friend still lives but with little hopes of recovery. I call to see him as often as possible, and have him the best medical aid known here. I will do every thing in my power for him, and if his life can be prolonged, it shall be done! I look daily for a letter, from our niece, Miss "Tene" Royston.[5] I wrote to Bro [Robertus] Royston, that so soon as Miss Tene would write to me, I would send her as long a letter, as my time would allow me to write.

The war fever here has some what "debated," as Burleson[6] would say. On yesterday I introduced a Resolution to meet hereafter at 10 oclock A.M. instead of 12 N. as has been usual since I came to the Senate. I will do every thing in my power, to get off from this great City, which by the bye, is by no means, a pleasant place to me. Nor can any place be pleasant, where you are not. For a week past I have

99 : MARCH 6, 1846—AUGUST 10, 1846

not heard from you. I received your letter on the 4th of June which was written on the 4th of May. It was mailed at New Orleans, on the 29th of May. [Judge Daniel] Toler has gone home, and I do hope mails will be regular hereafter, and that I may hear often, of & from my Beloved Margaret. Yes, and Sam, too, the "Great Big Boy." Do write to me all about, what he says, how he looks, what his manners are, how his disposition is. Indeed my Love, any and every thing, which you may wish to write, for all such things assuredly, do I wish to read. Every thing, even the least word, of yours is treasured by me, and is a source of happiness, which cheers me in the hours of night, when all is silent, and the world is asleep. You cannot I am confident my Love, appreciate my anxiety to see you, and all at home. Never am I alone, for a moment, but what my thoughts are with you, and our dear boy. You will not find it difficult to detain me, if we live to meet again, I will be, and hold myself at your disposition, and command. It is true my friends here think my presence needful, and it may be of some use, but at the same time, I owe you the first of earthly obligations! You are my own dear Wife. You are my better, vastly better half.

You will be so kind as to remember me to all, and to our neighbours. Hug Sam, & Betty! Commend me to Houston, and say to him that I hope, if he has time this summer, before I get home, to have Houses, for the negroes, that they may be comfortable hereafter, in winter. But I suppose he will have enough to do with the crops, until I get home.

Thy devoted & faithful Husband
Sam Houston

---

[1]General Winfield Scott had been given command of the army to be sent against Mexico. Instead of proceeding immediately to the Rio Grande, Scott lingered three weeks in Washington. For information about this matter see Bill, 114–16.
[2]General Edmund P. Gaines of Alabama.
[3]Former Senator William Larned Marcy of New York. *Writings*, vol. 4, 443n.
[4]For a copy of Houston's speech see Ibid., 483–84.
[5]Serena Royston.
[6]Edward Burleson, who was vice-president during Houston's second term as president of Texas. *New Handbook of Texas*, vol. 1, 837.

Washington
10th June 1846

My Love,

I have nothing new to write you, but I write to let you know, that all things are smoothe [sic], and a prospect of an adjustment of the Oregon Subject. The war with Mexico will be prosecuted with all the necessary vigor.

You will have made up your mind on the subject which I submitted to your decision.[1] Well! my Love, be that as it may, I will be satisfied, most truly so! I love you more, than I do the world beside!

I am sated, with all that I see here, and only sigh for the sweets, and quiet, of your woodland home.

Hug Sam, and Betty, and present love to all.

Thy Husband
Houston

[1]Accepting a command in the army.

Margaret wrote the following letter to her old friend, Almira Woods, and enclosed it in her letter to Houston.

Raven hill Montgomery co. Texas, June 12 1846

Ever dear friend,

I can not describe to you, my agreeable surprise on opening a package a few days ago, from my husband, and finding enclosed, a letter from one whose name is so intimately associated as your own, with some of the most pleasant reccollections [sic] of my life. You can imagine my feelings, I am sure, for you were once far removed from your native home, and doubtless received many assurances of the continued love of early friends. You were generally surrounded by so brilliant a circle of admiring friends, that I had scarcely dared to hope your reccolections [sic] of me, would be very vivid, but I rejoice to find that I am not forgotten. And I am so happy to learn that you and my dear husband have become acquainted with each other. He gave me a glowing account of it, I assure you, and I was more delighted than I could have been, by his meeting any other person. I expect he looked at you, a little curiously, for your name was a very familliar [sic] one to him, having often heard me speak of you, as one of my most highly esteemed friends. I perceive from your encomiums upon him, (every word of which I feel to be true,) and your lively account of the magic influence of my name, that you have not yet lost the secrit [sic] of making others happy. Do not suppose, that I take it merely as complaisance. Oh no, I mean to say, that you have the same happy faculty of turning things to good account. I always feel so much enthusiasm on the subject of my husband's character, that I am a little afraid to trust myself upon it, but I should say more in his praise, than you would deem proper for a wife to say, and as he is <u>my</u> <u>second</u> <u>self</u>, you know that might seem a little <u>egotistical</u>. But this much, you must allow me to say. The attractions for which he is admired by the world, are in my estimation his poorest charms, so poor in comparison with his domestic virtues, that I am sometimes half tempted to wish that I could divest him of the former, and then he would be "all my own." Do not think me selfish, dear friend, for if you could see him, in his little circle at home, you would not blame me. Did you observe the resemblance [sic] between him and Dr Woods? I have often remarked to him, that his features and the shape of his head, were both very much like your esteemed husband's. My dear little boy is a youthful miniature of his father, so if you wish to know how he looks, just fancy that he has his father's brow, (which I think remarkably like your husband's,) his grey eyes and delicate mouth, all lit up by the playful expression, the rosy cheeks and dimpled smiles of childhood. He was three years old, on the 25th of last month, and at that time measured 3 feet, 1 inch and a half. I do not feel anxious for him to read very early, but in that, I think I shall be governed in a great measure, by his own inclination. He does not know his alphabet yet, but is quite familliar with many portions of biblical history, and never grows weary of its interesting subjects. His little play, I believe would at any time be suspended for hours, if I would allow him, to sit so long, at my feet, and talk of the patriarchs, (among whom, he has particular favorites,) the creation of the world, the deluge, the prophets, but above it all—the meek and lowly Jesus. We pass many pleasant moments in discussing these interesting subjects. He also knows the names of a great variety of flowers, of which he is remarkable [sic] fond, and I endeavor to turn this fancy to good advantage. Occassionly [sic] when I see him delighted with some particular flower, I try to enter as much as possible into his feelings, and after pointing out its delicate hues, gradually lead his mind to the lovely flowers, that bloomed in Paradise, and the goodness of him, who made all beautiful things for our happiness. I am often rewarded by a sweet boquet, from his dear little hand. He came to me yesterday with a very pretty wild flower, and after looking at it earnestly, a few moments, he asked "Ma where are the flowers now, that bloomed in Eden? Are they all withered?" There was some poetry in this, was there not? I have told you, a great deal about our little boy, but you my dear friend are the mother of one son, and an only child, and I am sure, you will have an abundance of excuses for me. When you write, I shall expect quite as particular description of your son to whom, you must present me very affectionately. Bro. Vernal is at this time, on a visit to me. I suppose Gen. Houston told you, of his losing a young and lovely wife, a few months after thier marriage. It is now seven months since her death, but he continues very sad and devoted to her memory, but you would be delighted with his piety and meek resignation to the will of his Heavenly Father.

And now my dear friend, do you think you will ever come to the sunny west? Oh how happy I would be to entertain you and your dear family in our woodland home! Do give me some encouragement to hope, that you will make us a visit. I expect to accompany my husband, when he makes his next trip to Washington, and I hope to see you during our absence from home, but I must hear from him, how it will suit his business, before I can promise to go farther north. Nothing would gratify me more, than to visit you and your dear husband, and it may be, that I shall enjoy the pleasure, and in my next, I hope I shall be able to accept your kind invitation. I have omitted a great many subjects, about which I intended to say some thing, but our mail will leave very soon, and I must write to my dear husband before it leaves.

Ever thy friend
M. L. Houston

Raven hill, June 12th 1846

My Dear Love,

I address you with a much lighter heart than usual, for the time draws near, when I hope once more to be clasped to thy dear bosom, never never again to be torn away. On last monday I received four letters from you, and among the number, one enclosing a letter from my dear friend Mrs Woods. You were not mistaken in supposing that I would be delighted at the reception of hers, but I read all yours Love, before I broke her seal. I was truly rejoiced at your meeting her, and my pleasure was increased, on finding that you admired her, but I was a little disappointed at your saying nothing about her beauty. I fear you did not recollect that she was my model of female beauty. Years have passed, it is true since I saw her, (and she was then I presume, near forty,) but I must believe they have passed lightly over that polished brow and dovelike eyes, which I can never forget. Oh no, her face was illumined by the soul within, and I can not think it is less beautiful, than when I saw her.

Bro. Vernal is now with us. He was quite pleased with his visit to Houston county, which I mentioned to you in my last. The country he describes as being very delightful, and settling up rapidly, but a great deal of sickness is prevailing, amongst the people in that section. The inundation of the Trinity lands have been so repeated and so protracted, this year, that we may expect a great deal of sickness.

In the neighborhood of Col. Wood's[1] and Patrick's ferry the congestive typhoid fever (as Dr Evans terms it,) is already raging fearfully. Dr E. has lost one case—Miss Johnson, (a daughter of Mrs Johnson whom your friend Mr Mcagee has married since you left). His own daughter is very low with it, and scarcely a hope is entertained of her recovery. Mrs Wood[2] has brought her family out to spend the summer at Mr William Palmer's. I do not think you need apprehend any danger on our account, dearest, for not a single case of fever has yet occurred in our neighborhood.

Sister Eliza spent a day and night with me last week, and I enjoyed myself, more than when I have all the girls with me. Dearest, she does look so much like you, that it is a great comfort to me, to look at her, and think of you. Isabella and Mary are with me now, and Betty is with her mother. Her health continues to improve, and her sweet manners and piety are so soothing to her parents, that although I need her company quite as much as they do, I am always sorry to keep her from them.

I have been anxiously expecting the daguereotype [sic], you promised me. A true picture of my beloved, would be quite a companion to me. If his image would be so sweet, what be his real presence? The hope of seeing him once more, makes my heart thrill with delight. I was about to say—makes me almost <u>dance with joy</u>, but you know dearest I <u>never</u> was a very elegant dancer, and now from some cause or other, it would be a most <u>ungraceful</u> exercise. Oh, I wish I could tell you how I feel, when I think of being with you again, but language fails, and I can not give you the faintest idea of my feelings. I perceive that some of my first letters have missed you, as you say that I do not tell you any thing about Jose, and I have mentioned him in more than one letter. He and Maria gave us a great deal of trouble, but I will not weary you with details, so uninteresting. Houston fined him 5 dollars a month, merely to get rid of him, (for he says he had earned nothing,) which I expect he has spent in liquor, as he has been down at the river drinking ever since he left us. The consequence I expect will be, that he will try to get you to replenish his purse, as you come through Houston, which I sincerely hope you will not do. I enclose Mrs. Woods's letter to you, which I wish you to read and send to her. It is a miserably written thing, for Sam has been teasing me nearly the whole time that I was writing it, but I submitted to his annoyance, rather than send him out with the little negroes, for they are so corrupt, that I do not suffer him to play with them at all. Houston says he has about 15 acres in corn, which is now doing very finely. Bro. Vernal says with a good season, it will make 4 or 5 hundred bushels, but Houston begs me to say only 3 hundred, lest it should disappoint you. The two mules have done all the ploughing as we gave up Black hawk[3] and the Tennessee mare to Mr Moore. I expect we will have a fine crop of potatoes. Your wheat has been my special charge. The rabbits cut it down once, and then I had it staked in so closely, that they could not get to it. And now the bugs have assailed it, and I keep them killed off. You see, love, I am beginning to think of providing for a family, and taking <u>every thing</u> into <u>consideration</u>, I do not know, that <u>you need be surprised at that</u>. You will see in my letter to Mrs Woods, that I have said something about going to see her next summer. The first thing, I know you will think of, will be the crowd we will have to take along, but never mind that, if you can go, you can take care of Sam, and Anna (if I can get her,) and I will manage <u>the rest</u>. Mrs Woods begs me so hard, to go on with you and "let you shake hands with the Yankees," to use her own expression. I will be entirely governed by your decision in this matter. I shall indulge no wish to go, I assure you, until I hear what you have to say. This will go up tomorrow in the mail, and if Maj. McDonald is going on immediately, I expect he will take it to you.[4] He has promised to come down before he sets off, and if he does, I will write again. I have sent a very urgent invitation to him and Mrs M. both to come down before he leaves, for I know you would be glad to see any one, that had been with us.

[in the top margin:] I was caressing Sam, very affectionately a few days ago, when he looked up archedly [sic], and asked "Ma do you want a little baby?" I was rather puzzled at first, but finally answered a la yankee by asking him, if he would like for me to have one. He promptly answered "yes" and I then asked him which he would pre-

fer a brother or sister? "I would rather have a little sister," he replied.

Thy devoted wife

M. L. Houston

Dearest, I would be glad if you could bring me a very simple arithmetic and geography for Kitty. She will not understand any thing, that is not perfectly simple. I will seal this letter, for the reason, that I must request Maj. McDonald in case you should have left Washington, to break the envelope, and send Mrs. Woods' letter to her.

[1]George T. Wood. Identified in *Handbook of Texas*, vol. 2, 929.
[2]Mrs. Martha Evans Gindradt Wood. Ibid.
[3]Houston's horse.
[4]Houston wrote Margaret on July 17, 1846, that he had received the letter, but Alexander MacDonald did not arrive in Washington until July 28, 1846. See Alexander MacDonald to Margaret MacDonald, July 28, 1846, in the vertical files of the Sam Houston Memorial Museum, Huntsville, Texas. In this letter MacDonald describes his introduction to President Polk by Houston, and writes: "No man's introduction goes as far here as old Sam's. He is Polk's right hand man—in fact he has more of the cares of the government on his shoulders than Polk has, although Polk receives all the credit."

∞

Three weeks after his appointment to command the troops in Mexico General Winfield Scott was still in Washington. President Polk told Secretary of War Marcy that Scott's delay would not be tolerated and that Scott must either proceed to his post very soon or the president would place another general in that position. About the same time Scott received this ultimatum he learned that Polk was urging Congress to create positions for new generals.

With nerves frayed by working long hours to procure everything necessary for an invasion, Scott wrote a letter to Marcy outlining these activities. The letter went on to complain about the necessity of pausing to guard himself "against, perhaps utter condemnation" in "high quarters."[1] He continued that he had learned "that much impatience" was already felt that he had not left for the Rio Grande, but that he felt the importance of securing himself against danger in his rear. He concluded that he did not desire to place himself in the most perilous of all positions: "a fire upon my rear from Washington, and a fire, in front, from the Mexicans."[2]

On May 25, 1846, Scott received a letter from Marcy relieving him of his command and ordering him to remain in Washington. Scott replied that he had contented himself with no more than "a hasty plate of soup," as he wrote to Marcy before sending him a letter of explanation and apology. Scott's enemies immediately seized on this phrase to make him an object of ridicule.[3] Houston sent Margaret the newspapers concerning the incidents.

Washington City
14th June 1846

My very dear Margaret

This is the sabbath morning, and as the first Bell has rung for church, I intend, to go a little before the hour of visiting. The Baptist church is distant from my Quarters, or I would go, and hear the Pastor, as I learned he is an able man. For several days past, we have had incessant rain, nor have I seen the sun for the last four days. The like has not been known heretofore. We fear there will be much sickness, on the next change of weather! This summer, in all probability, will be sickly, and I hope the apprehension, of such a contingency, will cause congress to adjourn soon! I cannot think of staying here much longer! Of late, there has been no great excitement about any subject. I send you by every mail the "Herald" so as to give you the news. You will see that A General[4] has drowned himself in "a hasty plate of soup!" Our friend General Gaines is ordered here, for having done too much, but not too little![5] This is to be regretted, for the General is a good man, and a patriot! I hope when he arrives, that all things will go on well with him, and that his infirmities will be overlooked, and he excused!

Since writing the above, I have been to church, and expect to be there twice more, ire I retire to rest!! Mr. Miller I cannot induce to go to church. Eldridge & Thruston[6] go, but what their reasons are I do not know. For myself I go there hoping, that I may find something, that will enlighten, and impress me, as to my duties which I owe to the Father of mercies. My Sabbaths are employed in going to church— reading the Bible, and writing to you, my Love. These employments are surely better, than to idle, or waste my time! in idle conversation. With the best, & most rational employments to my time I feel, that it is heavy on my hands, while absent from you! I need say no more, on this subject, because I have before written so much, that I begin to fear, that you will think, I only wish to make fine profesions [sic], to relieve you from uneasiness, & that I can not feel so much, as I pretend! To tell you, that I love you more than all earthly things, and that I am miserable without you, would be to repeat an often told Tale! To say that I wish to see our "Great big boy," would only be to repeat what I have often done before! 'Tis true I might repeat it but to affirm any thing which has been once stated, is like swearing to a statement before it is questioned, by any one! Now dear, I feel sure that you do not doubt my love, nor my fidelity, and therefore, I will not reaffirm what I have often written!! I write almost entirely about home, and the reason is that I only think of home, and you Maggy! 'Tis true others come in, incidentally, but you are the magnet of attraction. You are my better half.

I came across a pretty piece of Poetry, which I send to you for our Boy, and hope if he is old enough to memorise [sic] it without too much exertion, that he will do so. I would like to hear him discourse about "my blue eyed boy." Dont my Love, oppress his memory, but if he is over roused to exertion, he will soon master the piece. Six lines one day, and four another, will soon enable him to get thro' it I hope!

I send you papers that you may see what is going on here! I know what the squad opposed to me at home are doing and have done! Well let it be, it is no matter of distress to me! I will if spared put all things to right and jerk the hide off, while I show the animal as it is. I very seldom think of what is going on. I will try, and do my duty here, and then I hope to do it at home, if I am spared to return again to our home. It is our home, our dear, dear home, or at least I

109 : MARCH 6, 1846—AUGUST 10, 1846

feel so!

My Love, I am just from church, where I heard one of the most able sermons that I have ever heard, and one that I hope I will not cease to meditate upon! It was from the 14th chapter of Job, and 14th verse! If we live to meet I hope to detail to you my Love the points!

15th My Love, I did not finish my letter last night, and will before the Senate meets, try and get thro' it this morning.

I have no additional news to send you. I will send either to you, Mr Moore, or some of the family, the "Herald." I will send you one of yesterday so soon as I return to my quarters. All the Texians here are well! My poor Indian friend was intered [sic] on saturday.[7] He suffered greatly in his last moments. Had he been attended to by by [sic] his Physician in the first instance, he would have recovered, I have no doubt.

No letters from you since yours of the 14th May.[8] I hope, and look daily for one or more!

My Love, I wish you to present me to all, in the most affectionate manner, and give Sam a good <u>hug</u>, if not <u>inconvenient</u>!

Thy faithful & devoted Husband
Sam Houston

[1]Alfred Hoyt Bill, *Rehearsal for Conflict* (New York: Cooper Square, 1969), 114–16. Charles L. Dufour, *The Mexican War: A Compact History: 1846–1848* (New York: Hawthorn Books, 1969), 89–94.

[2]John S. D. Eisenhower, *So Far From God: The U. S. War with Mexico 1846–1848* (New York: Random House, 1989), 94.

[3]Ibid., 95.

[4]Winfield Scott.

[5]General Edmund P. Gaines was facing a Senate inquiry for earlier calling up 12,000 troops without proper authority. *Writings*, vol. 4, 484n and Dufour, 95.

[6]Algernon Sideny Thruston. For a biography see *Writings*, vol. 4, 429.

[7]The funeral of John Rogers was held at Mrs. Eugene Townley's boarding house on June 13, 1846. Grant Foreman, *The Five Civilized Tribes: Cherokee, Chickasaw, Choctaw, Creek, Seminole* (Norman: University of Oklahoma Press, 1970): 374n.

[8]A letter for this date has not been located. Houston may have meant Margaret's letter of May 4, 1846.

My Love,

Before the committee on Military Affairs meets, I have a moment to write to you, but not to impart any thing interesting, other than what you will receive by the News papers. On yesterday there were some efforts made towards adjournment in July about the 20th. I consulted with some experienced Senators, and I came to a conclusion, that we cannot adjourn previous to the 1st of August. You may well imagine, how I realized this very distressing piece of news, and what I must feel in the contemplation of such a belief. It does seem to me, to be a most painful, and at the same time cruel, disappointment, to my hopes, and wishes. When I left home, you know my Love, that I hoped to be home, by the last of June. Now it is for me either to desert my duty, or to wait for the regular adjournment, of Congress. Yesterday I wrote to you, and Master Sam both,[1] and could write much oftener, if it were not that so many callse, are daily, and hourly made upon me. Calls of various character. Some for business, and others from curiosity. The latter are the most numerous by far. You know that I do not wish to be, in the "Menagerie line," and yet, I have to take a hand in that way. There was a <u>menagerie</u> here at one time, but it left. I did indeed wish for you, and a certain Great big Boy, that he could see all that was shown. The Elephants, the Lions (old and young), the Leopards and various other Beasts, as well as birds. You may tell him of Shetland Ponies, not taller [than] he is himself. These I well knew, would please him to a fraction. I did not enjoy the Show, as I expected. There were no lectures, on natural History, as I had before seen. It was a silent show, but not an exhibition, as I had hoped to see.

To day I learn, that a bearer of Dispatches, has come from England to our Government, and that the Dispatches have relation to our Mexican affairs.[2] If this is so, I will not be surprised, that trouble may yet grow out of the matter. I have never been at rest, on this subject. Nor do I by any means, think that we should feel at rest until we again see peace restored between this country and Mexico. England can not desire to see, the U States, have a foothold, on the Pacific such as the Californias would give us, and which <u>we must have</u>! Hence we may look out for some trouble. It will depend upon the condition of England, as to her situation for war! If her internal affairs, are such, that she can go to war, with us, and it is her interest, to do so, we may look out for a rupture! The Oregon matter, I doubt not will be settled, and so far, things will be well! I hope for the best, always, when things are in future! I did not my Love, set out to write a treatise on politics, but I rather slid into a train of reflection, in accordance with my "vocation." You will excuse me I hope, my Love, for when I write, or speak to you, I always think, and feel, as tho' you could appreciate, what I write, & say. I have been invited to Philadelphia, to speak on a subject of benevolence, and for the benefit of the poor, and needy.

I think I will probably go, if the Senate adjourns, as it has heretofore done, from Friday, to Monday. I will lose no time from business. If I speak, it will be on the 20th Inst. I know you will approve of my doing every thing in my power to lessen the ills of humanity, and increase the rational blessings of life. I have no other object, as I have refused to go, up to this time either to New York, or Philadelphia! I will not go to electioneer, as I am sated with offices, as I feel that, I never can be happy in any situation, which will ever produce a partial seperation from you!

I will not write about home, matters of the farm, but leave them to Houston with the advice of his Father, and Mr William Palmer. Let him consult them, and do the best that he can. I have made up my mind, to be satisfied, as I am compelled to be absent. I am looking with most painful anxiety, for a letter from you! There was none here received, by last nights mail.

Do, my ever dear Love, present me to all affectionately, and <u>hug</u> Sam, and if he does take "it with pleasure," give him a good <u>cuff</u>! Then kiss him for Pa!

Thy devoted & faithful Husband
Sam Houston

My Love, the dispatches from England are not important, nor interesting, as was supposed.

Thine,
Houston

P.S. Let Houston have the Piggis [sic] turned out, and do what he pleased with them. They are worth no great deal any how.

Thine,
Houston

[1]Houston may be referring to his letter dated June 14th, 1846. For the letter to Sam see *Writings*, vol. 4, 484–85.

[2]A war with England over the Oregon boundary line had been feared. A treaty setting the Boundary at 49 degrees was ratified June 15, 1846. M. K. Wisehart, *Sam Houston: American Giant* (Washington, D.C.: Robert B. Luce, 1962), 501.

Washington
19th June 1846

My Love,

I have only time, to say "good Morning," and that last night I had the happiness, and delight to receive your favor of the 17th Ultimo. I sent the letter to Madam Allen, with a polite note, and the subscription money.[1]

My heart was lifted up, and I kissed your letter soundly. I read your pretty lines, and read them to several friends. They were beautiful. I hope to see them in print. I am sorry, that I did not retain a copy. I will yet write to Mrs Allen for a Copy. I can get it in a day or two.[2] My Love, Mr Moore is sickly, and has to work hard. Could you not send him one of our hands. If Jose is there yet, I think you could spare <u>one</u>, and perhaps be a means of saving his life.

Tell Houston to send his Father help by all means, if he desires it, and to use no <u>delicacy</u> in the matter. I feel that we should help each other. I know you will order what is right, as you are both humane and benevolent. I know you will do what is right! I will look daily for letters from you, and as you will get enough from me unless you are very avaricious, you will be tired filing them away. You will please to thank Betty for her letter to me!

Give my love to all and hug Sam! Tell him to have a boquet for Pa, and give it to Ma, to keep for him.

I was happy that you wrote so much about Sam. It is interesting and amusing to hear of the lad. He has no doubt changed, and improved since I left home!

I wish I had time. I would write much. Miller, Col Eldridge, and all send their regards to you, and all the family.

Thy faithful & devoted Husband
Houston

[1]Houston was ordering for Margaret a subscription to *The Mother's Journal*.
[2]Houston had sent some of Margaret's poetry to be published in *The Mother's Journal*.

∞

Washington City
Friday 19th June 1846

My Love,

I find myself at the Room of the committee before the other members, so I write to you as usual.

There is nothing of stirring import to impart to you. All matters move on, in the same dilatory, & lazy way, which they have done, since I came to the city. I hope some impulse will be given to matters, so that we will get off to our homes. Some may prefer eight dollars per day, and to remain here, as it is more than they would make at home. For my own part, I would rather be at home, and to work hard every day, and be subject to occasional spats, than to be here with every comfort or pleasure, that I can imagine, to hope for to enjoy. I will [blurred] nothing to get home, but do every thing to expedite the joyful event, to which, I look with so much pleasure. To embrace you, and Sam, and all our Dear Kindred, would be to me the greatest happiness, which I can fancy of earth. Last night I went with Mr [Howell] Cobb, Genl Rusk, & two other Georgians to see the President on business, and found a band of "Harmonians" there ready to sing. (This is not intended as a reflection upon any one, but is stated for the purpose of explanation, for a Bill, which a Lady sent to you, and due to Master Sam.) Thus my Love, you see that you are regarded, on all occasions. Well, we sat for a short time, and broke off to leave the fine music, to those who had time to enjoy it, for we have not. Mr Cobb has recently heard from home, and says he has another fine <u>son</u>, and is rejoiced at it, for he says, that [he] wishes no daughters. If we live to meet, I will tell you his reasons, as they are rather too amusing. I am much pleased with him, as he is very moral, and genteel. Indeed he is very amiable.

I hope my Love, (for all my hopes are with you) that you will retain your health, and be happy. If any one is sick, you will find it a saving to send for Doct Evans. Let Mr Moore see him in relation to his health, and not defer it too long. I beseech you my dear Love, to let your mind be at rest, on all subjects of business. For I intend to be satisfied! Do not permit yourself to want anything. Get what you desire. My love to all our kindred, and do my Dearest, believe me your ever faithful, and affectionate Husband.

Houston

P.S. I think I will go to Philadelphia on this evening and return on Sunday.

⬯

The following letter written by Margaret is in the Houston Collection at the Barker History Center, University of Texas in Austin.

Raven hill, June 20, [1846]

My beloved,

As we expect Maj McDonald today, I have thought it best to prepare a letter to go by him, but I do most sincerely hope that when you read it, I shall be sitting, as in bye gone days, on your lap, with my arms around [your] neck, the happiest, the most blest of wives. Do not suppose that I intend to surprise you with a visit, and get to you before the letter. No—it is not that, but as Maj M's route will be a tedious one, I do indeed hope, that before he can get to Washington, you will have left the city, for home, and consequently, when my letter returns, as of course it will do so, you may have some curiosity to know what I said to you, when you were far away. I may be dreaming of bliss, never, never to be realized, but hope is whispering softly in my ear, and dropping sweetness from its dewy wings upon this lone, lone heart. Who would not listen to so sweet a charmer? I often reproach myself severely for wishing to hurry the moments of your absence, the precious moments given me to prepare for eternity, and I have no excuse for this sinful impatience, except that my husband is so inexpressably [sic] dear to me, that I cannot be happy without him. Alas "the time is short," and "in that day," nothing will serve as an excuse, for having defrauded our Heavenly Master of a single moment that was his due. Should we meet again, oh, may the main business of our lives be to prepare for Heaven!

We have few opportunities of doing good here, but I believe the Lord is blessing the little we have to do. Our sabbath school and bible class continue to flourish, and both teachers and pupils are much interested.

My friend, Mrs Merrit of Huntsville, has been with me a week, and has added a great deal to our enjoyment. She is very intelligent, and a fine musician, and as I have the piano at home, we pass our time rather pleasantly. We expect Mr Merrit down on tomorrow, with two of the girls[1] beaux, Dr Renfro[2] and Mr Wily.[3] We also expect Miss Mary Kenan. It will be quite a concourse for Raven hill. We have made one fishing excursion to the lake since Mrs Merritt has been with us, which everyone seemed to enjoy finely. Our party consisted of the two Messers Palmers' families, Mr Caldwell,[4] Mrs William Palmer, Mrs Col Wood and family, Mrs Merrit, the three girls, Houston, Sam and myself. Bro Vernal was also of the party. I do not think I ever saw a happier family. They all returned by Raven hill, and Mrs. Merritt gave us some fine music. Sam spent some time, very patiently fishing with a string and button attached to a small reed, which his cousin Mary had prepared for him. Never did I see such patience so poorly rewarded, for as might be expected—he caught nothing. He, after a while, seemed to determine in his own mind, that fishing was not his proper calling, and very quietly left the occupation. Not a word escaped his lips, but in a few moments, he was seen struggling hard to ascend a little dog-wood tree, which he finally accomplished, and I do wish you could have seen his bright triumphant eyes, peering through the leafy boughs, and heard his silvery voice ringing joyously through the wild-woods. Mrs W. Palmer and myself had prepared some refreshments, which added not a little to the life of the party. I am delighted with the scenery of the lake, and as Mrs Wood and I were appointed guardians of the children, I had abundant time for reflection and admiration. I have been very circumstantial about a small matter, but you must excuse me, on the ground, that in our retirement, we have so few incidents, that a single one seems very important. I spent the day before yesterday and night following with sister Eliza. We had gone over and taken Mrs Merritt to dine with her, and were detained until yesterday by a heavy rain. Sister E. has suffered much with a swollen jaw, but she is much better, and I hope she will have no further inconvenience from it. Mr Moore's health is very bad from an affliction of the stomach, and I fear he will never be entirely well of it. Betty, Isabella and Houston have all improved much in singing. The girls are beginning to play a little on the piano, and I intend to keep them at it, until they play well. We pass much of our time in practicing sacred music and in the study of the scriptures. Bro. Vernal left us on last Tuesday, with the promise that he would send mother up immediately, if he could get a conveyance for her. He did not think the buggy sufficiently firm, or he could have taken it down for her. He thinks he can borrow a barouche from Mr Henderson, Gen. Davis' son-in-law, and in that case, I expect Caroline D. will come up with Mother. I have not yet told you what I thought of your speech, though it came to hand several days ago. I was delighted, I assure you, (I mean the speech on the Oregon question),[5] the one on the war question,[6] I have not yet

117 : March 6, 1846—August 10, 1846

received, but I hope I shall soon have that pleasure.

Tuesday, 23rd. I laid aside my letter on Saturday evening, until the mail should come in, and agreeable to my expectations, it brought me a package from you, but dearest, I cannot say it added anything to my happiness, for the pleasure of hearing that you were well was counterbalanced by the apprehension of another absence from you. With the melancholy job, I can exclaim, "the thing which I most dreaded, is come upon me."[7]

Dearest, you tell me that I shall decide whether or not you are to go out with the army. Alas, what has always been my decision, when my own happiness or the good of the country was to be sacrificed? Have I not invariably ascertained your views, and then coincided with them, let my own sacrifices be what they might? And even now, though your personal danger will be far greater than it has been on any previous occasions, since our marriage, I will not express one word of opposition, but I cannot look around upon my widowed hearth and hear my poor boy's plaintive cry, "what makes pa stay so long?" and then tell you that I am willing for you to go. Other trials I have, and must have greater, but these are of such magnitude that the hand of God alone can support me through them. It is true your presence and sympathy would cheer me greatly, but my Heavenly Father alone can sustain me. I have endeavored to write to you as cheerfully as possible on this subject, that the few days of your absence might not be rendered gloomy by any uneasiness about me, but alas, when I spoke words of comfort, which found no echo in my own heart, I thought that but a few days would pass, and then you would be with me, and never, never leave me again.

My love, my feelings upon the subject are so intense, that I will endeavor to say as little as possible about it. I have none of that Spartan spirit that can equip for the battlefield the dearest object of my affection, not knowing that he will ever return, nor would I exchange one hour of happiness, such as we have had, for all the glory that may be won in the present contest. Poor deluded creatures! Born to wretchedness, and compelled to die for a country which has never cared for their happiness. If they must be slaughtered, why may not some other hand than yours perform the bloody deed? But I have said that I would not express one word of opposition, nor is it my design to bias your judgment by what I have said. I wish you to be governed entirely by your own judgment, and though the decision may bring misery upon me beyond description, I will try to bear it without a murmur.

On Sabbath morning, the whole of our expected party arrived and remained until yesterday. They seemed to enjoy themselves finely, but for urgent business of the gentlemen, would have made a longer visit. I think Dr Renfro is captivated with our niece Isabella. He is said to be a very fine young man, but as he has not yet proposed, we have not troubled ourselves to investigate his character. I do not think there is any probability of her marrying Mr Hobbs of Ala. as he is not yet come on, and delays are dangerous you know, particularly in "affaires de coeur." Maj McDonald made us a short call yesterday, and informed us he would leave on Thursday. Houston expects to go up to Huntsville on tomorrow, so that I must finish my letter to you, and some for Ala. to go by him. I will now tell you something about Sam. I endeavored to <u>show</u> <u>him</u> <u>off</u> as much as possible before Maj McDonald, that he might tell <u>pa</u> all about him, but as on all similar occasions, the young gentleman chose to be extremely uninteresting, so that I cannot promise myself much from his description of him. I think he grows more like you every day, and if you could hear our little conversations about dear, dear pa, it would almost bring tears to your eyes. His fondness for flowers seems to increase, and it is a singular fact, for one of his age, that he is always attracted by one that is new to him, let it be as simple as it may. He will pass the gaudiest cluster, to cull one which he has not seen before. Yesterday morning, before our company left us, he brought in a grass flower, which was something new to us all. He handed it to me first, and I told him to take it to Mrs Merrit, and ask her what it was. He did so, and she exclaimed, "young Linneus, it is a grass flower." Poor Sam looked up, quite astonished to hear so poor a station in the floral kingdom assigned to his new-found treasure. "It is not grass," he exclaimed. "Oh, yes, Sam" she returned, "it is one of the grasses, and it is a very pretty flower, too." "It is not grass," he repeated, and indignantly turning away, handed it to Miss Mary Kenan. So, you perceive, Love, he does not inherit his father's penchant for grass.

I send you a box and pipe of our prairie rock. It is some of Joshua's[8] work, and rather rough, but I suppose it will be a curiosity in Washington, and that it will give you some pleasure to present them to particular friends. I must have made a mistake about the glasses.[9] I meant "shields," either of india rubber or the skin of a cow's teat. They are designed to prevent soreness, from which you will remember how much I suffered before.[10] I would not have written for them, if I had thought they could be procured in this country, but I do not think they can. You may bring the glasses also, if you choose, but you misconstrued the word abundant. If you think it worth the time, you may put your guessing powers to work upon it. It was written from the want of something better to write, and I will not puzzle you again by anything so nonsensical.

In yours of the 21st, you say you had written to me on the previous night. I cannot tell what became of the letter, as I have not received it.[11] Your letters are generally a month old, or near that, when I get them, so that they do not afford me the same consolation that they would do if they came directly. My heart seemed to sink almost to despair when I found in your last no encouragement to hope that you would soon be at home. But I will indulge no longer in this melancholy language.

Ever thy affectionate wife,
M. L. Houston

I believe Sam has something to say to you.

My love, Sam has teased me so incessantly while I was writing, that I am afraid you will not be able to read my letter. You must make all due allowances.

My dear, dear pa,

Ma has been promising a great while to sit as amanuensis to me, while I sent you some of "my little words," but I apprehend she would get along rather better without my dictation than with it, as it consists principally in hanging around her neck, and other little teasing acts in which I am greatly improved, and which, I am sure, will not aid her much in her present occupation. Dear pa, you ought to come home and see the beautiful butterflys [sic] all over the yard. I chase them a great deal, and sometimes catch them, but I always handle them very gently and could not be induced to hurt one of them. Cousin Houston caught a pretty bird for me not long ago, and after I had played with it awhile, I sent it away to the green woods, and didn't I make that bird happy, pa? (his language to me.) Ma did say that I bragged a little too much about it, but I assure you dear pa, that I felt very pleasant to think how happy I had made that little bird. My kittens, too, are great things. They are my only youthful associates, (except when Cousin Willie [Moore] comes over to spend a few days with me,) as Ma does not allow me to play with the little negroes, and we have some fine romps I assure you. I have learned to talk to them, just as ma does to me, so that if my kittens do not use good language, it is her fault, and not mine. I must not forget to tell you my dear, dear, pa, that I have put away some pretty wood for him to cut when he comes home.[12] I asked Cousin Houston to put it away, high up, in the entry (true!), which he did, and then I moved all the chairs away, so that no one could climb up and get it.

I must not forget to tell my dear Father that his Christian name is always remembered in my evening prayers. Please give my love to Uncle [Washington D.] Miller and Uncle Joe [Eldridge]. My cousins are all in good health and I love them very much. We all made a visit to Aunt Eliza [Moore] a few days ago, and were detained all night, by the rain. Cousin Willie and I played in the mud, until at night I had to put on one of his shirts, and everybody was seized with an uncontrollable fit of laughter, which was increased by a little mistake which I made. I begged Ma for one little tale before I went to sleep. She consented, and related my own adventures through the day, ending with my change of apparel, and then told me to guess the hero of the story, and dear pa, I was thinking so little of myself that unluckily I answered, "Abraham!" supposing she had given me some of the early incidents of the patriarch's life. I suppose it was my ludicrous appearance at the time that occasioned the roar of laughter at your little boy. As to the coat and pantaloons, I believe I would prefer gray or green, at least, ma says that either would be more genteel than <u>red</u>, (although I acknowledge a considerable fondness for the latter!) and I think, sir (with all due respect to your taste,) that the ladies are, generally speaking, the best judges, in matters of dress! What is your opinion on the subject? Adieu, dear Father. I will try to be a good boy and obey my mother, and will remember all your good advice to me.

Thy dutiful son,
Sam Houston jun.

[1]Margaret's nieces, the Moore girls.
[2]Dr. E. D. Renfro. Identified in *1850 Census*, vol. 4, 2013.
[3]A. P. Wiley. He and Mary Keenan would later marry. Ibid., vol. 4, 2021.
[4]Thomas Calwell. Identified in Ibid., vol. 4, 1999.
[5]For a copy of this speech of April 15, 1846, see *Writings*, vol. 5, 451–72.
[6]May 12, 1846. Ibid., 475–76.
[7]Margaret is referring to the possibility of Houston's taking a command in the Army.
[8]A Houston slave.
[9]See Houston to Margaret, May 25, 1846.
[10]Margaret is referring to breast shields to prevent soreness while nursing.
[11]This letter would eventually arrive.
[12]Houston was in the habit of keeping a supply of wood handy for whittling.

⚭

Washington City
24th June 1846

My dearest Love,

I wrote to you on yesterday,[1] and sent you some little matters. Last night Mrs Cocke[2] arrived here with her mother, on their way home. I did not know that she was here, until, I was about to retire to rest. I was so anxious to see her, that I rose at 5 o'clock A.M. and escorted her to the cars, where I left her safely seated, and with good wishes for her safe, and speedy trip. I sent you enclosed a slip, for a highly respectable News Paper. You will see, if I am abused, I am also defended. This has arisen in part from my visit to Philadelphia. I send this to you lest it might reach you by other means, or it may in part have done so.

Don't you think, my Love, it would be better if I would write less, and send you news papers? You have to read my letters, and you abhor news papers, when I am at home. It may be that I tell you all the news,—when I am at home.

Be this, as it may, my Love, I feel assured that you will not quarrel, with me if I do write often. And if you were vexed at me, I woud [sic] write to Sam. I would like to see him the young gentleman, and mark his looks, when his Ma is reading his letters. I was much interested, with the lines which he dictated, and will so soon as I can, answer his letter! My Love, I fear from this mornings discussion, that Congress will not adjourn before the first of August. So you see now my hopes are dashed, by such a reality. I do yet hope that we may adjourn before that time. I have already written to Louisville to have a horse & buggy ready for me to put on board—land at the mouth of red river, and proceed home by land, with all possible dispatch. You see from these facts, that I think of home, dear home!

My wife—my son, and my friends!

Thy faithful & devoted Husband
Houston

[1]This letter has not been located.
[2]Mrs. James Cocke of Galveston.

⌘

Washington City
25th June 1846

My Love,

I wrote to you on yesterday, and since then, I have heard nothing new, unless it is the arrival, of some ladies, from Tuscaloosa. One I learn, is the daughter of my friend Judge Wallace,[1] of that place, who invited us to call upon him, and make his house our house while we stayed in that place.

I must, as matter of course, call upon the Ladies, and let them see, that you did not marry a Bear. This I will do, and in compliment to you my Love. All that I do is for you, and Sam and _____ such others, as may be interested. I care more about your feelings, and the innate propriety of my conduct than any thing else! This I design for two reasons, first that it will add to your happiness, and secondly, that I will have the solace, of a good conscience. This, I might have regarded, as the first reason, that I should keep myself at rest, within, well assured, that with you, it would be all, that you would require, to keep your heart at rest. My Love, you can not imagine how much I regret, that ever a cloud came, for one moment, came over the sunshine, of our joys, for joys we have had, and joys I hope for again, and sunshine, without clouds!

You speak of our dear Mother, and your wishes, in relation to my future conduct, where she may be a party! My Love, you may rely upon this assurance. Let what may take place, my pledge is given and I will redeem it. I love the old Lady as a Mother, and have resolved to defer to her age, and her disposition. The blood is much like my own, and we have seen in our dear boy, the commingled blood of the Moffats, the Houstons, and the Paxtons! Never was a son more like his Grand Mother, than Sam, is [like] Mrs Nancy Lea!

My absence from home, has inculcated, the love, of a happy, a peaceful, and cheerful home. This I hope my Love, is in store for us, and that my entire life (should I be spared) will evince the estimate, which I place upon domestic life. I know you will believe me my Love, for tho' I had many faults, they are not of the heart, but of the temper. I know its faults, and I feel its defects, but they are gradually coming under, the control of reflection. But enough of this! When we meet, which I pray Heaven may take under pleasing circumstances, you will see. I have been miserable, and must be so, until we meet again!

There has been an arrival here to day, of the Comanchee, & other Indians. Aquaquash,[2] with about 40 besides. I have not seen them, but hope to do so this evening![3]

I was happy to learn that Vernal, had been to see you, and was in good health, and very happy to learn that Mother was well. If she goes to see you, she will not take that little sinner, Virginia.[4] What will mother do with her? Mrs Cocke told me when she was here, that she thought it quite probable, that Vernal was well pleased, with Isabella. She said no more, but thought he spoke favourable of her! I hope your fears in relation, to Antoinette, will not be realized. I trust she will not forget, that riches are fleeting, and decay; or that the soul is immortal. If she should my Love, I hope we will not!

I hope she will show more wisdom, and reflection, than to throw aside her christian character, and assume, that of a thoughtless Lady of fashion. This is certain the most pitiable, of all respectable conditions of life, in which the destiny of society can be involved.

My Love, do present me to all the family. Hug Sam, and write me some smart saying of the lad. Pa thinks of him, and his dear ma, every hour.

Thy faithful and ever devoted husband
Sam Houston

[1]Houston is probably referring to Judge James B. Wallace. Identified in Willis Brewer, *Alabama: Her History, Resources, War Record and Public Men* . . . (Spartanburg, S.C.: Reprint Company, 1975), 566–67.
[2]The chief of the Wao Indians. Identified in Wallis, 104. The name is also spelled A-cah-quash, *Writings*, vol. 3, 363n.
[3]The Indians were invited to the White House. For an account of this visit see Polk, *Polk*, 100.
[4]Vernal's ward, Virginia Thorn.

Washington
28th June 1846

My Dearest Love,

Day after day, has passed and no letters from home. I am sure, you can have no idea, of my solicitude to hear again from you. *[in margin:* Love, I do not blame you, for I know you have often written! I blame the mail, & the U States in part!] To day, I did not go to church because, I was so worn down that as it was the Sabbath, I slept late, and after rising, and breakfasting, when I came to look at my watch, I found the hour had passed nearby.

I intend to go this evening at 4 P.M., as we have preaching twice each Sunday. I have no news of interest to impart, that would interest you. I send you every thing that, I imagine wou'd amuse, or please you. I do not read many news papers, & those which I send you, are handed to me, or accidentally fall into my hands. There is a calm now, in relation to myself, and I regard it only, as the calm, which precedes the tempest or storm. If such is the case you may rest assured, that I will not permit it to disturb me, any more, than those which have howled by me, in times past!

Long since, you have received my letter on the subject of my entering the army, and I doubt not my Love, but what you gave your negative, to the proposition. If you have done so, you may rely upon my faith, that I will be satisfied, for I would not give up the society of your dear self, & Sam, and our Kindred, for all the honors of this vast world! Each day I live, only endears to me more tenderly our wood land home, and disaffects me more, & more to the world, at large. I may truly say, the days are evil, & I have no pleasure in them! I can not be happy, nor can I have pleasure, where you are not! The wheels of time, ever rapid, seem to me, to roll, slowly on, as they do not bring me to thee! I often reflect upon the past, and anticipate the future. I think of home, our meeting, the self complacency of Sam, his exultation of heart, his joy, and the demonstrations, which he will make of his feelings. I dwell, too, on the bright, and lovely face, which you will wear, at our meeting! In all this I enjoy a pleasure, which is boundless, compared to the heartless scenes, with which I am surrounded in this place of fashion. When alone my Love, and in society, such thoughts, as I have imperfectly described, occupy my mind. The smile which I wear, is not the smile of joy, but wears, like the heart a tinge of sorrow. Sorrowful, I feel, because my even being here, was owing to circumstances over which, I had no control. I will say no more, on this subject for the present, as it can do no good and may increase the regrets of others, and only add to my own!

I went the other day to see Mrs Dyer, of Tuscaloosa, who was well acquainted with you, and who speaks of you, with great affection. She talked much about you, & Sam, and when I told her, that I wrote to you almost every day, she was much pleased, and said, that I could not help loving you, as you were so amiable, & interesting! She has two young Ladies with her, Miss Wallace, and Miss Banks. They are going North, and will pass the summer there. I think I wrote to you, about them on yesterday. If I did not, I intended to have done so, for really I write so often, and am so busy, that I hardly know, what I have, or have not written. I only saw them for a few minutes, and if they set out soon, I may not see them again. Miss Wallace was barely able to come to the parlours. She is pretty, & very modest. She met me as a relative, having heard her father, and mother, speak of me so often, and so kindly. She has one of the most meek, and subdued countenances, that I have ever seen with one so young!

She said that her Father, as well as the citizens of Tuscaloosa, looked for us last summer, with much solicitude, and would be rejoiced to see us there. I wrote to you in my last letter, that I hope to get home, by the middle of August, or to get off from here by 1st. I fear this will not be the case. There is a disposition, in Congress, to await the return, of the news in relation to the Oregon Treaty, which has been sent to England. How this will turn out, I cant say. I yet hope we will get off ire long! My intention is to set off in one hour, after the adjournment, and go with all haste, to embrace my wife, & boy. If I could fly, as the carrier Bird, I would pass this evening, in your dear society, my Love! This I can not do, but one thing I can, and that is to deserve all your Love, when I do reach your dear embrace! This I trust, and design (should Heaven permit us to meet again) to be the last time, that we will ever be so long absent from each other while we inhabit this world!

Nor my ever Dearest, do I regard our association here alone, but I look forward with devotional, and prayerful hope, to our reunion, in worlds beyond the grave. Were it not for this hope, I would be the most wretched of beings. To God alone, we must look with prayerful hearts for this happy and Glorious state of being! While I have reason, and a heart, I will never cease to pray for such realities, and hope for such enjoyments through the mediation of Christ Jesus! We surely are designed for another state of existence, than one of imperfection here! This world, with all its cares & joys, can not satisfy the cravings, of an immortal mind, for surely such is ours!

This evening, I intend to visit the Baptist Church, where I learn an able divine, will preach! Genl Rusk & myself have given Mr Huckins letters, to enable him to carry out his design, in raising contributions for Texas Missions. I put your name at the head of his list, and I learn that . . . *[incomplete]*

The following letter from Margaret has a large hole torn from the corner. It was probably written on June 29, 1846, as Houston refers to receiving a letter of that date.[1]

. . . But [I hope that you have] not for one moment indulged the thought . . . a delay an answer, when the subjects presented required such immediate action. But I must first thank you for the picture, which came safely to hand, the most welcome gift you could have sent me.[2] It is perfectly *[blurred]* except that the expression is a little disfigured by the sun. Oh how fondly I have pressed it to my lips and heart! Would that my beloved were as near me at <u>this moment,</u> as it is this moment. The countenance beams so sweetly upon me, that I almost fancy you were thinking of me when it was taken.

But you will be anxious to know what I have to say in relation to your joining the army. So long a time has elapsed since you were called upon to decide, that I know you have been greatly wearied, by the importunity of friends and the undecided state of your own mind. I regret exceedingly, that it should have been so, but it has been unavoidable. You call upon me dearest, to decide the case . . . *[torn]* I had long expected . . . I immediately fell into despondency, a state . . . which I fear was too perceptible . . . I assured you that I would not oppose your going *[torn]* by a single word, and even now I will say nothing against it, but I cannot give you a "cheerful consent" as you require. There are too many reasons why I could not. Many of them will suggest themselves, to your mind. Quite a sufficient number to satisfy you dearest, that it would be impossible. I shall now resign myself to the belief, that you are realy going, so that you need have no apprehension of the sudden effects of a surprise upon me, when I hear that you have taken the command. I am glad to hear, that you will be at home, previous to your departure, for I have much to say to you, which I can not write with freedom. As to my dreams, they partake so much of the melancholy, of the day, that I would dislike to treat them implicitly . . . I*[torn]* I have tried to banish from my mind *[torn]* all apprehensions of danger, but the *[torn]* approaching, and I am so helpless *[torn]* . . . make one request of you, which I would not do [if] I did not fear that something unforeseen might [prevent] another opportunity. But first I beg of you, not to indulge gloomy thoughts in consequence of it, as you know [it] can not hasten my death. In case, my approaching trial be the messenger of my Heavenly Father to call me home, will you allow my beloved bro. Vernal to be Sam's instructor? He is devotedly pious, and altogether capable of teaching him every thing, which it is necessary for him to know. His affection for him is exceedingly tender, and there would be no one in this wide world, except yourself, who would care so much for his immortal spirit. I would that you might never be absent from him, but with the career, which I can see before you, it is a vain and useless hope. But enough of this. Bright days and cloudless skies may be in store for us, brighter from the laughing faces, that may gather around us, and banish all recollections of the gloomy past. When I sat down to write, Master Sam was banished to Mr Thomas Palmer's that I might . . . *[torn]*

[Sam] has given his kitten the romantic name "Magnolia." She is the colour of her mother, and I think it is rather appropriate. Our relations here are all well. I expect to go over this week, and spend a few days with sister Eliza, while two of the girls stay here with Houston. I think the fresh water at Mr Moore's will do me some good. Do come home as soon as *[torn]*

I have said nothing to any one, about your joining the army, except our own family, but every one seems to expect it. Houston is so

129 : March 6, 1846—August 10, 1846

much afraid that I will dissuade you from it, that he has threatened me to write you that I am perfectly willing. You will know how much to believe of it, if he should write it.

[The signature is torn off the letter.]

[1] See Houston to Margaret, July 17, 1846.
[2] See Houston to Margaret, April 30, 1846.

3rd July 1846

My Dearest,

I have not written to you since sunday. The truth is, I wrote so much then, that I thought you might deem me idle, if I should be always writing. To day, as we have adjourned over until monday, on account of the 4th, I have concluded to go by Steam Boat, to Piney Point, as I think, I wrote. It is some distance below Mount Vernon.

We are to meet on monday, and go to business with all our might. I will vote for the earliest day of adjournment, and long to embrace my "treasure" again. You will find in a letter which accompanies this, from Mrs Allen,[1] which alludes to you, and I enlarge the term, not disclaiming the lady's application by any means. I will write to her, and request her, to send a copy to Mrs Woods, as I told her of your stanzas, which she was so anxious to see. I was so much hurried, and flurried, that I did not retain a copy of your verses.

I send you a news paper to day, in which you will see something gratifying to you!

I send to you the Book sent to Sam by Mrs Allen. He will be delighted. I will write to Mrs Allen, and thank her, as well for you as myself. It affords me a pleasure, next to seeing you, to impart, agreeable matters which concern you, as well as those, which concern our little circle. For some days no letters from home owing to the mails no doubt.

My Dearest Love, I can say no more of our Love matters until we meet, for fear, that you will think me a dying swain. My case will be to deserve all your love, and give you if possible a double portion in return! I have been invited, to Carlisle, the home of my ancestors,[2] and two invitations from associations in Philadelphia to spend the 4th, and politely declined them all. I was invited to deliver a Temperance speech at Westchester near Philadelphia in August. [*In the margin:* You get the credit of all this my Love!!!] I hope to be on my way home before the day will come.

I can only add a hearty squeeze to Sam, affection to all our kindred, regards to the neighbours, and all my love to Thee, dearest!

Thy faithful and ever devoted Husband
Sam Houston

P.S. Miller, Dangerfield, & Judge Hemphill[3] all send to you, their best respects, My Dear!

Houston

---

[1]Mrs. Eliza Allen, of Philadelphia, published some of Margaret's poems in *The Mother's Journal*. This letter has not been located.
[2]The Houston family originally settled in Pennsylvania.
[3]John Hemphill. For a biography see *New Handbook of Texas*, vol. 3, 550.

∞

Washington
6th July 1846

My Dear Love,

On my return last night from Piney Point, at midnight, I had the joy to find on my Table your letter of the 4th Ultimo.[1] I only took time to inflict upon it a hearty kiss—then torn it open, and literally devoured its contents. It was a letter from you, and you were not sick, so I was happy. Happy in <u>part</u>, only because, you were depressed, and I am not with you to offer to you the endearments of a husband, and friends [sic] affection. Were it not that the Tariff[2] is now before the Senate, and is one of the absorbing questions of the day, I would leave my place, and fly to you, did I believe that my presence, would afford you any certain relief! Miserable I must be, until I can be with you. My brightest, and only happy thoughts, are of you, & Sam, and our kindred. I need not tell you, what I have so often done already, of my love, & my hopes! You will confide in my love, and my fidelity! While reason, & soul exist, you will never be disappointed. No my Love, never!!

I am sorry that you have, I fear in two instances, mistook my meaning, in relation to what Major Cocke wrote about bro. Vernal.[3] The major was pleased himself, and thought others so too. He meant well, in what he said, and is our friend! I hope you think so! I may have said something, and cast too strong a light upon it. I felt strongly, and may so have written, as I felt excited. Next my Love, is your inference about our Sister Antoinette. I never for once, thought of breaking off your relations, as a Sister. No! My Dear, if you refer to my letter, you will see, that you have in some degree, misapprehended my words, or my meaning. I did say that I would not recommend you to visit her, in <u>my</u> <u>absence</u>, but if they came to see you, to treat her as a Sister, and Mr Power well, for he is a clever man! Truly I was wounded deeply in my feelings, and I expressed them when I was excited, which was wrong! You know my opinion of Galveston, and some of its inhabitants. Well! we need not speak of them. I wish I could forget them, as I have forgiven them!

I am depressed greatly by hearing, that in your situation, you can not have Sister Eliza, or your dear mother with you! Oh, I was so faulty, for ever coming from home, or leaving you!

My Love, do I beseech you, talk to our nieces, and the family, and induce the Girls to read, and to read History or travels! Tell them if I live to reach home, I will try, and have them <u>well</u> married. I hope they are sensible, and if they are, they will consider their relations to others. They are very unfortunate indeed, not to think of the improvement of their time and the advantages, which will result to them from such a course. Tell them to read, my Love, and do converse with them about what they are reading, or may read! I know their discontent will not add to your felicity, but on the contrary will make you unhappy. I intended to take to each of them, some matters of utility, as well as taste. Now I have no heart to do so! I looked upon them as my own children, and hoped in their prosperity to find happiness, & in their after life to feel justly proud. If they inflict upon their Parents a wound by discontent, or of complaints, they will reflect a cloud upon the bright example of their mother. Sister Eliza would never have murmured, in the presence of her Sainted mother. They are young, I well know, but the example of their mother should inspire with the saintly feelings, of filial affections. I will write to one of my dear nieces soon, but will be careful, not to say any thing, which will refer to your suggestion. I was happy to see the fact, that the Post office at Palmers is revived, and hope you will get your letters regularly! I am sorry to hear that Mother's feelings, were wounded by Sisters marriage. For my own part, I am satisfied perfectly, with Sisters & nieces marriages. It was their right, and "right wrongs no body!"

I feel the most lively, and anxious desire, that Mother should be with <u>you</u>, and <u>stay</u> with you. Get Mrs Tom Palmer to stay with you, or to visit you as often as she can! If you have not sent for mother, pray get Thomas Palmer to go after her, as you can not well spare Houston from the farm! Give Mr Palmer, whatever he may ask as remuneration for so doing. Dear, I wish you had sent for her, long since. I would have had her there, had I been at home.

I hope you will be enabled, to be comfortable, until I can get home, and that I feel satisfied (if spared) will be about the last of August. I can not be happy for one hour, until you are in my embrace. Not an hour passes that you are not present to my mind. Nor do I ever sink to repose, without invoking the blessing of our Heavenly Father, upon you, and to sustain you, in your afflictions & travail!

My Love, the God whom you adore will temper the breeze to the shorne [sic] Lamb; nor will he break the bruised reed. With the consolations which He has promised, to His followers, I pray, and beseech Him, that you may be sustained and borne through your afflictions, safely. In the event of a continuance, of the pains of which you speak, I think you ought to take small quantities of opium. Do send for Doct Evans, and consult him about your case. Dont fail, and let Sister Eliza send for him, and let him attend to the sick child. I pray you not to think of his <u>bills</u>, but of the good he may do, and the danger of delay in not sending for him.

Do Dearest, not by any means fail to take my advice. I will now say to say [sic] that I do not wish you to write to me—I mean after the 20 Inst, as I hope to be on my way before it could reach me! I will try, and send you some medicine by the bearer of this letter. My Love, as you complain of a nervous affliction, and pains, may it not be that, the medicine which I sent you, may produce these effects. Consult with Dr Evans if you think well of it. Should you feel a delicacy, in this matter, you can tell sister Eliza, and she can tell Mr Moore who can consult the Doctor, or you can write down the facts, and let Mr Moore submit the facts to him. I am confused, & so write. I hope you will understand me, and avail yourself of my suggestions. If any one is sick, by no means fail to call in the Doctor. It will be a saving, I doubt not!

Dearest, I found in my papers here, a letter which I wrote to you from Washington in Texas, and I now send it to you! You see my Love, that I am not easily wearied in "well doing" if it is well doing to write long letters to ones dear Wife! I am happy to hear of the prosperity of the wheat, and the cats! I regard both as good omens, and pray that our <u>tender</u> hopes, may be realised, in a mother's choicest <u>blessings</u>, or at least our fair daughter!

I am so sorry for poor dear Boy Sam. My Love, you will have to let him play with the little negroes. He will acquire disagreeable things, and the only way will be, when you find out the fact, to admonish him kindly, and teach him, that such things will disgrace him. This course will have the desired effect with him. I feel for the dear little fellow, and my heart bleeds. Shame will be the best corrective. His love of approbation, is so great that he will avoid impropriety or learn to do well, so as to insure the highest gratification of a proud son—a mother' smiles, and a mothers approbation, and her love.

When my wheat is cut, I wish it to remain in the head, and to have it put in a small bag, and hung up in some dry place.

Give my affectionate regards to Mr Moore, Sister & all the family. Tell them not to get the hypo, and if they do, not to keep it. It is a miserable companion. Kiss our dear son, & tell him Pa loves him and will have the Green Breeches & coat.

Thy faithful & devoted Husband

[1]No letter for June 4, 1846, has been located.
[2]The Walker Tariff. Morrison, 15.
[3]Houston to Margaret, June 25, 1846.

Washington
10th July 1846

My very dear Love,

Had I believed when I came here, that I wou'd have been kept here until now, I feel assured, that I could not have been reconciled to have entered upon my duties as Senator.

I see others, all others but Genl Rusk, sitting quietly, and not in any hurry, to leave this place. As to our anxiety, it is no fiction, but a melancholy truth. Some honorable Senators make more clear money here, than they wou'd at home, and for this reason in part, they are willing to remain, until the last moment. Just think my Love, that I have not seen you, nor Master Sam, for 135 days! To me this seems an age, an age of pain and woe. To me it does seem, if I could only be at home, that I would calmly, coolly [sic], and happily sit down, and repose in peace, contented, never again to leave my Doneveil, or my dear family.

From your own feelings, my Love, you can fancy, what mine must be. Even in society, I have not one pleasure, for I am singular, in this that my heart is not at rest. I always find something, something to remind me of you, and our love. I pass by no opportunity, to evidence my regard for you, when an Alabama Lady comes here. The other night I went to [a] reception at the Presidents, with Eldridge, & some others, and met Miss Goree, of Marion, or Perry, and for the evening was attentive to her, and her company. Thus evincing my regard for you, and that they cou'd see that I was no Savage. She spoke of you most kindly, and said that Lucy Ann[1] will receive the highest honors, at school. Our friends were all well, and Aurilea Blassengame is to marry Gov Fitzpatrick soon![2] I wrote a long letter to Bro Henry, after I saw them. Tene has not yet written to me, nor have I received any letters since I wrote. Your letter of the 4th June, was the last, that I have received, tho, I look hourly for more. Oh! my Love, to think, to hear, or to believe that you, are in health, and happy is my greatest joy, and bliss.

Could I only be again with you, and our dear boy, I wou'd be so happy. I often fancy that I see you look sad, as you now are, and poor Sam out in the sun with his face flushed, and bathed in swet [sic], toiling at some business, which seems all the world to him, and then reporting to his dear Ma, what he has done, while he looks and listens for approbation, from a mothers smiles, and a mothers lips! From even these fancies, I derive pleasures, far distant as the dear objects of my affection are from me.

My Love, you may rest assured, that should I live, not one moment, will be lost from the moment after we adjourn, until I will clasp you to my throbbing, & devoted heart! The Senate is meeting, and I must close my letter.

Do embrace my dear Boy. Love to Sister & family all, as I hope Mother is with you, I hope you will present her my filial devotion, and assure her of my future good conduct.

Thy faithful and devoted Husband.

Sam Houston

[1]Margaret's niece, Lucy Ann Lea, the daughter of Henry Lea.
[2]Benjamin F. Fitzpatrick, of Alabama. Thomas McAdory Owen, *History of Alabama and Dictionary of Alabama Biography* (Chicago: The S. J. Clarke Publishing Company, 1921), vol. 3, 163.

Washington
10th July 1846

My Dearest,

I wrote to you this morning, and since then I have received the enclosed a letter from my cousin.[1]

Judge Phelan[2] is here, and our cousin Judge Caruthers.[3] All well, and send much love to you & Sam and the family.

I send you my cousins [sic] letter to amuse you, and let you file it away. It can be of no use, but may at some future day gratify <u>our children</u>. I hope it will my love!

To day is fearfully hot. I am almost suffocated, with heat.

Thy faithfully Devoted husband
Houston

[1]Houston does not explain which cousin he means.
[2]Judge John Dennis Phelan. Identified in Owen, vol. 4, 1356.
[3]Robert Caruthers.

Washington City
Sunday 12th July 1846

My Dearest Margaret,

[In the margin on the first page]: There was a mistake in this letter!! Look at the paragraph on this sheet![1]

On last night, I was certain that I would have received a letter, or more from you, and you can not imagine my regrets. I ascribe it to the mails, as I have been informed that, there was none, south of New Orleans, or even from that point, so I hope to night to hear from you. The last week has been one of painful feeling to me. It must remain, a time of painful, and wretched anxiety for me, until I do hear from you, and in better spirits than you were when you last wrote. I will not repine at the past, for now I can not retrieve, what has gone by, and gone forever.

To day I went to hear a Baptist preacher, (the Revd Mr Sampson.)[2] He is a young man, but one of the most able divines, that I have any where heard. Well, as usual my Love, "collection" was the order of the day. I happened to have fifty cents, and put it in a small neat basket. My own opinion is that, I put in more at that rate, as much as one half of the congregation. People here use, and count cents! After this "Monsieur Touser," the Preacher proceeded, and gave us a rich feast, on the spiritual and practical duties of the followers of the Lord Jesus Christ. I have never heard any thing superior—extempore, or written. That he is a pious man, I have no doubt. It is my determination, while we are detained here, to attend his church, as often, as he preaches. It is usual for him to preach twice each sunday.

The weather here is hot, beyond any thing in Texas. At 9 o clock A.M. the thermometer, was from 87 to 90 for some days past. This without a breath of air. Now what do you think of this? It is oppressive in the extreme! When I think of your situation, I am distressed. You have no good water, I am fearful, and you will not be healthy. To console me, I have but one reliance, and that is upon the mercy of our creator God. He will guard you all, I pray. He noted the fall of the sparrow, and surely ye, are of more value, than many sparrows.

I do not permit one night to pass over my sinful head without reading a chapter, in the Testament, and kneeling in prayer, for your safety, & happiness and that of our dear Son, and kindred. I know and feel that mine are the prayers, of the wicked, but they are a part of the means pointed out by the scripture, and by Christ, & mine are at least an offering of the heart, for no one on earth, but yourself, is aware of my prayers. God sees, and knows the sincerity of the offering, & He knows that there is no hypocrisy in them, tho' they may be sinful, in the creature. I can only hope that the means, which I use may be sanctified, and my petition answered in much mercy. I feel assured my Love that you will not condemn me for the use of the means.

You will I hope feel confident, that I will see you (if spared) so soon, as the distance can be accomplished by travels. Nothing will detain me from you, for one hour, but some providential hindrance.

Every day which passes seems an age to me, and once reunited I can only guess my feelings. We need not think of parting again, but only of uniting! I trust your nerves, are restored, and that our dear Mother is with you, and as you get letters, from me every week, I hope you will be cheerful and tolerably contented. I could desire you to be entirely so. You will not agree to that, and I must indulge you my Love. As to our Dear Boy, I fancy that I can hear from him occasional complaints of "Pa, for not coming home, to my Ma, & my-self." Dear little fellow, how anxious I am to see him seated, on his Pa's knee, beside his dear Ma! The Lad, would feel so proud, and happy. Caesar never enjoyed a triumph more that Sam, does, one in his childish sphere! I hope he will be so directed that he will have many proud triumphs, and that they may be the triumphs of Virtues, over Vice. These are the best, and most glorious at last. All others are but vanity, and vexation of spirits. I find it so, and others will, who have time to reflect upon the past.

My Dearest, since I wrote the last line above, I have been at church, and heard an interesting sermon at the Presbyterian Church. I wou'd have gone to the Baptist, but no one was to preach until right this evening, when I hope to attend.

I will not close this letter until I see whether the mail of this evening, will not bring me letters, from the south, or in other words, my Love, from you, as really you are the only one, whose correspondence I wish kept up, with all my heart.

There is nothing in the way of news, which I can write, except that our relations, and every body else, sends their best regards, & respects to you, and kisses to Sam, but they dont give them to me for the young gentleman! I will continue to write, and whether congress adjourns early in August or not, I think I have so arranged matters here, that I will be enabled to leave by the 10th at farthest.

I hope my Love that you will be well, and happy. I am most sorry that you can not get exercise, in your present situation. I doubt not but what it is useful, and I hope you will be able to get some, when Mother reaches you!

To night I thought of writing to Sister Antoinette! I must soon write to Mr Power also!

Dearest it is past ten oclock at night. This moment I have returned from hearing a Baptist Preacher. He certainly is a very uncommon man. His name is "Dodge."[3] On my return to my room, the mail had been sent to me but no letter from my beloved Margaret! Well Dearest, I hope to get two tomorrow. Dearest kiss our dear Boy. Love to Mother if she is with you, and all our family.

Thy faithful husband
Sam Houston

[1]The word "retrieve" is written over an illegible word.
[2]George W. Samson. Wisehart, 548.
[3]Ebenezer Dodge. Identified in *Dictionary of American Biography*, vol. 3, Part I, 345–46.

∞

Washington
17th July 1846

My Dear Love,

Your two favors of the 12th and 29th ultimo reached me, with the enclosure for your dear friend Mrs Woods.[1] I lost no time, in sending it to the madam with a respectful note from myself, in which I said that I had complied with your request "as in duty bound." I read the letter and sealed it my dear. I was glad to see Sams [sic] hair in it, but was sorry to see it was so long. I mean the hair.

The Madam would be happy, I feel assured, for she loved you, most truly, and tenderly. The reason that I did not tell you that she was beautiful, was that I reserved that to talk about when we meet. She is beautiful, and looks to be about twenty, or between that age, and twenty five. I was disappointed in this, only that I expected to see, a large lady, at least as tall, as your dear self. Why, Indeed, I wou'd not know how to handle so small a lady, and therefore I looked at her as something not to be touched, and only fit for conversation!!! When she told me that she had a son reading medicine, I was astounded! I hope in a few days, that I will have the pleasure of forwarding to you a letter from her Ladyship. The balance I will reserve for you, when we meet, which I hope will not be long. Yesterday we resolved to adjourn on the 10th of August. You may guess, how I voted—My Love, the hours, and days move slowly on, and will until I can embrace my beloved Margaret. Your decision was right about army matters. I am not committed, and nothing but an emergency of great need, will induce me to renew the toils of camp, and then not until we have talked it over, face to face, as I truly hope, we will meet each other soon! So my love, you may be at rest. I most truly, sympathise with you, my dear Love. I know my ever dear Wife, that you must feel great depression, & melancholy, or you would not make the request which you have done, in relation to our dear Boy. My Love, I wou'd not have said any thing in answer to your request, had it not been, that you might suppose, that I do not feel, as I ought to do, on such an occasion. My Love, I hope it was made under a state of feeling incident to your situation, and that so soon as your Mother would arrive, that you will regain your usual cheerfulness. Be that as it may, and regarding, your solicitude on the subject, with all possible affection, I assure you, that your request shall be complied with, and carried out, to the letter. Should the will of the Great Giver of life, determine to seperate us, on earth, my prayers will be unceasing, as they have been, that we shall be reunited in Heaven! You do not my Love, estimate my intentions, should I be spared, to a longer life. I am not in Love, with my present station, only as it is necessary to our Posterity! I feel that I may now retire again to private life. For this reason, I consented, to leave the home, of my affections!! To leave you, my dear, & Sam, with those who are near to me. I do most truly Love, hope that ire this, you have recovered your spirits, and are cheerful, and happy. I cannot my Love, anticipate any thing, but the pleasure of again meeting a sweet, and cheerful welcome of yours, which has so often dispelled from my heart every care, and entirely absorbed my affections!

Dearest, I blame myself, necessary, as it seemed to be, that I ever left you in your present situation. It was not, without pain of heart. It seemed, like tearing me from all the ties of tenderness, and life. No one could have felt more truly, or more tenderly. It was the only time in my life, that I yielded so reluctantly, to what I thought a duty to you, and all of us! I pray daily, for our happy meeting, and and [sic] my Love, a night does not pass, but what I read a chapter in the New Testament, and invoke the blessing of our Holy Father upon us, and such others, as he has made it our duty to pray for. We are in His hands, and he can bless us. Our joint petitions, tho' we are far a part, may be heard, and answered, according to our Heavenly Fathers will!

I pray to be spiritually enlightened, and made pure, & holy.

There is a man here by the name of Minor, who says he was at Raven Hill, but I do not know how far to believe him. He had much impudence to go there, for he is not a man of good character. He is a man, who lives by swindling, and has two wives, one in Texas, and one in the U. S. I hear of other infamous acts of his, in the U States. Many will try to impose upon us, alledging [sic], that they are my good friends, and know me so well, and are so intimate with me. When any of that kind call, and have <u>not</u> conclusive evidence of character, keep a look out for imposters. Treat them well enough, but let Houston [Moore] know that there are wolves in sheeps clothing!

My Dear Love, I have written a long letter to tell you, that we are to adjourn on the 10th, and that your letters made me happy, and I hope weekly, to receive others. Dont think my Love, that I have in this been scolding! No, indeed my dear, nothing of the kind. My affections, and tender passions are all alive, and not an ungentle feeling!

Embrace Sam, and all our kindred for me.

Thy devoted, and affectionate husband
Sam Houston

[1]See Margaret Houston to Mrs. Almira Woods, June 12, 1846.

∞

The following letter is addressed to Mrs. A. M. Woods, Providence, Rhode Island, and is from the Alva Woods Papers.

Washington City
18th July 1846

Dear Lady,

The enclosed letter,[1] came from my dear Margaret, last evening, with command to forward it immediately. As in "duty bound," a compliance is most cheerfully rendered. I have by last mail received two letters from her. One since she wrote to you, and by which I find, her spirits quite depressed. I feel much disposed to abandon my past here, and return to her immediately.

If your Lady-ship should desire to write to her, as I know you will, be pleased to enclose it to me, and I will be most happy, to forward it to her direction.

Will you be pleased to make my very respectful salutations to your Sister, as well as my compliments to Dr Woods and your son.

I am with perfect
respect, truly your
obt serv't & friend
Sam Houston

[1]See Margaret Houston to Almira Woods June 12, 1846.

∞

Washington City
18th July 1846

My Dearest Margaret,

On yesterday I wrote you a long letter, but it contained little of importance but the fact, that we are to adjourn on the 10th of August.

On last night I received a letter from Genl Wallace,[1] enclosing a letter from our poor Sister.[2] From him, I learn that owing to her ill health, and affection of her head, she has become partially deranged, and talks, when her mind is affected, of going to Texas, and to Mr Penlands.[3] He represents her health, as too feeble to travel, nor does he mention much, if any, hopes of her recovery. I send you her letter which she wrote to me, and was enclosed by the General. By it you will perceive how painful must be her state of mind, and how much cause, we have of the Deepest sorrow.

I wrote to her a very affectionate letter,[4] and assured her if it were in my power, that I would visit her, but urged your situation as an excuse for my going home directly. It is a most painful thing to refuse her the pleasure which she asks. Genl Wallace ways that she said she would go to Texas with me, but said the reason she did not so write, was that I would not go by, if I knew of it to be her intention. But she says if she could once see me, she knows I would not leave her, but take her with me. If she were able, the Genl says he would take her to Mr Penlands where she wishes to go, but her Physicians, do not advise the course. My Dear, this is a melancholy visitation, and demands our hopes, and prayers. It has been the misfortune of my dear Sister, to set at naught, the advice of her friends. We can console ourselves, that we had no agency, in producing causes, which may have had some influence in producing, the sorrowful effects, which we have to deplore!

I suppose it will be proper, to let Sister Eliza know of this occurrence. Indeed you cannot conceal it, as I suppose. Tell Sister and Girls, & Houston to write to Sister. It may soothe, and gratify her, and be or real advantage to her! I advised the course, which I think best for her to pursue. So soon as I close this letter, I will write to Genl Wallace, and say more about, what I think of her treatment. The Genl is disposed, to do every thing in his power.

My Dearest, I have nothing of an agreeable character to write. I will suggest to you my dear, to regard this intelligence as you should do, but not to let it sink too deep into your heart. You cannot by sorrowing, relieve our dear Sister, and it is not our duty, to repine at His dispensations, in whose hands we are all, "as clay in the hands of the potter." Let us, by our actions, and prayers, deprecate his just wrath! My Love, do embrace our dear Boy, and give my love to all the family.

Thy faithful and ever devoted husband
Sam Houston

My Love I truly hope, that our dear Mother is with you, and will remain there always, or with you. I hope you will not let yourself become melancholy. You have to live, for Sam, and his Father.

Houston

[1]Houston's brother-in-law, William Wallace.

[2] Mary Houston Wallace. Neither letter has been located.

[3] N. A. Penland, who was married to Houston's niece, Phoebe Jane Moore Penland. M. W. Hearne Papers. Phoebe Jane was close to Mary and her first husband, Matthew Wallace, and was mentioned in his will. Worth Ray, *Tennessee Cousins* (Baltimore: Genealogical Publishing Company, 1994), 303.

[4] This letter has not been located.

Look at the pages!!!!

Senate Chambers

21 July 1846

My Dear Love,

Since I wrote to you, several days have passed, but as I wrote to Sister Eliza, I was assured that you would know the contents of my letter. And as you receive the mail in large parcels, this letter may reach you, as soon as she may get hers. The hour of adjournment I look to, with much anxiety. I have been pressed to pass home by the South, and to return by the North. You can fancy my reply. I will not repeat it. I cannot with all my haste, reach home, so soon as I wish to do, but trust I will reach there by the 1st of Sept, or the 5th, tho' the water in the Ohio, will be low, as it is at this time. Yet small Boats run, and will, all the season. So if I should not make my time, you need not be surprised, as Boats, at times, lay on the sand bars for several days. You know one thing my Dear, that I will not delay, one moment. You say in you letter that you have many things to say, that you will not, or cannot write. I guess such is my situation, and should kind Heaven be pleased to grant us the happiness of again meeting, you may rely upon my talking at least a week, if not two. But I will be happy to listen, first to all that you have to say, and Sam, you know, must "talk," or all does not go well. Has he given you any late lessons in "singing?" At one time, he had some ambition in that way. I hope he has improved his own taste in music.

I am very happy my dear, that you were gratified, on receiving, the Locket, and likeness! You see I was not selfish, or I would have kept, and taken it with me. I might have done this, had it not been, that I hope you will be as well pleased with the original, hoping that it will be more responsive, in feeling than the likeness, and thereby be more interesting to you. You need not my Love, suppose me jealous of the picture, for if you do admire it, you gratify me much. You say it is defective, and so rendered by the "Sun" or light. In this, it only resembles the original, I fear, as when he is seen he is seen, and knows most intimately, I fear he is injured by the "light." I hope this is not the case! I would not care my Dear if the light of your knowledge were to shine upon me, and all my words, and actions since we parted. I hope my dear, always to act, in such a "light," that it will gratify you. And if it were possible, I declare to you, that I wou'd be willing that you should know every thought, and action of mine, since Sam pointed to the tear on my cheek, and said "Pa what is that?" My dear you may be assured, that my heart, & my conduct, has been in your keeping. You from this will be satisfied, that the original in your estimation cannot be prejudiced, by too much light.

You my Love, have been afflicted by my absence, while I have been punished for leaving you. But I trust most sincerely, and devotedly hope, we will never, be so punished and afflicted again. In all the confusion of debate, and my speaking some, too, I have written this letter. You will see that it is truly confused, and that I did well to page it! Had it not been for frequent interruptions, I wou'd have written with more order, or arrangement. You will infer at least a disposition to think, of you, and to write to you. Yes my dear, I will not think, so poorly of your feelings, and wishes, as to believe that I have written to gratify you, as well as myself by writing to you! I am like Sam. I love approbation, and try to deserve it. I hope Sam, may also make, that condition in his self approbation. Bless the little Boy. Oh with what pleasure, do I anticipate the meeting with his dear Mother, and the "young man." How does he come on with "Abraham," and (as he conceives) his misconduct? I have not yet said any thing about his cat of "Romance." I supposed he would be rather rude, with the little pets. I hope soon to see his capers with them! Tho' my dear, I do confess, that the time appears to move slowly on. If it were possible for me to reach you in an hour, I would even then, feel that it was an age. Yes, to reach my home, my woodland home, where all my earthly hopes, and treasures are! Yes, my Love, your heart is the Casket of my feelings, & my love while Master Sam enjoys a large portion of my hopes. Not my dear, the hopes of ambition, but hopes which arise, from a wish, to see him more virtuous, and more enlightened than others. This I trust will arise from the early principles, and lessons, with which his dear Mother, will imbue his young mind, and heart. Dear having reasons, and treasures of such character, I <u>guess</u>, you will believe me anxious to reach our home. These are some general reasons, but my love, I have others, which I hope to tell you of when we meet! They may be of minor class, but they are <u>my</u> reasons, and will be under consideration until we meet.

I would like to see Mother at home. And I wou'd like to see Sister Eliza at her new home, as well as our dear nieces, and all the family. I would be glad to see how Isabella looks in Texas, and to see if Mary still humps her shoulders, or is fond of reading. Nor as I without some care, about the appearance of Sams "Tosen Betty." Whether her health is restored, and whether she retains her dignity, and her decent attitudes? Taking all matters into view, I have a <u>thousand reasons</u>, to wish to be at home, and not <u>one</u>, to be absent!

There are others my Dear, which I may allude to! For instance, Sam's question to you, relating to your wish about a "little <u>babe</u>"! I would like to see the change in <u>appearance</u> of <u>some one</u>, which must have been, his reason for making the enquiry.

He must be a lad, not only of observation, but reflection. Had he not been so, I take it the enquiry [sic] wou'd not have been made!

I am anxious to see, and enjoy with Sam, the agreeable and delightful <u>cause</u> of hope, and expectation. I regret above all, my Love, that I can not be with you constantly, to soothe, gratify, and cheer you every hour! If spared, the like of my absence, shall never again occur! I hope to be in a situation soon to press you to my devoted, and faithful heart.—To repay the pain of absence by the presence of pure affection. To make you happy, if in my power. Give my love to all, and my regards to the neighbours.

Thy faithful Husband
Houston

Washington
24th July 1846

Dearest

    Knowing that you will not reply to this letter, as I hope to be on my way home before the time which I expect it to reach you, I write it. Congress has commenced business in good earnest, and of course we are quite busy.

    I trust my Love, that I may not be detained by any accident, an hour, on my way home. You, I can assure you, are not more anxious to see me, than I am to press you to my ardent heart. Not an hour passes when I am awake, that you are not present to my thoughts and ever and anon our dear Boy, comes in for a share of my intense affection. He would not envy his "dear Ma" in a preference, but wou'd not wish to be posponed [sic], in his rights by another on earth.

    Should we be so blessed, as to meet again, on earth, I hope to find that you, and our dear Boy, will each require, a greater reach to embrace you, than when I left you! Yes, my dear, tho' it is true that I think of you, as I left you, I nevertheless, fancy many things about appearance and in size of both. This you will readily account for, as I have gained some thirty, or forty pounds. You will be surprised, if I should retain my size until we meet, and you, I hope, will retain yours.

    I am trying to procure your Books, and all other things which you desire. The dress I will [not] get, for fear of a <u>bad fit</u>, and because you do not wish me to do so.

    I did not go to New York, but sent an apology of business. Sarah Ann, our niece, and her Lord[1] I hear are there, and Genl Rusk, and myself may run over there during the session, and return before the adjournment. If I should do so, I will call, and see our "Kin" if they are in the city, at the time.

    On tomorrow, I hope to have time to write Sister Ann, a letter! I have been greatly annoyed this session, by calls.—Some I doubt not, from respect, and many from curiosity.—No matter, I have been dismayed by the show. If you were here, I wou'd wish you, to hold my Levees. You could sit, as a lady has a right to do, if she either thinks it unelegant, or not pleasant to stand in company. As you say you would not cut a handsome figure, in a dance, you might fancy that you had best remain seated, to receive your company.

I hope to discourse with you soon, on these subjects and many others. Never did [a] poor exile, sigh for the home of his birth, or the companions of his youth, as I do, for our woodland home. The sweet breezes of the south, and their music, in the tall pines of Raven Hill visit me only in fancy, while my heart is with you, and the inmates of our quiet home. I trust a happy home! You I hope my Love enjoy health, and cheerfulness in the society, of our dear Mother and our kindred. You will, I am assured, think from the tone, and tenor of my letters, that I am courting you either for a reunion, or at least to get you in love with me. At all events, you must (if you believe me sincere) think that I am not indifferent, to your love! Well to be candid my own one, I am as much, if not more in love with you, than I have ever been, in my whole life. And if you do not find it so, you may "nail me as base coin to the counter," to admonish other dear women to beware of counterfeits!! It all amounts to this, my dear, that I do, most truly, sincerely, and devotedly love you, more than all, & every other human being, and esteem you, as my good angel, sent by a kind Father, & Friend, to be a mentor, to my heart, and a light to my path, and indeed my Love, Sam, adds to the light, of my ways, by his little lamp. While blest with these temporal lights, my path way seems bright, and my heart is cheered.

My dear One, I wish you to give my love to all—hug and kiss Sam. Salute the neighbours.

Thy Faithful Husband
Houston

[1]Thomas Power.

⌒⌒

149 : March 6, 1846—August 10, 1846

Washington City
Sunday [26] July 1846

My Dear Love,

I have just returned from the Baptist church where I heard an able sermon by Mr Sampson, & this evening, I am to hear him at 8 oclock preach on the subject of predestination. As I had sought for the Books, for which you wrote, and could not obtain them, I made a request of him, and he said he could get them he thought for you. So soon as he can my dearest, I will take pleasure in sending them on to you, as I will carry but little baggage, with me in a carpet bag, so that I may not be detained on the way home. I have not told you, how I spent last Sunday. I was twice at Mr Sampsons Church. He is a very pious, and excellently good man, in my estimation.

I sincerely hope that I may have reason, to think as well of all the clergy, with whom I may become acquainted, for recently I believe, two at least have been expelled from the church, for awful crimes. One of this place, for seducing a young girl, tho' he was a man of family—six children. The other was of the North, and after seduction, he had the girl murdered. Such things as these are awful, and call for punishment on earth. Different from such men is Mr Sampson in my opinion. Those preachers who behaved so badly, I am happy to say, were not Baptists. You, I feel assured, will also be gratified at the fact. For the sins of others we can not be accountable, only so far, as we may participate, with them in their crimes, or so far, as we may induce their errors. For my own part, I have not, nor will I ever, solicit mortal being to sin in this world, while my heart is as it has been, and now is. Our frailties are humiliating enough without bedaubbing [sic] them with crime.

There has been, and still is very great excitement about the Tariff, and I think it will be defeated. The Bill was not a good one, and its friends are not willing to let it undergo any modifications, and I have not ventured, to do any thing, which could distract the democratic party, or the Bill could have been improved, and carried into a law. The upshot will be that the Bill, in my opinion will be posponed until next session. This will arise out of the fact of Mr Secretary Walker,[1] having recommended the proposed Bill, and relying on the strength of the democratic party, intended to crush the whigs & the present Bill was drawn, for a state of peace, but not war. We are now in a war, and he will consent to no modification, to the measure. In this way he puts the democratic party in jeopardy, and at great hazard. Mr Haywood[2] a democratic Senator, on yesterday resigned, rather than vote for the Bill. Others cannot, and will not vote for it. This state of things destroys the unity of the Party, and at once, disconcerts its action. Mr Haywoods place will be filled by a whig Senator.[3] This, we say in our country is awful, most awful!!!

Well, my own One, this plagues me, but I will not let it distress me. I am most happy, because I want nothing but to see my country happy, and retired with you, and Sam and such other family, as a kind Providence may be pleased to afford us. I feel most gratified to my Creator, that I have no disposition, to aspire to any station, nor even to retain the one in which I now am! If I were in the state of mind, with some poor wretches which I see here, (who would in my opinion, sacrifice a portion of the dearest, & best interests of the country, to procure their own advancement to the Presidency of the U States,) I ought to be miserable, in my own want of esteem for myself.

You have seen, and I have purposely sent you many news papers, which would show you what was said of me, (to gratify you,) as I thought it would do so, but I declare to you my Love, it was not intended, for the purpose of appealing to you, nor preparing your mind for events, connected with a canvass for the Presidency. No, this was not my object, for all that could be done, by an election to the Presidency, has resulted, by my coming here, and if I could now command the Presidency, or any earthly situation, at the hazard of your health, or happiness, I do my Love, assure you, I would spurn all! These remarks arise from a reflection, or thought, in one of your last letters, where you say, "I see that you, are doomed to politics." My Love, you may not think so. I was never, in my life, so little disposed to them, as at the present moment. I love home, & idleness too much, ever to wish to be in public station. I do not dread the responsibility of office, for I am vain enough to believe, that my troubles, and labours past, are equal to any, which could result hereafter in any station, if I were doomed to fill them. I hope the time is at hand that you will see that I live for you, and not for empty breaths of fame, & noise.

You must allow me to tell you an anecdote my Love, although [it] is the sabbath. Soon after I came here, and one night at the circus, I saw a young lady, seated several seats above me, and behind me. I looked at her, again, and again, until I was ashamed of myself. I saw that one of the gentlemen, who waited upon herself, and other Ladies, was an acquaintance of mine, and asked him to make my apology to the Lady for my seeming impudence, in looking at a strange lady, and gave this reason as an apology; that she was "much more like Mrs Houston, than any lady, I had ever seen"! After this, I saw her on the first of May, and was introduced to her.[4] I made my apology in person, and her Father, and Mother, who were Mr Seaton,[5] (Mayor of the city) & Lady,[6] old friends, invited me to call often, and see them! I have never called, and to day, as I was returning from Church, I met Miss Josephine, returning from another, and walked with her Parents, and her home. I was rated for not calling upon them, when I assured them of the true reason, that the young lady, so much resembled you, that as I was doomed to stay here for a season, I was only made more miserable, as she recalled you, & Sam so vividly to my mind, & heart. So after seeing them to the door, I made an elegant bow, and came to writing. The young Lady seems flattered, and considers it a fine compliment, for you must know, that a great part of my standing here, is on your account, I assure you! Your last letter my Love, was dated the 29th of June. I am uneasy, but I hope it is owing to the mails, as I get no letters from Texas.

My Love to all! Hug, and kiss young Mr Houston. Thy ever faithful, and devoted husband.

Houston

[1]Secretary of the Treasury, Robert J. Walker.

[2]William H. Haywood, Jr., a North Carolina Senator, resigned July 25, 1846. *Biographical Directory*, 140. For Polk's conversation with Haywood on the subject see Polk, *Polk*, 128–30.
[3]George E. Badger. Ibid.
[4]Josephine Seaton. Identified in *Dictionary of American Biography*, vol. 8, Part 2, 541–42.
[5]William Winston Seaton. Ibid.
[6]Sarah Weston Seaton. Ibid.

Washington
31st July 1846

My Dear Love,

Only ten days, have I to stay in this city. I may set out sooner, if I live. You may guess how anxious I am to be with you, and Sam Houston Jr. I hope he will receive me in becoming style. As for you my dear, I feel no apprehensions, as to how you will greet me. But he has been so absolute, and controlling, that he may not desire any conflict with his authority. I wish now, as I hope, he will be disposed to accord to me, a share of his authority. If he shou'd not, I must call in his Ma, to my interest, and if needful, an umpire. Oh my Love, how often is my heart with you, and borne, by fancy, to scenes which are hourly passing at Raven Hill. I can not, I will [not] attempt, to describe my feelings, my hopes, and my wishes, in relation to you and the lad. I had no idea, when I was telling him about Abraham, that I was making so deep an impression, on his ready mind, or that he would ever identify him with the incidents of "a [blurred] day." I like such blunders in our Boy. They show his intensity of feelings, and will render him more careful, as he can never bear ridicule. In this he is like Napoleon, who could face the cannon of the world, but could not stand the shafts of ridicule. If Sam, is only good, I do not care how great he is. There's none, that's truly great, But those, that's truly good! Dear, learn him these lines, & explain them to him! They may be of incalculable advantage to him, if he should possess emulation, to a great extent.

153 : MARCH 6, 1846—AUGUST 10, 1846

I only intended to write you a few lines, and I find that I have run into a long letter. I will not take time to apologize for the error. I will reserve that for our meeting, and if you say so, I will ask pardon on my knees!

I wrote a long letter to Bro Vernal a few days since, and told him to meet me at home, from the 1st to the 10th of Sept. Dear fellow, I am truly anxious to see him. But I need not say <u>him</u>. I am anxious to see all our relatives.

You will please to send my Love to all, whom you may not see. Kiss the Girls who are with you.—hug Sam, and salute the neighbors, with my compliments.

Thy faithful
Houston

I received your welcome favor, and the <u>presents</u> by Maj McDonald.[1] He went on to New York two days since! I thank you!

[1]For an account of Alexander McDonald's visit with Houston, see McDonald to Margaret McDonald, June 1846, vertical files, Sam Houston Memorial Museum, Huntsville, Texas.

∽

The following letter is addressed to Doct Alva Woods, and is from the Alva Woods Papers.

Washington City
10th Aug 1846

My Dear Sir,

Your very kind and acceptable letter has just reached me. I thank you for it. The enclosed from Mrs Woods will be borne to Mrs H. with much pleasure, and if I had otherwise been doubtful, as to the agreeable character of my reception, at home, I would feel confident, that by becoming the bearer, of Mrs Woods letter, I should secure a kind, and agreeable welcome from, my wife. On the present occasion, I feel more pleasure, in becoming the organ of the Ladies, or their Diplomatic agent, than I shou'd feel honor'd by becoming a Minister to the Court of St James. My present commission will take me home, and the other would consign me to a longer exile, from our woodland home, where I can only be happy, or even satisfied.

I had the pleasure to receive the mementos so kindly sent to our little Pioneer. I intended to have written to Lady, and yourself, but I was overwhelmed with business. To day at 12 M. the congress adjourned, after doing enough, if not too much, business. It will render me very happy to hear from you, and to know that Lady, and your son are well. I do sincerely hope, that my dear wife, and Mrs Woods will cherish their affections, for each other, and cultivate them by increasing correspondence.

It will, if possible, be an object of my ambition, to afford the Ladies an opportunity of embracing each other. Mrs H. says, she will refer the matter to me. This being the case, I will be compelled, to maintain my allegiance, to our better halves.

I pray you, to do me the kindness, of presenting my salutations, of affectionate respect, to Mrs Woods, & assurance to your son, of my friendship, and regard.

I am very truly
Your Friend
Sam Houston

Chapter II

November 21, 1846—April 4, 1847

January 30, 1847: Sam Houston to Margaret Houston
February 1, 1847: Sam Houston to Margaret Houston
February 3, 1847: Sam Houston to Margaret Houston
February 5, 1847: Sam Houston to Margaret Houston
February 8, 1847: Sam Houston to Margaret Houston
February 9, 1847: Sam Houston to Margaret Houston
February 10, 1847: Margaret Houston to Sam Houston
February 11, 1847: Sam Houston to Margaret Houston
February 12, 1847: Sam Houston to Margaret Houston
February 16, 1847: Sam Houston to Margaret Houston
February 19, 1847: Sam Houston to Margaret Houston
February 20, 1847: Sam Houston to Margaret Houston
February 22, 1847: Sam Houston to Margaret Houston
February 23, 1847: Sam Houston to Margaret Houston
March 5, 1847: Sam Houston to Mrs. Almira Woods
April 4, 1847: Ashbel Smith to Sam Houston

Houston returned to Texas in August, 1846, when the first session of the Twenty-ninth Congress adjourned. He spent the summer at Raven Hill with Margaret, Sam, and the new baby Nancy Elizabeth, who was born September 6, 1846. He purchased a new home a mile from the center of Huntsville, and made arrangements to move his family there as soon as improvements were completed. In late November, he began his journey back to the nation's capital for the second session of the congress.

Houston
21st Nov 1846

My Dearest

I was detained here as you will see by the date of my letter. There was no Boat. The General and Miss Caroline[1] went down the evening before I came in. Our trip down here was awful.

You will see that I send you Prunes, the flannel, a little cap, a large cap, Sams check (not such as I wished) Nannys "little shoes" Sams shoes, candy, 2 apples, and one orange, last I believe, I send you a fine Safety. The Lobelia, I send to our dear Mother. I am sure there is enough to vomit every body, and every thing on Trinity. If I have not named every thing, you will dispose of them as you find them. A Boat has arrived, and I hope to get off this evening. I presented you to all the Ladies which I have seen. I went to see Mrs [James] Reily and met Mrs Nicholls[2] and others shopping. My time has been much occupied, and yesterday the friends here would compel me to take a dinner. I did not even drink cider at it. Made a speech. Only fair.

I will (if spared) write to you from Galveston. Mr Holliman[3] is waiting. I would write a long letter if I could or had time. Tell our dear Boy to be good, that I love him more than "Ten thousand bushels." Kiss a thousand times our dear little cherub. Give my best Love to Sister, Bud, and to our Dear Mother commend my most grateful affection.

Write to me <u>always</u>. The day is fair & pretty.

Thy ever

Devoted Husband

Houston

[In the margin:] Sugar Cane will cure your cough.—I believe.

[On the outside:] All the Ladies reproach me for [not] bringing you, and the balance down.

Thine

Houston

---

[1] James K. Davis and his daughter Caroline.
[2] Mrs. E. B. (Margaret Stone) Nichols.
[3] Howell H. Holliman. Identified in *1850 Census,* vol. 3, 1286.

∞

Galveston

25th Nov 1846

My Dearest Love,

Seated at a Table quietly, in the private parlour of our friend Mrs Betty Culp, and our Niece Mrs Tose[1] Power, at the Tremont,[2] I am determined to write to you on my departure tomorrow morning. The [sic] Sarah Ann is making "<u>chimis</u> [sic]" for our dear little Babe, Nanny. Having no <u>small</u> sewing, to do for herself, she has leisure to help her friends. Mrs Betty is pretty well, and making a dress for her Ladyship. They are both boarding here, and happy. I have not seen any persons more happy in my life than Tom, and Tose. It has added not a little to my gratification, and what to me is equally pleasing, I doubt not but what their happiness will continue. I hear from Antoinette, & Mr Charles [Power], and they are entirely happy, and love vastly, each other. Our dear little Nephew, Martin Royston[3] is here, and in fine health—and nearly grown. I forgot to say that I like our Nephew Tom, extravagantly. He is a <u>prime gentleman</u>!!!

My Love, I sent you some trifles, from Houston, and from here, I will only send you some Baby socks. They are pretty, and not by any means expensive. I will go on in the way of business. I told Mr

[James] Huckins to draw on me, at Washington for your subscription, to the Baptist Church at this place. You can draw on Major [James] Cocke at any time for Elizas[4] hire. I will not use any of it. You can if you need more money, draw upon Mr Torey (D. K.) for any amount, as I left Shacklefords[5] note with him for collection. The amount which I drew from Major Cocke, on Vernals note, was $50.00. I will make [no] disposition of Eliza, but leave her with Major Cocke subject to your commands. She told me that she would like to go home, or she would rather live with Mr Stuart[6] than Mrs [Anne] Maffett. I hope to see Mr S. in the morning, and I will let him have her, if he wishes her!

Since I came here, I have seen most of your Lady friends—all your particulars. I spoke to Mrs [John S.] Sydnor[7] about the Books, and she said it was all right. The dinner went off well. I made a decent speech, so some say! Ladies attended! and a large crowd. To day an opposition dinner was got up by some body, or some body else. I was not invited, but was invited to a party to night but declined, and I am sure you can guess the reason! It would have deprived me of the pleasure of writing to you my Love!

You can have no idea of my mortification, in not being able to get off, on my journey. At the same time detained so near you, and not able to return, and pass every hour with you which I had to pass, in Houston, and this place. I will not my Love, attempt to express my conflicts of feeling, with a sense of duty, to my pledges. By way of vanity my Love, I will send you a political letter, with one, which has, and ever, will be regarded as far more dear to me, and my affections.[8]

You will recognize, and [sic] old acquaintance. I let Sarah Ann, Madam Betty, and Mr Tom Power read it—Mrs Hotchkiss[9] was greatly distressed, for by accident, she threw your other letter into the fire, with some of her own, as it was written on white paper and this one being double, she thought when she threw it in the fire that it was one of hers, as they were all on white paper. So you have the case. I forgave her, and as the letter was mine it is ended, much as [I] regret the misfortune. You can my Love, so soon as you get this, write me two letters, and that will make up for the loss.

I will not detail to you the enquiries which are made about you, and Sam, and our relations all. I promise them if we live to visit here in April next. I say this as neither our Sister, nor our niece will keep house here, before then, if they should at all. In a few days, Mr Tom, & Sally, will set out for Matagorda, but say they with A. & Mr Charles,[10] will be to see you all this winter and about Christmas if possible. Business tho' may prevent them. Sally says she is crazy to see our dear sweet Babe. To tease you, I have forborne to speak of her. I will now tell you, that every body asks for you, babe & Sam. I tell all who ask me, that "I have never seen a more beautiful babe." Now is this letter complete? Well my dearest, I have seen Mrs Allens[11] babe, and it has not been well. I will only say that, her little Maggy is not so pretty as ours. Mrs A has not been well, but is now better.

My Love, if I could only see you again, and press you to my heart, with Sam, and our dear babe, I would be the proudest of mortals. Aye, & the happiest too. My Love, it is late, and if I do not get off in the morning, I will write again. I could write all night, if it could afford you pleasure, to read more. Dont think I will assent to any think [sic], that will keep me from you, and our dear, dear pledges. Tom, Tose, and all friends send love to you and all the family.

Thine ever

[in margins:] You will my Love, present my affections to Mother, Sister & Bud[12] the first opportunity, that offers. Some things will be sent up for you—Eatables etc.

My Love, hug and kiss our little one a thousand time[s]. Dont whip Sam. He will do better without it, I think.

My Love, I was beau to Miss Caroline [Davis] in going to and returning from the speech making. You will please to kiss Sister, for me. & Mother.

Thy ever devoted Husband
Houston

[1]Tose was a family nickname for Sarah Ann Royston Power.
[2]The Galveston hotel where Houston frequently stayed. For a description see William Bollaert,

William Bollaert's Texas, ed. W. Eugene Hollon and Ruth Lapham Butler (Norman: University of Oklahoma Press, 1989), 19–20.

[3]Martin Royston was the son of Varilla Lea Royston and the brother of Sarah Ann Royston Power.

[4]Margaret's slave.

[5]Jack Shackleford. *New Handbook of Texas,* vol. 5, 983–84.

[6]Hamilton Stuart. For a biography see *Writings,* vol. 4, 420–22n.

[7]Sarah White Sydnor. Identified in *New Handbook of Texas,* vol. 6, 184.

[8]These letters have not been located.

[9]Mrs. R. Hotchkiss, the wife of a San Jacinto veteran. Identified in De Witt Clinton Baker, *Texas Scrapbook* (New York: A. S. Barnes, 1875; Austin: Texas State Historical Association, 1991), 600.

[10]Antoinette and Charles Power.

[11]Mrs. John M. Allen.

[12]Catherine and Vernal Lea.

The following letter, in the holdings of the Texas State Archives, was written by Margaret from her mother's home.

Grand cane Nov. 27, 1846

My own dear husband,

Yours by Mr. Holliman[1] was handed to me on monday morning, with the accompanying articles. I felt some concern at your disappointment at getting to Galveston in due time, but also my grief at parting with you, was so great, that I had scarcely a feeling left for minor troubles. Old Mr. Holliman left here for Galveston a few days after yourself, and at the time of his departure my breast was in such a situation, as to throw the whole family into consternation. I fear he may have given you some concern, and if so, I regret it sincerely as our fears proved groundless. I told him to tell you that if it proved serious, I would try Col. Williamson's[2] remedy, and in case of failure, would proceed directly to Memphis, and have an operation performed by Dr Thomas.[3] My reason for telling you any thing about it was that I apprehended there was no time to be lost in awaiting a letter from you on the subject, and I did not wish you to be surprised by hearing that I was in Memphis. Sister Katherine[4] had agreed to accompany me, and the children were both to be left with Mother, but the Lord has been exceedingly merciful unto me, and my breast is nearly well. I had it lanced on the day Mr. Holliman left here and it has been discharging ever since that time. The tumour is now much smaller, and I think it will soon disappear entirely. My cough has also ceased to trouble me, and I have great hopes, that the Lord will restore me to health. Our dear children enjoy fine health Sam is quite as loquacious as always, and "baby" grows more beautiful every day, but no one has succeeded yet, in drawing from her, those sweet notes with [which] she entertained "dear papa."

I wrote to Isabella [Moore] on last sabbath by Mr Ben Ellis, who expected to leave for Gen. [George T.] Wood's on the next day. He said it was possible, that he might call at "Raven hill," but if he could not do so, he would send my letter.[5] I urged Isabella to come down with her father and if she comes, we will all unite in trying to make her visit pleasant.

Oh my Love, when I think of the cloud under which you left me, it wrings my heart with suffering. Would that I could recall every word of mine that has ever given you the least anxiety! God is my witness that there is no sacrifice of mere pride, that I would make, to reinstate in your good opinion those whom you once loved, and make them worthy of that opinion.[6] Time is passing rapidly, and we shall all stand ere long, at the "judgment seat of Christ," and "receive every man according to his deeds." If I have not exercised enough of that spirit, which turns the left cheek, when the right is smitten, I hope the Lord will forgive me, and help me here-after to make his blessed precepts my constant rule of action.

Bro. V. and sister Kate are making a farewell visit to the Gen.'s family,[7] as they are about to leave for thier new home.[8] If they were here, I know they would send a great deal of love to you. I mentioned to you dearest, that I like to divide your note against Mother and bro. V. for the money loaned to them, but I have determined to say nothing about it.

We hope soon to have Antoinette and Sarah Ann with us, and I think it is very probable, that Mother and I will return with them.

Sister Katherine also speaks of visiting Galveston during this winter.

Mother and Sam send thier love to you. Do write often and very long letters. I will write whenever I can.

Thine devotedly

M. L. Houston

[1]See Houston to Margaret, November 21, 1846.
[2]Houston's friend, Robert M. Williamson. For a biography see *New Handbook of Texas*, vol. 6, 992.
[3]Margaret is probably referring to Dr. Isaac J. Thomas. Identified in Silas Emment Lucas Jr., ed., *Obituaries from Early Tennessee Newspapers 1794–1851* (Easley, SC: Southern Historical Press, 1978), 471.
[4]Katherine Davis Goodall Lea. She was the daughter of Gen. James Davis.
[5]It appears that the Moore family was now living at Raven Hill.
[6]Margaret is referring to an estrangement which was growing between the Moores and the Houstons.
[7]The family of James Davis.
[8]Vernal and Katherine Lea had purchased property northwest of Huntsville near the town of Coldspring.

∞

New Orleans

30th Nov 1846

My beloved Margaret,

It is past two oclock, really A.M., 1st Dec that I sit down to write you a letter from this place, tho it is dated on yesterday. Since I wrote to you from Galveston, I have had but little pleasure. Our trip was no less than seventy hours. Our delay was owing, [to] the failure of a wheel. Had it not been for that our trip would have been more pleasant. The Boat arrived here yesterday at 10 oclk [sic] A.M., and we were to have taken our departure for the City at 6 P.M., but the Boat did not get off. I had the pleasure to meet Genl [Thomas] Rusk, and Col Kaufman,[1] who have waited four days for me. We will take the Ohio route to the City.[2] The travelling by the Southern route would be the most speedy, but much the most fatiguing. We will be detained, or rather delayed longer, by ascending the river, than by

Charleston, if the Stages are arranged on that route. They may not be, as the changes, may be making touching the stages which are said to take place in the fall Season. We expect to reach Washington about the 14th Inst.

Since I came to the city I have been engaged, either in business, or in company, until now. There seems to be much curiosity, and more kind feeling, towards me than heretofore. All persons seem to regard me, either with friendship, or respect, and I demean myself with great propriety, and sedateness. On your account I dressed in the "black suit," as I did at Houston & Galveston. I wear too, a handsome new hat, which was presented to me!

All persons of my acquaintance assure me, that I have not looked so well in ten years, and our dear friend Mrs [Katherine] Christy says, that you are the cause of it, and I ought to thank you for it. I dined to day, or rather yesterday, at our friend [William] Christys, and the Madam had many questions to ask about you, Sam, and our little cherub. Madam, as every one else, told me, that she heard that you had the prettiest daughter in any country. To which I <u>modestly</u>, replied, "we think her very pretty indeed!" I have not told you my dear, that William Christy, is lying in the last state of consumption, and seems, as tho' he can only live a few days.[3] Poor fellow he appears, meek, and subdued, and his Mother never leaves him, but seems cheerful. My Love, she is a dear Lady! What a treasure she is to her husband and to society.

Little as I have slept for many days, and nights, my Love, I cannot cease writing, without telling you the oft told tale of <u>how much I do love you</u>, and how often you are present to my affections, as well, as our dear little ones. You are all present to my mind, whether I am alone, or in the cowds [sic] or company. Yes truly, my Love, you form the circle of my joys. My whole heart is filled, with love of you, and the pledges of our love. I fancy myself talking, with the dear babe, and seeing her little eyes, sparkle, while responding to my questions. Yes, and I see, and hear, Sam, engaged in baby talk, with his little sister, to command her attention to "brother Sam." And full, to my hearts vision, is exhibited the fond, and doating [sic] mother, in the person of my devoted, and lovely Margaret—my own, and only one, on earth. I look past all the anticipated troubles of the coming session of Congress, to the time, when I shall again clasp you to my heart, and have the little dear ones, on my knee. Regarding as I do my family, can you, for a moment, believe, that I can be happy while absent from you? No my Love, I am sure you will not.—If I wished to forget you, I can assure, the thousand kind enquiries which are made about you, would not let me forget you, for an hour, unless, it is, when I am sleeping!

My Love, I will write to you as often, as I may have it in my power to do so. I hope to see brother William,[4] and his little family, as I pass up the river,[5] when I hope to brag of our Girl. I must not fail my dear to tell you, that I had two Ladies placed under my care at Galveston for this place. They were the Mrs, & Miss Gantier of Brazoria County, the wife[6] & daughter[7] of Doct Gantier,[8] a planter of Brasos. They were elegantly sick on the voyage, and kept their state Room. This you know my Love, I could not help. The Doctor was a good Houston man, and I could not refuse the honor. They are very intelligent & highly respectable. They are pious and I think Baptists. I behaved, so far as was in my power most <u>elegantly</u>.

Now my Love, present my affection to our dear Mother, Sister, & Vernal. Embrace and kiss our dear children.

Thy ever devoted Houston

[1]Texas Representative David Kaufman. *New Handbook of Texas,* vol. 3, 1039.
[2]Washington, D. C.
[3]Christy recovered and lived until 1865. *New Handbook of Texas*, vol. 3, 1039.
[4]Houston's younger brother lived in Memphis.
[5]The Mississippi River.
[6]Lucy Gantier. *1850 Census*, vol. 1, 216.
[7]The Gantier daughters were Harriet, Ariadne, and Lucy. Ibid. It is unclear to which daughter Houston refers.
[8]Dr. Peter W. Gantier. Ibid.

167 : November 21, 1846 - April 4, 1847

The following letter is from the Margaret John Houston collection of Houston materials in the Center for American History, The University of Texas at Austin.

Grand Cane December 5th, 1846

My Dear Love,

Your most welcome package from Galveston[1] came to hand yesterday, and I have been much happier, I assure you, since the reception of your letters than at any time since your departure. The fact is, I did not like your letter from Houston. I could perceive that it was a very hurried thing, yet there was about it a tone about it of despondency "je ne sais quoi" which pained me exceedingly. After reading it again and again, I still folded it with an uneasy sensation about the heart. I have since come to the conclusion, that it may possibly have originated from the omission of that very important expression "I love you," but of this I am not quite sure. I do not jest dearest. Oh no, I never was more serious. I have spent much of my time lately in the study of my own heart, in the careful examination of its different emotions, tracing each to the source, and endeavoring to cherish the good and reject the bad. But I am often enveloped by clouds of gloom, which I can not understand, and this is one of the occasions. Of one thing rest assured. I am much comforted since the reception of your affectionate letters from Galveston. I reviewed my old letter to you with a melancholy pleasure. Ah, how different are my feelings now, from those of girlish romance that dictated that letter. I loved you then with all the enthusiasm of my nature, but my heart was free from care. I had never felt a mother's anxiety. I had never borne upon my heart the weight of immortal souls. But the lord has given them to me, that I may train them for a higher and never-ending existence, and I shrink not from the task. Oh that he may bring them early into the fold! Our sweet babe with her violet eyes raised to Heaven, hath drawn my heart thence more than ever. Ah what peace hath a mother's heart for the love of the world! Dearest our baby knows me! Yes, I have received from her, that first look of recognition, which stamps itself upon the mother's heart, never never to be erased. Mother says I must tell you, that when you left us, she was just half as beautiful as she is now. I think myself that she improves every day. She preserved melancholy silence for several days after your departure, but she has now a pretty smile and soft tone for every one that speaks to her. Sam also grows more interesting each day. I am delighted with his developments of character. He is truthful, generous, affectionate, and magnanimous. With all he is circumspect and considerate, more so than any one of his years that I have ever seen. But facts will best speak for themselves. You know that he was perfectly familiar at home with the name of "Virginia" [Thorn], and the unpleasant association connected with it that he identifies her. I can not doubt, for he never speaks to her, but I perceive him occasionally at a distance casting a cautious glance toward her. He has perceived, that from some cause unknown to him, I never allude to the "poisoning," and strange to say, though he often spoke of it at home, he preserves a cautious silence respecting it here. She has been confined ever since you left, with a rising on the knee, and just now is recovering from it. This morning as I was sitting at the breakfast table, Sam was standing at my side, and saw her come out and seat herself in the entry. "Oh ma," he exclaimed "Jinny is getting well." "Yes my son" I answered, "and I am happy to see it, are you not happy?" "Yes ma," he said, "I am so glad," and drawing a little nearer to Virginia, he tenderly inquired, "Jinny are you getting well?" She answered "Yes," and his eyes sparkled with real joy. It was the first time I have heard him call her name, since we came here. Sam and Sister Katherine's little Ann Eliza[2] are almost inseparable. He never quarrels with her at all except when she steps on his toes and it is a little inconvenient, as she wears shoes, and he rarely does, and I can not make him understand yet the nature of an accident. This morning I read to him, from Gen. a portion of the history of Cain and Abel. When I came to the question "Where is thy brother Abel?" Sam exclaimed, "Ma when I go up to Heaven, I will tell God that Cain had killed him!" Here was a fine opportunity for some remarks on the omniscience of God, and I endeavored to impart it.

I have understood that Mr [Joseph] Ellis spent a night at Raven hill during his visit to Gen. Woods, and found the [Moore] family well, but I did not see him after his return as I only spent a few days at home, and then set off for this red lands. Mother, sister Kate and bro V. send a great deal of love to you.

[On margin:] I send you the promised lock of hair. I presume you will need no necromantic skill to tell you from what head the little lock of silk was taken. Sam said as I was cutting his "Oh, ma, pa will be so glad, don't you hope so?"

ever thy devoted wife,

M. L. Houston

P.S. Dearest, I will try to make up to you the loss of the old love letter, and you must write whenever you can. Oh, how inexpressibly dear you are to my heart! I am sad and cannot be happy without you. Please present my compliments to Mrs. Graham,[3] and tell her I design writing to her very soon. My breast is not yet healed, but still discharges like a boil, and I think the tumor will disappear in that way.

Sam's shoes are just the right size, but he does not seem fond of wearing them. Rebecca Maxey, the daughter of our old friend[4] is dead. She died at Independence on last Sunday week. Mr. Knight of this neighborhood, is also dead. Sam says to come home, and "baby" crows very meaningly when asked what message for dear pa. You will perceive that this letter was written with the impression of your having received a previous one.

[1]See Houston to Margaret, November 25, 1847.
[2]Ann Eliza Goodall.
[3]Mrs. George (Jane Watson) Graham. Identified in *New Handbook of Texas*, vol. 3, 272.
[4]William Maxey. Identified in C. L. Greenwood, *Index of Deaths,* Center for American History, University of Texas, Austin, Texas.

∞

18th Dec 1846

My very dear Love,

I must tell you how happy your letter has made me. I had on last night received a letter from Mr Tom Power telling me, that Mr Holliman had reported "all well at Grand Cane, but Mrs Houstons [sic] breast." Whether it was only the asthma, or the tumor, I could not tell. Fearful it was the latter, tho' I had not anticipated anything when I left home of the kind, I could not sleep until 3 oclk this morning, altho' I had been worn out, for the want of sleep on my journey. When I arose this morning my mail came to me, and I discovered, and tore open, your letter with intense solicitude to see, and read its contents.

I felt pained that you my ever dear Love had suffered, and I was not by you to soothe & support you! I could well fancy the pain, which you experienced, of body and mind. You would have done right to have sought a remedy, and that promptly. I thank the Divine Father of Mercies, that you had so far recover'd, as to be satisfied that you are out of danger. But my Love, you may imagine how miserable I will be, until I can hear from you. My heart is drawn more nearly, and dearly towards you, and our children, if possible, than it was ever done before. I am sorry, that you have any uneasiness, about the matters which we had discussed about my kinfolk. You did right. It was fit that I should know all matters of the sort. They were unpleasant it is true, but the fault was neither yours, nor mine. Others did wrong. We did right. Our motives were kind, and good! I approve all that you did, and could not do otherwise, and be myself.

I will be glad, if you have room, that Isabella [Moore], should come down, and spend some time with you.

I have heard a most melancholy account of my dear Sister Polly.[1] I do not suppose, that she is now alive. Genl [William] Wallace wrote to me that she was in the asylum at Lexington Ky, and he was there to attend to her wants. She has refused to eat or drink any thing, but what is forced down her throat. She is melancholy and distressed. Indeed she remains in a state of stupor. She is emaciated and a skeleton! Her mind seems to decline with her body. Her memory affords but a glimmering reflection upon persons, or things. How fearful is the visitation. We must all feel solemn, and accountable to our God, and Father, and we must pray for His grace, and mercies. I will send

Genl Wallace's letter to Mr Moore, and I hope it will have a salutary influence upon the mind of Sister Eliza. I hope she will soon learn, that Religion is of God, and abides in the heart, but not in forms, or sects. I forgive them all, but I will not write to Sister, because if she is not changed, she could not appreciate the act![2]

My Love you must excuse me, for the clock has now [struck] two of another day. I only slept about three hours in 24, on average, on my route here. I was one month from home. I was on the car from the west, when by carelessness, it met the one from the east, and broke both engines, but injured no one.

My Love, do present me most affectionately to our dear Mother, Sister, & Vernal. To our dear, dear, little ones, bestow a Fathers love, and kindness. Tell Sam of the breeches, which I am to take him, and sisse, something pretty. Every one here asks for you, and the dear daughter. I declare to all that she is "beautiful," as Sam says.

I can only add my Love, that you are more near, & dear to me, every hour. Write to me, as often as you can, without trouble to yourself, or injury to your health. I have been kindly met here by all persons.

Thy faithful and devoted husband,
Houston

[In margin:] I send a scrap for Mother.

[1]Mary Houston Wallace.
[2]Family tradition holds that Eliza Moore was opposed to Mary's marriage to General Wallace.

Washington
25th Dec 1846

My Dearest Love,

This is Christmas day, and I forego every thing else with pleasure, that I may write to you, and recur to the dear little circle in which I left you, with so many, & such painful regrets. After I arrived at Houston, I reflected seriously, on what course I should pursue, whether to resign, and return home, or come on, and pass the winter here, overwhelmed in business, and harrassed [sic] by anxiety. Eight nights have I passed in the City, and I solemnly declare to you that I have never laid my head on my pillow, until after two oclock, but last night, I lay down after twelve. Five out of the eight I did not retire until after three o clock A.M. With all this fatigue and want of rest, my business only seems to accumulate. Mr [Washington D.] Miller assists me much. The reason why I am so much oppressed, is because it is supposed, that I have influence with the Executive,[1] and tho' I disclaim the supposition, it has no bearing on my fate. I have now fell on a plan by which I hope to send you a few lines every day, or every other day. I hope to have something agreeable to write you as the season advances. Until the Holy days are over, very little will be done in Congressional matters. In a few days, I expect to set out for New York, & spend a few days! I will not be absent from business. I rejoice that nearly one third of my time has passed, which I expect to be absent from all that I love on earth. I see and every day behold persons here, who have their wives, and many their little ones about them, and they seem, and no doubt are happy. If I could only be with my own little family, I would be more happy, than they ever seem to be. I would learn our dear little babe to talk, and tell me of the bad treatment of her dear ma.

I was sorry to hear from you that she would not talk to any one since I left home. It was my voice which caused her to talk. Yours is more fine, and did not effect her nerves. Try a different tone! Don't think that I have forgot our boy! Ah no, I cant forget Sam. I hope he is a good boy to his Ma, & Sister, & his Grand ma, His Uncle, Aunt, & Missie.[2] In my life, I have not felt so lonesome and lost. No, not even in my exile, as I do now. Every demonstration of respect, and regard which is tendered to me, only presents in more vivid characters, the vanity of all earthly pageants. The only earthly pleasure which I can enjoy, is blended with my family, and home affections. I am beset by many of my friends, to go into the army, but as you may suppose I most <u>obstinately</u> refuse to do so. It is in contemplation to appoint a Lieut Genl, for the army, and even this will not tempt me to forego my love, of you, and your society, with the smiles of our children.—to this I add also, the association of friends & kindred.

I can tell you little of the gay, & fashionable world. I have seen your friend Rev'd Mr [George W.] Sampson & will try and hear him preach as often as possible. I have seen a Revd Mr Tinsley, a Baptist Divine who says he will go to Texas with me in the spring. He was once a chaplain of Congress I learn. He is a man of some wealth.

I have seen your friend Mrs Gaines,[3] and she gave me an awful raking down, as she had heard that I had been opposed to the General last session, but when she knew the facts, she became penitent, and sent vast love to you. In her accusation she said, "Genl Houston, your angel wife was not with you, or you would never have done wrong." So you may infer that she controls the General, & that was no doubt the course of his getting him, into a bad <u>snap</u>! She became perfectly satisfied, and I think some what sorry! You would be amused to see how she does move about, and score some of our big <u>buggs</u> [sic]. It amuses one greatly. I wrote to Doctor & Mrs [Alva] Woods,[4] and for you, & Sam & Nanny, as well as myself sent the compliments of the season. I hope you will write my Love, to her Ladyship & to Mrs Jane L. Graham. It will gratify them, if you can do so, with ease to yourself. I have seen my God Daughter[5] and the family. They are all well, and have a thousand kind enquiries to make for you, and the little ones. They really seem as much interested in you, as tho' you were a near relative, and I doubt not if you were here, you would receive from them, every evidence of affection, which they cou'd bestow.

My Love, I do really think if you were here, that there would be as much regard evinced for you, as any other lady in the city. Not because you are Sam Houstons wife only, but because, you are esteemed his good Angel. You have all the credit, of my good conduct, and great propriety of action.

The impress, which your association makes upon me, at home, is supposed to bear me company abroad. Is it not a pity, that I can not share a portion of the credit of my reformation? My only merit is supposed to consist in obedience, and love of you. This character I have incured [sic], by once (as they hear) having been wild, and careless of the worlds opinions. I have not the least disposition, ever to leave my room, only on business. This is now midnight, and I have not witnessed a gay scene to day. I have heard of Balls, & amusements, but have seen none, and wished for none. My thoughts, and affections have been with you, and our young Barbarians, on the Trinity. You are far more dear to me, than all the gay scenes of a thousand cities, of a thousand kingdoms.

I did not go to church to day, as I wear pumps, not having had it in my power to get Boots, or thick soled shoes, since I came to the city. As yet, I have got no new garments, but hope soon to do so. It is owning to my negligence, more than economy, I fear. However, I will try, and be very saving, but my dear, I must send or take you home a dress, this time, if I live. I have seen a piece of pretty silk, and it seems to me, that it will suit you well, and I have some taste, as I fancy. You will not let me take you a velvet, and I have a right to take you silk.

Tonight I learn, that Genl. Bailey,[6] and Mr Davis[7] of the House of Representatives, are to meet tomorrow morning, near Baltimore to fight a duel. The difficulty arose in debate, but there was an old grudge, as they say here. I hope there will be no damage done, tho' a strong probability is that it will end seriously. They are married gentlemen, and Mrs Baily[8] is here, tho I do not know that Mrs Davis[9] is. Had I known of the affair in time I would have endeavored to have reconciled the differences. Such things are to be deplored.[10] You will be desirous to know of what character the Session will be. I suppose it will be quite angry, as from some indications, the debates will be heated. For my own part I intend to be quiet, and at this time, I have no intention to make even one speech. Should I make any, the necessity must be urgent. Poor little Texas is to be a bone of contention still. Rusk has a disposition, not to hear much, and if he comes out it will be well done. He is a man of good feelings, but on the subject of Texas, he feels quite sensative [sic], and if he is brought out he will be bitter, and forcible.

I have written until near one oclock, and must close. Before I retire to rest, I will read the XXVII chapter of Matthews Gospel. Since I left home I have advanced that far in the New Testament. I will as I do each night, invoke of our Heavenly Father, a blessing upon us, and our dear children, and such as it is our duty to pray for.

Give my love to Mother, Sister, & bro Vernal. Embrace our dear, dear little ones, with a Fathers love and with them, kiss little Missie.

Thy ever devoted Husband
Houston

P. S. My God Daughter had the shoes, or slippers made, and they are on my mantle.
All the Houstons, and all my friends send their regards to you. Since I came here, my mail brought me the letters which I wrote last session to bro [Robertus] Royston and Cousin Columbus [Lea]. So I must write again soon.

Houston

---

[1]President James K. Polk.

[2]A nickname for Ann Eliza Goodall.

[3]Myra Whitney (Mrs. Edmund P.) Gaines. Identified in *Dictionary of American Biography*, vol. 4, Part I, 92–93.

[4]See Houston to Almira Woods, December 25, 1846, the Alva Woods Papers, The Rhode Island Historical Society Library, Providence, R.I.

[5]Mary Houston.

[6]Thomas H. Bayly of Virginia. *Biographical Directory,* 592.

[7]Garret Davis, representative from Kentucky. For an account of the feud see Polk, *Polk*, 179–80. They were accompanied by Louisiana Senator Andrew Barrow who died during the proceedings. Of Barrow's death Polk said, "I am a firm believer that it was a judgment of heaven upon the immoral, unchristian and savage practice of dueling."

[8]Evelyn May Bayly. Identified in *Dictionary of American Biography*, II, Part I, 79.

[9]The former Mrs. Thomas Elliot. Identified in *Dictionary of American Biography*, III, Part I, 113–14.

[10]Houston had fought in an earlier duel with William A. White and had suffered a feeling of regret for many years. For more information see Marquis James, *The Raven: A Biography of Sam Houston* (Indianapolis: Bobbs-Merrill Company, 1929), 65. Margaret's older brother Martin had been killed in a duel.

The following note to Doct A. Woods is from the Alva Woods Papers.

Washington
25th Dec 1846

[no salutation]
Genl Houston has the pleasure of presenting to Mrs, Doct Woods, & Son, the compliments of the season for Mrs Houston, as well as his own.

Mrs H. and her daughter (which Mrs H thinks very pretty) send their <u>best love</u> and Master Sam, his homage, to Mrs woods, and tenders a thousand thanks for the many interesting mementos[1] sent by Doct & Mrs woods. With salutations of sincere esteem, & regards.

I am most
Truly & sincerely
Your frd & obt Servt
Sam Houston

[1]It is unclear to which objects Houston is referring.

∽

Baltimore
26th Dec 1846

My Dearest Love,
    I am this far on my way to New York. It is the visit of our delegation, as we are all, this far on our way, but Col Kaufman, and he is to join us in the morning. We arrived here at 8 oclock P.M. & all went to the Theatre but Judge Pilsbury,[1] & myself. You know my Love, that I do not go to Theatres, nor Balls, unless you would say that I could not do otherwise. Circumstances might render it proper for me to attend a Ball, so far as to be present, but not to partake, in the amusements. We have all been invited to attend, a Ball on the 8th of Jany at

Tamany hall in New York, but we do not intend, to remain there until that time. Our intention is to return by the 2nd Proximo, if we can as we are anxious to be present in Congress, that we may get all our business done, that is possible for our dear little Texas. We will have to use every exertion, in her behalf, for I assure you my dear, that we may look out for all that I apprehended, of danger to her interests. All that we can do, by union, in her behalf, will be done!

I feel well assured my Love, that you will blame me for what I am about to tell you of. It is now half past two oclock P.M., and I am writing to you, rather than to retire to rest. Judge Pilsbury has just retired, and so soon as I found myself alone, I began to commune, with you, distant as we are from each other in presence. You are always present to my heart, and with you, are our dear little ones. You can have no idea of my devotion. I have no doubt but what you will accord to me a reasonable share of affection and regard, but I am sure, you cannot suppose, that one, who has so many cares of business, can so often withdraw his thoughts from them, and dwell, with almost constant meditation upon those who are not present to the senses, as I do, upon you, and our children. When I contrast the sweets of home, with my toils, and vigils, here, I resolve never again to be absent from you again. If I did not cherish the most perfect, and enduring affection for you, and our dears ones, I might again have my thoughts recalled to the "Camp and battlefield," but as it is I am deaf to importunity of friends who daily urge me to go, that they may become heros [sic]. Never have I seen a fairer opening for fame, than the present moment presents.—Notwithstanding all this, I assure you my Dearest, I do not harbour one latent wish, or desire to engage in any thing, which could seperate [sic] me from you. At the same time, it is true that I have seen no time in the History of our country, when efficient leaders, were more needed, than at present. Matters in the army are a sad plight, I fear. I hope they will soon be mended. We have all the means necessary to success, if they are only well directed.

I am amused sometimes at my reflections. When I think of our dear Mother, and the composition of her mind, and disposition, I feel assured, if all matters were laid before her, she would say, "Genl you ought to go to the army, and Margaret, don't you say a word against it. How will Sam or his little Sister look, at some future day, to be told that their father could have taken Mexico, and his country wished him to do it, but their Mother would not let him enter the army." Now don't I pray you construe this as any oppression of desire, for my Love, I do declare to you it is not, but I know Mothers disposition so well, and besides, heroism is a part of faith you know. The old Lady wou'd think, that "Conqueror of Mexico" would tell finely in our childrens ears, or look well in the Historic page. You may read this to Mother, and see if I am not right in my suggestions. I will not envy those who may "revel in the Halls of the Montezumas," and I am frank to confess, if I were not blessed with a family, as I am, I think it more than probable, that I would try, and realise, a part, of the reputed prediction. Without the endearments of home, a dear Wife, and little ones, I would, only be fitted for the music of the Camp, or the exercise of the battlefield.

But as it is, home supplies me superior pleasures, to those of the martial toils, and my joys, of Wife, & children, are incomparably greater, than, all which, have arisen, or could ever, arise from victorious achievements, of arms.

Good morning my Love, as it is half past 3 A.M.

Give my love to our dear Mother & all the family. Kiss our dear little lambs, and press them to your bosom for me.

Thy ever devoted & faithful husband
Sam Houston

[1]Thomas Pilsbury a member of the House of Representatives from Brazoria, Texas. For a biography see *Writings*, vol. 3, 59–60n.

∞

Washington City
5th Jany 1847

My Beloved,

After presenting you, and our dear little ones, with my warm embraces, I will add the salutation of the Season—wishing that you may enjoy, many happy returns of the New Year.

I thank you for the dear locks of hair sent to me. I kiss them, and must kiss them, until I return to the dear objects, on whose heads they grew. My Love, I went to New York, and spent nearly a week. Never have I seen persons more kindly treated than was the Texas Delegation. I did just as you wou'd have wished, me do. I would not go to a theatre, except a "horse theatre." At that place, I only sat a few minutes—received "nine cheers" by the audience, & left for my quarters. You will see by the news papers, all the news relating to our visit. All seemed pleased, and gratified, that we turned out, not to be savages. You may rely upon it, that Genl Greens, & Miss Corinne Montgomerys Books,[1] are not in demand, nor one word believed, which they had published to my prejudices. I tried to see your friend Mrs [Eliza] Allen, but could not get time to do so. I met her husband at the "parent temperance society" on the night of New Years eve, where I was taken by a committee—introduced, and made a speech, which was received with great, very great enthusiasm. The next day Mr A came to take me to his house. As I did not go, I sent your love, and my best respects to the lady—said much of your appreciation of her worth, and your intention to contribute some pieces to her periodical.[2] A thousand thanks were returned to you, and blessings to the children.

My love, I could well make a temperance speech, because during the tremendous festivities of the season, I did not take even a glass of Egg nogg, or any thing else stronger than pure water!!! My Love, I rejoice that, one third of my term of service is out, and I pray that by the last of March, if not before, I will press you, and our dear pledges to my heart. I would inexpressibly, rather have spent my Christmas, & New Year with you, and others, than in the hurly burly, of New York. I have not seen our kindred here since the season of gayity [sic] commenced, as I was absent from all the scenes here. On the first as usual, I learn there was a great show at the President's.[3] Messrs Miller & [Joseph] Eldridge tell me all the news. They behave very well, and attend to their business. They are much respected.

They send regards to all. My Dearest, I rejoice that our little Dove, has renewed her cooing, and talking to her dear mother. You speak my _dear_, of the babe's look, of <u>recognition</u>. For this I pant, as the hunted hare does, for the cooling brook.

I have laughed, again and again, about Sam's impulsive indignation. In my opinion Sam's object was to rid society, of a dangerous subject, lest he might some day come within his power, and he be the sufferer. He is the most cautious, and wary, of all human beings. If he lives, he will be an extraordinary personage. His conduct too, with Virginia, demonstrates, a wonderful degree of wisdom, & prudence! I admire his circumspection, and magnanimity. I am happy to see that, he has had no whipping. He is not of the cast to bear chastisement by the rod.

I rejoice, much more than I can express, that your <u>dear breast</u> improves. You may laugh at this expression, but when you reflect upon its relation to the heart, you will approve the association, in which I bring it, with my affections. I have heard from my poor dear Sister, and there is no hope that she will survive, even a few days. Her afflictions are the most distressing, & melancholy that can exist. She is not in the asylum now, but in the vicinity of Lexington. Her disease arises from, an enlargement, and pressure of the bone, upon the brain. There is no possibility of her recovery. No circumstances so fearfully distressing, has ever befallen me, as to think that a sister is to leave this world, with a mind shattered, and not capable of reflection, nor placing any estimate, upon the awful transaction from time, to Eternity. I pray God, that she may not be lost but redeemed, thro' the mediation, and free Grace of our Savior, Jesus Christ.

My love, I will tell you (not claiming any merit) that I never retire to my repose, without reading a chapter in the New Testament, and kneeling in prayer to our Creator God, and invoking his blessing upon my wife, and our dear Lambs. Nor do I fail to own myself a sinner, & beseech my God, to change my heart, and renew my nature. His kindnesses are infinite, and I try to render to our dear Saviour, some return for his merciful protection, and favour. I will not cease to seek an interest in the atoning blood of our Redeemer. My

Beloved you will please present to Mother, Sister Kate, & Bud, my regards, and hug nearly, and dearly, our little ones. Kiss Missy and salute our friends. I send you some scraps, but not one half which I have seen, in relation to myself.

You need not be alarmed my Love about any impression, which may be made upon me, by such things, for I assure you, that my affection for you has not been clouded for one moment, nor would I exchange even a woodland <u>with you</u>, surrounded by our babes, and friends for any earthly situation. If I were silly enough to seek for farther distinction, I admit that appearances, of my success, are as fair, as those of any other names before the sovereigns. I seek no station higher, than the possession [of] your affections, for I esteem that the hight [sic] of mortal bliss.

I will try my Love, and write as often as I can, but really I have much business on hand, and on my table some thirty letters, not even read.

Thy ever devoted Husband
Sam Houston

[1]Corinne Montgomery was the pen name for Jane McManus Storms, who wrote *Texas and Her Presidents, with a Glance at Her Climate and Agricultural Capabilities*. Both this book and Thomas Jefferson Green's *Journal of the Texian Expedition Against Mier* were unflattering to Houston. *New Handbook of Texas*, v. 1, 1053.
[2]*The Mother's' Journal*.
[3]For a description of Polk's New Year's Day reception, see Bergeron, 226.

Washington City
10th Jany 1847

My dear Love,

This is sunday, and as it is snowing, I will not go to church, but pass a part of my time in writing to you, and thereby bring a ray of sun shine to my heart. While I commune with you, it brings you with all the dear little <u>attendants</u>, present to my imagination. I see our dear little babe with her sunday finery, upon your knee, smiling in your face, and our Boy toying with his little sister, and demanding of her if she "does not love her other Sam"? If I could fly to you, my Love, I would be with you! Last night, altho I sat up until 3 oclock, as usual, I did not fail ire morning, to dream, that I was with you, & happy. Yes, my Love, but few hours, if any, pass that you and our dear pledges are not present to my mind and my heart. I have an old, and valued friend here, Genl A Anderson[1] of Tennessee, with whom I often sit until 3 oclk in the morning, discoursing of our families. He is anxious for me to go to the army, and in that event he would march a Brigade from Tennessee. Altho the President, Genl. Rusk, and many friends are anxious that I should go, I nevertheless decline, all solicitations, solely because I love my Dear Wife, and little ones, more than I do fame, and all the honors of this world. To fame and to the world, I have generously dedicated a great portion, of my life, in the hope that I was promoting human happiness. If I have not succeeded, a farther pursuit of the object would be vanity, and if it calls me from my home, & my family, it would be vexation of spirit. The only hours of pleasure, which have cast sunshine upon my heart, in manhood, (where no cloud, could dim its brightness,) are those which I have passed with you, and I would not exchange, my hopes of future joys, and happiness anticipated, for the triumph, of a Hero, who had dictated peace, to a conquered nation, even in the "Halls of the Montezumas." Were it your request, I would freely, tho' not willingly, essay to do it! I will never attempt it, but from a conviction, that necessity enforces it upon me, as a sacred duty, to my Country, & my family. You will see that my inclination, receives no great violence, nor do I wish you my Love, to think that I am imposing any great obligation, upon you, for which I claim high merit. And to convince you of the fact whenever, you tell me that you, think it dear to your happiness, or to the advantage of our dear pledges, that I should dedicate a Laurel wreathe to your care for them, in future life to look upon, I will do so!!

You may write me, what you please on this subject. I do not require to touch upon the subject of war, but write about every thing else, and that if you please. I count each day, as it passes. Fifty two days only remain, until the session will be over. Yet every day seems a week, or a month to me. You I hope have enjoyed (if a quiet) a happy christmas, & New Year. By last mail, I sent you many scraps from News papers. In this letter I will send you one from an abolition print, by which, you will see that "wounded pigeons are known by their fluttering." I send you this, to manifest, that politics like "true love, never run smooth." Don't be provoked my Love, for really, I have had a pleasant laugh, at the temper of the fellow. He is angry, "jist" (as Sam would say) as certainly as he is a man.

Contrary to my wish, I was a manager of a Ball on the 8th of January and of a Committee to wait on the President to the Ball. I was a submember, and without my knowledge was selected to discharge the duties mentioned. Soon after the party met, the Jackson Hall, a most splendid building in which the Ball was, took fire and produced great alarm to the Ladies. I was free from them, as I had the President in my charge, and he took care of himself.[2] As usual, I did not dance, nor was I gallant as I would have been, had I been attending to Miss Lea, on such an occasion, I would rather reflect on any one scene, which transpired with Miss Lea, (unless our adieu,) than to pass, weeks in the most pleasant circles which, I have been placed, since I was with you. My rule is to decline Balls, & every scene of amusement which I can possibly. If I live, I will never attend, a Ball, nor be present at one, unless it is a national anniversary, at which duty would require my presence. And when ever you desire it, and so express yourself, I will desist, altogether, from all recreations, or supposed amusements, for then I will know, that I will be promoting your happiness.

Since I last wrote to you my Love, I have not heard from my dear afflicted Sister. I am prepared to hear of her death, under most distressing circumstances. God only has power, to cure, and save her. My prayers for her, I am sorry to say, are not "prayers of the righteous."

Life, is at best a fleeting show, and we can only render it profitable, and our latter end happy, by virtue, and active piety. I pray God to enable me to impress this conviction, upon the minds of dear off-spring! I feel more, and more, each day anxious, to imbue, their young minds, with lessons of such character. If spared I will draft a code, for our son, and hope he will read it at an age, when he will imbibe such feelings, and sentiments, as will guide him in after life. The palladium, of all virtue is the Scripture!! It is now evening, & the snow storm continues. From present appearances, the people will have sleighing enough for some time. I do not expect to join them, in any amusements after this. The fire was extinguished, and the fine Jackson Hall was saved. Many of the Guests returned, and danced, until a late hour. I daily resolve to make a total change in my disposition of time. Now if spared, I will not sit up, as I have done, but will go to bed, at an early hour, and not be at home, when people call to see me. To enable me to attend to my business, it will be necessary, that I shou'd do this. A press of company, has prevented me from writing to you, as often as I wished to do. I must be very <u>interesting</u>, for it seems that people never get tired writing to me, or speaking to, or staying with me. I like the compliment, but I do not like such a waste of time. I am not the property of the people, as they seem to think, but belong to Texas, and my wife, and <u>weans</u>! The joys of home, tho' rude that home, are worth more than all the varnished Halls of Power, and are far more dear to me. I hope it is within the providence of God, that we shall once more meet, and pass days, and weeks and months, and years, with those dear objects of our love, and give to their young minds impressions, which will never be irradicated [sic], but take root for Eternity, and grow for Heaven.

You my Love, regard rightly, the important charge which you have, in the care of immortal souls. We cannot be too careful, of our charge, and I feel assured, that I will never forget, my duty to them, and their dear mother. Could you only realise my anxiety to be with you, you wou'd I am sure desire me more happiness, than I can enjoy, while absent from you.

I think I can fancy how Sam looks, but I can not suppose, how the dear babe looks, owing to her rapid improvement, for the month preceding my departure. I do not hope that she has improved, for I could see no possible chance, to be more <u>beautiful</u> as Sam would say. I hope the dear little one has not taken a <u>relapse</u>. You know, at one time, tho I loved her, I did not think her pretty, but the reverse. You tho' were of a different opinion always. I have been interrupted since writing the above, until 9 oclock, and it is snowing very freely. I must close this letter, and only fear, that you will be weary, & end it unsatisfied.

You will my Love, please to present my love to dear Mother, Sister, & Vernal. Kiss, & Bless our dear children. Salute our friends, & tell Kitty [Hoffman], and Virginia [Thorn] to be good girls.

Write my Love, until 20th of February, if the Boats run from Galveston to Orleans, and you have a direct conveyance to Galveston.

Thy ever devoted Husband
Sam Houston

P.S. My Love,

I have said nothing about your <u>breast</u>. I could do no good by condolence, but if sympathy could relieve you, or restore you to perfect health, you command it. I hope, and will believe, that you are now well, and will remain so until I can, again take you to my heart, and feel that I again [am] happy.

Thy devoted
Houston

I hope in a few days to send some trifles by Mr Rose[3] for you and <u>others</u>!

P.S. Great anxiety is felt here about the fate of our army, in Mexico. Say my Love if disaster has befallen it will you consent for me, to take charge of a campaign? Write soon as I <u>will not</u> until I hear from you. All deem the present a most important crisis, in our national affairs, and national Honor!!!

Thy ever devoted
Sam Houston

[In the margin:] This was written at the request of a friend!

---

[1]Alexander Anderson of Knoxville, Tennessee. Identified in *Biographical Directory*, 533.
[2]For a description of this event, see Bergeron, 226–27.
[3]Robert Rose, a Galveston lawyer. Identified in *1850 Census*, vol. 2, 789.

Senate Chamber
11th Jany 1847

My Love,

I wrote to you last night and I hope my letter will soon reach you. The mail of yesterday brot us no army news, which was very desirable. But what was more desirable, to me, was a letter from you my Love, which did not come. I am consoled by the condition of the mails,—they are very uncertain. To day we have a white mantle cast over the bosom of Mother Earth, or in other words, we have a snow about eight inches deep. The tinkling of Bells, keep quite an excitement. They are placed on the sleigh horses so as to keep them clear of each other at night. Sleighs are substituted for Hacks, and tho' the sun shines most beautifully, it is cold!

I only write you this note to let you know that you are always present to me.

Give my love to all, and kiss our dear ones. Bless their violet eyes, I mean Nanny's. Sams are cold grey eyes according to Mrs [Jane McManus] Storms.

Thy ever truly and faithfully devoted
Houston

Washington City
12th Jany 1847

My Love,

We have met in Chambers this morning, to announce the death of one of our body. Senator Pennybacker[1] deceased last night, at 4 A.M. He was an amiable, intelligent, and I think a pious Gentleman. This is the second member of our Body, which our Heavenly Father has been pleased to call hence forever.[2] They were among the most robust, and healthy members of the Senate. It shows that in the midst of life, we are in Death. These warnings, are direct, and immediate, and therefore more impressive. But it ought not to be so. We know by a law of nature, & the declaration of the Eternal God, that we shall die, and not live! My hope, and prayer is that we may be enabled so to get in life, that when the summons shall come, that we may be prepared, for a mansion above the skies. How very thoughtless we are, and prone to idleness. If we are not sinful, we are not <u>as active in piety</u>, as those who have immortal souls to save, should be.

There is no news of a pleasant character to write. The snow which fell, has not thawed but remains, notwithstanding the sun shines clearly.

Every day only increases my Love of you, and home, where I hope to see the treasures, of my earthly happiness. Our friends all send their regards, and good wishes to you, and the little ones. They are too many to enumerate. My love to all.

Thy devoted Husband
Houston

[1]Isaac Pennybacker of New Market, Virginia. Identified in *Biographical Directory*, 142.
[2]Alexander Barrow of Louisiana had died on December 29, 1846. Ibid., 139.

∞

Washington City
17th Jany 1847

My Dear Love,

This is Sunday, and I have been to church, in the forenoon, as the day was fine. The Sermon, was an excellent one, and the Preacher was a man of ability. He was of the Unitarian persuasion, but preached from a text in Corinthians.

I have had the happiness to receive but two letters[1] from you since my arrival here. So my Love, you can well imagine my boundless anxiety to hear of your <u>treasures</u>. I am half crazy. The situation of your breast, and its unhealed state when you last wrote united to the silence which has ensued, gives exercise to my fears, and increases my solicitude. But I deserve it all for leaving you and our little Loves. I will not make promises about the future should we be spared, but I will enclose to you a slip from a news paper, which has no less than 30,000 subscribers, and is one of the most respected in Penna. Where I resist much more, and direct influences, to accept such place, you will be able to some extent to judge of my affection for home, and for yourself. You will I apprehend, deem me uxorious, or some what nervous, when I think of war. I see in proud men, daily panting for such, and humbler stations, yet I wish for none. I sigh for no place but home!! Sometimes, I fear that our dear Mother will think, that I ought to accept a command, and she wou'd "make you behave yourself!" If it is to be done the time has not yet come! When we parted, I had not confidence in the skill, or energy of our Generals, and since I came here it has greatly diminished, and if the war is not ended in twelve months, some one must take hold of matters, who can end the war. You need not think, my Love, that I intend to forget you, our weans or my love for you so far as to engage in any thing without your advice, in which your happiness is concerned, or my own affections. If I were not happy at my home, I might seek some resource of the kind. But as it is my Love, I freely confess, that I have no earthly wish, to divert my affections, or my attention, from the dear object of my love. Those very ties which bind me to earth, and confines [sic] my thoughts to the sweets of home. Yes, my Love, it is so, that all my wishes, and ambition, are confined to, or connected with you! If spared, in a few days, I hope to be with you, and our little ones, and our kindred. We are to have great excitement on tomorrow, I expect! It will be with Col Benton,[2] & Mr Calhoun.[3] So soon as I can, I will send the result to you, not because you love news papers, but that you may judge of the times as they are passing. There is to be propositions of a serious character, and affecting the war. For my own part, I intend to move on in a most amiable mood. I have no wish to be engaged in any excitement but, to spend the balance of the Session as usefully, and quietly, as possibly [sic]. I will write as often as I can.

Give my love to all, and embraces to our dear, dear little ones. I am crazy to see you all.

Thy devoted husband,
Houston

[1]See Margaret to Houston, November 27, 1846, and December 6, 1846.

[2]Senator Thomas Benton of Missouri. Identified in *Biographical Directory*, 139.

[3]Senator John C. Calhoun of South Carolina. Ibid., 140. For Calhoun's slavery resolutions and Benton's arguments see Thomas Hart Benton, *Thirty Years View; or, A History of the Working of the American Government for Thirty Years, From 1820 to 1850 . . .* (New York: D. Appleton and Company, 1856; New York: Greenwod Press, 1968), 696.

The following letter from Margaret is in the Houston collection at the Texas State Archives, Austin, Texas.

Grand Cane, Jan. 18, 1847

My ever dear husband,

By last mail your most welcome letter from Washington was received. By the previous mail, I received the one from Louisville Ky.[1] I can not tell you how happy I was made by these kind proofs of affection. That you love me dearest, unworthy as I am, I have not one doubt, and within my own heart, I can read, that neither [*torn*] nor absence can ever efface such love as ours, but to me, the oft told tale will never grow tiresome. Every word of affection from you is soothing to my heart, and I read your letters again and again, lest I might overlook <u>some</u> <u>little</u> <u>word</u>. I am beginning to count the hours that are to pass, ere we can meet again. Hope points with a sunny smile to the future, when around our own fireside, we may enjoy the prattle of our little ones. May no feeling of selfishness or worldly ambition ever disturb that little band! I am not afraid of ourselves, dearest, but I tremble when I think of our children, and all the snares and temptations which they must encounter. May the God of purity and innocence shield them, from the assaults of "the world, the flesh and the devil!" I can not describe to you, how deeply I was pained at your account of sister Polly's situation. I had entertained great hopes of her recovery, but alas I fear, that all we can ask for her now, is a breif [sic] interval before her departure. The Lord is merciful, and oh my husband, let us plead with him, to prepare her for an entrance into his presence! In my last letter to you, I did not mention my breast, because it was still slightly inflamed, and continued to discharge a little, and I did not wish to mention these facts lest it might give anxiety. I now take great pleasure in assuring you my love, that it is free from inflammation, and I think out of all danger. I have also great hopes of recovering entirely from the asthma. I have had nothing like it lately, though I have suffered from a violent cold and sore throat. Heretofore these have always been followed by a fit of asthma, but at present, I have not the slightest symptom of it.

Wednesday 20th Dearest, on the night after I commenced writing to you, our darling son was taken seriously and dangerously ill, but is now much better. About 10 o'clock, I was roused by hearing his deep groans, and found him cold and stiff, and his flesh all in a tremor. This was very soon followed by a scorching fever, and for several hours, he was hardly conscious of any thing, but when asked where he was suffering, would lay his hand on his head or neck. Towards the latter part of monday night, with the palm of my hand, I could cover on his face and neck, burning and icy spots. The next day his [torn] assumed a dead purple hue, which has not left [torn] entirely yet, but unless he takes a relapse he is cer[tainly] out of all danger. I have never seen a family mo[re d]istrest than ours, when we all thought Sam was about to be taken from us. The remark of every one was "I always said he never would be raised," and "we loved him too much." "He was our idol" was the heartbroken exclamations, that greeted me on every hand. The threatened calamity was considered a general one, and each member of the family felt too intensely on his own account to offer consolation to another, so that there was no one who would say unto me, "be comforted." Of my feelings on the occasion, I will not attempt a description and oh my Love, I can give you no idea of the joyful gratitude, that fills my soul this day, for the restoration of my child. What shall we render unto the Lord, for his goodness and mercy towards us? Oh let us dedicate ourselves and our children unto his service, and let us never never wander from him. The relations were all anxious to send for a physician for Sam, but mother would not consent to it, and I rejoice now that she did not,—for every dose of medicine she gave him, had the desired effect, and he is now almost well.

The weather is intensely cold, and it has been so, for several days. Every thing out is covered with icicles, and the earth looks dreary and sad. I wish you were with me my love, for I feel very lonely without you. My relations do every thing in thier power, to promote my happiness, but my heart pines for your gentle sympathy. Sister A. received letters on yesterday from bro. Charles. He and [*torn*] are to be with us on next monday. They are expecting Isabella and Betty [Moore] at Gen. Davis's soon, to spend several days. I designed writing you a much longer letter dearest, but Sam still requires my attention. If he is well enough, before the mail starts, I will write to Mrs Graham, but have no fears for him dearest, for this evening he is as lively as a cricket, and would be out in the yard, if I would suffer him. I send you two pieces for the "Mother's Journal" which Mr Ellis was kind enough to copy for me. All send their love to you. Farewell my ever dear Love. Write often and long letters.

Thy wife
M. L. Houston

Mother was delighted with scraps you sent her.

"Missy" says tell uncle Houston, if he would bring me a little ring, I would rather have it than a doll!

[*on the outside:*] 21st Sam is still improving.

---

[1]This letter has not been located.

The following letter from the Alva Woods Papers is addressed to Mrs. Almira Woods.

Grand cane Liberty co. Texas Jan. 18th 1847

My very dear friend,

A long time has passed, since your welcome letter was recieved [sic], and I am just now taking my seat to repy to you. It may seem strange that I have not done so before, but I assure you, my silence has been occasioned by circumstances, over which I had no control, for I am not so indifferent to my own happiness, as to neglect wilfully [sic], a correspondence, which has given me so much pleasure. You know something of a mother's duties towards an infant, and how monopolizing they are. Then, with the inconvenience of a risen breast, and consequent debility, have rendered me really incapable of replying to the letters of my friends and kindred, but my health is much improved, and I hope that it will not hereafter be necessary, to devote so much of my time, to the infant daughter, (whom I would be delighted to introduce to you,) as she is becoming quite strong and sprightly, and does not now require so much attention.

I have been again compelled to give up for a time, the society of my dear husband. The sacrifice is truly a painful one, for although I believe I am at heart a true patriot, I have none of the *[torn]* spirit about me. I am now with my mother and brother Vernal, and expect to remain with them, during Gen. Houston's absence. My time is passed as pleasantly, as it could be, when he is far away from me, but one who has never seen him, with his little family, can not imagine how much he is missed by them. However I spend some cheerful moments in talking with our little pratler [sic], of the happy time, when dear papa will come to us again, if the Good Father should spare our lives, and am thus cheated of some sad hours. We are in a retired part of the country, but at present, our family is quite a large one. My sister Mrs Charles Power, formerly Antoinette Lea, and my niece Mrs Thomas Power, whom you probably recollect as Sarah Royston, are now on a visit to us, and we are all truly rejoiced at meeting each other, after a seperation of several months. Bro. Vernal is married again to a very sensible and amiable lady, and has I think, a fair prospect of happiness.

My husband made me very happy, by an account of your meeting in Washington, and I was delighted to find, that in his opinion, I had not exaggerated the attractions of my dear friend Mrs Woods. In truth he seemed quite as willing to talk about her, as I was anxious to hear of her. So you may readily suppose, that your merits were discussed with a great deal of interest. Oh how I wish you could make another visit to Washington! It would be a source of comfort to me, to know that he would see you again, and your presence to him, would be like that of a sister.

The "gazettes" for our little boy have been regularly received, and I have been highly entertained by them. He does not read yet, but I have given him the contents of his papers, and he is quite delighted with them. He says "tell Mrs Woods, she is very kind to send me the pretty papers." He still gives evidences of an absorbing and contemplative mind, but I suppose every mother can discover some signs of genius in her child. The subject which you gave me for a poem, (his question abut the flowers of Eden,) I am holding in reserve, but do not know when I can undertake it. In truth I have so poor an opinion of my poetical talents that I feel great diffidence in attempting any thing of the kind. The greater part of the time, which I can spare from my domestic duties, is spent in reading, which is such retirement as arises, is truly a delightful employment. One of my favorite writers, is "Charlotte Elizabeth."[1] What do you think of her? It is my opinion, that she fills a place in the literary world, hitherto unoccupied. Other writers may have exercised talents of a higher order, but who hath so sweet a balm for the wounded heart! or who can bring so vividly before "the mind's eye," the *[blurred]*, the mad, the unforgotten? Many of her own church, think she is to [sic] severe against "the womanists," but I do not think she is more severe, than St Paul, against the "man of sin." Alas I fear, that spirit of tolerance will much endanger the dearest privileges we enjoy. I have no fear, that superstition and idolatry will ever gain an entire triumph over us, but I think the parent hazards much, who sends his child to be educated in the midst of image worship and all the allurements of the popish church. The custom is becoming fearfully prevalent amongst us, and I shudder, when I see a young immortal, thus consigned to ruin, by the hand which Prividence placed over it, to guard it and shield it from all contamination. "The mystery of iniquity" is beginning to work in our own fair land, and protestant parents are aiding it! Truly the true worshipers should be watchful and prayerful.

You will percieve [sic] my dear friend, that I have written with a feeble and tremulous hand, but I hope my rough scrawl will not be the less acceptable to you. Prove to me that it is not, by writing to me very soon. Mother and brother Vernal send thier regards to yourself, Dr Woods and your son, in which I by leave to unite most affectionately.

Thy true friend
M. L. Houston

[1]Margaret's volume of *The Poetry of Charlotte-Elizabeth*, with her signature on the fly leaf, is in the Sam Houston Memorial Museum, Huntsville, Texas.

∞

Senate Chambers
19th Jany 1847

My Dearest Love,

I have leisure to write a line. Since I last wrote no letters from home. I am distressed, to have something that I may look upon, which you have lately seen, or touched, and that has been breathed upon, by those I love.

I think I can see Sam, approach the elbow of his dear ma, and say "Ma are you writing to my Pa?" How happy, supremely happy would I be if, I cou'd but embrace you all, and be happy. If spared, forty two days, will release me from this prison. I will fly, with all speed to meet, and greet my Love, and embrace our little ones. You are all, continually clustering around my heart, & mingling with my best affections. My whole heart is thine, and every day, the desires of preferment, which I ever had are deminished [sic], or swallowed up, in my rustic love of home! I will write every leisure moment, and I will constantly think of, and love you all.

To day the Senate is wasting time, and I hope the members will go to work in good faith soon. Tomorrow, I may speak, on the army Bill. I have my own views on these subjects, and track no one. My measures, have been, & ever shall be, directed to my countrys good. I will not wear the "collar" of any man. It is enough my dear, to wear the "collar" of a wo-man. That I do with pleasure. Render my love to our dear mother, and the family.

Hug and kiss our own, our dear ones!

Ever thy devoted Husband
Sam Houston

P. S. I have heard nothing of our poor unhappy sister, since I last wrote, but daily look for a letter. I have no hope of her recovery.

Thine
Houston

Washington City
20th Jany 1847

My very dear Wife,

Last night, when I felt lonesome, and unhappy, I was delighted by the arrival of your letter, written two days after Christmas.[1] I was so happy to hear, that all were well, and delighted that your breast is well also. Had that not been the case, you would have told me so.

You dwell with delight on the charms of our babe. I thought her beautiful when I left home, and could not fancy any improvement, nor can I now imagine how she will appear, if I live to see the dear little being. I rejoice to hear that our lad is interprising [sic], & reflective. That you are, and have been happy, I am truly gratified, and soothed to some extent by the fact. It is not an unwelcome assurance that our dear Sister,[2] and Niece[3] are very happy, as well as their Lords.

They ought to be happy, for I think them all, worthy, of the good fortune which they enjoy!

I will write to Mr Charles [Power], for really, I always liked him as a gentleman, and as a relation, I am sure, I will not like him less. I regret that I did not write to him, but as I wrote to Sister, and spoke of him with regard & esteem, I thought it enough. I have a sincere regard for both the gentlemen, as well as their wives, for I was once, most prodigiously in Love, with a Sister, of one of the ladies, and an aunt of the other. Now you see here is Love & Reason united to remain so, in no one else, than your Ladyship. I hope you will now my Love, be satisfied that I love the Powers, and will submit, to the powers of Love. So you see, that I esteem my relations to you, and hope they will soon be more intimate, and near!!!

Isabella, my niece, wrote to me, and as her letter, was too formal, I took the liberty to write to her a lesson, which she will not forget. Among other things she said "Aunt wrote to me, and I wrote to her a kind letter." I wished to know of her, whether she conceived, her so doing, an act of duty, or condescension? They are strange people, to my apprehension. [Samuel] Moore wrote to me a coarse letter. I did not answer him. I may do so, or may not as it happens. Dont you be unhappy, my Love, about it, for I will not! I will treat them right, & with due kindness, but no more!

I send you by Judge [Daniel] Toler, a pair of slippers from our God Daughter,[4] with much love from all the family. To Sam, a pretty pair of shoes, and to Sister, and you some hair oil!

I have only time to conclude as the Judge will soon start. Give my love, and a kiss to each of the family. Hug, & kiss the children.

Thy ever devoted Husband
Houston

P.S. I sent your letter sealed to Mrs Allen after seeing the pretty poetry, and I sent the subscription also. I wrote a polite note to her Ladyship.

Thine truly
Houston

[1]This letter has not been located.
[2]Antoinette Bledsoe (Mrs. Charles) Power.
[3]Sarah Ann Royston (Mrs. Thomas) Power.
[4]Mary Houston, the daughter of Houston's cousin, John Houston.

Washington City
24th Jany 1847

My Beloved,

I have just written to our Boy,[1] and I now proceed to write to you my Love, and apologize that I have not written oftener in the last week. I had to attend to our army Bill, and took a pretty active part in the discussion. You will see my speech in part, but not in whole.[2] And I will also send you some remarks of the Editors of the Intelligencer, which you can judge of, as they do not compliment a Democrat, more than once in ten years. You will see my Love, that I can not wear the Collar at all times! Some things can stand, as for instance, if I were at home, weary, and fatigued, and when I had sat down, you were to ask me, to let you sit on my knee, that I would stand, my Dear. Or I would be happy, even to gratify Sam, in any little harmless conceits, but I will not gratify grown children, in mischievous fancies. So I have been obedient to a sense of duty. Too much was required of the party. A sacrifice of principles, as I thought, demanded of me, so I dissented from the wishes of the administration, in its desire to raise a Regular, and standing army. To this I will never assent, so long as I live in America!!!

Dearest, I have been interrupted for four hours, by company, and have just resumed my letter. Tomorrow, the debates on the army, will be resumed, and I expect to join in the debate. You need not entertain any fears, as to the result, for I am right, in my opinions. They are the only ones, suited to our institutions. They are all that can maintain the rights of the people, against Executive patronage.

I hope my dear, that you will be gratified with my speech, which I send you. It has not been corrected, but I intend to have it published, and other remarks appended which I made in debate. You will deem it a plain common sense affair. So as it is, I hope you will approve it. The principles are right.

I need not renew any assurances, of my boundless anxiety to get home that I may again be happy, with you, and our dear little ones. At times I fancy, that I can see you all, and Sam claiming the smiles of his "dear little Sister, for brother Sam." I was not at the last drawing room, for really, it is a flat business to me, & I am free to confess, that if I am any judge, there is but little beauty there. I am busy, beyond any thing, which I have heretofore experienced, and each day, only increases my business. Mr Miller & Col Eldridge, assist me in my business, and by their aid, I get on pretty well. It is nearly two oclock in the morning, and tomorrow if I live, I am to have a busy day. As this is the case, I must close my letter.

You will give my love to Mother & the family, and if you write to our Power-full relations, give them my love also. Kiss our dear little ones.

Thy faithful and devoted Husband
Sam Houston

[1]This letter has not been located.
[2]For a copy of the speech see *Writings*, vol. 4, 504–22.

∞

Senate chamber
25th Jany 1847

My Love,

While a prosing, & sawing speaker is going on, with a silly speech, & no one listening to him, I chuse to employ my time in writing to you. It is true, that I have but little of interest to narrate. A letter from Genl Taylor[1] to Gen [Edmund P.] Gaines, has been published. It will make some excitement before it is over.[2] I think it will take place on tomorrow. I learn that our friend Mrs Gaines advised its publication. I have not seen her for about three weeks, altho' she is not a hundred yards from my residence. This I will say. No one thing could have been done at this time to the reputation of Genl Taylor. The Genl thinks he has Glory enough, and is a bidder for the "white House." If he were in it, he would make a bad tenant, unless he has first rate luck. I know my Love, that you, take but little interest in politics, nevertheless, I venture to try, and interest, by way of creating curiosity, as to how matters will turn out! If you are not interested, you will do me the justice, to suppose, that if I do not instruct you, it will at least, employ you in reading—or in a "bushel of chaff, you may find a grain of wheat." When I look out of the window, the air, and earth looks gloomy to me. I think of the sunny south, my wife, my young barbarians, and our friends, and sigh for our rustic home. I sigh that I cannot recal [sic] the joys which are passed, and for the reality of those, which I hope are to come!

My heart is purified by these holy, and cherished influences. So long as I am within the influences of exciting subjects, so long as I am in public life. You will be aware of my love of home, and to return here again, without you, and our weans, I wou'd not, for a throne!

Altho' my time hangs heavily, yet I know, the sand of life is wasting, by hours, and days, and years, and when once exhausted, it can, never run again. I feel it a duty, to meditate upon this all absorbing interest. One that is worth all other subjects in time. It is the business of eternity.

It is late my Love, so Adieu. Thy devoted & faithful

Houston

I have not time to read this letter.

[1]Zachary Taylor.
[2]For the contents of the letter written November 5, 1846, see Eisenhower, 167n. Polk and his cabinet condemned both Taylor for writing the letter and Gaines for publishing it. Polk, *Polk*, 191–92.

Washington City
26th Jany 1847

My Love,

I am here in the midst of a trifling debate, and to let you know that such is the fact, I write. Since yesterday, I have no news, nor does it appear, that the army Bill, will come up for a day or two. The Senate to day is engaged, upon the subject of <u>Finance</u>. This you know my dear, is not suited to my capacity, so you will not expect me to speak upon it. Last night, I wrote a long letter to our Nephew, Tom Power.[1] It was partly upon business, and partly friendly. They are clever Gentlemen, and I so esteem them. They are enterprising, but I am fearful they will get into some snap, or in other words be taken in by sharpers. They will find that men in Texas, are different from men in England.[2] Business is different here, and they should be on the alert. I hope they will need no suggestions of mine.

To day I am suffering much from cold. My head aches very much. We burn coal fires here, and they are less healthy, than wood fires. I was busy last night as usual until long after midnight. Each day I set a resolution, that I will retire at an early hour. As often as I resolve, I violate my resolve. I receive letters from so many persons, that if I were to answer them all, I would not have time either to eat or sleep. I only attend to those which have merits in them. I feel quite patient, and will try and get thro' this session with a resolve, that I will answer no letters but on business. Yes Love, on business, for all my letters to you are on the <u>business</u> of <u>love</u>!!

So you will please give my <u>love</u> to all, and kiss our little ones.

Thy faithful and devoted husband
Sam Houston

[1]This letter has not been located.
[2]Both Thomas Power and his brother Charles were from England.

Senate Chamber

29th Jany 1847

My Dear Love,

I will quit prosing about my business, and complaining of things which I can not avert. I will do the best I can, and try from time, to time, to write you such matters, as may amuse, or interest you.

The Army Bill is up to day, and Col Benton will speak. He has risen to speak, and has just begun. He will make a good speech, and I will send it to you, so soon as it is published. I will try, from day to day, to send you such papers, as contain speeches. I do not expect you to read them, but Vernal will.

I hear of much gaiety in the city, as reported by Miller and Elderidge, tho' they do not join in them! Eldridge has received the appointment of Purser in the Navy, and I expect will soon go to Sea. Miller is busy, day & night. He is often with me as well as Eldridge, until eleven o clock.

At this time I have a very bad cold, and a few days since I was very ill. This is the most changeable climate, in America. All have colds, and are hoarse. You will please make my love to all the family, and embrace our dear children.

It is sometime since I heard from you. I am very anxious, yes, crazy to hear again.

I have not heard from my poor sister. I am waiting in painful solicitude, to hear [*torn*]

I am faithfully

[*signature has been cut off*]

Washington

Senate Chamber

30th Jany 1847

My Love,

As I am at my desk, and do not take part in debate, I feel pleasure in writing to, as well as in thinking of you. It is impossible for me to be a moment silent without thinking of you, and our little ones. The dear little creatures. When I look out on, the snowy earth, or hear the howling blasts of winter, I think of you, and our little nestlings, and ask, are they comfortable? is [sic] my Love happy, and in health?

Time passes slowly by, and leaves my feelings, still a prey to anxiety. Only thirty three days remain of the session. There will be but little done, I fear, of the remaining business of Congress. Much ought to be done, but the Senators must talk, & will not act. I find a difference between the statesman, and the soldiers to consist mainly in this. The statesman relies upon talking, and the soldier upon action. Whenever I see any thing which may interest you, or will add to another "Cabinet of scraps," I will send them to you. To day I will send you a paper. One I sent this morning to our dear brother.

Render my affectionate regards to our dear Mother, Sister & Bud. Give the little girls howdas. Kiss our young Barbarians, & bless them! Kiss Missy!

Thy faithful and devoted husband
Sam Houston

Washington City
1st Feby 1847

My Love,

Tho' it is past midnight, I can not retire, until I write a line to you. You have often said my dear, that you were somewhat jealous of Sam, and thought I would love him more than I did you! I fear the contrary is the case, and, that is your devotion to Sam, and our babe, that you are so much engaged that I have some reason to complain, of your silence. I am painfully anxious to hear of you, and the children! It has been for days, that I have looked for letters. None lately have come, and southern mails have been regular! If you had known how happy your dear letters make me, you would have written very often. It will not be of any use for you to write after the 15th Inst.

To day I made a speech on the 3rd reading of the army Bill, and my friends think that I sustained myself well. I would think better of the speech, if my friend Miller, did <u>not</u> approve it. He I am informed thinks well of it, and says "it was a grand speech." It had two qualities of a good speech. It was truthful, and patriotic. How many bad ones it had you can judge of when you see it, as I will send you a copy so soon, as it is out. The press of business will increase, as the session draws to a close. I will try, and have my business complete when we adjourn, so that I will not be detained an hour, in this city. You know that I have said, I will make no more complaints about business etc. Well, I know, you allow me to complain of absence, from you, and from home. Great as is my wish to see you, and our young Barbarians, I will not ever harrass you, with complaints—but I will say, that above all things earthly, I would prefer to see, and embrace you all with a husbands, and father's affections, and tenderness.

No important news, now on hand, but look out for some excitement among the "cliques political."

Salute, all with affection, and embrace our little ones.

Faithfully thine ever
Houston

Washington City
3rd Feby 1847

My Love,

You have no idea how unhappy, I was this morning. I heard from a fellow Senator, who sits behind me, say that every other day, he received a letter from his wife. He resides in Indiana.[1]

Weeks have now elapsed since I have heard from you, or home. I have received letters from Swarthout, and from Galveston, and as none came from you, or any person at Grand Cane I am left sad, and melancholy. I am not complaining my Love, of neglect, but of disappointed hope! Vernal, (my Love,) could have written to me a single line, if you were sick, or could not write. All the happiness which I have enjoyed since I came here, has arisen from your letters. I have not, as often, written to you, perhaps, as I would have done, if I had not hoped to have letters from you, to answer. You would have been amused, could you have been present, and seen me, tear open the mails, as they were laid on my table. I say amused, because after you had witnessed my anxiety, and there by presenting yourself, you could have relieved my anxiety, and made me, supremely happy.

Not a night passes, but where I, upon my bended knees I implore the great Father of Mercy, to grant, His protecting care, in the preservation of my wife, and our dear children. This brings you all present, to the minds vision, and my heart. I can see you all as I fancy you to be—You my Love, seated with the babe, on your knee, while Sam, with his rude, but affectionate caress, toying with her, and wishing to secure her approbation, and impress her, as well as all present, with the importance of his attentions. My time, I thank my Good Father, is now reduced, within thirty days, which I have to stay in this place. I am not unmindful my Dear, that each day I live, only brings me nearer to my final account. For that time, I know, and feel, that I have to render a strict account which no condition can evade. That we may all be prepared, and keep in a state of constant, and earnest preparation!

I know you will not have it in your power to answer this letter, as I hope to leave here, before an answer could reach me!

I send you papers often. Give my love to all our kindred, and embrace out little ones.

I am thy faithful and devoted husband
Sam Houston

---

[1]The senators from Indiana were Edward A. Hannegan and Jesse D. Bright. It is unclear to which one Houston refers. *Biographical Directory*, 144.

∞

Washington City
5th Feby 1847

My Dear Love,

205 : NOVEMBER 21, 1846 - APRIL 4, 1847

The mails or some other cause has kept all letters from me. Weeks have now passed my dear, since I have heard a word from you, or from home. Yet, I get letters from all parts of Texas. I am painfully apprehensive, that you are ill, or that our dear little ones are suffering. Unless I get letters in a few days, I will despair of hearing again, until I reach home, if I shou'd be spared, to do so. Night after night, I sit up until three oclock. Long as I am awake, I reflect upon you, and the dear little creatures. I thought when I was at home, that I loved you all tenderly. I did so, but I find that absence has changed the character, of my affections, from tenderness, to wildness. At times I wish that I could fly to your dear embrace, and once more, to look upon our dear children. The day has been, when I could feel, an interest here, and cared, only to be amused. Now I have, as I before said, in former letters, no pleasure in being here. I have no ambition to gratify, nor do I think of any substitute, for the joys, and happiness of home.

Parties are occuring [sic] nightly, and yet I do not go to them. I could not be happy there, and have no wish to be there. The last one which I was at, was given by the Secretary of the Senate.[1] I looked on for a short time, and returned to my room, relieved, and satisfied, that I cou'd be more happy, in solitude, than society, when absent from my home, & from you Dearest. The Ladies which I saw there, seemed adorned for the admiration of many, and my heart, and thoughts recurred to <u>one</u>, and but <u>one</u>!

By recurring to my habits in Texas, where I traveled in dark forests and deep swamps, after Indian guides that I might be with you, & Sam, you can have some idea of my desires, and my anxiety to see you, and others. Then I was prompted by double affection, but now my Love, it is treble. The dear little Nanny. Yes I fancy how she looks, and how strange, she would regard me. She would not converse with me as she once did. She wou'd not prefer me to all others. You say my Love, that she will now talk freely—Ah yes, but I can neither see her, nor hear her sweet voice. How much happier would I have been, never to have left home, nor been absent from every object of my affections. I will look dayly [sic] for letters, and hope

many letter[s] are on the way. It may be that they have been pur-
loined, as statesmen are in some instances jealous of me, and may
suppose, that I am writing treason to you, and that your letters would
render a key to my designs. That they should think so is reasonable,
when we reflect, that the idea is afloat, that you are really my "confidential adviser." The <u>treason</u>, of which I might, or may be suspected,
is only, treason against great men, who wish to be greater. If they
knew me better, they would find, that really they have nothing to
fear, from my desires. If we are so blessed, as to meet again, I will
have much, yes, very much, to tell you of.

You will my dear, present me affectionate regards, to our Dear
Mother, and the family.

Kiss Sam, & the dear babe for me. I[n] doing this, I wish you
double joy.

Thy affectionate & faithful Husband
Sam Houston

[1]Asbury Dickens, of North Carolina. *Biographical Dictionary*, 138.

∞

Senate Chambers
8th Feby 1847

My Dearest Love,

Weeks have passed, & not a line from you. On last night I received two mails, and letters from Texas, but none from home. I
would fain hope, that the Bay has been in a rough state, and that
owing to the fact, letters were not sent to Galveston, by mail, or private conveyances. In my state of anxiety, I bear up as well as I can.
'Tis true that I am very unhappy, or rather miserable, indeed. I must
bear my trials, with all the fortitude in my power. I will look with
increasing anxiety, until I can hear from you. At times I am almost
maddened, and my brain burns, with solicitude. My heart, too, seems
as if it would burst, and then it sinks in depression.

You can now judge my Love somewhat of my condition of mind,

and heart. Night after night, I dream of you, and home. I fancy the joys, of your society, and the prattle, of our children! These fancies vanish, when I awake, and leave me the victim, of disappointment, and sadness. I declare to you my Love, that when I reflect upon my wife, or children, & our kindred, in Texas, I feel, that I should never have left my domestic endearments. A poor, very poor, requital would it be, for the pain of absences, if I cou'd acquire, the largest share of <u>fame</u>, which any man can possess, or acquire, in the Senate of the U States.

Others seem crazy to acquire the distinction, of third rate renown, and to do so, economize thoughts, and words, and struggle hard, to render them palpable in the forum of a set speech!!!

I will look with more . . . *[The bottom of the page is cut off]* that Lieut Tennison,[1] of Texas Navy, is to be married tomorrow night in this city. All the Texians here are invited but Comd [Edwin] Moore. I expect to attend and see the torch lit, and Hymen preside, while cupid will drop his wreathe of flowers, on Neptunes brows. I do not know, that my metaphors are exactly right, or according to classic taste. <u>You</u> can judge!!!

Give my love to all the family—Kisses to the babes, and salutations to friends.

Thy faithful and . . .
[signature has been cut off]

[1]William Tennison married Mary Virginia Brooks on February 9, 1847. *District of Columbia Marriage Licenses Register,* compiled by Wesley Penninger (Westminster, Md.: Family Line Publishers, 1994), 292.

Washington
9th Feby 1847

My Beloved,

Since I wrote yesterday, no less than three mails have arrived, and no letters. My anxiety increases hourly, and I feel almost certain, that sickness, is the cause of my not getting letters. Until I can hear from home, I will be without happiness, for I declare to you I have not enjoyed an hour, since we parted, unless you, or the children were the subjects, of my thoughts, or my hopes. There surely is nothing here, which can afford me happiness. By way of coming as near home as possible, I have ordered you a sort of cloak, which is worn here by Ladies. Some little matters for Nannie, and for Master Sam, a Sack coat, with many buttons, which of course will suit him precisely. Whether I can take them with me on horseback, I do not know, but I will try, and do so. I expect to send my Books, etc by water to Galveston.

If spared, I can not say, when I will be able to reach home. It may be, by the last of March, at least I hope so, if not before. You will I hope, not think me tardy, no matter when I may get home! Since I rec'd your last letter, my mind has had some (almost) unpleasant forebodings. I will not state them, until we meet[.] I hope you will find me by no means, querulous, on my return home I trust, but so happy, that I will be unusually amiable, and pleasant, in our intercourse.

I have nothing of interest to impart, but hope, ire another day passes, that I will have to announce to you, the happiness of having received a letter from you, saying "We are all well, and happy," or at least cheerful.

My affection to our dear Mother, and all the family. I send to our Bro Vernal Documents often.

Kiss our dear Weans.

Thy faithful and ever devoted husband
Sam Houston

Grand Cane Feb. 10th 1847

Dear Love,

I have suffered two or three mails to pass, without writing to you, for the reason, that my breast was in such condition, that I could not write without detriment to myself. It has risen three times, and the last time presented such an angry appearance, that Brother Charles prepailed [sic] on us to send for Dr Smith,[1] who was fortunately at his plantation on the bay, and on the day before yesterday, he arrived here, and remained until this morning. He has decided that it must be operated upon, and so soon as I can dry up the breast, with the help of God, I hope to sit down to it, like a soldier. I would not tell you anything about it, but I fear that each one of the thousand tongues of madam rumour will report to you, that Dr. Smith had been up to see my breast. Now my precious Love, let me entreat you, not to be anxious about me, for the Dr assures me that the operation will be a mere trifle, and easily performed in two minutes, and what could I not endure for my husband and children! The Dr prefers waiting until your return, but I prefer having my breast sound and well, when you get home, and we have fixed on an early day in march for it. Sister A. and Sally, and thier husbands expect to leave us, on tomorrow, and brother Charles says he will bring Sis back with him to be with me. I think [blurred] and Cary[2] will come also. Every one is so kind and affectionate to me in my illness, that my heart is not troubled by it. Our dear children are in fine health and much grown since you saw them.

I must not forget to mention that by yesterday's mail, I recd yours of the 5th to the 12th ult. I would give you my opinion on the war question in this, but it is not necessary, as I have already written at length upon it. However, lest my letter should have missed you, I will merely mention that I left it entirely to your own discretion. How much my happiness depends upon your society, I need not repeat, but if the path of duty is plain before you, I would not dare to place an obstacle in your way. Mother is exceedingly anxious for you to go, and says she will take care of us, while you are away. And now my love, I know you would not expect a long letter from me, as you will easily suppose, that I am feverish and nervous about drying my breast. Dr Smith tells me, that my health will probably be entirely restored by operating on my breast. He speaks with more certainty that I like to repeat, and says I will [*blurred*] as large as Mother. My husband, my darling one, farewell.

Thine devotedly,
M. L. Houston

[1] See Charles Power to Ashbel Smith, February 3, 1847. Ashbel Smith Papers, Barker History Center (Center for American History), University of Texas.
[2] Caroline Davis.

∞

Washington City
11th Feby 1847

My very dear Wife,

What to think, or how to account, for my not receiving letters, are matters, of painful uneasiness to me. I received a letter from Galveston, dated 29th Jany,[1] and learned that the people there, had not heard from you for some time. Since I came here, I think only three letters have reached me. I am at the Capitol, and may not be correct, in saying, <u>but three</u>. It is now two months, & I have written not less than <u>twenty</u>, and keep writing!

I surely have the gift of continuance, and I doubt not, but you will so think. The last letter which you wrote, was when our kinfolk were with you. Why it was so, I can't tell, but I felt, as I thought, something like a cold sensation of feeling come over my heart, when I read your letter. This is no fiction, I assure you. It was a painful sense, but why the emotion was, I can not yet resolve! As you have spoken of my letters from Houston, as having a something about them which gave you uneasiness, so it was with your last letter, my Dear. Hope is left with me that my fancies are but fancies, and bode no harm to us, or ours. It may be that this night, I may receive quite a bundle of letters from you. I get abundance from those, for whom I care nothing! as I know nothing. Time passes slowly, so far as my anxiety to get home, is concerned—yet when I regard the amount of business which ought, to be transacted before Congress adjourns, it is very brief.

The last <u>Levee</u> went off last night. I say the last, because I learn, that there will be no more this season. I was there for a while. It was a great squeeze, and I suppose persons were dressed very fine! You blame me for not noticing your finery, when you assume to wear. Now I can assure you my Love, if <u>you</u> have cause to censure me, others are less noticed. I assure you, that at this moment, I can not say, whether the Lady President, had a head dress, or curls, or neither. Thus you can judge, how much I was attracted by finery. When I go to the Levees, or receptions, it is a round of introductions, to Gentlemen, with now, and then a lady. This season, tho', several Ladies are boarding at the Hotel where I stay, I have not been in the Ladies parlour, since I came here. My room is crowded whenever I am in it. Indeed, I have so much company, from all parts of the U States, that I am compelled to sit up every night, with the exception of three, since I came here, on the 16th of December.

The date of your last letter was at Christmas. Is not this a very great while? It is possible my Love, that my letters, may not have reached you! But I hope this is not the case.

To day we are to have speech making, on the 3,000,000 Bill, and as it is a whig who is to speak, I look for bitter things against Mr Polk. In a few days I hope to send you a full report, of my last speech.

Do present my love to our dear Mother, and <u>all</u> the family. Kiss, and bless, our dear children.

Thy faithful & devoted
Houston

[1]It is unclear who the writer of this letter was.

Senate Chamber
12th Feby 1847

My Love,

It was my hope, that I shou'd ire this, have enjoyed the pleasure, of thanking you, and congratulating myself, on having received a letter from you. None has yet been received.

It is not by way of complaint that I now write to you. No my Love, I assure you, it is only in sorrow, but not in anger, that I tell you my mind is tortured, and I fear some cause, other than a failure of the mails. Each day I receive, no less, than two mails, and you can imagine, with what avidity, I seize, and open my letters. For tho' I would recognize your handwriting, and do not find it, in the hope that others may contain some news of home I do not cease this search, until it ends in total disappointment.

Each day ends, as it begins, in hope, that I must soon hear from you, and when I do hear, the intelligence will be that all are well, and happy. If I have happiness, it arises from the hope, that I will soon see you, and embrace you, with our dear little ones. Not a night passes, but what I most fervently invoke the Father of mercies, to bless, and preserve you all, from the evils of this world! My heart is absorbed, with love of you, and our little ones. Life has no joy for me, in which you are not associated, and is hightened [sic], by expectation of the future. Twenty-two days, only remain, for our detention here. Already, I have begun to prepare, for our being off, so soon as Congress adjourns. If there should be a called session before we were to leave, it would not detain me, as my term expires on the 4th of March. Do not think there will be a call session. Matters might require such a thing, but the President, I think will be disinclined to do it, as he is not a great favorite with Congress. I do not say, that he ought not to be a favorite, but I do not think that Congress is entirely disposed to render him the aid which he requires, to conduct the wars.

Since I commenced this letter we have had more excitement in the Senate, than I have before seen. It was between Mr Turney[1] of Tenn, and Mr Calhoun![2] I have taken no part, in the matter, tho' it concerns Texas. My time has not yet come, but in a day or two, I hope to vindicate Texas, and the conduct of her public men. Not as one who acted a part, but as an American Senator!!

Give my love to all, and hug, & kiss the children.

I am thy faithful and devoted husband

Sam Houston

P.S. Genl Geo S. Houston[3] is looking over my shoulder, and sends his best respects to you.

Houston

---

[1]Hopkins L. Turney. Identified in *Biographical Directory*, 141.
[2]For information on Calhoun's views see Irving H. Bartlett, *John C. Calhoun: A Biography*, (New York: W. W. Norton & Company, 1993), 341.
[3]The Democratic Congressman from Alabama. O'Brien and Martin, 193.

Washington City
16th Feby 1847

My Love,

You can have but little idea, of my state of mind at this moment. Only think, that I have not heard a word from home since the 27th December. I have so often written, in hopes that I wou'd get responses from home, or at least hear some thing, that I am almost in state of despondency. I must have written at least, some fifty letters. Indeed I have on one or more occasions, written to you, two letters in one day. I can not but hope, that my letters may have reached you, or some of them, at least. I find that the only pleasure, which I have, is to read over, and over again, your three letters to me. Never before have I so forcibly felt, the solitude of heart, as I have done for the few last weeks. When a mail is handed to me, my heart sickens. So often, have I been disappointed in seizing, and looking over my letters, that now, I am unprepared to sustain it longer. Oh my Love! I declare to you, that if I have flown from guilt, or crime, I should deem that my punishment would be replete, in the suffering which I endure!

Well I can not amend my present position, by indulging vain

regrets. I hope for a happy future. It is in the society of my <u>wife</u>, my children, and friends, and not in the hustle of this wide, and noisy world! I doubt not, but you will duly, and kindly, appreciate my feelings.

I intend to write to you, on tomorrow, or day after, if I live, and will send you some poetry—but I don't say it is of my own composition. It is original, and it is for <u>you</u> only. You may judge of its merit, and you will think the inspiration most natural.

Present my love to our dear Mother & the family all. Kiss, and bless our little ones. Press them near your heart, & say "a father loves them, and their dear, dear Mother."

Thy faithful & ever devoted Husband
Sam Houston

Washington
19th Feby 1847

My dear dear Wife,

Your favors of the 5th, and 27th of Jany,[1] have reached me, and you can not imagine the happiness which they imparted to me. It is true the indisposition of our lovely boy, pained me, to think of his sufferings, but as I read the letter announcing his recovery first, it was less painful to me. I know his noble, and enduring disposition, and I was rejoiced, that he had not disappointed my hopes of him, in his late sickness. My Love, may it not be possible, that Virginia <u>may have given him something</u>, that caused his sickness? Can not she be seperated [sic] from our dear <u>jewels</u>? You know my fears, ire we came down? It may be that she was not the cause, but as it has doubt, and mystery about it, I am willing to suspect her, from past events! Judge ye!!²

I was pleased with his mexican triumphs, but I must confess to you my Love, that it gave me no singular gratification, to know that trait, in his disposition.³ If the author of our being, has directed him, a warrior's toils, and perils, there is enough, for him to do on this continent, to eclipse twice told, his Fathers fame! The harvest of Glory, at his proper age, will be ready, for the conquerors sword. I would rather see him a holy man, with high qualities to serve his Great Creator, as he ought to do!

Dearest, I intend to speak tomorrow, as I have not spoken on the subject, as I proposed.[4] I hope to succeed, as well, quite as I have now. I am not anxious to speak, but feel it to be my duty, as Texas, has been called in question. You, would say to me—"speak"!

Our dear babe, I can well fancy, to be the most beautiful, that I have ever seen. I thought so when I left home! Your enclosures to me, will be strictly attended to. Mrs Graham has received her letter with delight. She says, that she has "half a notion, to go to Texas, to see you." She is fitting me out, with various matters for you, Sam, and Nannie. I agree to pay for all she gets, and thus far only, am I responsible. The dress, she says, you shall have, and so say I. Sam is to have a sack coat. That will be nice, no doubt. It has many buttons on it!

I would write much, but the clock has struck 12 at night, and I must speak tomorrow. It is not so late, as my usual bed time, but I wish to take much rest to night.

Give my love to our dear Mother, and all the family. Kiss our dear, dear, very dear children; and be assured of the devoted love, of thy ever faithful and affectionate husband.

Sam Houston

P.S. In all the month of March, I hope to reach home. It would be unsafe by the Gulf, as I think, therefore, I intend to go by land, on horseback.

Thine ever Houston

[in the margin:] P.S. I am so fat and large, that I fear you will not know me.

H.

---

[1]These letters have not been located.
[2]For more information on the problems the Houstons had with their troubled ward Virginia Thorn see Madge Roberts, *Star of Destiny: The Private Life of Sam and Margaret Houston* (Denton: University of North Texas, 1993), 112, 130, 144–45.

[3]Houston is probably referring to information given about Sam in Margaret's missing letter of January 27, 1847.
[4]For a copy of the speech see *Writings*, vol. 4, 523–47.

∞

Washington City
20th Feby 1847

My Love,

On yesterday I made the speech, which I contemplated, and I can only say to you, that my friends were all <u>extremely</u> gratified. For myself, I was not in love, with my effort. I furnished to the world much new matter, and information relative to Texas. The audience was immense, and perhaps the best evidence, which was rendered in favor of the speech was, that none left, tho I spoke for more than two hours. I was not personal to any one, but treated the Subject, as a Texian, and as an American Senator.

There was no one here to personate [sic] you. If this had been the case, I would have done much better. You can not imagine how solitary I feel, and restless, in my absence from <u>you</u>, and home.

When I fancy you seated with our dear children, and listening to Sam's inquisitive prattle, I am almost deranged. Dearly, Dearly have I paid for my absence from all the indearments [sic] of life. So soon as I can set out for home, I will do so, and with a healing heart. You will suppose, I have no doubt concluded, that I am in a hurry, to embrace you, and our little ones. I hope that I may be guided, and guarded by a kind Providence. I will make no more promises about what I will, or will not do, but I will state my intentions, and they are these. I never will be absent from you again, nor our dear pledges, for more than a week, or two! This I hope you will ratify, and approve!

I can only be happy, when I am with those who love, and those whom I can love. At home I hope to find them, for I fancy that some instinct, will cause our dear little Nanny to love me. It may be, that she will not, but I hope she will, and at once recognize me as her Pa.

If she should not, I am sure, that Sam will be distressed, and so manifest his feelings.

My Love, I have not yet copied into pretty hand, the poetry which I promised you to do. It is in the rough original, and at times my hand is so unsteady, that I can not at all times write so well, as I do to day. I hope to have time soon, & I will not authorize you to decide whether it is mine, or not until we meet. I was happy to hear from our nieces, and I hope they will do well, and be happy. I will do all which I fitly can, to aid them, as a relation.

Since I last wrote to you my love, I have not heard, from our poor unfortunate Sister. I look daily for some intelligence, and will impart it to you so soon as I receive it. I have not any hope that, any news which I can receive, will render to me hope, or joy.

I am very busy, my Love and will cease writing.

My regards to all the family. Kiss the babes, and Missy, and thank her for her remembrance of me.

Thy ever devoted, and faithful Husband
Sam Houston

Washington City
22 Feby 1847

My Love,

To day I have listened with great pleasure to Mr. Soule[1] of Louisiana, in making a speech on the subject of the 3,000,000 Bill. It was a fine, very fine effort. Tonight the 22nd Ball, or rather the Birth night is to take place. I see by the notices, that another gentleman, and myself are to wait on the President, and accompany him to the Ball, and there introduce him to the company. By the bye, I have, if we live to meet, my dear, something amusing to tell you of!

If I had time, I would write you about the events. I have now two letters to enclose to you. You will see my Love, on your account, I have been patronizing your friend Mrs Allen. I never fail to do any, and every thing, which I may suppose will gratify you, and do nothing but what would gratify you, if you were cognizant of my actions, and my natures. In twelve days, we are in hopes, that we will get off from this city. Then my Love, as the old saw says, "I will let no grass grow to my heels," until I can embrace my own, my beloved Margaret. And then her dear little <u>pets</u>, for really I am some what fearful, they will be wild to me. Should this be the case, I assure you my Love, I will spare no pains, to domesticate them <u>suddenly</u>! I say suddenly, because I hope to stay at home, and to be with you, and them. To be with you, and stay with you, is the proudest earthly wish, which I possess, or entertain. It is a most delightful hope for me to encourage, that we shall soon be again united in health, and with all our dear friends around us to see Sam, with all his importance, and at the same time deferring to his Ma! and setting forth his claims to a hearing! Poor little fellow, my heart has bled for him, and I am not without fears, as to what the cause of his illness may have been! I fear Virginia!!! If she had not burnt the letters, and cut the Bible, I might entertain hopes of reformation, but as it is, I have no hope of her, or any thing, which could be expected, of other children! If you should deem my suggestions of any value, I pray you, that you take some measures, to guard the dear little <u>loves</u>, from her dreadful disposition. I pray you my love, to watch, with increasing vigilance, our treasures!

My dear Love, I was sorry, that you did not let me hear all, <u>all</u> particulars, about your breast. If you had known, how anxious I was to know, the exact prospect of your entire recovery, you would have been minute in your details! I trust however, that I will have the pleasure of meeting you, in perfect health, & in perfect happiness also. You my dearest are the subject of meditation, with which my mind sinks to repose, and the first which bursts upon my waking imagination. I dream of you, but not of our dear babes. Thro' the day, my fancy, as my memory embraces you all in our group, and Oh! how my bosom swells at the thought. I laugh to myself, at poor Sam's military display, and martial glances. If we live to meet, I hope to hear his very interesting history, of his achievements, his battles won, his slaughtered foes, and all his martial feats of glorious war! My love to all. Kisses to Missy, and our babes.

Thy devoted & faithful Husband
Sam Houston

[1]Senator Pierre Soule of New Orleans. Identified in *Biographical Directory*, 139.

∞

Senate Chamber
23rd Feby 1847

My dear, dear Love,

As a large speech is making in the senate, I take more pleasure, in writing to you than listening to a thousand such speeches. I waited with the President last night, at the Ball, and introduced him, in handsome style. Mr Sevier[1] of the Senate, and myself were his props. You see he, at least, was in good company, and for myself, I can assure you, that I never enjoyed my self <u>less</u> than at the Ball. Should we live to meet, I will promise to you, if you should require it, that I will never again go to another. This resolve you need not be astonished at, when you reflect, that you will not go, & where you are not, I can not be happy.

This is no "love letter," tho' I am speaking of things, and persons lovely to me! I might well send to <u>you</u>, love letters, for surely, there is no one here, by me regarded, in the light of loveliness. My heart is like that of the Parent bird,—thru things, its thought command. Its home, its mate, and its young. I love my home, because you are there, and illumine every joy, and soothe every care. I love my young, because you are their mother, and the centre of all my affections!

The speech is enclosed, and it is near 5 oclock P.M. when we must adjourn.

Render my love to all the family. Kiss the babes. I hope to get a letter from you this evening, when I will be so <u>appie</u>.

Thy faithful, and ever devoted husband
Sam Houston

[1]Ambrose Sevier of Arkansas. Identified in *Biographical Directory,* 138. For Polk's description of the ball see Polk, *Polk,* 199.

The following letter is addressed to Mrs. Doct. A. Woods, Providence, and is in the Alva Woods Papers.

Washington City
5th March 1847

Dear Lady,

Some days since, I received, from Mrs Houston a letter for you,[1] and by some means it disappeared from my table. It may be that Mr [Washington D.] Miller may have enclosed it, and my frank was put on it, without observing the address. I hope this has been the case. Since, it came, I received another letter, from my dear Margaret, in which she informs me, that before I can reach home, she will have had an operation, on her breast. It has risen, and broke, three times, from a tumour. For several years, she had felt some inconvenience, & pain, but when I left home, I hoped, it had ceased to annoy her. Until I can reach her, my feelings will [be] agonized. For several days, I have been, in a painful state of mind. It does not arise, from any alarm expressed by her, for she assures me, that there will be no danger, and that she will bear the pain "like a soldier."

The little ones, were very well, when Mrs H. wrote. I hope you will be so kind as to write to Mrs H. enclosed to me at Houston Texas. It will find us. I am under many and cherished obligations to Doct Woods, and your Ladyship. I doubt not, if I ever enjoy the pleasure of meeting him, that I will (if possible) love him, as much as Mrs H. does her "dear friend Mrs Doct Woods."

You will be pleased Lady, to salute the Doct and your son, for me, and be assured of my affectionate esteem, and regard.

Most truly thine
Sam Houston

221 : NOVEMBER 21, 1846 - APRIL 4, 1847

∞

On March 3, 1847, President Polk wrote in his diary that he offered Houston the appointment of major general in the army.¹ Houston declined the offer, and about the same time, he probably received the news of Margaret's illness. He left for Texas immediately. Upon arriving home he found that Dr. Smith, assisted by Dr. Bauers, had performed the surgery and that Margaret was slowly recovering.²

Dr. Smith had returned home where he wrote the following letter to Houston.³

Galveston Bay April 4, 1847

My dear General,

I hope this will find you at home, after a pleasant journey, and satisfied with the state of Mrs Houston's health. Her care seemed to offer a favorable prospect of entire recovery with improvement of her general health, and I trust confidently we shall not be disappointed. It was with some anxiety that I undertook so severe an operation in your absence, but an operation offered the <u>only possible</u> cure and its necessity was urgent. It is useless to mention to you that Mrs H. bore the pain with great fortitude. I rec'd Mr Power's letter a few days since—three days ago—saying that the wound was healing fine. Dr. Bowers⁴ goes to Liberty tomorrow. I have urged him to make a visit to Grand Cane. He was present at the operation, and is fully competent to dress the wound and give it all the attention it may require. If necessary I would make a visit.—I am moreover hoping to make you a short visit in the course of the spring apart from considerations connected with the health of Mrs H.

The letter you kindly forwarded to me came to hand. It was from Dr A. R. Terry, an old and dear friend of mine; we were roommates in college. He stated he had written to you respecting a surgeonery in the service. I should be sincerely delighted could he get one,—he is highly competent, of excellent habits, a scholar, and a gentleman. His acquaintance with the Spanish language, having practiced his profession three years in Peru, particularly qualifies him for the Mexican service,—that is service in Mexico. I hope you have felt authorized to speak a word in the right quarter.

I have been passing some two months or more on the Bay, for the benefits of my health. It seems now quite restored. I wish to resume an active life—but Galveston appears to me a narrow field whether for my profession or indeed any thing else. My life here is one of busy indolence—wading and looking after my planting operations. I had agreeable society in the company of Mr Allen & Mrs Ives who have been passing some weeks with me. Your course in the senate has of course commanded much attention and has given universal satisfaction. Your fellow citizens will again call on you to fill the same place whatever your private wishes may be. We are also looking to your being the candidate for the White House.

I am aware my letter is dull—but the "Bay" you know is not very <u>newsy</u>.

Allow me to present my us'l comp: to Mrs H. and Mrs Lea and believe me

Dear Gen. as ever, very truly yours, A. S.

[1]Polk, *Polk*, 200.
[2]For more information about Margaret's illness see Roberts, 150–53 and Vernal Lea to Ashbel Smith, February 24, 1847 (Barker History Center).
[3]Smith to Houston, April 4, 1847. Ashbel Smith Papers, Barker History Center, University of Texas.
[4]Dr. Bauers's name was also spelled Bowers.

Chapter III

August 7, 1847 to November 27, 1847

Houston wrote the following two letters to Margaret while away on business trips during the summer of 1847. The handwriting on the first part of the next letter is very difficult to read.

At Rankins[1]

7th Aug 1847

My Love,

I did not go to day. It is raining, and it would be senseless to expose myself. It has rained every day since I left home, and more-over I have been using Quinine, as you will see by my attempt to write.

You know my dear Love, when well or in health that I never stopped, but when sick, it seems I stopped. Today I have taken a dose of Oil. I think it is about the last medicine, that I will have to take. I will start home at the first moment in my power. Dont be alarmed at any reports of me. You *[The rest of the letter is in an unidentified person's handwriting, apparently dictated by Houston.]* could not come down at this time. For two weeks I am satisfied that no person will be able to cross the Roberson or Danville Road leading across the San Jacinto. I think it probable that travelers will have to swim to get to Davis' bridge on said river. Unless the weather continues un-commonly bad, I will be enabled to get home in a day or two. I am free from pain, and also from any like fever, and if it were a fair day, I would certainly start for home, in company with Mr Wood, a young friend of mine, who will hand you this letter.

Dr Price[2] has advised me not to write to you at all. The quinine has so deranged my nervous system, that I can not write at all, hardly, and you will find it so when you attempt to read this letter. My love, I left two letters, one for Mr. Stockbridge[3] and one to Mr. Brice in Sam's hat on the Piano. Which I forgot to send to the office. I hope however they are gone to the office. Present my love to all, and kiss the dear children twenty times.

[In Houston's writing:] Thy devoted

Houston

[1] The Polk County farm of Frederick Rankin. Identified in *New Handbook of Texas*, vol. 5, 444.

[2] Dr. John Howland Price. For a biography see Robin Montgomery, *The History of Montgomery County* (Austin: Jenkins Publishing Company, 1974), 150.

[3] Elam Stockbridge who fought with Houston at San Jacinto. Baker, 630.

Montgomery [Texas]
7th Sept 1847

My Love,

I am here, and will as I expect remain until the last of the week. I have seen Genl [James] Davis, and was happy to hear that all were well, and by him received Sam's command "not to stay to long, but come home." I will try and gratify him if possible.

If the hands are not engaged in getting in the corn, I wish them to be getting 3, or 4 feet boards, and making rails until I get home. The Boards will be important to my cribs, and stables. Let the sheep be kept up in the lot, or if they are let out, at all do not permit them to be alone for one moment, or they will run off, and mix with the flock, from which they came.

I have no news to tell you of, my Love, except that I have been offered some good fees, and there is a prospect of more. Your friends in Houston are all well. Dr [Charles] Keenan will take this letter.

My Dearest, I am most anxious to meet you again, and embrace you, and Sam, and kiss fat Nannie. Poor Sam. I hope his foot is well. Has his nose bled any since I left?

Give my love to Mother, hug Nannie, and kiss Sam.

Thy devoted Husband,
Houston

P.S. No news from the Army by mail.

Houston decided that Raven Hill was too remote for his family and purchased a farm with a small cabin in Huntsville about a mile from the center of town. While the cabin was being enlarged, Margaret visited with various friends. She wrote the following letter while Houston was at court in east Texas.

Gen'l Sam Houston
San Augustine, Texas

Huntsville Oct. 3rd, 1847

My beloved husband,

On yesterday, I enjoyed the unexpected pleasure of welcoming to our rude cabin Mrs [Ellen] Reily and the Maj. [James Reily]. I trust they will soon be with you, and I know you will be glad to learn they have been our guests. I am extremely anxious to be with you again, but this, I need not tell you. I left Gen'l Davis's on tuesday morning, accompanied by Carry [Davis] and the Gen'l. Our dear bro. V. [Vernal Lea] was very low, when I took leave of him, and I fear he is not long for this world. On yesterday, we received a messenger from the family, stating that he was better, but at the same time, we learned that he was under the care of Dr Baker.[1] When I arrived at home, I found Mother very ill, with an inflamed leg, which I realy [sic] feared was dangerous, but it is now much improved. The children seemed to have become almost wild during her illness, and I found my presence much needed. Mother's situation alone has prevented us from going to bro. V. Carry remained with me, until friday morning. I must not forget to tell you, that we came by Raven hill, and took our lunch in the old house. The family[2] were gone, and the scene was desolate indeed. I hope I shall be able in a short time to send a waggon [sic] for our furniture, for I do not like to let it remain there without protection.

Smith[3] met Joshua and took his waggon from him, so that Mr Moore was under the necessity of borrowing William Palmer to bring up his own things. Mother sent Bingley[4] and Brassos[5] down with Mr Moore two days ago, to assist in driving the cattle, and I am told that they brought up all except about 30. But I presume Mr Moore will write to you and tell you, all about matters. The children and myself enjoy fine health. Nanny talks a great deal about you, but can not make herself quite intelligible. With Sam, of course papa is the favourite theme. I send you two letters, which according to your request, I have opened. I supposed the contents might be of some importance, and therefore thought it best to send them. And now dearest, as it is sabbath evening, I will take leave of you, and endeavor to spend the remainder of the day in reading and meditation.

Thy devoted wife,
M. L. Houston

[1]Dr. Edward Baker. Identified in Emma Haynes, "A History of Polk County," 1937. Bound manuscript in the DRT Library, San Antonio, Texas, 21.
[2]The Moore family.
[3]Margaret may be referring to one of the Smiths from Huntsville.
[4]Nancy Lea's slave.
[5]Brassos was either a workhorse or a mule.

Nacogdoches
3rd Oct. 1847

My dear Love,

I wrote to you the other day,[1] and intended then to have gone by this time to San Augustine. This is sunday, and last night the court sat until after midnight, so that I did not get off. To day we intend to go part of the way, and be there when court opens.

I find my matters here in good condition, and entertain no fears, as to the result of my suits. The house & lot have become valuable, and the tract adjoining town of 325 acres for which I have sued Starr,[2] ought to be worth from $5 to $10 per acre. I was out to see the "silver spring" place, and found it a melancholy waste, but by nature alarming situation. I found the scite [sic] surrounded by springs, and bordered on the south, and east, & west, and north by piney woods. Yes, all around and in view of the house we could have a beautiful fountain, to play in the beams of the Rising Sun. There is no place in Texas more beautiful.

I regret intensely my dear, that you did not accompany me, on my trip. In the first place, it would have saved a thousand enquiries. In the next place, I hope it would have proved beneficial, to your health, and last, it would have added, inexpressibly to my happiness. As it is, I find that I am compelled to stay here, and experience a weary time. It was my intention, as you know to return in three weeks. I yet hope to do so, and nothing can detain me, but sickness, or the trial of Tom Palmers suit. I hope that you will excuse me, if I should detain for a <u>purpose so benevolent</u>, and kind to his wife & family. I hope it may be tried on the first week, and if it should, I will able to get home, by the time proposed.

I find that home is the only sphere of my earthly happiness. I hourly think of you and the children, and fancy how each one looks. I see Sam, the great, ruddy and Boatswain looking fellow, some-times exulting in a fancied triumph, and courting admiration and poor little Nannie retains her composition, on riding horse with her hands full of eatables, and smiling at her Ma's departure.

I will not (at so great a distance), tell you of the twofold charac-ter, in which I contemplate you. I hope the time is not distant, when I will enjoy the expressible happiness, of pressing you to my bosom. Present my best love to mother, and say I can judge of her manage-ment if I live to return. Smother Sam, & Nannie with kisses, for me. Tell Virginia howda, and say to the servants, that I will expect them to be industrious and faithful.

Thy devoted Husband
Sam Houston

P. S. Judge Sterne,[3] the Ladies, and all persons send their respects, and regards to you.

Houston

---

[1] This letter has not been located.
[2] Dr. James H. Starr. For a biography see Best, 337–38.
[3] Judge Adolphus Sterne.

To
Mrs. Sam Houston
Huntsville Texas
Captain A. Beck[1]

At Shannons[2]
27th Nov 1847

My Dearest,

I write to you with cold fingers. If Mr Royal[3] should come to work at the chimneys, you can tell him to wall the foundations well. Make the hearths large, and the fire places to suit you. About five feet wide, and by all means well floored.[4] But after these suggestions it is left with you so far as you may chuse to direct. What ever you do, I will be satisfied with. Do what you may think best. If you think well of it, I would have Robt Birdwell[5] to stay, at our home, until I return. If Mother is to shut the windows, of our house, and no one is to sleep there, I would have it nailed inside. If the servants don't do as they ought please to call on Mr Kelsey[6] to put them to <u>rights</u>.

My love to mother, howda to Jenny, and hugs, and kisses to our children. Tell Sam, that I wanted him to hug up in my bosom last night, and you may guess the rest.

Thy Devoted
Houston

[In the margin:] If necessary send for Mr [Thomas] King to cut out the places for the chimneys!

---

[1]Alexander Beck. Identified in Pauline Murrie, *Early Records of Nacogdoches County, Texas*, (Waco, 1965), 50.

[2]The Montgomery County plantation of Jacob Shannon. *New Handbook of Texas*, vol. 5, 993.

[3]Peter Royal, a brick maker. Identified in *1850 Census*, vol. 4, 2021.

[4]These fireplaces are still in place in the Sam Houston home, Huntsville, Texas.

[5]Robert Birdwell, the eighteen-year-old son of a close friend and neighbor, Thomas G. Birdwell. *1850 Census*, vol. 4, 2020.

[6]Thomas C. Kelsey. Identified in *1850 Census*, vol. 4, 1724.

Chapter IV

⌇

January 3, 1848 to August 11, 1848
The Thirtieth Congress (Second Session)

January 3, 1848: Sam Houston to Margaret Houston
January 4, 1848: Sam Houston to Margaret Houston
January 9, 1848: Sam Houston to Margaret Houston
January 14, 1848: Sam Houston to Margaret Houston
January 17, 1848: Sam Houston to Margaret Houston
January 24, 1848: Sam Houston to Margaret Houston
January 25, 1848: Sam Houston to Margaret Houston
January 26, 1848: Sam Houston to Margaret Houston
January 27, 1848: Sam Houston to Margaret Houston
January 27, 1848: Sam Houston to Margaret Houston
January 29, 1848: Margaret Houston to Sam Houston
February 2, 1848: Sam Houston to Margaret Houston
February 3, 1848: Sam Houston to Margaret Houston
February 4, 1848: Sam Houston to Margaret Houston
February 6, 1848: Sam Houston to Margaret Houston
February 9, 1848: Sam Houston to Margaret Houston
February 13, 1848: Sam Houston to Margaret Houston
February 14, 1848: Sam Houston to Dr. Alva Woods
February 17, 1848: Margaret Houston to Sam Houston
February 17, 1848: Sam Houston to Margaret Houston

February 19, 1848: Sam Houston to Margaret Houston
February 24, 1848: Sam Houston to Margaret Houston
February 26, 1848: Sam Houston to Margaret Houston
February 27, 1848: Sam Houston to Margaret Houston
February 28, 1848: Margaret Houston to Sam Houston
March 4, 1848: Sam Houston to Margaret Houston
March 5, 1848: Sam Houston to Margaret Houston
March 5, 1848: Sam Houston to Dr. Alva Woods
March 9, 1848: Margaret Houston to Sam Houston
March 10, 1848: Sam Houston to Dr. Alva Woods
March 21, 1848: Margaret Houston to Sam Houston
March 25, 1848: Dr. Ashbel Smith to Sam Houston
March 26, 1848: Sam Houston to Margaret Houston
March 30, 1848: Sam Houston to Margaret Houston
March 30, 1848: Margaret Houston to Sam Houston
April 3, 1848: Sam Houston to Margaret Houston
April 3, 1848: Sam Houston to Margaret Houston
April 5, 1848: Margaret Houston to Sam Houston
April 6, 1848: Sam Houston to Margaret Houston
[undated note]: Margaret Houston to Sam Houston
April 11, 1848: Sam Houston to Margaret Houston
April 12, 1848: Margaret Houston to Sam Houston
April 14, 1848: Sam Houston to Margaret Houston
April 20, 1848: Sam Houston to Margaret Houston
April 23, 1848: Sam Houston to Margaret Houston
April 26, 1848: Sam Houston to Margaret Houston
April 27, 1848: Sam Houston to Margaret Houston
May 1, 1848: Sam Houston to Margaret Houston
May 2, 1848: Sam Houston to Margaret Houston
May 3, 1848: Sam Houston to Margaret Houston
May 3, 1848: Margaret Houston to Sam Houston
May 7, 1848: Sam Houston to Margaret Houston
May 8, 1848: Sam Houston to Margaret Houston
May 8, 1848: Margaret Houston to Sam Houston [excerpt]
May 10, 1848: Sam Houston to Margaret Houston

May 12, 1848: Sam Houston to Margaret Houston
May 12, 1848: Sam Houston to Dr. Alva Woods
May 14, 1848: Sam Houston to Margaret Houston
May 16, 1848: Sam Houston to Margaret Houston
May 17, 1848: Sam Houston to Margaret Houston
May 18, 1848: Sam Houston to Margaret Houston
May 24, 1848: Margaret Houston to Sam Houston
June 2, 1848: Margaret Houston to Sam Houston
June 11, 1848: Sam Houston to Margaret Houston
June 12, 1848: Margaret Houston to Sam Houston
June 19, 1848: Sam Houston to Margaret Houston
June 20, 1848: Sam Houston to Margaret Houston
June 22, 1848: Sam Houston to Margaret Houston
June 24, 1848: Sam Houston to Margare Houston
June 26, 1848: Sam Houston to Margaret Houston
June 28, 1848: Sam Houston to Margaret Houston
June 28, 1848: Margaret Houston to Sam Houston
July 1, 1848: Sam Houston to Margaret Houston
July 2, 1848: Sam Houston to Margaret Houston
July 9, 1848: Sam Houston to Margaret Houston
July 14, 1848: Sam Houston to Margaret Houston
July 16, 1848: Sam Houston to Margaret Houston
July 21, 1848: Sam Houston to Margaret Houston
July 21, 1848: Sam Houston to Margaret Houston
July 22, 1848: Sam Houston to Margaret Houston
July 26, 1848: Sam Houston to Margaret Houston
July 27, 1848: Sam Houston to Margaret Houston
July 30, 1848: Sam Houston to Margaret Houston
August 2, 1848: Sam Houston to Margaret Houston
August 5, 1848: Sam Houston to Margaret Houston
August 8, 1848: Sam Houston to Margaret Houston
August 10, 1848: Sam Houston to Margaret Houston
August 10, 1848: Colley & Ballove Publishers to Sam Houston
August 11, 1848: Sam Houston to Margaret Houston
August 11, 1848: Sam Houston to Margaret Houston

Houston began his trip back to Washington around the first of the year, traveling through East Texas.

San Augustine
3rd Jany 1848

My Dearest Wife,

On the evening of the first, we reached here safe. I had only slept about four hours. We travelled day, and night, and sometimes stopped in the road, and remained until day light. The horses could not see, or would not keep the road. The second morning, we came to Nacogdoches, at day light, and so soon as the mail could be opened we left for this place, and reached here at night, in hopes to start on at day next morning. Instead of this we will be detained until tomorrow morning, [as] the stage omits one trip from this place to Natchitoches. This was to Mr. McCleny, & myself some disappointment, and we sought a private conveyance, but did not obtain one. We hope to have a speedy trip, but not by any means a pleasant one. I have now given you a detail of events. They are not very interesting. By stopping here I hope it has been some advantage to us, for I hope I will be able to find some 4 or 5 town lots, which I own, here. I will write to Mr Kelsey, and tell him, how and where to get glass, etc. If you want pickled Pork to support the hands, you will write to Torrey Bro. for it, or anything you may want. The Smiths have promised to get us such Glass, as you may want for the windows.

You may imagine that my journey was as gloomy, as it could be, for my affections, were with you, while I was wending my way, far from you.

Indeed, I was almost sorry, that our dear little Nannie had shown a fondness, for me, before I left home. It was enough for me to feel the loss of your dear society, and Sam's <u>fellowship</u>, without the dear smiles, and imperfect prattle of our dear little one. But I will, as far as it [sic] can, enjoy the hopes of hearing often from you all, and again seeing you. As for yourself, I will look, & hope for you in June.[1] I can hardly write, or think coherently, for my regrets, and anxiety about you. I hope all things will go on well. If they do not it is too late to mend them now, unless, I were to return. You must take some responsibility upon yourself, and in the event of any trouble in law matters, call on Col Yoakum.[2]

Write to me as often as you can my dear Love, and be cheerful. If you are lonesome, get some genteel young lady to stay with you, so soon as you have room, or even before then.

I have been in a hustle here as every person wished to see me, and they even wished me to make a speech, which I refused to do. Every person asks for you, Sam, & Nannie. My replies are that "you will be on in June," that "Sam is <u>not pretty</u>, but <u>good looking</u>, and Nannies Ma says she is the prettiest child in the world."

Present my kind love to Mother, and to Sam, with a kiss and "squeeze" our dear little one, and kiss her often. Tell Virginia howda, and tell the Negroes, that I hope they will all behave well, and assist in making a good crop.

Thy affectionate, and devoted husband
Sam Houston

[in the margin:] I will write at every port, at which I have time.

[1]Margaret was planning on joining Houston in Washington in late spring.
[2]Huntsville lawyer Henderson Yoakum. For a biography see *New Handbook of Texas*, vol. 6, 1121–22.

∞

Town of Sabine
4th Jany 1848

My Dear Love,

It was tuesday, this morning. To night I have been busy. I called to see Mrs Kaufman,[1] with my old friend, Col [James] Gaines. She says, "It is too bad for wives to be absent from their husbands so long." She will be on in May or June, and was delighted to hear that you intend to come on. In this place I found a relation, as we suppose. It is Mrs Austin,[2] the member of an old Firm at this place. They live in pretty style, and she played for us, on the Piano. They are remarkably genteel, and Pennsylvanians. Col Gaines, Mr McCleny & myself supped with them, and were most kindly treated. Mrs K. wished us to sup, with her, but we had been previously invited by Mr Austin. It is now after two oclock A.M., and the stage will start at 4. Tomorrow, we are to reach Natchitoches. The water is in fine stage, and there is hope that we may reach Orleans in three days. I wrote you from San Augustine.

Dearest you can have no idea of my unhappiness, caused by my absence from you, and our dear little Barbarians. I really enjoy no pleasure, in the society of any one. Some are more agreeable to me than others, but none can add to my happiness. I have not slept one half my needful time since we parted, nor do I expect to do so. You will think strange that I have not slept to night. Well, I will answer the enquiry. I met Col Gaines the first time for years, to day at the town of Milam. I induced him to come here with me. He has been here for 36 years. Was here at the commencement of the Revolution when Mexico declared her Independence, and has been here ever since. He knows more about the History of Texas, and its boundary, than any man now living. I have been taking notes of his knowledge of facts, as they may be of use to me in Washington.

If I close this letter now I will have time to sleep an hour and a half, before the stage will start. As I have said my Love, I will write, whenever I can.

Oh, if I could only see you and our dear dear, little ones again, how happy, supremely happy, would I be. I feel as tho' I had done wrong in leaving you, and yet I can not exactly condemn myself for so doing. At least there seemed to be a necessity, which I thought I could not eschew. I must now submit to the sad adversity. It was intended for the best, and for all of us.

Present my love to Mother, & Sam. Kiss him, and our little cherub. You are all present to me, continually, and I love to cherish the communion, tho' I know, and feel that you are distant, far distant from me. Tell Sam that I know he will be a good boy, and try to make his Grand Ma, & Ma happy, and love his little sister. He must take care of you all, as his Pa is not at home. If I live, I must try, and bring him a pair of boots, of the right sort.

Tell Virginia howda. Present me to all our friends. I have not failed to present you to many persons. Write when you can.

Thy ever devoted & faithful
Houston

[1]Jane Richardson (Mrs. David) Kaufman.
[2]Houston is possibly referring to the wife of Norris Austin. Identified as a resident of Sabine County in *Poll List,* 6.

∞

The following letter is in very poor condition. The bottom part is torn away, and some of the remaining words are blurred.

Steam Boat Heda
9th of Jany 1848

My very dear Wife,

It is now 4 oclock A.M., and we are about 110 miles above New Orleans. Since I reached red river, I have been detained, on account of Boats loading etc two days. I hope we will reach the city in a few hours. For fear that I may not have time to write from there, I have concluded to write to night. I hope to meet Bud [Vernal Lea] & Mr [Washington D.] Miller there. As it will be very cold on the Ohio, my inclination is to take the southern route. Should I do so, and it is possible . . . *[torn]* I will call . . . *[torn]* and see our relations . . .

[bottom of page is torn off] . . . travelling every night on the stage, while I travelled on land. This is the second Boat I have been on since I left Nachitoches. The passengers have been pretty nervous . . . *[torn]* general . . . *[torn]* My anxiety is so acute about home, as well as to reach Congress, so soon as possible, has been . . . to prevent my taking much part in conversation. I have suffered much from the pain in my eye, which was in part owing to a want of sleep, & have caught some cold. It is now well, without taking medicine, or

bleeding. Boat was detained . . . *[torn]* When I can have time, and will not be shaken twice by every revolution of a steam Boat wheel, I will try and say more to you, of my wishes, & my plans. I did not retire to night, as I slept an hour or two to day. The hands have risen to put the cabbin to rights, so I must case [sic], until I reach the city. The Mississippi is very high. It had backed the red river above Alexandria 140 miles. The Freshets up the Ohio, and some of its tributaries have been greater (as stated) than they have been previously and within the memory of many, and have done much damage. I am fearful, you will not be able to read this letter. There is no political intelligence of importance. I apprehend a boisterous, and angry session. The partizans [sic], of both parties, are to have great trouble, confusion, and dissentions [sic].

11th As I anticipated my Love, I arrived safe yesterday at 12 M. I was busy thro' the day, in arranging matters to be off by two oclock to day. I persist in the hope, that I will see our relations.[1] Yesterday, I dined with our friend [William] Christy, and the good dear Lady cherishes all her love of you. I received two tickets to the Soiree, from five Ladies. I went. Gen [Zachary] Taylor was there & Gen [Memucan] Hunt. These were not all—but some fifty others. I never saw so many Lions & Lionesses. I looked out of Cages, but did not enter the arena of wild beasts. Gen Taylor, Gen Hunt, Col Christy, *[torn]* hundred others, bade me present their esteem to you, and to Sam, & Nannie kisses.

I was pressed to visit the Theatre, and see the Dancers. Mrs Christy heard my reply, and positive refusal. It of course referred to your feelings, and your happiness, and the effect it would have upon them, on hearing that I had visited a Theatre. Then she decided that I was a clever, & very dutiful husband. The Soiree passed off, and I saw, and met many persons, of high character, which I have not seen in 18 & some in 20 years.

It is now 11 A.M., and at 2 P.M., I must be off. I have many things to do. As I pass, by stage, Steam Boat, & Cars, I will have but little time to write until I reach the city. If I live, I will write to you at every point, of the journey, if but a line.

240 : CHAPTER IV

Salute Mother with my love. Hug Sam, & kiss Nannie. So soon as I can have time I will write to you about a proposition, for you to come on in May, or June.

Thy faithful, and ever devoted husband
Sam Houston

[1]Houston was planning to visit the Leas and Roystons in Alabama.

∞

Priara Bluff[1]
14th Jany 1848

Dearest,

On yesterday at 3 Ocl P.M., I came here, and at half past 4 Ock. I was on my way to the Cane Brake.[2] I arrived at Bro Roystons, at 9 ocl, & surprised them as you may suppose. They were about to retire. Sister Virilla, & Tene,[3] almost smothered me with kisses. All were glad. Young[4] was at Columbus',[5] and was sent for. Robert was surveying, in the upper part of the county. I told them that I came for a moment, and must be here at two to day.

I answered all their enquiries about Mother, yourself, and the little Houstons. They were delighted. About 12 Sister disappeared, and Tene, until half past one. Bro R. until two. Young who had come in the meantime, & myself sat, until half past 4, and slept until half past six. Columbus came to breakfast and in company with Young, and him, I set out at 9 for the Bluff. They came about nine miles with me.

Columbus, and Cousin,[6] with the children,[7] will go down to Mobile tomorrow. Young, Tene, and Neantha,[8] are to accompany them. Tene has had the chills, and hopes the trip will help her. Neantha is to enter the Convent there to be educated. I told them that you and Mother, would be horror stricken at the idea, and tried to make objection, but it will be done. Tene looks pale, and a tinge of melancholy. I told her not to get in love nor marry but to visit us, and her relations in Texas. Nannie does resemble her. Their noses are precisely alike.

I had not time to see Aunt Lea.[9] Of course, I sent all love for you, & Mother to her and cousin. Aunt Eiland[10] is well. They are all well. Lucy Ann [Lea] has returned after a 12 months absence, grown, <u>improved</u> & beautiful. She is as large & tall as Tene. The family all talk in raptures of her. She must be a fine Girl. Bro Henry [Lea] has undergone no change for the better. I told <u>why</u> you did <u>not</u> <u>come</u> with me.[11] I told Columbus. His Daughter will be two years old in April, and he says in about five months from this time—you can guess!

My Dear Love, I have hardly slept since I left home, on account of stage, & Steam Boat. In Mobile Col McGhee, & myself called on Mrs Levert,[12] who had a thousand pretty things to say of you. I think she told us, that she had five daughters. Mr Jones[13] called to see me, when I presented your regards to him, & love to his Lady. I came up the river with Parson Hearn,[14] a methodist divine. He spoke much of you, and wished to be presented. Hundreds have asked me to present them to you, & mother.

The relations all send boundless love to Mother, you & Sam & Nannie. Her fame as a beauty, is not confined to Texas. Present my duty and affection to Mother—love to Sam, & kisses to our dear Nannie. A Boat is looked for every moment, as the hour has come. I am impatient to get on board. I will do all in my power to reach the city soon.

Thy ever faithful & devoted husband
Houston

[1]Alabama.

[2]The plantation home of Margaret's sister Varilla and her husband Robertus Royston. M. W. Hearne Papers, "Notes on the Lea Family," n.p.

[3]Serena Royston, Varilla's twenty-year-old daughter. Ibid.

[4]Varilla's twenty-six-year-old son, Young Lea Royston. Ibid.

[5]Margaret's cousin, Columbus Lea, the son of Margaret Moffette and Green Lea. Ibid.

[6]Elizabeth Parker (Mrs. Columbus) Lea. Flora D. England, *Alabama Notes*, (Baltimore: Genealogical Publishing Co., 1978), vol. 3, 3.

[7]The children of Columbus and Elizabeth Lea were Margaret, Knox and Wayne E. Ibid.

[8]Neantha Royston, the eighteen-year-old daughter of Varilla and Robertus Royston. M. W. Hearne Papers, "Notes on the Lea Family."

[9]Margaret Moffette (Mrs. Green) Lea, the sister of Nancy Lea. Ibid.

[10]Gincy Moffette Gray (Mrs. Asa) Eiland, the sister of Nancy Lea. England, vol. 3, 1.

[11]Margaret was expecting a baby in April.
[12]Octavia Walton Levert. For a biography see Brewer, 395.
[13]William Giles Jones. Identified in Brewer, 412–13.
[14]Houston is possibly referring to the Rev. William C. Hearne, identified in Wilson, Woodyerd, and Busby, 113. There was also the Rev. Ebenezer Hearne, a Methodist minister who lived in Camden. For a biography see William T. Hearne, *A History and Genealogy of the Hearne Family* (Independence, Mo.: Examiner Printing Company, 1907), 468–69.

∽

Griffin

17th [Jany 1848]

My Dear Love,

Yesterday morning I left Montgomery, and at half past ten A.M., I reached here after travelling 40 miles by rail road, and 100 by stage. In a few minutes I will set out by the cars for Augusta. Of course I sleep none, on the route only what I get in stages. I was one night at Montgomery. The Legislature was in session, and many of the Honorables called upon me at the exchanges. Among them, some of your old Beaus, and many of your friends. I was very kindly treated, and pressed to stay, a few days. This I could not do.

I met your relation Major Hubbard.[1] He has no children. Says she[2] is at Nashville, and he will let her know, why you did not come on. My trip has been as pleasant as it well could be, to have little, or no sleep. I constantly think of home, of you, and the dear ones. At times I am ready in heart to turn around and go <u>home</u> never again to leave Texas without you. *[torn]* . . . ask for you that you were coming on in June, and some the reasons why you are not along—others that you fear the <u>climate</u>, in winter.

I have only a moment to write, and will at every where I have time, to scribble a line. If you want Glass for the windows, as you must, call on Mr Smith,[3] or let King[4] do it. Have the House finished to your liking.

I am anxious to reach the city, as I hope to meet letters from you, on my arrival. Order the Servants to take care of the horse, and harness, of every <u>kind</u>. Mr Kelsey told me he thought he could sell the carriage for $240.00. If he can, let him do so. You have an excuse, to refuse lending them to any person.

Give my love to Mother, & kiss again, & again, for me, our dear children. Write to me all about them. Tell Jenny howda. I heard from her aunt, Mrs Dyer of Tuscaloosa. She is well.

Thy ever fa[ithful] & de[voted]

[signature is torn off]

[1]David Hubbard of Kinlock, Alabama. It is unclear how he was kin to the Houstons. For a biography see *Biographical Directory,* 1223.
[2]Rebecca Stoddert Hubbard. *Dictionary of American Biography,* Vol. 5, Part I, 322.
[3]Either carpenter James Smith or cabinetmaker Lemuel Smith.
[4]Thomas King, a carpenter. Identified in *1850 Census*, vol. 4, 2020.

Senate Chambers
24th Jany 1848

My Dear Love,

I have just taken the Oath of Senator for six years.[1] I have been very kindly received, by the Senators, & indeed by all persons, and all parties. On the evening of the 21st, I arrived after a singularly urgent journey. From the time I wrote you from Griffin, I never lay down until I reached this place. Notwithstanding this, you would be astonished, to see how much my health has improved. Every person remarks that it is improved since last session. There is a vast crowd in the city. So great is the press, of company, that I declined writing until I might have something to say, that might indicate how my time is to pass, as to personal comfort. Now I can say, that I hope to have a comfortable room, and my colleagues, near to me, so that we can often confer on business, & policy.

Our Presidential aspirants are on their <u>tiptoes</u>. If I were one, I would desire things to be as they are. The nation, has not spoken on the subject, nor has she even reflected. I <u>guess</u> Mr Clay,[2] will be the whig candidate of the convention. Genl Taylors friends wish him to run, but Clay will control the Party, as I think, and it is the general opinion Gov [Lewis] Cass is now managed to pass me up, but many changes will take place before matters will take a final direction. I will not my Dear Love, trouble you about these matters, as I do not think you feel much on the subject.

So far as I have seen any of my old city friends, they are well. Jack Houston & family are all well. Mary is in Philadelphia, so that I have not seen her. You may rely upon my writing as often as you may wish, I am sure. All that I can promise to write, is that I love you, and the children ten thousand times more (if possible) than I ever did. If it were not that I hope to see you in June, I would not be able to bear the absence, to which I would be doomed. What, eight months absent from my dear wife, & children? This would be insupportable! Order things as you please. You must do the best you can. I will approve what you may order, or direct.

I made such arrangements as I thought best, but I could not see all that was, or may be useful. So you must do, what I could not.

Present my love to mother, and kiss, oh kiss the little ones a thousand times. Then write to me, and tell me that you have do[ne] so. I know you have done it, and will do so, without my bidding, but the words in which you will tell me of the performance—the words spoken, and the little cherub's looks! I fear Nannie has almost forgotten me? I will write.

Thy ever devoted Husband
Houston

Dearest. Tell Sam I have already made arrangements to have a coat sent him.

Houston

[1]Houston had been re-elected to the senate on December 18, 1847. Friend, 187.
[2]Henry Clay.

∞

Senate Chambers
25th Jany 1848

My Dear Love,

245 : JANUARY 3, 1848 - AUGUST 11, 1848

As I promised, so will I write, if but a line. We have had a long prosing speech to day. In an hour, we hope to adjourn for to day. At 5 oclock, I have promised to dine, with the Secretary of State.[1]

Last night we had a meeting of the Democratic members of the Senate & H Representatives. I was called to the chair. The object was to appropriate a day for the meeting of a convention. It will meet on the 4th monday in May, to nominate a Democratic candidate for the Presidency. So you see this much is done. The Party are disposed to harmony, and I trust it may obtain.

My Love, I have nothing particular to write, only to present to you, assurances of increased affection, for your dear self, and our sweet "two children."

Present my love to mother, and give howda [to] Virginia. Tell Sam, not to be impatient about the coat & pantaloons.

Bless the little fellow. I see him hustling about, and his countenance beaming with exultation, about some fancied exploit, and little Nannie, dear love her life [sic], stumbling about, in imitation of her Grand Ma, and her countenance, lighting up at appearance of bro. Sam, or assuming a just preference, to her Ma's, or Grand Ma's lap. You have no idea my love, of my anxiety to hear from you & home. I have not heard a word, since I left my home, and the absorbing objects of my affections.

My Love, do write when you can. Begin to contrive with Mrs Reily, about coming on in June, or May. Don't regard the expense, or cost, if you can come. If you do not come, I will [be] miserable. Miserable because, where you are not, I can not be happy. No society, no charms, no pleasures, nor any thing on earth, can supply your presence. But I need not assure you of this. So soon as I can be at leisure, I will try, and write you, a right down "love letter."

Thy faithful and devoted husband,
Sam Houston

---

[1]James Buchanan, *Biographical Directory*, 16.

My Dearest Love,

It is raining. To day we had a fine speech on the war from Genl Dix[1] of New York. This being the case, I could not write, with any degree of respect for his situation, so I write this evening. There is a <u>Levee</u> this evening, and I may go after a while. The President would think [it] strange if I did not attend. I have not asked, but I think it is the first this session. To day I was called on by the "N. Y. Recorder" man. I will send you the account, and if it is right I will pay it. This will be as you say. I think you ordered it to be stopped, and Mr [James] Hutchins received the money to pay the subscription from Maj [James H.] Cocke. Let me know dear if you recollect how it was. I will write to Major Cocke, and ask him. If I should not, or should, do you write to him and ask him to write me, if you have not a perfect recollection, of the matter.

I do not recollect that I told you yesterday, that on friday next, the 28th inst, I have to go to N. York by invitation, to a Grand democratic meeting. I hope to return to my duty on monday. I tell you with much pleasure, that I heard from Major [Andrew] Donelson at Berlin, and he with the family, send a thousand regards to you & Sam. They have not heard of Miss Nannie's advent. Mrs D. has a fine son, and they are all in fine health, and pleasantly situated. Their Boy is named Martin, his mothers maiden name. Donelson alledges it was for "Martin Luther." So much for Diplomacy!

I hear the rain pattering at my window, and am carried back to Liddesdale in heart to my own dear fireside. Are you in a house with a "brick chimney and glass windows?" If I knew you were,[2] I would be less pained in my absence. I will at least hope that you are. There are rumours of peace here, but I place no reliance upon them.

My Love, I must tell you a most agreeable incident. Doct Mowry[3] of Rhode Island, wrote to me, and hoped that you, and the children were here. They sent much love to you, and press us to visit them. I will answer the madam,[4] or rather the Doct, and say that I hope you will be on in June with some delicate, and suitable apology. I may say, that "family matters will necessarily detain you until that time," that you will expect not to bring Sam & Nannie, but a <u>small portion</u> of the children! I will try, and say what I do so delicately my Love. Commend my affection to all.

Thy faithful
Houston

[1]John A. Dix. *Biographical Directory*, 140.
[2]The Houstons had been expanding their one-room house, and Margaret may have been staying in a cabin on the place.
[3]Dr. Samuel Mowry. Information furnished in a letter from Rick Stattler, The Rhode Island Historical Society Library, to Madge Roberts, April 21, 1995.
[4]Mrs. Robe Bellows Mowry. Ibid.

◯◯

Washington
27th Jany 1848

My very Dear Love,

As I suggested last night, I went to the Levee, and there I saw very many. It is needless to say, that in all my life, I never saw as few pretty ladies. I saw there Mrs. [Myra Clark Whitney] Gaines, and the good Lady as usual made many kind enquiries, about you. She has lately gained her suit, or at least in part.[1] She looks well, & the Genl[2] as usual, still erect.

I came home, and at 2 A.M. this morning retired from business to rest, was up to breakfast. I read before I retired the XV c. of Romans. I yet preserve, the forms of duty, but I fear tho' proper, in all the externals, that no change of heart, has taken place, and for this, I am not at rest.[3] I know, and feel, that all my hopes, & wishes are vain. I hope the prayers of the righteous, may be heard in my behalf, and answered in the salvation of my soul. I will omit no night, nor morning, to pray for those, who are so near to my heart, as you, and our dear children are. I awoke this morning dreaming of you. If the dream were not too long, I would relate it. I am sure you would not be offended, if you were not amused, at it. The scene was affectionate, for I thought I was kissing, and <u>you were not angry</u>!

I am, as you may suppose, busy, and business accumulating, instead of diminishing. Will you not get tired reading so much, & frequently, for so little? Often as I can I will write, and you will do so likewise.

Ladies are always good at invention! Write to me, and let me know if you cant devise ways, and means to come to the city with Mrs Reily. Draw on me, thro' any of the merchants for what money you want at <u>any time</u>, and for any purpose.

Love to Mother, Hug Kiss and "squeeze" the dear children. Tell Virginia howda.

thy faithful & devoted husband
Sam Houston

[1]Myra Gaines was involved in a lengthy litigation for many years before the U.S. Supreme Court ruled her the daughter and heiress of wealthy New Orleans businessman Daniel Clark. *Dictionary of American Biography*, v. 2, Part II, 124.
[2]General Edmund P. Gaines.
[3]Houston is referring to his struggle on deciding to join the Baptist Church.

∞

W City
27th Jany 1848

My Dearest Love,

I was about to retire, and found on my table, your note of the 5th Inst.[1] I was happy to hear from you, and distressed also. Poor dear little Nannie. I was distressed, because you, must have felt great anguish, and Sam poor dear lad, to think of his sad dream. I know how the boy must have been pained, almost as much as the reality. His bright mind suffers, in dreams, I fancy the most acute pain, and sorrow. I feel every day more sad that I pass from you. I would give thousands, if I could spend but a single hour with the treasures of my heart. When shall I do so? Ah when? From Col [Henderson] Yoakum

I received a letter of the 8th. He told me our little cherub was better, and told me what Sam said about the workmen. I do wish you were all comfortably [sic], in a house with "brick chimnies & glass windows." I hope ire this you are all comfortable, & happy in the new house. Have matters so fixed, as to make you so. I was happy to hear that Sister Ann, has a prospect of doing well. I will send you bro Charles'[2] letter again, as you may wish to have it. It is after 12 midnight, and I have to be off at six in the morning, as the Cars will start then.

I will write to bro Charley soon.

My Love, present me to mother, and kiss, & bless our weans.

Thy devoted & ever faithful

Houston

---

[1]Margaret's letter of January 5, 1848 has not been located.
[2]Charles Power.

Huntsville Jan. 29, 1848

My dear husband,

It is now three weeks, since I was violently attacked with pneumonia or winter fever, and I have never been able to write a letter since that time. I sat up long enough once to write a few lines to Maj Cocke and also to Houston [Moore], about Eliza's[1] baggage, hoping that on the next day, I would be able to write you a long letter, but I relapsed immediately and became quite ill again. I have suffered much anxiety lest you should be distrest at my silence, but I knew it would not do for any one to write for me, as I apprehended it would give you more concern than my silence, so I determined just to let you charge to the mails with it all.

On yesterday I rec'd yours from New Orleans.[2] It was a great source of happiness to me, and I will here tell you how rejoiced I was, at your refusal to attend the theater! Huntsville is pretty much as you left it. The people have had a good deal of sicknesses, but no deaths have occurred amongst our friends. We are not in our new house yet, but the mechanics seem disposed to hurry it as much as possible.[3] They had a good deal of biser's [sic] work to finish but one room is ready for me now, and I expect to go into it in a day or two. Our overseer took a fancy a few days ago, to run away and get married. He married a daughter of the widow Gilespie,[4] (herself a grass widow.) They were married in Crockett, as they could not get a license in this county, and from thence proceeded to Shrevesport—or somewhere. I do not know where. Col Birdwell[5] says if he does not come back, he will give our hands all necessary directions, and they seem so ambitious to make a good crop, that I think we will have no difficulty. I refer particularly to Prince and Joshua.[6] Albert I expect I had better hire out. Mr. [Thomas] King speaks of hiring him, and I expect he would give a good price. Now do not, my dear love I entreat you, do not give yourself the least uneasiness about the farm or any thing else that appertains to us, for we have the best friends in the world, who will attend to anything that we need.

Col. Birdwell, and his dear wife,[7] and Dr Evans and Mrs Evans[8] have been such constant untiring friends, during my illness, that I can never forget them, and I feel that the Lord has blessed me particularly with friends. I wish I could repeat to you, some of Mrs Birdwell's quaint remarks during the last few days. It is certainly true that she sometimes caused me to smile, when I did not know but in a few hours, I should be in eternity. Her soul you know will always speak out, under all circumstances, and one other great evil which she seemed to apprehend, was that a <u>prospective</u> branch of the family might be lost, and that must be prevented if possible![9]

Sister Katherine [Lea] came up to see me during my illness, but only spent one night, as she had left her baby[10] at Gen. Davis's.[11] The Gen'l's two daughters Manerva [sic] and Eliza are staying with me and going to school. I would not take them as boarders, but agreed that the Gen'l might pay something into the church fund. Now don't you scold, for I wanted company, and you know he would never let them stay on any other conditions. I expect Carry [Davis] up soon to make me a long visit. Mr Moore's family and ourselves are on the same footing, on which you left us.[12] They are doing very well I believe. They have hired a negro man, from Dr. Branch[13] and I am told are getting along finely. It is expected that Mary[14] and John Lehr will be married on his return from Miss. The little servant of thiers that was so afflicted, died soon after your departure.

Mary Wily[15] is the mother of a fine son, and I have heard that her suffering was trifling when compared with others. Truly the Lord is merciful to the afflicted, and my heart swells with gratitude, when I think of his goodness to her. I have not yet mentioned our little Sam and Nannie. They are growing finely and improving in every respect. Sam sees every thing about the place, that needs attention, and is a great help to me in this way. Nannie takes up your letters and pretends to read them, repeating again and again "papa papa." I have only rec'd three, but hope soon to get another. Mother and I were rejoiced to hear that you were going through Ala. She unites with me in much love to you. Virginia [Thorne] went home with sister Katherine. Sister Kate tells me, that she can not make any thing of Kitty [Hoffman]. I was grieved to hear it, but if she is preserved from vice, it will be something. Our preacher Mr Creath[16] has left his wife[17] to spend some weeks in our neighborhood. I am quite pleased with her. She is intelligent and agreeable. The members speak of buying a lot for them in Huntsville, and settling them here. Would you be willing to give them the lot you offered them for the church? On account of its nearness to the church, it would suit very well for a parsonage, but I will say nothing about it without your sanction. Do write as often as possible. I send you a carte blanche, to fill with the names of those to whom you would wish me to send messages of regard. My love is so entire that I am sure you have a right to distribute it amongst those whom you love. I could write longer, but I must economize my little strength, and take care of myself, for your sake and our children.

Thine devotedly
M. L. Houston

P.S. Did you meet a little note from me, on your arrival in Washington?

[1]Eliza was Margaret's slave.
[2]See Houston to Margaret, January 9, 1848.
[3]It is unclear where Margaret was living at this time.
[4]Elizabeth Gelespey. Identified in *1850 Census*, vol. 4, 2002.
[5]Col. Thomas Birdwell. Ibid., 2020.
[6]Prince, Joshua, and Albert were Houston slaves.
[7]Tirza Birdwell. Identified in *1850 Census*, vol. 4, 2929.
[8]Dr. William Evans and his wife Jemmia. Identified in Walker County Genealogical Society, *Walker County History* (Dallas: Curtis Media Corporation, 1978), 276.
[9]Margaret is referring to the child she was expecting.
[10]Temple Lea.
[11]Katherine Lea was the daughter of Gen. James K. Davis.
[12]The Houstons had apparently become estranged during the summer from the family of his sister, Eliza Moore. It was possibly brought on by the Moores' objection to the marriage of Mary Houston to William Wallace, the nephew of her first husband Matthew Wallace, on January 13, 1846. M. W. Hearne collection.
[13]Dr. John Branch. Identified in *1850 Census*, vol. 4, 2010.
[14]Houston's niece, Mary Moore.
[15]Mrs. A. P. Wiley (Mary Keenan). Identified in *1850 Census*, vol. 4, 2021.
[16]Rev. J. W. D. Creath. Ibid., 2010.
[17]Frances Creath. Ibid.

∞

Washington City

2nd Feby 1848

My Beloved,

I am happy again to write to you. The reason of an omission in my writing, was absence to New York. To save you the trouble of reading too much, I will refer you to the news papers for matters in general. You will see what is said by neutrals, and enemies, for no one has yet written as my friend. You will see in the N. Y Sun "what Mrs Storms[1] says of me, (as I am told she wrote the article)." It is different from "Corinne Montgomery."[2] Well, I returned in good health, and on last evening, I dined with the Prest. of the U. States.[3] The duty was assigned to me, to see Mrs President[4] to the Table. If you are not pleased with this matter, I am sure you will be pleased, when I tell you that a Miss Cobb, a Sister of Howell Cobbs, was there, and asked an introduction to me. After it, she made a pretty apology, and laid it to the score, of relationship, through you,[5] and said that thro' our Niece Lucy Ann [Lea], she felt well acquainted with us both, and Master Sam too, as the smartest child in the world. She is a very genteel young lady, & very unpretending. She is comely, but not pretty, (for really no one seems to me pretty, or lovely but yourself.) Dont think that I am consoling you, for I declare to you, I am in earnest! She really spoke of you as a relation, and regretted your absence. I found her that far congenial to myself. I told her you would be here in June, and mentioned the "asthma," "cold climate," and such matters, as would seem reasonable—but not a word of <u>truth</u>, or <u>falsehood</u>, did I tell!

I send you a letter from our brother William [Houston], that I know you will be happy to receive & peruse. <u>He is a brother</u>! I am pained, not to have received, but one short note from you, and that brought me such unpleasant tidings, of our dear little <u>one</u>. My heart, and life seem to be centered, in home, our own dear, dear home. If there were any substitute for home, I might hope to find it in the approbation of my public sentiment. Yet this has not one charm, only so far as it may reflect pleasure to you, or benefits to our dear off-spring. It is not ungrateful to me individually, but it has no charm for me. It has been my way of life, when I have felt conscious, of acting well, not to feel myself indebted, to the world for its good opinion.

I expect my Love, to make a speech on the subject of the war within the next ten days. In view of this, I must reflect some, but even this I hope, will not prevent me from writing often. The press of letters upon me is great, as you may suppose.

My love to all

Thy devoted husband
Houston

I have about 150 letters to answer now on my table. H

[1]Jane McManus Storms. *New Handbook of Texas*, vol. 1, 1052–53.

[2]Corrine Montgomery was Mrs. Storms's pen name. Ibid.
[3]James K. Polk.
[4]Sarah Childress Polk.
[5]Serena Lea was the aunt of Howell Cobb and his sister. "Lea Genealogy," the M. W. Hearne Collection.

Washington City
3rd Feby 1848

My dearest Love,

As it is very late, and I have had company until this moment, I have concluded to perform my daily task ire I retire to rest. A long speech by Mr Bell,[1] Senator from Nashville, which occupied two days, was concluded today. Mr. Sevier[2] of Arkansas, will speak to-morrow. The vote on the Ten Regiment Bill will not be taken for some 10, or 15 days, as I suppose. The Bill, I imagine, will pass without much difficulty, tho' a desperate effort will be made to defeat it. You care nothing about matters of State. Since I commenced this letter, my mail of the evening has come in, but no letter from my dear Wife. I saw in one I thought a female hand and upon opening it, I found it was one from a cousin.[3] You have seen her letters, I think before. I will enclose it for your perusal. She is a fine woman, and you will hardly doubt her politics. They are democratic clearly. On tomorrow I have promised to meet a family circle, at Old Mrs [Elizabeth] Watson's, and eat a piece of mutton. Should I see Mrs [Jane L.] Graham there, I will tell her to guess again! But my Love, you know that I have guessed already. The finery, I will send home I think by Mr Gray (Pleasant), if he should go directly home. I hope you will excuse me for taking the liberty, as I claim some right, in the matter. Tomorrow evening I will try, and write to you, and if I get any news, I will try, & tell it in an agreeable manner. I have no news to tell you, of the fashions here, for really, I know not what they are, only I see blue, & white bonnets very small. I will send you a letter from a brother of Mrs Hadleys,[4] who resides in New York. It will please you to some extent I know, and therefore I send it. Purdy[5] is the great democratic Chief of New York. He moves the masses, more than any one man in the city.

Present my love to our Mother. Hug Sam, & Nanny for me, and write what they say. Does Nannie change in her appearance?

Thy devoted Husband
Sam Houston

The steel pen is wretched!

[1]John Bell, identified in *Biographical Directory*, 145.
[2]Ambrose H. Sevier. Ibid., 143.
[3]Narcissa B. Hamilton, who corresponded frequently with him. Her letter of February 1, 1848, is in the M. W. Hearne Collection. In it she spoke of Houston's re-election to the Senate and the possibility of his being a candidate for the presidency.
[4]Mrs. T. J. B. (Piety Smith) Hadley. Identified in Karen Thompson, ed., *Defenders of the Republic of Texas*, (Austin: Laurel House Press, 1989), 24.
[5]Elijah Purdy. For Houston's correspondence with Purdy see *Writings*, vol. 5, 12–13. Houston to Purdy, June 3, 1847.

∞

Washington City
4th Feby 1848

My Love,

Today I ate dinner with Mrs Watson, and found all well. I saw there a little girl, her Grand daughter, of Nannies age prettily dressed, and asked Mrs Graham, to go tomorrow, and get Nannie one, also a plaid suit for Sam. I want to have them, and send them by Mr Gray,[1] if they can be prepared. If I only knew what to get for you, I wou'd send it, no matter what. Mrs G. said she would look out for some things to <u>suit</u> you. I did not tell her my <u>guess</u>, or <u>my reasons</u> for <u>guessing</u>. Whatever she gets, I will send it to you. If you want any thing let me know what it is.

I enclose you my Love, two slips, from the papers. One is from a N. York paper, and the other a "communication" to the "Union" which shews [sic] that a change has come over some people. My friends say it is strange the Union should publish any thing in my favor. I just give you these hints, for what they are worth. It is 2 oclk A.M. and so I must close, my letter. My Love no letters have yet reached me from you, since your note of the 5th Ult. I will not complain, as I hope to receive many letters, at once, and soon.

My love, do present my affection, and kisses to all.

Thy faithful and ever devoted husband
Houston

[1]Pleasant Gray of Huntsville.

⚭

Washington City
6th Febry 1848

My Dear Love,

On yesterday I did not write. I was not well, and remained in bed until 5 P.M. I took some medicine, and to day I am well. I think my indisposition was caused by cold. To day (sunday) I went to the Capitol, to hear a Lecture, by the Rev'd Doct Mathews.[1] It was to shew [sic] as I understood, that science was corroborative of the Christian Religion. It was clever enough, but I regret that I did not hear my Baptist Brother, as he would have interested me more I think. Washington is like Athens when Paul visited there. "They spend their time in nothing else, but to tell, or to hear some new thing." And they know more, than they are willing to perform. Hereafter, if I live, I will go to some church of your order. I have no prejudice against any thing intended for advancement of Religion, or Science. There is a very proper way to advance either, or both.

My Love, I wrote the above at three oclock. It is now eleven, and my time has been taken up with company in my room, and to no advantage. I learn to day, that Pleasant Gray started two days since for his home. I will soon I hope have, another opportunity to send you some articles, which I have named. I have no news, only that all my friends, send their respects to you, and hope to see you here in the spring, or summer. I need not say, who of all mortals, is most anxious to see you, and remain forever with you. Could you guess my Love? Try! I am crazy to see my home again. I dream of you, and our "wee ones." As yet no letters have come to me! I dont blame you Love, but I do the mails. I am certainly in a state of painful anxiety. I hope, and pray, for such news as will respond to my careful, and unceasing affection. Oh, my Love, the word affection embraces, every thing which relates to you, and the children. But of you, I often think when you alone are present to my mind. Your interesting situation requires all the kind, and soothing offices of affection, and tenderness. These it is not in my power to render, to you, when I am far distant, in every thing, but love, and devotion. It was vanity, in part at least, for me ever to leave my peaceful, and happy home. We thought it duty. Was it really so? It may have been right, but I doubt it. If you, and those I love, were with me here, I might be better satisfied than I am, yet not so well, as if I were at home. You know I dislike city life. Write to me my Love?

Thy faithful & devoted Husband
Houston

[1]Houston is probably referring to Rev. James M. Matthews of New York. Identified in *Dictionary of American Biography*, vol. 6, Part 2, 402.

⚭

Washington City
9th Feby 1848

My Dearest Love,

For two days past I have not written. The reason was that I had not heard from you. To day I did hear my dearest, but the news was truly distressing. Col Yoakum wrote to me (on 15th) that "you have been ill, but was convalescent, and poor Sam, has been afflicted with sore eyes." I will not attempt to describe my feelings, nor my distress. Before I heard, I had been painfully anxious to hear some news, from you, and when I did hear that you had been dangerously ill, for

I know it was so, I only had my fears realised. My self reproaches are increased, as well as my tenderness, and affection. The Col only wrote me a few lines, which did not place me at ease. I could not know how long you had been ill, how ill you had been, nor what your want of comfort had been. Had I been at home, I could have rendered some aid to make you suffer less than you did. I cou'd at least have given my presence, and sought to soothe your pain and suffering. I pray that we may meet again, and never be doomed to part while we are spared on earth. I drag a miserable existence. It must be so my Beloved, while I am absent from you. I feel that I am but half myself, and every day, seems only to protract my misery, and multiply my cares, and anxieties. You, I hope, are restored. I pray our dear Boy may not be injured by his affliction. Oh! I would fly to relieve you, or at least to minister assurances, of affectionate tenderness, of heart, if I shou'd be so unfortunate, as not, in some measure to alleviate your sufferings, and cheer poor Sam. In fancy, I have wittnessed [sic] both your sufferings, & his. I will hope by every mail to hear from you. I will write & write.

My dearest, commend me affectionately to Mother & kiss the dear little ones. Tell Jenny howda.

Thy ever devoted, and faithful husband
Houston

∞

Washington
13th Feby 1848

My Beloved,

Another Sabbath day has passed, in which, I was employed in reading the scriptures. I did not attend church. For two days I have suffered with the pain in my eye, as you know I am sometimes troubled with it. It is now easy. I did not have recourse to bleeding, but lay down, and was as quiet as possible, for me to be, in this place.

There is some fatality attending our correspondence. As yet my Love, I have received no letters from you. You can imagine my dearest, what my anxiety must be. I have not written every day, because I hoped each day would bring me some news from you and Home. This day I was oppressed, with care. I reflected on our Sunday mornings at home, when we could turn to each other, and feel, and see, that we were in the midst of our little ones. We too were society for each other, our thoughts were matters of expression, and one could sympathize, and feel happy, and contented, tho' our habitation was rude, & homely. We felt, that it was home, our own home. I will not complain. There is no one to blame for my absence, but myself. All that I can derive here, will be a poor recompense, for the deprivation of your society. I would not, for all the honors, however distinguished, barter your society, for the space of ten minutes. I could, & ought to be satisfied here, if it was possible for me to be so where you are not. Balls, and theatres, and soirees, are here, but I attend none of them, nor do I wish ever to be at any place of amusement, where you could not, or would not attend, if you were with me.

I have not seen your friend Miss Cobb since the first evening, and for this I reproach my self. I must do it, as she claims relationship with you. I will do it, on your account, but you know my Love, I ought not to tell her so, or she would set me down for a "Hoosier." Have you written to Mrs Reily about her trip, this coming spring, and reflected about coming on. Write to me my Love all about it, as well as every thing else.

I have seen the plaid dresses for Sam, and Nannie. They are pretty indeed. You may rely on my sending them by the first chance.

Give my love to Mother, and kisses to our treasures.

Thy ever faithful and devoted husband
Sam Houston

[In the margin:] I intend soon to write to Sam. The discussion on the ten Regiment Bill continues.

[Cross writing:] You will see my Love, that in attempting to save my paper, I used the inkstand in lieu of the sand stand.[1] It is midnight or I would write again, and from this letter, I know you will readily excuse it, as I have stated the reason of the blot. I have not written to Doct [Alva] Woods yet in the hopes that I would hear from you, and

have something particular to write. The Doct with many others wish me to visit Yankee land. When you can go with me, I wish to do so.

[1]Houston is referring to a large ink blot on the top righthand corner of the letter.

The following letter is addressed to Doct A. Woods. It is from the Alva Woods Papers in the Rhode Island Historical Society Library, Providence, Rhode Island.

Washington
14th Feby 1848

My Dear Sir,

Until now I have defered responding to your welcome letter. It has not been for want of a disposition to do so, but from a hope, that I should hear from Mrs Houston, and have something of interest to impart, to your excellent Lady, as well as to yourself. I have been disappointed. From a friend,[1] (for I have not heard directly from Mrs H) I have learned, that she had been quite ill, but was convalescent. Sam too was afflicted with sore eyes. Mrs H. has been attacked, with an epidemic called "winter fever." It has heretofore, in many instances, proved fatal. You can well imagine my a [sic] painful anxiety, until I can hear from my dear wife. I labour under self reproach for ever having left my family. I grant it was from a sense of duty as to my constituents, as I conceived, but that affords but little solace, for my absence. It was our intention for Mrs H. to have accompanied me, this winter, but it so happened that she did not deem it fit, or convenient, to come on, before the month of June. I pray that her health, and circumstances will enable her, to come on at that time. She will not expect to bring Sam, & Nannie, with her, nevertheless, she will expect to have <u>another</u> member of the family.

I need not assure yourself, & Lady, that one motive for coming on, will be the hope, of meeting her most valued friends, for such you are esteemed by her.

I will be unhappy until I can hear from home. So soon as I do, I will write to you again. In the meantime, I will be most happy to hear from you. Mrs Houston, sent by me, her love to Mrs Woods, and her best regards to yourself, and son.

Be pleased Sir, to salute Mrs Woods, with my most respectful compliments, and your son with my regards.

I am truly your obt
Servt [sic] & friend
Sam Houston

[1]Henderson Yoakum.

∞

To Gen. Sam Houston Washington city D. C. By Mr. Smith[1]

Huntsville Feb. 17 1848

My ever dear husband,

On yesterday, I recd 4 letters from you, all nearly the same date, proving to me, that you think of me very often, and I need not tell you, how welcome to me, is every assurance of affection from you. On tomorrow or the next day, I expect Mr Smith will leave for the north, and I have commenced preparing this letter for him, but my eyes are so much inflamed, that I fear I shall not make myself inteligible [sic]. They have been very bad ever since my attack of neumonia, which seemed to affect the whole system, and particularly the head and throat. When I last wrote to you, Mother's negro woman Vina was expected to die of the disease, but I did not mention it to you, lest it might excite your fears on my account, as I had had one relapse, and was then just able to sit up. She only survived a short time, and I can say with safety, that her death was one of the greatest trials I ever endured, first on account of the state of mind in which she died, and secondly because I knew she had died from the want of medicine, for Mother was so alarmed about me at the time that she had neglected her on my account. My dear Mother bore it with so much fortitude, that I felt like a mere pigmy by her side. But enough of this sad occurrence. I hope ere this you have seen brother Charley, and that he has told you about his great boy.[2] I recd a description of him yesterday from Mrs Dawson's[3] pen, and also an amusing account of Antoinette's management of him. There is truly great joy amongst them. I hope we will get a sight of him and of Sally's girl[4] during the spring, as I expect a visit from them. But I must say something about our own ones.

First on the list comes Master Sam, who says "Ma be sure to tell pa, that I go to the post office for his letters." So you will perceive he is realy [sic] becoming useful. I have never seen such a boy for business, and he sees everything about the place, that is not just right. When I read your letter to him, he was perfectly silent until I finished and then took it and of his own accord pressed it several times, closely to his lips, and exclaimed "this is a precious little letter!" He then handed it to me and said "Ma now do you kiss it." I took it and put it to my lips, but not forcibly enough to satisfy him, and he exclaimed "Ma that's not kissing at all." When the ceremony was ended he asked permission to put it in his trunk, which was granted, and there it is safely deposited. The boots although they are considerably scratched have not yet lost thier novelty, and whenever any removal of furniture takes place, from one room to another they are sure to go along. The most amusing change of locality took place not long since. I was fitting up the parlour, and in a great hurry, as I had the field hands engaged in lifting the furniture, when behold poor Sam walked in with the boots in his hands and with the greatest solemnity placed them in the first right corner of the room! But what should I say of Nannie, our little rose-bud? Well I will first tell dear papa, that he does her great injustice in supposing she has forgotten him. Far from it, I assure you, for she prattles of you asleep and awake, and when any one says to her, "let us go and see papa," she extends her little arms and looks bright with joy. Her pronunciation is very fine. The only word in her little vocabulary which she does not pronounce perfectly is "Jack."[5] She still calls for "Dack," and looks around with mournful anxiety. You must not feel yourself too much complimented when I tell you that she calls the man on the "aunt Eiland hunting bag" papa, and the dog "Dack."

Saturday 19th

Owning to the inflammation of my eyes, I have been unable to finish my letter, and I must now hasten to a close. My general health is good, and I hope will soon be firm. On yesterday evening, Gen'l Davis arrived with Carry, and she expects to spend several weeks with me. About going to Washington, I can not say much, until the great trial[6] is over. Then if the Lord brings me safely through, we will talk about it. I am sorry I can not see to write more, for I could say a great deal. I hope soon to write again, until then adieu my dearest love.

Thy affectionate wife
M. L. Houston

P.S.

All are well and send thier love to you. Albert is hired to Mr. King and the rest of the servants are working well. Kelsy is not returned and it is not expected that he will come back. Mr King's work is finished in neat style, and I am sure you will be pleased with it. We are now living comfortably, and pleasantly, and Sam thinks in princely style. He often asks "Ma don't you wish pa knew we were in the new house?" My love, can you not contrive some way to stop the "recorder."[7] I never subscribed for it but one year, and that was certainly paid by Mr Huckins.[8] I hope you will not pay for it, as I ordered it long since to be stopped and have only recd a few scattered numbers since that time. I will write to Maj Cocke or Mr Huckins about it.

Thine,
M. L. H.

[1]Margaret is probably referring to Huntsville merchant J. C. Smith. Identifed in *1850 Census*, vol. 4, 2002.
[2]Thomas R. Power, born July 3, 1847. Roberts, 381.
[3]This is probably Mrs. W. N. Dawson, who was a neighbor of the Bledsoes when they lived in Red River County. Identified in *Poll Lists*, 42.
[4]Sarah, the daughter of Sarah Ann Royston and Thomas Power.
[5]Houston's hunting dog.
[6]Margaret is referring to the birth of her third child, due in April.

[7]*The New York Recorder,* a Baptist newspaper.
[8]Rev. James Huckins of Galveston.

⚭

Washington
17th Febry 1848

My Beloved,

You can have no idea of my felicity, on the arrival of your welcome letter, of the 28 Ult. You were right in suffering that I had
"charged it to the mails" in part, but not entirely. I was fearful, that
you were too unwell to write, and that my friends did not wish to
distress me, until the result of your illness shou'd be known. Now I
feel as tho it was best that I should have been in wretchedness, for a
while. I am now so happy when compared with my distress, that I
feel, as tho it were best. Had I not sorrowed, I could not now rejoice,
as I do.

I will not attempt to depict, my joy, or my fears, until I heard
from you. Poor dear Mrs Birdwell. I can now feel amused at her
care, and solicitude. Did I not know her, I could not appreciate the
scene, nor fancy her quaint remarks. I was much delighted, at what
you say of Sam's usefulness to you, and his observation of all passing matters. Nor was I less happy at Dear Nannie's reading her Pa's
letters. I have fondly, nay, almost wildly, thought upon the scenes of
home. Dear little creatures, neither they, nor their dearer mother can
conceive of my feelings, my wishes, and my hopes, in relation to
them.

As to business matters my Love, do as you may think best, with
the advice of Mother. I am not, & can not be there, and I have made
up my mind to be satisfied! As to other matters my dear, in which
you feel much interested, I have to say, that I will not give the lot to
Bro. Creath (as Sam says) but my dear wife, shall, and I will ratify
her act! Now my love, the matter is your own! In the first place he is
welcome to it, and in the next place it will recompense me richly, if it
can add to your happiness, as I hope it will. Please see what Sam has

to say, about it, and write to me? I doubt if you present the subject fairly, and abstractly, that he will object!! Keep good works out of view, and see if does not!

I am rejoiced my Love, that you have taken, our young friends[1] for company. Leave it to the General, and me to settle the price of board, and I will make him pay a round sum, as the <u>church</u> will be the recipient, of benefits!

I now come to a matter, which touches me to my soul. I have a Wife, and a Sister, to the first, devoted as a husband. To the second as a brother, <u>indeed</u>. To think that my wife whom I dearly love,—the mother of my children, should be afflicted by Providence and I was absent, that my Sister[2] did not fly, and seek to relieve my wife, has confirmed me to the belief, that she has been mainly instrumental, in driving an excellent sister to madness.[3] I have wittnessed scenes of horror, and distress in the human family, but I deplore the fact, that none has [been] so distressing to me, as my own blood, or has ever so much distressed me, as the conduct of Mrs Moore. I have read the last sentences, and I know they are hardly intelligible,[4] however my Love, it is distressing to me, when I contrast the conduct, and feelings of bro William, with that of Mrs Moore. I never was able to do any thing for him, and his attachment is boundless to <u>us</u>. I have done every thing for her, and she will not exercise to <u>you</u> in sickness, the kindness of a stranger.

Do not my Love, suppose that I will take these matters to heart. I will blot them out of remembrance. I am rejoiced to hear, that <u>they</u>, are prospering, and getting on well. I feel yet, all the tenderness for Betty, and Mary,[5] that I ever did. In them there is no fault, and I will not visit the <u>sins</u> of the Parents, upon the children, for they have enough to repent of, and I pray that they may be forgiven! I feel grateful my Love, to our good friends, who have so kindly, sustained you, in sickness, and in trouble. Pray commend me to them, with all affection. Tell Col B.[6] that the farm is given up to him, if Kelsy does not return. Or if he shou'd return and you chuse to dismiss him, but it might be well to think of the sheep & goats. Consult Mother, & Mrs Birdwell, and see what they say. If <u>they</u> cant keep you out of difficulty, I am sure, if they were to try, they could get you into it, and a half dozen others!!! Expound this to them.

I was truly happy my Love to learn, that you were about to get into a home with "Brick chimneys, and glass windows." That will be nice. My Love think of this. If you do not wish, with the company, which doubtless you will have, to come on, in the summer this far, how would you like to come as far as the Cane brake?[7] If you fancy this, and I live, I will go there to see you, and spend a week. If I remain in the Senate, I will go on in the fall, and bring Sam and Nannie to you. Can't you leave them with Mother? Think of these matters, and let me know. Do as you think best, but my Love, you know how painful my absence will be.

Commend me affectionately to our dear mother, and a thousand kisses to our babes. Salute our friends.

Thy ever devoted & faithful Husband
Sam Houston

[1]Eliza and Minerva Davis.
[2]Eliza Houston Moore.
[3]Mary Houston Wallace.
[4]Houston had crossed out words in these sentences.
[5]Houston's nieces, the daughters of Eliza Moore.
[6]Thomas Birdwell.
[7]The Royston Plantation in Alabama.

∞

The following letter is from the Sam Houston Hearne Collection of Houston materials in the Barker History Center of the University of Texas.

Washington
19th Feby 1848

My Love,

I will not retire to rest, without saying to you, that I love, yes, dearly love you! I love Sam, & Nannie too, some, but you an infinite deal! I send you a ticket. You will see what is to be here. I knew nothing of the affair until Col [David] Kaufman bro't it to me. You may rely upon it, that I have no pleasure in such things, and if I go, it will be to bow . . . *[blurred]* and leave it. They can't get me here, <u>by urgency</u>, to attend the Theatre, tho, I hear there are two in the City. I assure you my Love, that I have not even seen the buildings to know them! It is only a sense of propriety, and regard for the feelings of my dear, that keeps me away. Tho, I have no earthly wish to go. Yet, were I otherwise situated, I have no doubt but what I might attend them.

I have sent tickets to our nieces, Tene, & Lucy Ann, and a kind note to each. I have seen Miss Cobb, and she sends much love to you. Her brother[1] has lately lost a child and has another quite ill. Poor fellow looks sad!

Salute Mother, & kiss our dear Cherubs.

Thy ever faithful and devoted husband,
Houston

[1]Howell Cobb.

∽

Washington
24th Feby 1848

My dearly beloved,

On last night I wrote you a long letter, of several pages, and after two oclock was about to scatter the last sand on it, when I made a mistake, and took up the ink stand, and poured the ink on the letter. In this plight I wou'd not send it to you, and burned it. To night, tho, it is after 12 M. I will try and do better. Two days since I received a letter from Cousin Columbus [Lea], and in it he said all were well. He was just from Marion, and said Bro. Henry had joined the "Brothers of Temperance." He had kept his pledge for five days, and his prayers, and hopes were that he might stand to his pledge. I write this my Love, because I know you will rejoice indeed, and to our dear mother, it will give real solace. We must hope that it will be effectual, under Gods blessing!

My Dearest Love, you can have no idea of my press of business, and the number of letters which I receive, and I declare to you, that one letter from you, gives me more real pleasure, than the hundred which reach me, no matter whether they are of <u>praise</u>, or <u>business</u>. I was in hopes that I should by this time have word from you again. I need not write to you every day, for you would hear from me as often if I only write twice a week. I will to be sure write oftener, but you will not hear from me more frequently! You may, my dear, if you will blame me, and I will hear it all, if you will. I have only seen Miss Cobb twice, and have never called upon her yet, but—I saw her in the Senate, and told her of your letter. Seeing I was so happy on its receipt, she expressed a wish to see it. I told her she could not understand, but as she insisted, I told her, she should see it, and I accordingly sent it to her. Since then I have not seen her. I feel queer, for fear I will have to explain the expression of "a prospective branch of the family" for which our dear friend Mrs Birdwell was so much <u>concerned</u>! You see my Love, how liable I am to get into difficulty! She, may not press the enquiry, or explanation, and if she does not, I will get clear of the embarrassment. I will send you a news paper, which will announce the death of Mr Adams.[1] From time to time, I will send you such news, as I hope will interest you!
My love and kisses to all!

Thy faithful & devoted Houston

I have declined going to the Ball, and had refused to visit the Theatre, and see the battle of San Jacinto performed. Is not this wonderful?
Our Cousin Jack[2] has written to you!

[1]For an account of the death of John Quincy Adams see Benton, 707.
[2]John Houston.

◯◯

W. C.
26th Feby 1848

My Love,

I send one of our dear Boys papers, & as I got Genl Rusk to send you a speech of his,[1] I concluded to write this note, lest his <u>frank</u> might make you feel for an instant, unhappy. To day we interred Mr Adams, & it is the 3rd day in which nothing has been done.[2]

Tomorrow is Sunday. You will see that there is a Treaty before Congress.[3] I can't tell you any thing about it but what you see. I have only received one letter my Love, and you may judge how I feel in consequence of the fact. I declare that you are the last object, that leaves my mind at night, and the first, that I greet in the morning. You are present to me a thousand times in the day. Dear Sam & Nannie too are often present with us. I would rather see you all for one day, than realise all that this place cou'd afford me in years.

Do my Dearest Love, present me to Ma, and your young companions. Kiss the dear children, and believe me ever thy devoted & faithful husband.

Houston

You see how much my hand is altered. Tho, I am fat, and I fear becoming much larger than usual, I get no exercise!
Do my Love write me all about your health etc.?

[1]This was probably Rusk's speech of February 17, 1848. For excerpts see Clarke, 168–70.
[2]For a description of the funeral see Polk, *Polk*, 311–12, and Benton, 708–709.
[3]The Treaty of Guadalupe Hidalgo which ended the Mexican War. For the terms of this treaty see Benton, 710–11.

Washington
27th Feby 1848

My Beloved,

To day, I went again to hear, a Lecture by the same Divine,[1] on the subject of Theocratic Government—That of the Israelites. He failed in imparting the interest, which the scene between Saul, and the people of Israel would do, if well read by a man, who could embrace in his mind, and heart the interesting occasion. I surely, if spared to another sabbath will go to hear our Baptist Brother.[2] He is always interesting, and unites, (I hope) evangelical piety, with his preaching. I received to day, an invitation to go as far [as] Portsmouth N. Hampshire, to make a democratic speech. I fear the business of the Senate will detain me. The Treaty will come up on tomorrow for discussion. I am preparing for the occasion, as I presume there will be a contest. You may my Love, rest assured, that I will be as I have always been, (when even at your side) always on the side of my country. That I may find it my duty to oppose the Executive, I think most probable. I tell you this that when you hear it as you may, you will be prepared for the event, and not suppose me taken by surprize [sic]. All my actions arise from reflection, and are not the result of accident, or impulse. I would write about some other matters, but as they, are properly of things which pertain to men, I will reserve them for a week day.

At church I saw many mothers, and little children. You will fancy my feelings, when I was far from you, from home, from Sam, & Nannie. Yes, all that I love. Since I came here the weather has been fine. Not colder, than our sunny home. You have warm weather, I hope unless you are in <u>Sam's</u> <u>fancy</u> <u>house</u>! That house, Oh how I do want to see it, and be in it, and stay in it my dear, and talk of seperation, but never feel it more. My Love, I wish you would tell the Boys to take care of the harness, saddles, etc. I think I wrote to [David] Torrey for three blind bridles, if they have not come please write for them. They will be useful in ploughing.

Order, and use whatever you want. Tell Jack Davis[3] to leave Davy Crockett, as he comes home, or to send him back. He is a fine plough horse, and he will be killed at Genl Davis. Dont make a fuss on my account, but if proper let matters rest. I hope the corn ground, will all be planted with peas, & pumpkins, when it will not injure the corn. Let as much be put in Sweet Potatoes, as can well be. They are said to do as well from the vines, as the <u>slips</u>!

You will please present me kindly to Dr Evans, & his family for their kindness to you my dearest Love. I will always love them, and all others. I feel almost crazy again as no letter come [sic]. I am beginning to hate Cave Johnson,[4] & every Postmaster, and mail contractor between this and Huntsville. It will be best for you to send your letters, "Via Natchitoches." In this way, I hope they will reach me.

Give my love [to] Mother, & the Miss Ds. To Col & Mrs Birdwell. If any travellers shoud [sic] represent themselves as my friends etc receive them with many grains of allowance, & let them pass.

My dearest I can not tell you how much I love you, but I can assure you, that it is enough, while absent to make me miserable, and when present happy.

Kiss our dear <u>ones</u>, and write to me what they say, and as Sam says, "Ma what did I do when I was a little baby." Let me know, what he does, when a "gate b-e-g-e" boy.

Thy ever faithful & devoted husband,
Houston

[1]Rev. James Matthews.
[2]George Samson.
[3]The son of General James K. Davis.
[4]Postmaster General during Polk's administration. *Biographical Directory*, 16.

∞

Huntsville, Feb. 28, 1848

My Dear Love,

When you left me, I little thought I should ever be so much in your epistolary debt, and I feel pained, when I recollect, that this is only the fourth time, that I have written to you, but that which is providential needs no apology, and no other hindrances dearest, I assure you, could have restrained the expression of my continued devotion to you. I have been a constant invalid since a few days after you left, and have had a sick family, but we have all now the promise of good health, white and black, except Mary, and I fear she is consumptive. I have sent her to Dr [William] Evans (our neighbor,) that he may have her constantly under his care. By the last mail, I recd quite a package from you. I can give you no idea, how much I was cheered. Until then I did not receive yours from Ala, and was quite at a loss to know whether or not you had visited our relations, but I discovered from the postmark that the letter had been to Huntsville once, and miss-sent.[1] By the same mail I recd one from Serena [Royston], that was full of your visit—short as it was. Carry Davis is still with me, and is a great comfort to me in your absence. Mr and Mrs Creath spent last week with us. They left us on last monday in fine spirits. Thier little boy was then in blooming health, but since that he has fallen asleep in Jesus.[2] He died at the widow [Katherine] Hatch's and the bereaved parents seem almost deranged. Our dear little Nannie was attacked at the same time, in the same way, (from cutting the eye-teeth,) but with the blessing of God, the disease was checked. How merciful is he unto the weakest of his servants!, for I tremble for my fortitude, should it be tried in the same way.

Bro V. has just made a visit. He left sister[3] and the boy[4] well, and looks exceedingly well himself. I wish you could have looked in upon us, a short time after his arrival. Little Nannie suddenly discovered that it was a joyful occasion, but watched us all very closely, for a length of time, now and then casting a sly glance at her uncle. At length she seemed determined to fathom the mystery, and peeping from behind her grand ma's chair, she looked at him with a most bewitching smile, and exclaimed "papa!" Poor little thing, it was almost too much for me. Sam and I have many a long talk about you. He wished me to store away every smart thing and good act of his, until you come home. He is as fond as ever of flowers, and watches with care, those that are planted, that they may bloom for dear papa. Our home is looking cheerful and pleasant. The rubbish is cleared from the yard and every thing looks neat and comfortable. The woods too are glowing with the first smile of spring. How I wish you were with us at this balmy season! But it can not be, and I will not sadden you with my regrets.

My Love, when you left us, you were anxious to get some one to look into your land matters, and I discover that bro. V. would be willing to undertake it. He has rented out his farm, and he tells me, that if you would like to entrust it to him he would ride over the country and arrange everything that is unsettled. You can write to him, if you think proper, and give him the necessary instructions. Our family is a <u>growing</u> one, and we must not be insensible to thier interest. I know that you will not be. Hereafter I hope to write to you every week, and every mail to get a letter from you. Mother sends her love to you. Farewell my ever dear Love.

Thy devoted wife

M. L. Houston

P. S. Our boys commenced planting corn on yesterday. Several of our neighbors are ahead of us, but we had such a cold spell of weather, that I do not think they will gain anything by it. Kelsy[5] is evidently run away, to the great detriment of many persons.

[1]See Houston to Margaret, January 14, 1848. The letter had been sent to Huntsville, Alabama.

[2]Samuel W. Creath died February 22, 1848. Lucy Alice Bruce Stewart, Verna Baker Banes, and Anthony V. Banes, compilers, *Walker County Cemetery Records* (Huntsville, Tex.: Walker County, Texas, Genealogical Society, 1992), 144.

[3]Katherine Lea.

[4]Temple Lea, born July 3, 1847. Roberts, 381.

[5]The overseer.

Washington

4th Mar 1848

My very dear Margaret,

For days past in the hope of hearing from you, I have not written. The mail comes twice every day, and for many days past I have, with eagerness seized, and tore open, many letters from Texas. But one letter from you has yet reached me. As late as the 12th of feby, Col. Yoakum wrote to me, and told me all were well. This was great gratification to me. He also stated that the hands were getting on well, and that you had all enjoyed spring since I left home. If I had only enjoyed the happiness of hearing from you the same things of that date. If you have not time, or can [not] by any means write to me at length, just write me three words, "all are well," and I will be happy, compared to what I now am. Only write in pencil, and that will satisfy me, when better can not be done! I wrote to you my Love to send your letters by Natchitoches. Owing to recent arrangements of the mails, it may be well to let them (the letters) run their chances by the Gulf.

My dear, I am truly at a loss to know, what to write. We have a Treaty of peace before the Senate, but my opinion is that it will, if ratified by the Senate of the U. States, amount to nothing. This is private, as I have to act on the instrument.[1] I want peace,—an honorable peace, or war for a thousand years.

My dear, I see that my speech at Tamany [sic] Hall in N. York,[2] is published, in all the democratic papers which have been received here since it occurred. I sent to Col Yoakum a pamphlet, published by the Albany convention, to which an imperfect copy of my speech was appended.

There is a severe contest, in N. Hampshire, between the Democrats & Whigs, in the coming election, which will take place, on the 14th Instant. I have been invited, by a committee at Portsmouth, and by the representation here to go on there, and make a speech, which will embrace the rights of Texas, and the justice of the War. At the instance of these considerations, and the advice of my friends here, Genl Rusk & others, I have concluded to go on. I intend to set out on Monday, or Tuesday next. I expect to be absent some eight, or nine days. I will call, I think, and see Dr Woods & Lady[3] and show him, that I can be (for a short time at least) a decent man, and as madam said to you "Shake hands, with the Yankees."

You may rest assured my Love, that I had no hand in this contrivance, in this matter. At first I declined, and did not think that I should visit the East until I shou'd have the pleasure of your company at some future day. We have snow here, about six inches deep, yet the weather is mild, and is now thawing rapidly.

The winter is quite gay, and I hear of parties every night in the city but sunday. I have been at but one private party here, and that was at Mr [Thomas] Ritchies. It was proper that I should be there, as some notice would have been taken of it, of political character. I have to watch here, and be seen without <u>seeming</u> to see! There is much casting about here, amongst the <u>wire</u> workers. I intend if you will say so to me, to write you about politics, of this region!

Major Reily is here, and will sail for Europe in a few days. He is very well, and in good spirits. Your friends by the hearing of the ear here, send you a thousand regards to you [sic].

I want you <u>dear</u>, to write to me, at least once a week if but a word, and let me hear that <u>you are well</u>! I am sure my Love, if you only knew, or could realise how often, how ardently, I think of you, you would minister to my love, as far as distances can, or will permit. Of Mother I am anxious to hear, and how she gets on with her farm. How is her health—is she happy? and has she become satisfied with the prospect of having Sam & our "wee Nannie" curtailed in their prospect of fortune, by multiplying their <u>competition</u>. This was to my mind, one of the strangest reasons, that I ever knew of in my life. It is a most "restrictive system" in family matters. For my own part I can not subscribe, to it, no more as husband, than I would as a statesman subscribe to the doctrine of the Tariff of 1842. If we are to judge of the future by the past, we have not much to dread! I can say to Mother, as a scotchman once said to a friend, who was reproaching him for something which he could <u>avoid, "It is a very easy matter for bystanders to make observations</u>." Persons who reason abstractly, and not actors, in matters, do not feel the influences, which will to a greater, or less extent control <u>the actors</u>. I wish you would my Love be so good as to refer this whole matter, to our excellent friend Mrs Birdwell. I will abide by her decision, and if any doubt arises, you can call in Mrs Doctor Evans, and I will wager any amount, that Mother will be over ruled, in her opinion, or I had better say her objections. Her opinions, she never changes. It is certainly a matter of thrilling anxiety to me, the fate of those interested in the matters referred to. My very dear Love, I constantly desire to know how you are <u>getting</u> on. About the result, I have no evil forbodings [sic], but hope you will do well, and have a good time! I hope your cheerfulness remains, and will continue. At times, I reflect until I am ready to fly, and leave Washington, and all here behind me. My love, my hopes, my all are with you. The idea of distance, and the pain of absence, at times, almost burst my heart. Yet I look to my God, and pray for your safety, happiness, & preservation.

My dear Love, present me kindly to Ma. Kiss our dear children. Salute all friends. I do hope, that I may yet hear from you before I go north.

Thy devoted & faithful Husband
Sam Houston

I cant get time to read this letter.

[1]Houston was opposed to the Treaty being negotiated by a private citizen, Nicholas Trist. Eisenhower, 366–67. His speech was recorded in the *Senate Executive Document* No. 52, 5, and is quoted in part in Faulk and Stout, 190, 232n.
[2]For a copy of this speech see *Writings*, vol. 5, 29–36.
[3]Dr. Alva Woods and Elmira Marshall Woods.

Washington
5th Mar 1848

My dear Love,

As I know, or believe it is in my power, to make you doubly happy by writing, I will certainly do so, by enclosing a letter from our friend Doct Woods. Truly it is late sunday night, and I ought to be reposing. To day I was to hear the Rev'nd Mr Cushman[1] preach a fine practical sermon, on the subject of offerings. "If thou bringest thy gift to the altar, and rememberest, that thy brother hath aught against thee, etc" was his text. It was the first sabbath, in Washington, which I recollect, that I had no <u>change</u> to give a mite to the church. As I expend none in going to Theatres, and Balls, you will desire me to give a portion of my savings, to the ends of Religion, and education.

My Love, I have not received any letter, or letters, since I wrote last tho' a mail has arrived from Texas. This is not said in the language of complaint, or reflection, but in the kindest feeling of regret. Either tomorrow, or the next dawn, I intend to set out north, and will give the Doctor (Woods) notice when I expect to be in Providence. It will be on my return from Portsmouth, & Concord. You may rely upon it my Love, that I will do my best to be very clever, on your account, as well as my own. So that if Sam, should ever wish to marry in the East, it will be of advantage to him. This is rather a remote calculation, but you know, it is statesmanship, to look far ahead, if results should fail.

I intend to take on to New York, the articles for the little ones, and send them by Mr [David] Torrey. I will direct him to send them direct to you, as he will take them in his Trunk.

In the hope that tomorrow I will hear from you, I will not say more, intending to inflict upon you a long letter, some other time. You will recollect Master Sam's "purple boots," I am sure! I wish you to take the measure, of the length (heel, & soal [sic]) of those which he had, when I left, and sent [sic] it to me—a slip of paper.

Nannies shoes, sent by Mrs Graham are "right red" as Sam used to say. The other articles which she has sent, she says were for "Miss Margaret Lea." I guess she is mistaken, but I was so modest, that I did not tell her so.

My affection to our Mother, and love to the dear dear children. I have not room to tell you how much I do love you.

Thine ever
Houston

[1]Rev. George L. Cushman. Identified in England, vol. 3, 42.

∞

The following lettetr was written to Doctor Alva Woods and is from the Alva Woods Papers.

Washington
5th Mar 1848

My Dear Sir,

I thank you most truly for your kind favor, which I forwarded to Mrs H. an hour ago. I do not expect to pass by Providence, on my way North. So soon as I can reach my destination, or before, I will with great pleasure say when I can have the pleasure of seeing Mrs W, and yourself. I apprehend my stay will be much shorter from necessity, than it would be if my inclination were to limit the period. I hope, when I have the pleasure to meet you, that we will be able to make the most of time. I do not care about, what is called "good eating," and as for repose I am always willing, to exchange half the hours allotted to it, either for talking, or listening.

I pray you to render my homage to Lady, and beg her to accept my thanks for her intention to write to my dear Margaret. My salutations to your son.

I am most truly
Your obt Servt & friend
Sam Houston

Huntsville, March 9th, 1848

My dear love,

On yesterday, I recd yours of the 13th ult. I feel so pained to think of the suspense, which you must have endured, during my long illness, but my dear husband I am sure will attribute to my affection for him and regard for his peace, the silence that was present during this time. We had not a friend that could have written to you and explained with candour, more than a faint hope of my recovery. But it is past, and I have now abundant cause of thankfulness to my Heavenly Father, for the fine health, with which I am blessed.

I have not yet written to Mrs Reily about our trip to Washington. I hardly feel that it were right to say much about it at present, but I am perfectly aware, that if all the arrangements are not made before the great trial[1] is over, it will then be too late in the season, to begin them. So I will just say, that it is my present calculation to set off the latter part of may or first of june. If I go, I must take Sam. His character is developing so rapidly, that I think nothing ought to induce me to leave him. That he is uncommonly talented, no one can doubt, but he has a disposition, which I fear will imbibe too readily, the character of things around him. I have never seen a child so devoted to a mother, and I believe for the sake of being with me, he would resign any play or amusement, though my conversation might be of the gravest character. I am sometimes accused of partiality, but it is not just. A mother like a good Gen'l, ought to watch that part of her little force which is most exposed to the foe, and it is this, which causes me to feel more concern about our dear boy, than the little cherub. My Love, she is perfectly beautiful, and realy looks like the embodying of a poet's dream. Oh, if the Lord will only make her soul as lovely, how blest will be her parents. Let us plead with the Shepherd of Israel, to bring our little lambs safely into the fold, ere the world has stolen thier young hearts. I must hasten to close, as I believe the mail will start very soon. By the next mail, I hope to write you a long letter. Oh, My Love, if you could only know my anxiety to be with you, I believe you would almost drop every thing and come to me. I am just about starting to Col. Birdwell's with the children to spend two or three days. Mrs B. thinks I am yielding too much to despondency, and you know that is contrary to your rules. We are working the crop with Prince, Joshua, and Bingley.[2] Mother thinks they will do well. She bids me tell you, that the work shall go ahead, and medicine too if it be needed. The notable <u>Brasos</u>[3] does his duty well in the field. What shall I do about my expenses to Washington? You tell me to draw on you, but please say how and where. You know, dearest, I am not very wise in money matters. Gen. Davis says Col. Williamson[4] will let me have some when he sells his cotton, but I do not know about it.

[In margin:] Mr Smith is getting corn for us as a result that Kelsy had none. I used all mother's money in buying meat which fortunately was driven into our lot at 4 cts. We saved it very well.

[letter is unsigned]

[1]Margaret is referring to the impending birth of her third child.
[2]Bingley was Nancy Lea's slave.
[3]A mule.
[4]Robert McAlpin Williamson.

The following letter is addressed to Revd Doct A. Woods in Providence, and is from the Alva Woods Papers.

Concord N. H.
10th Mar 1848

My Dear Sir,

I will be engaged, or rather detained, from Providence, Rhode Island until, the morning. Cars from Boston on the morning on the 15th Inst. I regret truly, that it will only be in my power, to remain until the 16th, as on that afternoon, I have to be at Norwich. I have been invited to address, the people of Boston, on the evening of the 14th in relation to Texas. If I shoud do so, I intend to set out by the first train of Cars, thereafter.

I pray you, my dear Sir, to present me to Lady, in most acceptable terms, and salute with my regards your son.

I am Truly
Your Friend
Sam Houston

Huntsville, March 21st, 1848

My own dear Love,

I was quite enriched by the last mail. The treasures which have been detained from me, by the high waters, until I was almost in despair, at length were received, and I had the exquisite pleasure of reading <u>more</u> than once, quite a number of letters from my beloved husband. It is no little comfort to me, to learn that you have at length received a letter from me. I can well appreciate your anxiety, during the long interval, but it is ended now, and I sincerely trust we may here after hear from each other regularly. Sam and I are still troubled with weak eyes, but they are gradually becoming stronger. At one time during my dangerous illness, I had the most awful apprehensions of his entire blindness. For several days, he never beheld the light, and his sufferings were intense. You would have been delighted with his patience and fortitude. He seemed perfectly resigned if only permitted to lie on my bed. We used no remedies except the Irish potatoe [sic] poultice and cream. During his temporary blindness, his mind seemed to dwell much upon the restoration of the blind, by our Saviour, and often, when I was scarcely able to reply to him, he would beg me to tell him the story of the blind men, by the wayside. He still retains his love of scripture narrative, and I trust that it may increase with his years. Oh that the Lord may call him, to labour in some portion of his vineyard! I care not, though it should be amid the wildest tribe of indians. I ask for him, no earthly honours or wealth, but this sacred calling, I crave from my heart. I must now say something of our Nannie, or you will think with others, that Sam is my favorite. Ah my love, if you could see her now, you would be more apt to conclude that she was one of those little charmers, that endanger a parent's heart. Yes, the greatest danger is loving her too much. She has so many little fascinations, that I look upon her with "fear and trembling," and ask myself, "what if she were to die?" This is wrong, I know, for she should never doubt that the Lord hath a balm for every wound. When she saw the picture of Washington, on the ticket which you sent me, she exclaimed "papa" and seemed perfectly delighted with it. I wish you could witness the scene, when I am teaching Sam to sing. She invariably puts in her little bird notes, and in spite of all Sam's efforts, will sing the loudest, and I should not be at all surprised, if she learned to sing first, for poor Sam has yet given no evidence of musical genius. I consulted with him as you directed, about giving the lot to Mr Creath. He seemed quite pleased at the idea, and I think his feelings were truly benevolent. I made a tender of it to Mr and Mrs Creath and they were very grateful, but have since bought a situation from Mr Rogers, a little further in the country, which they thought suited them better. Mrs Creath spends a good deal of her time with me, but since the death of her little boy, (which I mentioned to you,) she is not the joyous being, that she was. She is naturally one of the most cheerful beings, I ever knew, but she seems as if a blight had fallen upon her. I have conversed a great deal with her, and read to her, but how vain are the words of comfort to the bereaved mother! The Lord reserves unto himself, the power of healing her wounded heart.

I was delighted with the letter from our cousin Mr [John] Houston. You must present from me, a great deal of appreciation to him and his family. I do not know any family, with whom I would like better to become acquainted, and if it were possible, I would certainly comply with his solicitation to visit Washington, but to be frank with you my love, I do not think it will be in my power. I have tried to lay plans for the journey, merely that I might have something on which to rent my thoughts, and not allow them the dreary range of six or seven months absence from you, but when the subject is brought closely to view, there are so many things in the way, that I do not think it will be possible. I would, however, as soon set off for Washington, as Ala, and I think the best plan will be for me to remain quietly at home, until you return.

Mr [Thomas] King is very anxious to go on with our galleries and rooms, but his calculation is that the lumber will amount to five hundred dollars, independent of the work, so that I have concluded to let it alone for the present. I am improving our yard very neatly. I have set out a great many shrubs, and they are budding beautifully. I had the most of our shrubbery brought from Raven hill, and have not lost any of it. I expect I should get a little scolding if you were at home, for I can not keep away from my flowers.

Present my love to Miss Cobb, and when you write again, tell me her given name, as I would like to know which of the girls she is. Please ask her, if her cousins the Misses Jackson are married, and if they are, thier husbands' names. I would be glad to know how many children her sisters Laura and Mildred have, and if they are very pretty <u>and smart</u>. If you would not like to ask her, you can ask her brother.

My dear Love, it grieves me to see that you are unhappy on account of the course pursued by our kindred.[1] It is true, they have been unkind to me, but from you, my ever precious husband, I have received gentleness and devotion enough, to atone for a world's unkindness. They are comfortable, and I am rejoiced at it. Did you ever hear from sister Polly?[2] If you receive any intelligence of her, do not forget to give it to me. Mr [Archer B.] Worsham is here from Liberty. He left all well at bro. V's. By the bye, I must tell you that the latter had curiosity enough, while in Galliton [sic], to take a good look at Mrs D.[3] He stopped at the same hotel and saw her at the table. He thinks she is very fine looking. I can not express to you my love, how rejoiced Mother and I were at your news of bro. H[enry]. The Lord grant that he may remain firm.

You must not expect too much from the farm, as we have only three hands, Prince, Joshua, and Bingley. Hosea left for Houston soon after Vina's death. I did not intend to say any thing to you about the sheep as I know it would cause you some regret, but as you have mentioned them, I must inform you of thier fate, lest you should suppose that I have not thought of them. Soon after your departure, they were scattered in various directions, but I did not feel privileged to interfere with them, until I found that Kelsy had run away. I used every effort in my power, to collect them, but only succeeded in finding 13 sheep, (besides the two from Roberson's,) and 3 goats. The rest we suppose were all drowned at Calhoun's[4] mill, as we have heard of a flock being lost there in the high waters, and we can get no other trace of ours. Those that we have recovered, seem to be perfectly domesticated again. and I am getting a fine pasture for them and the calves on Mother's lots.

Thomas Palmer is making a fine crop. Mr. Worsham tells me that the Raven hill corn is knee high. Farewell My Love. Do not miss a mail if you can possibly avoid it, and I will try to write once every week.

Thine with true devotion,

M. L. Houston

P.S. Mother sends her love to you and says she thinks we will do well. I do not know what I would do without her.

[1]Margaret is referring to the Moore family.
[2]Mary Houston Wallace.
[3]Eliza Allen Douglas, of Gallatin, Tennessee, Houston's first wife.
[4]William Calhoun. Identified in *1850 Census*, vol. 4, 2026.

⬯⬯

The following letter from Dr. Ashbel Smith is in the Ashbel Smith Papers in the Center for American History, Austin, Texas.

Galveston, March 25, 1848

My dear General,

We have no local news of interest at this time. Our Legislature is about adjourning—I need not tell what they have done or omitted to do, as you will see their proceedings in the news-papers.

There has been a tolerably general expression of opinion in regard to the next Presidency. The friends of General Taylor expected at first to carry their candidate by acclamation, following herein in the footsteps of the Whigs of New Orleans. They will be disappointed. I wrote you some time since of the abortive attempt made here in Galveston to inveigle your friends into a pledge to support General Taylor. I am pretty well satisfied now that this state is disposed to accept the candidate who shall be selected by the Baltimore Convention.—Gen Taylor will not, I believe, be the choice of the people of Texas.

I delivered by request of the citizens a speech on the 22d of Feby. I have been flattered with the opinion that it gave great satisfaction;— some correspondent however of the "News" along with some compliments intimated that the Hero of San Jacinto so floated before my vision that I could not see General Taylor.

Peace however procured, as peace will give universal satisfaction; yet for my own part I would have repudiated and disavowed the whole of Mr [Nicholas] Trist's proceedings; sending nevertheless immediately to Mexico able and dully [sic] empowered Commissioners. If we ever become embroiled in another war, as we undoubtedly shall be, this business of Mr Trist will become a precedent for irregular, unauthorized and embarrassing negotiations. A departure from established usages of international intercourse and especially between nations at war is fraught with much obvious inconveniences immediate and remote, that I will not weary your patience with their enumeration—and especially as I could mention none which have not already suggested themselves to your own reflections.

I see you have been on a tour northward—it was wise—I shall look with interest to the accounts of it in the newspapers.

Major J. W. Simmons[1] communicated to me a letter from Col Talcott in which it was intimated that a depot or arsenal may some time hereafter be established at San Antonio for the State of Texas. My dear General, this occasion for placing an establishment of the kind in question on San Jacinto ought not to be neglected. If something of this nature be not done, the great battlefield of Texas will in a few years be a sugar plantation, or may be a cow ranch. The appropriation of San Jacinto to some public use is due to the State—it is due to yourself.

I have also wished that the Federal Government would establish at Galveston a marine Hospital—it is the most suitable point for this purpose between the mouth of the Mississippi and Vera Cruz. And if this should be done, I should be glad to be appointed Hospital Surgeon—though by no means solicitous on this last point.

Things are truly quite dull in Galveston—numbers of houses to rent—property has depreciated more than one half in twelve months. I am practising [sic] medicine—rather nominally or as the phraze [sic] is, ornamentally. I have commenced sugar planting on a moderate scale on the Bay—having bought Gen Bakers's[2] Evergreen place.

I am obliged to you for the Report of the Secy of Treasury—are the documents of the Institute at Washington distributed gratuitously?

And now one word in conclusion for myself. I should be flattered to receive the appointment of one [of] the West Point Visitors. I think something of this kind is due me.—Besides my life is passing idly, amid books indeed, but still idly. I want something to do.

I am, dear General,

Very truly Yours,
Ashbel Smith

[1]Smith may be referring to James W. Simmons, whom Houston had recommended for the position of Keeper of Naval Stores in Galveston. *Writings,* 4, 398.
[2]Mosely Baker. Elizabeth Silverthorne, *Ashbel Smith of Texas: Pioneer, Patriot, Statesman, 1805–1886.* (College Station: Texas A&M University Press, 1982), 59.

∽

Washington
26th Mar 1848

My Dear, dear Wife,

Your favors have reached me, for which I render to you, ten thousand thanks, and all affection, that is inexpressible. I had been so long, without hearing from you, that I was heart sick. On my return from the Eastward, I received your last letter, and the next day Mr Smith arrived, and hand[ed] me the one sent by him. When I left for the East, I directed any letters from Huntsville, to be sent to me on the route. When I returned tho' it was three o'clock in the morning, I would not retire, until I had made search for letters, from you, and like an anxious Lover I did not sleep. The next morning I found, that my letters had been retained at the Capitol, by the Sergt of arms.[1] I was sorry to hear of Mothers misfortune in the loss of Poor Vincy, and yet more sad to reflect, on her dying situation. God is merciful to those on whom He will have mercy, therefore we must submit to his dispensations. How much have I a very sinner, to thank our Heavenly Father for, in the Preservation, and recovery of my dear Wife, and children. I am as grateful, as an unregenerate man can be. The bereavement of Poor bro Creath, and his dear spouse, truly distresses me. They have the consolation of religion, and that alone can sustain them.

I was truly rejoiced to hear, that after your severe illness, that you had recovered, and likewise the returning freshness of our dear little rosebud. Your graphic description of her scene, with brother Vernal affected me nearly as much as the reality did you. In fancy, I saw her, heard her sweet tones say "papa." But I reflected on our [son], and my feelings, are not to be described. I could not eschew the most painful anxiety. That dear "precious boy Sam" to think of his goodness to his Ma, and little sister, as well as to all others I hope, cheered me, and recalled me to home, and happiness once enjoyed, and made my resolve, if reunited, never again to part, while we live. I will not attempt an expression of my feelings towards you, and the dear pledges of our love. I can essay, to express many feelings of the heart, but that which is associated with home! The soul alone, can entertain a passion so pure, and sacred! Dont you my Love think so?

I am truly glad, that you and Sam, are all in "a house, with brick chimneys and glass windows." Poor Sam! I have often told of his fine taste, and the reason of it, to the amusement of many persons, and none below the first circle.

You will see that I have been to the East,[2] I saw your great friends Dr & Mrs Woods. I dined there, was with them about five hours, and had to leave for Norwich, as I had an appointment to speak there. I was sorry, because a party had been invited to meet me there, on that evening. In thirteen days, I made nine speeches, and attended three sermons, in Yankee land. I spoke in the Athens of America (Boston) and had you been present, I will only say you would have been much gratified. It was much better than any speech you ever heard me make. Before I rose, I thought of you my Love, of Sam, of Nannie, and of myself, & friends. I will say no more but refer you to the papers. I will send by this mail a letter from our dear Niece Teen [sic] Royston. You can see all. I will also send you scraps, from the most respectable Journals in the U. States.[3] It is not vanity my Love, which causes me to send them, but because I think they will gratify you, and Mother much more![4] You can tell me whether they will or not.

I sent by Mr Torrey, some articles to you, and the children, but did not write I was gratified to see the Doct and Lady Woods. Our talk was altogether about you, and the children. I gave her your letter to read, in which you spoke of Mrs Birdwells anxiety. Are you angry? At the moment I only thought that it was a letter from you, but not its <u>contents</u>. This being the case, it was no breach of faith, or betrayal of trust.

I am glad to hear that all things are going well at home. If you are all well and happy it is consolation to me. Let them plant Pumpkins, peas, and sweet potatoes. The two first in the corn! You can have some idea of my engagements, when I tell you, that I found on my return about 70 letters, to attend to. I want the hands to keep planting while there is any place to plant, and to the 4th of July, but not to neglect what is planted, that they may plant more. Let them attend <u>certainly</u>, what is planted. So soon as I can, I will write to Brother Vernal, about my business, and propose to him terms.

You will think strange of this letter, as it appears. Well, the whole matter is, that I took up the inkstand to sand with, and lost one leaf thereby. It is such [a] stand as I took home. I will send you such scraps from the papers, as come [to] hand, for indeed, I do not look for them.

I hope Love you will write as often as you can, if but a line to say "all are well."

My love to Mother, and kisses to our dear children. Send me the measure of Sam's boots—The sole I mean only. Present me kindly to Miss Caroline Davis, and tell her to stay with you until I come home. I will write to you my Love, as often as I can. My arm, at times is so, that I can hardly write.

I am thy ever devoted and faithful Husband

Sam Houston

P.S. Commend me to all our dear friends. If not done, let Genl. Davis, & Yoakum, bring suit against William Palmer. You will see I write in much haste & collusion.

Thine

Houston

[1]Robert Beale. *Biographical Directory*, 143.

[2]For information about this trip see Friend, 188.

[3]In the Sam Houston Hearne Collection there is a clipping from the Hartford, Connecticut *Daily Times*, March 20, 1848, which describes Houston's speech of March 18, 1848, as a "regular old fashioned jam."

[4]It was reported to be "the largest gathering in New Haven" in the reporter's memory and that "hundreds went away, unable to gain admittance." Ibid.

∞

Washington

30 March 1848

My Dear Love,

To day I had the pleasure to receive your letter of the 9th Inst. I was truly happy to hear from home, from you, from all! I will write soon, and in less haste. I now write to enclose you a letter from Mr Burrows[1] containing, or rather accompanying the present which I sent to you by, Mr Torrey. I will give you the history of the pretty thing. You will see it—a pretty thing, and I hope you will admire it. Nannie will if she lives.

I was delighted to hear your sentiments, about Sam & Nannie. They are worthy, of their mother.

Matters here are moving on rather briskly, in the political world. Who will be the nominee[2] of the Convention at Baltimore no one can say, but many suppose, that a southern man may be the individual. Matters are now gliding, to that point, unless an eddy, should take place in the current.

You will hear as the subject progresses. I will send you news papers occasionally.

I assure it is of much less interest to me, than the anxiety, which I feel to be at home.

My love, commend me kindly to all, and kiss our babes. My regards to all our dear friends. I will send you many Garden seeds, & some flowers by mail.

Dear salute our friends kindly for me.

Thy ever faithful and devoted husband

Sam Houston

[1]Houston is probably referring to James Burroughs, a Texas Legislator. For a biography see *Handbook of Texas,* vol. 1, 256.
[2]The Democratic nominee for president.

To Gen'l Sam Houston Washington city D. C.

Huntsville March 30 1848

My ever dear husband,

By yesterday's mail, I recd two letters from you, one the 4th inst, the other the 5th, and would have answered them last night, but was too unwell to do so. I am scarcely able to sit up this morning, but I am so nervous and agitated by learning that you have recd no letters from me, that I should suffer more from not writing than writing. I have written to you once every week since I recovered from my tedious attack of neumonia, but my heart sinks within me, when I find that they (my letters) have not reached you. Why it is, I can not tell. There must be something wrong in some quarter. My Love, you ought not to have said, "If you have not time to write." I never felt more pained by an expression. Can you believe for a moment, that I would put off writing to you, for any other occupation? I know you can not, and let me here remind you that we are too far apart, for home explanations. We have often made friends over a slighter affair than that cruel expression of yours, and I do not know that the wound will ever be healed, until we meet.

I have suffered much within the last few days, from depression of spirits, and sometimes my weak spirit shrinks from the sufferings before me, and I long for "the wings of a dove, that I might flee away and be at rest." Not even our Nannie's prattle, which every day acquires a new word or two, can entirely banish the gloom that gathers around me. But I will trust in the Lord. Under the shadow of his wing, I know that I should fear no evil.

I was much pleased to learn that you expected to visit Providence during your tour, as you would see our friends Mrs Woods and the Dr. I shall look anxiously, for her account of you. I recd a letter yesterday, from Antoinette. She and Sarah Ann expect to set off for Huntsville, so soon as thier husbands get home. They are exceedingly anxious to exhibit the young ones, and like all young Mothers, of course, think there was never any thing like them before. I sent my last letter to you, according to your advice, by Nachitoches, but I fear it will not reach you. If you get no more letters from me, you may rest assured that if I am living and can use a pen, it is my regular business, to write to you once every week. There is no news of interest in Huntsville except that Dr Keenan[1] brought home a wife from Austin. He married Miss Ward.[2] As to politics, my Love, whatever interests you, must interest me, and although in a general way, I feel no great interest in matters of that kind, whatever you write, I will read with pleasure, unless you give me some reason to scold you, as I have done in this.

Mother is well and sends her love to you. Gen'l Davis's daughters are still here and seem very happy. They are making Nannie a great romp. Sam is still the same grave old fellow, and talks a great deal about you.

Thy devoted wife,
M. L. Houston

[1]Dr. Charles Keenan. Identified in *1850 Census*, vol. 4, 2010.
[2]Eliza Ward. Ibid.

∞

Washington
3rd Apl 1848

My Dear Love,

To day I was at church and heard a good Baptist sermon. It is now late at night, but I can not sleep with[out] indulging my feelings in writing a few lines to you ire I sleep. If I live tomorrow, I wish to write you a long letter.

This morning at 6 ock Charles, and Tom Power left here by way of the Ohio River for home. They have been North on business, but did not succeed, as well as they wished. For several evenings in my room, I had the pleasure of their company. We went to the Reception at the Presidents. Charles and myself waited on two young Ladies. My God Daughter[1] who has been at Philadelphia all this season, was to have gone, as she had just returned, and as she did not go, we went with two of her friends. I threw them pretty much on Charles' hands, as I had the gentlemen, who were present to make my court to. The evening was a drag so far as the ladies were concerned. Mrs Polk, and all the ladies of my acquaintance, make constant enquiries for you, as it is here understood that, I am your obsequious husband.

Miss Cobb, I have not seen, since I wrote to you about her. Howell, her brother, has lost two fine Boys here this winter. I have not learned of what they died. I will ascertain. It may be my Love that this circumstance will alarm you about coming on this summer. If it should my Love, I would not have you to feel any compulsion, if we can live apart until Congress may rise. Or if you wish to come on as far as the Cane Brake, where we could meet and spend a few days together, I would be most happy. The idea of travelling with a babe, and not having me along, and Sam too, with you, as you say he must come, if you do, seems to overwhelm me. When I think of his attack when he was an infant in Hatfields[2] house, really alarms me. When you might [be] travelling amongst strangers, and without Mother, have a babe, thus attacked, would place you in a most deplorable condition, & this too, on my account. I declare to you, that it is all that I can do to keep from resigning, and forthwith returning home, when I reflect on our situation, and the distance, which I am from you. I hope this letter will reach you ire the hour of your trial comes on.

I never lay my head to rest on my pillow, without beseeching the Father of mercies, to have you in his holy keeping, and that He will bring you thro [sic] your trial in safety, and with joy. Nor do I ever fail to beseech His mercy, and his grace in behalf of our little Lambs. Yea, I even pray for those, who have not the claims of affection, or kindness upon me. Then how much more will I feel, and pray for those who are interwoven with every fibre of my heart, and every covee [sic] of my affections.

In a few days from this time I hope my Love Mr Torrey will send you, the articles which I confided to him for you. I have sent you some seeds, which I hope will please you. I sent some to other Ladies.

You may say to our son, that I have a white Terrier presented to me in New York, which sleeps in my room, and I call his name Jack. My dear, do have Jack sent home to you. He will be a good guard.

If you want money for any purpose, all that you have to do, is to draw an order on me at sight for the amount, and let some merchant give you the cash for it. Mr [J. C.] Smith will do it. I will send you the form of the order. Give my love to ma, and the family. Kiss the babes.

Thine ever
Houston

[1]Mary Houston.
[2]B. F. Hatfield of Washington-on-the-Brazos.

∞

Senate Chamber
3rd Apr 1848

My Dear Love,

On last night, I wrote to you, and promised to write to day. It is inclination which induces me, and not to redeem a promise, to write to you at all times.

I can tell you one thing, which will gratify you. Since I have been to the North, successive assurances have arrived, bringing conclusive evidences, that my trip there, has had the effect, of convincing the people there, that Texas is a fine country—the inhabitants are clever people, and that I am a first rate [*blurred*], and well behaved gentleman, and that my wife, must be very amiable, and excellent, as she has been mainly instrumental in making me so. All but the last, will gratify you, and that I do not begrudge you.

I will tell you an anecdote which occurred at Portsmouth in New

Hampshire. Many Ladies were present in the audience, and I deemed it fit to allude, to the provisions made, in our constitution, favorable to the Ladies in their rights of property. As I did so, a voice was heard in the crowd saying, "I will never be under petticoat government." I replied, "If you should not, you will never be properly governed." This was cheered most vociferously! This you know, would have the inference that I was (or that I was well governed,) and ergo my wife ruled me. By this course, all the Ladies, as it was understood, were in favor of removing to Texas. They all wished to be introduced to me, so soon as the meeting concluded. I do not my dear, boast of any thing, but I assure you, that in my life, I never saw such enthusiasm, as I did on the trip. I do not recollect my Love, that in former letters, I have told you that I had to make nine speeches in thirteen days, and travelled thousands of miles, by Steam Boats, cars, & carriages. I travelled two of the coldest days, this winter, and in snow, with open vehicles. I have never seen so much kindness to a stranger mani-fested in any part of the U. States. I have been invited to a Demo-cratic State mass Convention to be held, at Raleigh N Carolina on the 11 Inst. I can, by the cars go there, in 30 hours. Rusk, and all my friends are anxious, that I shou'd attend the Convention. Carolina was once a strong Jackson State, but since his day, it has gone over to the Whigs. There is a hope that the state may be brought back to its democratic faith. That it can be done, I have no doubt if a proper person is run as President in the Democratic Party. If I go my Love, I will write to you from Raleigh. In that State, I have had a full share of abuse, and now may be the best time, and opportunity that I will ever have to alleviate the calunies [sic], which malice or meanness, may have cast upon my character. Our children may travel there, and if I owe any thing to posterity, it is to my children, and I feel assured, it will be so regarded by you. I am uneasy here, and any thing but the routine of my duties, will enable me to reflect upon home, upon my dearly beloved wife, and our Lambs.

This is not the last letter which I intend to write to you my Love, until the 11th, for I hope to write several times. I write as often as I can, and never feel so happy in business, as when I am writing to you, or thinking of you.

Since I came to the City, I have had a visit from Major David Edmundson, of Rockbridge, who married a cousin of mine. She was Miss Hannah Paxton, & was the daughter of my mother's brother.[1] They have been married, some thirty, or thirty five years, & have no children. He has raised a fine house, and prays if you should come on that you are able to spend your time with them when I get home, after Congress rises. The Major was a member of the Democratic Convention, at Richmond, and went home full of the idea, of have [sic] one of his relations President at the next election. Very many persons, are getting in the same way of thinking. We can't tell what will take place, but it is probable, as any other event. I have also heard from Col Jno Hopkins, a cousin on my Fathers side.[2] He is wealthy, and has been a whig but is prepared to take the field in support of his kin, and says if I could return by Ohio, I wou'd carry that state, if I were nominated. If you wish me to write you more fully on this subject, you must write to me, and say so. I will write to you whatever I conceive will make you most happy and is in its-self [sic] true. At the first moment, that I have time, I will write to our dear Boy, as he thinks so much of my letters. You do not know how often I have told of Sam's "precious little letter." It is certainly my duty, and my highest pleasure, to add to the happiness of my dear treasures of home!

I fear my dear Love, that my letters are not written in a tone to make you happy, & cheer you, in your present depressed state of feelings. I can only say my Love, that you deserve, and command, my perfect and entire affection. Give my love to Mother, and the family, and Kiss our little Lambs.

Thy ever faithful and devoted husband
Sam Houston

[1]Joseph Paxton. W. M. Paxton, *The Paxtons: We are One!* (Platte City, Mo: Landmark Print, 1903), 90.

[2]John Hopkins was the son of Margaret Houston (Mrs. James) Hopkins, a sister of

Houston's father. Dr. Samuel Rutherford Houston, *Brief Biographical Accounts of Many Members of the Houston Family* (Cincinnati: Elm Street Printing Company, 1882), 21.

∞

Huntsville April 5 1848

My ever dear husband,

No letter from you by today's mail, and I am sad indeed. The reception of your letters is a thing of so much importance to me, that after the mail arrives, I am in a state of painful anxiety until I know whether it has any thing for me or not. How heavy then is my disappointment on finding that there is no word from you. I can imagine many reasons for your silence, (or rather the non-arrival of your letters, for I know that you have written,) but they can not entirely console me. But I must not distress you with my melancholy. We are all enjoying good health (after a long season of affliction,) with the exception of that very inelegant disease from mumps, which has commenced among the negroes, and I suppose our little ones will be apt to have it, but we will take great care of them, if they should.

We are enjoying a delightful spring. You can not image how beautiful our forest here appears. The hillside is clothed with the loveliest verdure I ever beheld, and our little prairie is dotted with flowers of every hue. Oh shall we ever sit together under these sweet shades, and look around upon the lovely gifts of our Heavenly Father! God alone knoweth, and oh may He prepare us for every dispensation of his will! I must soon descend into the dark valley of suffering, and my weak nature shrinks from the contemplation of it, but He who sees the end from the beginning, I humbly trust will sustain me through it, or provide for them who are left behind, if he should call me to my Heavenly home.

I am anxious to hear something of your northern tour. By the next mail I hope to receive your own account of it. So you are looking out for a yankee wife for Sam. Well I have nothing to say against it, for they are far ahead of us in many respects, and to be frank, I would like to have Nannie brought up in some northern state.

297 : JANUARY 3, 1848 - AUGUST 11, 1848

I am now without a hope of seeing you until august or sept. If the Lord spares my life, I shall have cares enough, to keep my mind employed, but nothing can banish the loneliness and dreariness of my spirit. But you will doubtless like to hear some little home details. Mother bids me tell you, that she has been looking at the corn, and never saw any that was more promising. Her pet Brasos has done some very hard work for us, but so soon as he could be dispensed with, she exchanged him with Mrs Leach,[1] for a beautiful mare and colt. The former is perfectly gentle and accustomed to the range. I mention this, because I know you have been uneasy about Mother's riding him. We have planted a great many potatoes, and they are coming up beautifully. We have not been under the necessity of calling on our neighbors for advice, as every thing seems to go on well. Sam and Nannie talk more about papa than any thing else. You would be much amused at Nannie's prattle. She is just beginning to frame sentences, and has every thing backwards. For instance, instead of "papa's baby Nannie" she says "baby papa Nannie."

Mr Creath requests me to present him kindly to you, and thank you, for the offer of the lot. I mentioned in a previous letter, that he had purchased a situation a short distance from town.

I enclose two documents with this which I do not understand. What is the meaning of them?

I have written to you regularly once a week since I recovered my health, and you may calculate on my doing so, during your absence.

Thine affectionately
M. L. Houston

April 9th

I was disappointed in getting my letter mailed on thursday owing to a change in the mail hours. No letter from you on yesterday! My fortitude is failing. I must hear from you regularly, or you must come home. I know I ought to conceal my feeling of distress from you, but I am so disappointed, that my heart sickens. You say I must tell you all about my health. Well I still think I am cured of the asthma, and I am sure you will be delighted to hear it. If I could get your letters, I should be cheerful.

[1]Margaret Leach. Identified in *1850 Census*, vol. 4, 2005.

Washington City
6th Apl 1848

My Beloved,

To day, I was made truly happy, by the receipt of your dear letter, of the 16th March.[1] On the day it was written, I was at Norwich in Conn making a speech. Your letter made me happy, because you say, you are comparatively happy. I was happy too, to hear that Mother is satisfied, or more so, than you anticipated, at any house but her own. I wish her to feel that it is her own, and we must be boarders with the old Lady. Sam, and Nannie must come in as sub-boarders. I will try if I live to return, to submit to the old Lady, and let her manage all matters, in the yard, & garden. Out of that, I will <u>ask leave</u>, and be content.

Say to our friend Mrs Doctess [Jemima] Evans, that I will give her a Diploma, for what she had done, and hope, that her success will be complete, in a cure of my dear wife. I regret to hear of our dear Boys chills. Dont let them start on him again. I fear them, on his sanguine constitution. He was bad with them once, and had a third one taken place he cou'd not have survived. Our dear little rose-bud, I hope is well, and ruddy, as you have said nothing to the contrary.

Had I fancied, my Love, that you derive so much pleasure from the receipt of my letters, as you describe, I would have written oftener, than I have done. Indeed, when for many weeks, I would not hear from you, I thought, my writing, and announcing the fact, or not alluding to letters received, would only make you less happy, than if I were not to write constantly. You I know have not had much reason to complain of me, as a negligent correspondent. Had I wrote as often to you, as my affection dictated, I cou'd have done nothing else. I would be willing that you should look into [my] heart, and there read the emotions which I cherish for you, and our dear little ones. You wou'd see that I regard all things here, as vapid, and vain. I wou'd not exchange, one day of the joys of home, for a throne, or exchange the cheerfulness of my family, for the proudest sceptre in the world.

I feel that I have made a fair experiment, by leaving home, and at this time. If it were possible my Love, I would start this night, so that I might be near you in your hour of trial. I am, and [have] been the creature, of necessity in my life, to a great extent, and never more so, than at this moment. I hope, and pant for the day when it will be in my power to remain with the dear wife, of my bosom, and my love. Our children too, they are to me every thing. They are <u>ours!</u> My reflections, and my fancy are always busy, and you are all presented to me most vividly. When I kneel every night, and invoke [sic] the Father of all mercies, in our behalf, and beseech Him, to pardon our sins, and bring me "from darkness, to His marvellous [sic] light," I do not feel my ever dear Love, that God through Christ Jesus, has pardoned my sins, or that He is reconciled to an object so unworthy as I am. I am not by any means discouraged, for in the Gospels, which I read every night, I find His promises of Grace, and mercy. Thus through faith, in the Savior, and the promises of mercy, and free Grace, I hope for salvation! It is my duty, to use the means appointed, in Gods word, and that I will try, and perform, to the saving, of my soul. I know that for all my efforts, I will deserve nothing but condemnation, and that, if I am saved, it will be thro' the merits, of Jesus Christ, and him crucified. All the forms of piety, are due to my station, as a man, but they will avail me nothing. The blood of the atonement alone can purify, and redeem the souls of men. I feel, and know this, and you may be assured my dear Love that I will strive for the favor, and forgiveness of my God, and Creator. I pray for you my Love, your health, your preservation, your happiness, and salvation. I pray for our dear Lambs, and ask God in all sincerity, that they may be preserved, and that they may be reared, in the nurture, and admonition of the Lord. I pray for all, for whom it is my duty to pray. I reflect more upon the subject of death, and eternity, than I have ever done before. I feel that it is appointed for all men, once to die, and after death the judgment.

I am gratified my Love, that you are not depressed in spirits. It is pleasing prognostic of the future, and I will pray, and hope for its realization. I will my Love, write to you often, as it makes you happy, and also to my dear Boy. He too, will be gratified, and happy. I hope my Love, you will be able to write to me, and that you may be safely brought thro your trial, under the care of that God, under whose kind providence, we have seen, and enjoyed, days, and years of happiness. I do not go into society here, but on a few occasions. I have only dined out three times in company. I have been at neither Balls, nor Theatres, tho' others go almost every night to such amusements. I first trained my actions to your wishes, and now my Dear I assure you, I have no wish on such concerns, only to advance your happiness. My love to mother, and the family. Kiss our dear children.

Thy faithful and ever affectionate
Houston

[1]This letter has not been located.

⌾

The following note from Margaret is not signed or dated and may be incomplete. It is believed to have been included in the letter of April 6, 1848.[1]

I have just returned from a ramble with the children on the hillside. It was a charming scene, truly a fairy picture. Sam amused himself by climbing the bending trees, and Nannie had a great deal to say about the pretty flowers. She is getting to be a saucy little lady, and when I speak quickly to her, she says "Nannie mamma cold." (scold) Confidential

In a few days, I suppose if all turns out well, there will be a great discussion about names, and in order to abridge it, I have determined to bring this question before you at once. What do you think of Temple Lea for a boy? If a girl's name should be required how would you like your mother's maiden name.[2] We could substitute Lea or Moffette for Elisabeth in Nannie, you know. Do not say you leave it all to me. You must be frank about it.

[*unsigned*]

[1]Houston answers this note and refers to it as "her dear letter of the 9th Inst." See Houston to Margaret, April 27, 1848.
[2]Paxton.

∞

Raleigh N. C.
11 Apl 1848

My Dearest Margaret,

Since I last wrote to you from Washington, I came to this place. To day, as I supposed the Convention was to have been held. It will not be until tomorrow. This is one of the most whig-ish places in the union. Wherever I find Whigs, my welcome is not "first rate" as you say, but in the proportion of the whigs dislike, I find the zeal, and attachment of the Democrats. My Dear, learn Sam to say, "I am a Democrat."

I will not my Love trouble you about these matters, but advert to other matters, in which I feel a ten fold interest. I wrote to you my Dear, about your trip here, or to the city, in June. I do confess in suggesting the difficulty, of your coming on, and bringing our Boy with you, that I was activated by a wish for your comfort, and indeed for the safety of the "prospective branch of the family." When I reflect on the certainty of your being sick in crossing the Gulf, and again in crossing from Charleston to Wilmington, if you come by sea, or travelling in stages, if you come by land, for 230 miles, and this in two nights, and a day, I would expect it to be done at infinite hazard, of your own, or at least, the life of your Babe. There would be no society in the city, by the time you could arrive. And again you would find Washington a hotter place than Texas, during the summer months. A Senator has arrived here, since I have, and he says Congress will adjourn in July, as he is satisfied. If this should be the case, and you were to come on, you would only be in Washington about a month, and if I have to return to Texas, as I ought to do this year, I will have to take you home with me, or if I should leave you either in Virginia, or Alabama, I would be absent from you again for months. Now if you remain my Love, and I return to Texas, so soon, as Congress rises, I hope to be able to get all matters so arranged, that we will be able with our little flock, to reach the city, before the weather is inclement, either from heat, or cold. At all events my Love, I will not again be seperated again from my family. No, I can not bear the anguish, of mind, which I dayly, and nightly feel, & experience. I am satisfied my Love, that you will appreciate what I say. If you would come by this place, and not by Charleston, and by sea, you would be wheeled along, at the rate of six miles an hour, and only stay fifteen minutes at any one place. The passage by sea is unsafe, & very rough.

If your mind has been inclined to come on, you will feel disappointed, & depressed. I hope my ever dear Love, that you will appreciate what I say to you, & ascribe the course suggested to the purest, and abiding affection. If I live, and you do not come on, I will leave for home the hour that Congress adjourns, if not before. I will not now forget to send you the form of a Draft, so that if you should wish to come on, you can do so. If you come on, you ought not to start with less that $300. It will take that to bring you, with Sam. But, (and if you come you must do it) you bring a servant, you must start with $400 (Dollars). I thought that Congress would sit until some time in August, when I proposed you to come to Alabama. If you do not come on now, but wait until fall, and you desire it, we can come by Alabama, by a carriage. If we live to come, we must travel by private conveyance. For a Lady, and two or three children to travel by public conveyance, and be subject to the coarseness of stage drivers, and Car conductors, is too painful to contemplate. My love to Mother, and all, & kiss our Lambs. May Heaven shield & protect you my ever dear Love.

Thy Faithful
Houston

Margaret wrote the following letter telling of the birth of the third Houston child. A copy of it may be found in The Raven.[1] *James lists the original as part of the Madge W. Hearne Collection, but it has not been located.*

Huntsville April 12, 1848

Dearest Love,

Another mail and no letter from you! I am distrest at it, but feel that in a few days, if I live, and nothing serious has befallen you, I shall get a great package from you. I can only write you a few lines, but I must write a *[The sentence is incomplete.]*

Saturday 22nd

There is no doubt about it, my dearest Love, she is one of the loveliest little creatures you ever beheld. I mean our second daughter,[2] for we are now the parents of three children. . . . You must look upon the unfinished paragraph of this letter as a great proof of my devotion to you, for I had endured much suffering, for a day and night, and in about 8 hours, the little one was added to our circle, but I thought I would make out a letter, as the mail was to go the next day. . . .

What shall we call the little one? All I have to say is that it must be a family or fancy name, as we have too many friends to exercise partiality in that way. I enclose a lock of her hair [and] . . . a little white rose which she held in her hand, the first nap she ever took.

Thy fond and devoted wife
M. L. Houston

[1]James, *The Raven*, 367–68.
[2]Margaret Lea Houston (Maggy) was born April 13, 1848.

Raleigh N. C.
14 Apl 1848

My Dear Love,

On yesterday the show went off. Judge Dunlap[1] of the Senate, and my self addressed the Democracy, and they <u>say</u>, did the cause good service. The people here, have treated us with much consideration, and kindness. In two hours, we will set out for Washington, and I at this time, do not intend again to be absent from Washington, until I set out for home, unless I can not avoid it. You will see all that is said about what we have done. I will send you the first account that I get of the matter.

My hand is so excited after using the arm a good deal yesterday that I can with difficulty write a scrall [sic]. So soon as I reach the city I will write again.

Daily, nightly, and hourly, I think of you, and our dear little ones. I reflect upon what you have to pass through in a short time, and beseech our Creator, to be with, & sustain, and preserve you. I sicken, and become sad, when I feel that I can not be near you, to sustain and comfort, or cheer you. I can only say my Love, that every hour of existence renders you more dear to me, and increases my affection, and my love.

Give my love to Mother and kiss our children.

Thy ever devoted Houston

[1]William Claiborne Dunlap of Tennessee. For a biography see *Biographical Directory*, 937.

Washington
20th Apl 1848

My ever dear Wife,

I have the happiness to thank you for your letters of the 13th[1] and 30 ultimo. These I received soon after my return from Raleigh. While there, I wrote you two letters, but not of great length. I was not happy while I was there, for I thought letters wou'd arrive from [you], and I would not receive them, so soon as they arrived. The letter of the 13th refers to Miss Mary Cobb, for her to answer the questions, which it contained relative to her Sisters. I called to see her this morning, and she says she will send me a letter to day, that I may send it with this. I let her see your last letter, that she might know how well you could scold me!

My Love, I am as much pained as you could be, at my expression "to write if you had time." When you reflect, you will at once perceive it was reasonableness. When Sam or Nannie are sick you know they are always in your arms, or have you seated beside them on a pallet or bed. So my Love, I really did fear as they had been ill that you might not have time to write, unless you taxed your constitution beyond your strength. Thus I apprehended you might not have <u>time</u> to write but seldom. Col Yoakum had written to me of the families health, and I had revolved the subject again, and again in my mind. I reproach myself for not writing, as often as I ought to have done, had my hand been in order. To day, I fear you will not be able to read this letter. We had ice this morning, and my hand or arm feels the effect of cold. Nothing on earth gives me more pleasure than to impart to you any, and every thing which can create one throb of pleasure, or gratification. Long ire this letter can reach you, you will have been confined, and I will pray, as I have done each night upon my bended knees, that our God may sustain and preserve you, and make you the happy mother, of a perfect Babe.

You can have but an imperfect idea of the anxiety, which I feel, and must feel, until I can hear of your safety. If I could, I would fly to you, and be with you, and remain there, until you wou'd tell me to leave you.

You have my Love, told me about the Sheep, & Goats. Well, I assure, it caused me no regrets. So long as Providence mercifully preserve my Love, and our little Lambs, I will make no complaints, about our Lambs out of doors. So you see my Love, I am not in a complaining mood. I hope my dear Love, when you receive this letter, I hope you will forgive my indiscreet expression, to which you took exception. Could I have anticipated the effect of the expression, it certainly would not have been used. I would not have caused you pain for the world. I do hope my Dearest, that your mind will be at ease, and if you do not excuse me, that you will pardon me. The distance—your situation, and my anxieties, for your welfare, & that of our dear family, had almost run me crazy. If I did wrong it arose from the excess of love!

Miss Cobbs letter is just sent to me, and I will conclude. As it will please our dear son, I will write a letter to him.

My Dearest Love, I embrace you, with my whole heart. My love to Mother, & the Miss Davises. Kiss Sam and the Rose-bud.

Thy devoted husband & Lover
Sam Houston

[1]No letter from Margaret on this date has been located.

∞

Washington City
23rd Apl 1848

My Dearest Wife,

I have just returned from a visit to our friend Dangerfields,[1] about nine miles from the city. It is sunday, and as I went down on yesterday, to day I went to church in the neighborhood, and witnessed a sacrament of the Episcopalian church. It was an interesting scene, and it was the first time, that I had seen one, that I recollect. It took place in a church, which had been built, (if I mistake not) more than, one hundred years ago. It stood, in a sequestered place, a spacious enclosure, and every yard of the green sward, seemed to cover the portion of the "narrow house" of some one who had mingled in the busy scenes, of other days. It was a volume of instruction, and a place for meditation indeed. For years, I have not reflected, so much, upon the solemnity, of the change, which must, and will take place, with all living. For days past, I have not passed an hour without reflecting upon your trial, and your danger. I can only hope, & pray for your safety. This I have not, and will not fail to do. This affords me some solace,—but I am not comforted, by the assurance, that I am one of the righteous, & one whom Heaven will answer. This day, My Love, you recollect, (if Heaven has mercifully spared you, to me) that I calculated you would be confined. I have never ceased to think of it, and the more, as you seemed to apprehend, as I thought, great danger, from the occasion. No one, who has not loved, as intensely, as I do, can ever know what I have felt, and yet must feel, until I hear from you. And one cause is to me, most distressing, is that you could not receive, an assurance that the unguarded expression (which was made by accident,) could not be explained to you before your travail wou'd come upon you. I can only hope that my subsequent letters would convince you that, there could have been no intention on my part to wound your feelings! Then this is not all. If you are satisfied of this, you will then regret, that you had said any thing to me, which by possibility, might wound me. You have not done so, but yet if you have apprehended it to be the case, your regrets will be of a painful character. I will know, from a knowledge of your heart, and its affections. And again Dearest, I have relatives near to you,[2] whose affections, and devotions, you have the highest claims upon, and, whom, if you were no more, unless, from selfishness, I fear (and it is a painful thought,) would not pay the tribute of decent respect to your memory, nor cherish, our dear little orphans, if they were friendless. These things, my ever Dearest, must wring my heart, and render my solicitude, if possible, great, and more painful, than if you, had all their sympathies, their affection, and their kindnesses. It does seem to me, that I am the only one on earth, who is so peculiarly, and miserably situated, in this respect. I loved my clan, as you well know, nor did you my Love, feel less towards them, than myself. I hope it may all be for the best. I forgive them, but it has put me upon my guard, and the past will live with me, as amongst the most painful of all my reminiscences.

When I began to write this letter my hand was so unsteady that I would not have attempted to write, if it were not that I was writing to you. It was a little selfish in me too. I hoped it might give you pleas[ure], and I am never happy myself, only when I am communing with you. For then, I live over the past, and hope derives new life of the future!

My ever dearest Love, I will say nothing of business. I can not tell why my hand is changed, unless it is that I only exercise occasionally, for in my life, I was never more healthy, nor have you ever seen me so large as I am!

I hope my Love, that this letter may find you, in health, and a happy mother, with increased objects, of affection, but not with increased cares.

Present my Love to Mother, and hug, oh hug, our dear, dear little ones. Salute the Miss Davis', and all our friends.

Tell the Blacks, that I do not forget them, and I hope they will be dutiful.

Thy ever devoted, & faithful husband
Sam Houston

[1]William Henry Daingerfield's home was in Prince George County, Maryland. *New Handbook of Texas*, vol. 2, 474.
[2]Houston is referring to the Moore family.

∞

Washington
26th Apl 1848

My ever Dearest,

I snatch a moment to write to you. I am in the hustle of the Senate. In my last I did not reply to that part of your letter, which spoke of your not coming on, or to Alabama, this session, because I had suggested to you the same thing, in some of my former letters. You my Love, have come to a proper conclusion. To travel with Master Sam, and I hope a little "Temple," or "Margaret" would be at imminent risk of your safeties, if not your lives. I am aware of the pain of absence, and this I feel, in the most acute manner. Not one night of my life do I sink to sleep, but what you are present to my thoughts. When I awake you are present to my mind. As I returned from Raleigh, I saw two Ladies travelling in the Cars, with their Brother. One was the wife of a member of Congress, the other her sister. The wife had a son, about our Dear boys age, or older, and I assure you, I pitied her, and the lad. I thought of you, and what your situation would be, when my heart sank within me.

When I received your letters on my return to the city, I felt relieved much. Until I can hear of your safety, & restoration, I will not cease, to hope, and pray for you, and feel incessant, and painful anxiety. Under any, and ordinary circumstances, I would <u>feel</u> much, and tender solicitude, but now it is <u>boundless</u>. I will in future, if I live, never sacrifice my family attachment to official place, or station.

My dearest, I want you to draw on me for any money that you may want for any purpose, either for yourself, or the family. In that I <u>especially</u> include our Mother. Her peculiarity of disposition, or temper, is not, to be considered, only with filial regard. I often regret, that I ever felt, the least irritation. I ought not to have done so. Her kindness of heart, and not her manner, ought to be noticed, and esteemed. The interest, which she feels in our welfare, can not be questioned, and for this we ought to be grateful, as well as dutiful.

Dont allow yourself to want any thing. If you wish stores of any kind, or supplies, please write to Torreys at Houston for them, and the Smiths will have them brought up to you at Huntsville.

I am using all the economy in my power, that you may have the more to use, for family purposes.

To day, I have come to the conclusion, to write to you, even when I have nothing to write, but to tell you, that I <u>cannot tell you, how much, nor how devotedly, I love you.</u>

I will hope to hear from you, (not from yourself,) but make some one write to me, so soon as you are confined. No this [is] not possible! That is over, or will be ire this is in the mail. I can only hope, that I will have been anticipated, in my anxious desires, and prayers.

Give my love to our Mother, and kisses to our dear Babes. Regards to Misses Davis. When you are able my Love, let me know, what you have received from Mr. Torrey. I mean of the articles, which I sent you and how you like them! I have seen no pretty Boxes, this time, but will look out for them. I have bought you a pretty trunk, and I am now adding to your Religious Library.

I am my ever dear wife, thy faithful & devoted Husband.

Sam Houston

P.S. I can not find out the reason, why hand write[ing] is so bad. It may in part, be owing to my coat sleeve being too tight.

Thine
Houston

∞

Washington
27th Apl 1848

My beloved,

The first thing which I engage in this morning is to write to you. I am fearful, that while on my Northern trip, my not writing to you has caused you uneasiness. My tour was one of incessant travel or speaking. I did not intend to have been so long on the trip, but the Democracy kept me as long, as they could, and at last, I left them in despite of their wishes, and urgent solicitations. Since that time I have been pretty dutiful in my correspondence. I ought to be so, for I assure you my Love, it is a pleasure to me, to write often, to you. I feel at times, as tho' I was conversing with you, face to face, or side by side. I can not forget the incident of our dear little Nannie's coming to me while I was writing at the Table, and soliciting, a place on my knee. I will remember the remarks on the subject, and the feelings, which were inspired in my bosom. It was on the eve of <u>my departure</u> <u>from home</u>.

Nor have I my dear, ceased to remember, our Boys anxiety for me to explain to him the duration of my absence! I recollect all, and every thing, which is connected, with my dearly beloved Wife, and the agony of mind which I felt, at having to seperate myself from, the object of my unchanged affections. Yes my dearest, they are, and will ever remain unchanged.

I beg you my dear, not to think me trying to compose a love letter. No my dear, I will only write affections, but make love in person!

When I reflect upon what your situation has recently been, my hopes however, have been more bright, and if possible, my feelings more fervent. Until I can hear from you my Love, and what your situation is, and has been!

My love I will try, and atone, for the past, so far as I am culpable, on the score of delinquency.

Give my love to Mother, and the Misses Davis. Kiss our dear, dear children for me.

I am thy faithful, and ever devoted husband.

Sam Houston

P.S. Dearest,

Did you ever write to Major Cocke, to learn in which Bank your cash is deposited in? This is useless, when I reflect that you have the certificate of deposits!

Thine

Houston

My Dear Love,

Just as I was about to fold this letter on my desk, I received your favor, yes, your dear letter of the 9th Inst. I thank you my Love for the "precious little letter" as Sam would say. About the names my Dear I can not determine. I am candid. I thought you would call the expected, would (if a daughter) be called Margaret, and if a son, Temple Lea. By a letter of date prior to this,[1] you will find the allusion accordingly. If you will reflect my dear, you will see of how little use, a family name is with a young Lady. You my dear, when I courted you, were Miss Margaret M Lea. By some means, I dont say what, but I assure you very satisfactory to me, you became Mrs. Margaret Lea Houston. If Nannie should ever marry would she not become Mrs. Nancy Houston _____? If a daughter should bless her parents, or has already done so, and she should be called Margaret, and any middle name which you may chuse say, (as it is a dear name to me) Lea, and she should ever marry, would she not become, Mrs Margaret Houston _____? My Love, these suggestions are made for your reflection, and not by way of objection, to any arrangements, which you may make. I confess that I have some superstition, about changing <u>childrens</u> names, as Sam wou'd say.

You told me to be candid, and to express my wishes, and not to leave it to you. I can only say My Love, that I have given you such reasons, as I think will have some bearing on the subject. If now, Nannies name were changed our <u>kindred</u>, would charge it upon you, as an act of disrespect to the memory of my sainted mother. Now my Love, I am sure that such a thought, has never, for one moment entered your thoughts. I am particular in <u>this</u> because, I am fearful, you will feel distressed when it strikes your mind! I pray you not to be, even perplexed.

As for Temple Lea my love, should a "man child be born," [it] is a fixed fact! To my mind, that will be the name of the <u>expected</u>! It may be that you will have, or now have, a Temple Margaret Lea. Such things have been shadowed forth!

My Love, the mail is about to close, and I must send this letter, without looking over it. I am so happy to hear of you, and Sam & Nannie among the "flowers."

Thy ever devoted
Sam Houston

P. S.
The protests sent to me by you, have all been settled. There was money in the Bank, but the certificate was not here, until I came.

Thine truly
Houston

[1]See Houston to Margaret, April 26, 1848.

∞

Senate Chamber
1st May 48

My Beloved,

To day we have the melancholy duty of perform [sic] of inter-ring a brother Senator, Mr Ashley[1] of Arkansas, deceased on saturday last about 2 Oclock P.M. He was an amiable, and useful member of the Body. It is said his end was a fearful one, and such a one as ought to admonish us, to be always prepar'd for deaths summons, and not to rely, upon a death bed repentance. His illness was less than a week, and his apprehension at the approach of death was fearful. His wife,[2] and a grown daughter were with him. We will inter him to day, and it may be, that it will have a happy influence, upon the asperity of feel-ing, which often manifests its-self in this chamber. Since writing the above, I am happy to learn that Mr Ashley departed with lively hopes, of Salvation. I will send you my Love, the announcement of his death by his Colleague! On yesterday, I was a[t] church as it was sunday. I did not go to church in the morning, as I had lain too long, in bed. In the afternoon, I went, and found that there was only prayer meeting in the church. The Sermon last night, was able, and impressive. I will attend church whenever I can, and I will use "every appointed means of grace." I try to bring to my understanding, and heart, that I must die, and as I can not know the time, or manner, it is fit that I should be in constant preparation, for death, and the judgment.

I feel less careful, not to let the love, of this world engross my thoughts. By this I mean, the love of objects of ambition. It is true, if I were to try, I could not with draw, my cares, my thoughts, and my affections, from you and our dear offspring. But this is required, by the very precepts, of our Holy Religion. These feelings correct, and purify the affections, of the heart, and render as grateful to Provi-dence, for His preservation of our earthly treasures.

At times, I am almost maddened, by the reflection, that I did not write to you, while I was on my Northern tour. I am fearful too, that when I returned, my letters might have been delayed. I am apprehen-sive, that your last letter written in much anxiety, was the commence-ment of the long silence, which had only begun. I hope it may not.

There would be a space of twenty days, or more, in which you probably would receive no letters. Could I have anticipated this, I would have written. Indeed I was so worried, that I could not well write. I might though have written a single line, and that would have been enough to have let you know that I could do no more. This would have satisfied you. I think you will find my Love, that I told you, I would not write while on my tour. I expected to be absent for ten days only at most, and I was detained more than twenty days. I hope that I may be mistaken. Indeed my Love, I did not think in the constant care of your little family, that it was so important, that I should even write by every mail. I did it more, as a matter of self gratification, that I might evince to you, how much I loved you, and our little ones. Nor do I think myself, an elegant or interesting correspondent to any person, unless it is you, or Sam.

If the mails are regular, my Love, you shall not have reason to complain of my silence, while we are seperated. My hopes, are great, that you have passed through your troubles, and are in health.

About the names, my Dear, I hope you will be satisfied and happy. I am fearful that Mother has been so much displeased, that she will take no part in the matter. Well, indeed it is a most unreasonable ground of quarrel. I hope she will think better of it, next time, if we should live.

My Love, I wish you to present me affectionately to mother, & Misses Davis. Kiss all our dear, dear children, and tell Sam, I will [write] to him, and may-be, I will send a little letter to dear little Nannie, and tell Nannie that her Ma must not, "Nannie Mamma cold." My dear don't whip Sam for any thing he may do! His reason and his heart, are to be appealed to, but not his fears! He is noble, and manly, in his feelings.

My Love, I have not time to read this letter, as the mail is just about to close.

Thy ever faithful devoted and affectionate husband
Sam Houston

[1]Chester Ashley. Josiah H. Shinn, *Pioneers and Makers of Arkansas* (Baltimore: Genealogical Publishing Co., 1967), 189.
[2]Mary Elliot Ashley. Ibid.

Washington
2nd May 1848

My Dearest Wife,

I have just returned, from the funeral, of Senator Ashley. It was truly distressing to see his wife, and grown daughter, and son, dressed in the habilaments [sic] of woe. With them, it was no ostentatious sorrow, but grief unmeasured. I heard but one sob, during the obsequies. Every honor was paid to his remains, and to his memory; but how empty were they all. I thought upon the vanity, and viewed the pageant with sorrow. So soon as the members, of the procession, turned their faces, from performing their sad office, all care for the dead seemed to cease, and the solemnity vanished as a dream of the night. The family will return, to their home without their affectionate head, and in seclusion deplore his loss. How inscrutable are the ways of Providence, and how careful should we be in preparation, for we know not, when the summons shall come unto us. I will try my Love, and be ready, by preparation before it is too late. If my own prayers, should not avail, I know that many pious prayers are offered up, in my behalf, and the prayers of the righteous availith [sic] much.

My mind my Love is constantly embracing you, and our little ones. So far as fancy can enable me, I am with you in our home, tho' homely, I will fancy it sad, because, it is the desired home, of my affections.

I hope, and believe that you have passed safely thro your troubles, and then I contemplate the joy of all. A mothers, and the delights of our little ones. The importance felt by Sam, and the assuming pertinacity of wee Nannie, the grand looks of Mother, and her deep sigh, after calculating the subdivisions of property, among "such a parcel of brats." Thus am I, borne in imagination, to our woodland home! If it is the will of Heaven, that we meet again, I can not reconcile it to my heart, again to part. Nothing but distance prevented me from being with you, in your troubles! If you could have been in Alabama, I would have been with you, and stayed by you. I hope all things are for the best, and that Heaven [may] guard you, and preserve you from harm, with dear cherubs. As I pray that all things may be well, and that a stranger has come, kiss the youngster for me, and give him a Fathers blessing, or if a Daughter, do likewise. But my Love, I have no idea, but the stranger is a Boy. If it should be otherwise, I will not be in the least mortified, for I declare to you, that I have no choice, unless it were that we might have a dear little Maggy. I have often regretted, that I did not call Nannie, Margaret. You can never have a babe, with eyes more like yourself, than that afore said young lady, whose pugnacity caused her to rap poor Sam, on the head. I hope [you] will have no trouble about names. Tho, the Shandy family thought there was much in a name! If a Maggy should be in the family, I only hope that she may be all that her dear Mother is in excellency, and many amiable qualities.

My Love it is now late, and I am pestered with a man who is half intoxicated, and he has just standing enough to prevent me from ordering him out of my room. Don't make a fuss about my writing too often, for I intend to write, just as often as I can, to you, & Sam.

Give my love to Mother, and the Misses Davis. Kiss all our dear little ones for me. Tell the servants to be faithful. I will rely upon them to take care of all the property. I would like to hear about the Pigs, etc. etc.

I am thy faithful and devoted husband
Sam Houston

P.S. My Love, you will see how much change, there is in my hand writing. I do not suffer from my arm, yet the nerves are often affected.

Thine ever
Houston

∞

My Dearest,

I have written to Sam,[1] and can not deny myself the pleasure of saying some thing to you, if it is only to say, how much I love you, or that I love you more, the longer I am absent from you! It is my intention to visit Baltimore this evening, and attend a "Sympathising [sic] meeting." I may speak on the occasion but I am not certain that I will say any thing. You know I sympathize more more [sic] for <u>Ireland</u>, than for <u>France</u>. The Irish are kinsfolk, and if I speak, I will talk of them. I trust long before this will reach you, that your health will be restored, and your cheerfulness will be complete. I mean as complete as it can be until I become the recipient of your <u>smiles</u>. Until then, I assure you my Love, that my happiness will be very incomplete. I permit myself, to fancy, and hope for the time, when there will be a contest between Sam & Nannie, for pa's knee. I hope to be most agreeably worried by them, and fancy might add more to the contest. You know my Love, that I have a great love for <u>children</u>, and now, it is restricted, to our own.

Thy faithful Husband
Houston

[1]This letter has not been located.

∽

Huntsville May 3 1848

My dear husband,

I recd your two letters from Raleigh[1] today. Many many thanks for them. I wish I could write you a long letter, but it is not in my power to do so, as I have arisen from a sick bed, to prepare this scrawl. I was so very smart after the baby's birth, that I contracted a violent cold, attended with some symptoms, that with any medicine, but the botanic would have been serious, but I will try to be more prudent hereafter. My precious babe grows finely, and is a perfect beauty. Sam and Nannie are the rosiest children, I have ever seen in Texas. With the exception of a cold, Mother enjoys fine health and spirits. I am careful to tell the servants all you direct about the farm, but the fact is, they are tolerably lazy and stubborn, and you know my love, that there is no one to control them. They will not be governed by Mother, and all I can do, is to remind them, now and then, that you will expect a good crop from them. Mother says the corn and potatoes are doing finely, but I fear you will be disappointed in the quantity of ground that is in cultivation. I can not ascertain exactly how much they have taken in, but am inclined to believe that it is considerably short of your calculation. As far as I am concerned, I am determined not to make myself miserable about that or any thing else, but I sometimes feel a sort of apprehension that you will be dissatisfied with your farming arrangements when you get back. The negroes have had such a taste of freedom, that they would be very insolent, if we exercised any authority over them, but no such a thing is attempted, therefore I trust we will get along peaceably at least. This is certainly not very interesting matter for a letter, but my object is to prevent your making great calculations upon a crop. Mother says I must tell you what fine irish potatoes we have. They are really very fine. Our yard looks beautiful. I wish you could see my circle in the front yard bordered with pinks and chrysanthemums. It is lovely indeed. I enclose a boquet from it, which you may give to any one you please. I suppose before this you have recd my letter, in which I informed you that I had declined going on. It was always against my judgement [sic], and I am glad that you now see the obstacles that frightened me from attempting it. My dear Love, I do rejoice to hear that there is a probability of congress adjourning in july. Time will move slowly, until I am with you again. Mother sends much love to you. Do you get a letter from me every week? If you do not, the fault is in the mail.

Thine affectionately
M. L. Houston

[1]April 11, 1848, and April 14, 1846.

Washington
7th May 1848

My Dear Love,

You have no idea of my extreme happiness, when I received Mrs [Frances] Creaths letter of the 15th of April.[1] I had been for days, desponding, as you will see from my letters, and was truly miserable. An incident that took place, I will relate to you. About eleven oclock in the day at the capitol, I had my mail given to me, & of course run over my letters to see if any were from you. I saw none, and did not look at the Post mark of the letters. When I came down to my room I brought them with me. After I had eaten my dinner about five oclock, I commenced reading, and the first letter, on looking at the signature, as well as the date told me all. I was resting on the carpet in my room, and my old friend Major Graham of Tennessee,[2] was in my room assisting to read my letters. I was very soon delighted, and announced to him the advent of another little Houston. The major was greatly pleased, for your sake, and mine. He has been married, more than twenty years, and has no little Grahams. Well my Love, I was very happy. We rode to tell Mrs Graham,[3] and Mrs Watsons family. So soon as that was done, a fuss began about the name. I told them, by advisement, it would be Maggy Lea, or I was greatly mistaken. You will soon receive my letters already written on the subject of names. I hope they will be satisfactory to you.

The first thing my Love, upon which I felicitated myself was your good turn, and the prospect of your well doing. The next thing, was that the Babe was a precise resemblance to you, and lastly, that it was a daughter. Poor Sam will be happy that little Maggy resembles her Dear ma, and indeed My dear, I do also rejoice, for you must [*blurred*] suppose, I will think it a very pretty "baby," as Nannie calls it.

I feel very truly obliged to our Sister Creath for her very acceptable letter. I woud rather have received it, than a mine of Gold. I hope you will my Dearest present me to her, and as earnest, you may kiss <u>her</u> <u>for</u> <u>me</u>, as she is neither old nor ugly, and is not in the class of those, whom you allow me to kiss, so you must attend to that yourself. I will look with great anxiety, for your next letter, and only feel concerned, least you may have undertaken to write, before you were quite able. I expect, and hope, you will have much to say, and tell me a thousand little matters. There is some talk of the session adjourning soon, and meeting earlier in the fall. I would be rejoiced, at this of course!

To day I was at church, & heard a fine sermon from my friend Mr Cushman. Our friend, Mr Sampson, has gone to Egupt [sic] (I think it is) as a missionary. The Sacrament of the Lords Supper will be administered at 4 oclock to day.

I have heard from General [William] Wallace, and the news is truly distressing. There is no mitigation of her (Sisters) mental malady, tho her health is considerably improved. I will enclose the letter to Mr Moore that the family can know her situation, tho I fear they will not sympathize with her. Yet, I pray God, that their eyes may be opened as I fear they were the cause of her derangement. Unbridled passion is a terrible fury. I can only hope, and pray for Sisters recovery, but I can not expect it. It is a fearful calamity! I will write to Genl Wallace soon, and advise him to try electricity.

I will close as it is near dinner, and I intend to go to church this evening. My Love, before I close I must let you know, that I hope Albert[4] is religious, but have no confidence in him. He is the most deceitful fellow in the world. I did not think to tell you of some things, of his deceit. Let an eye be kept upon him. I fear he meditates some mischief. Don't let him know that he is suspected. It is my intention my dear, to say to you something about politics, in my next. You have not told me my Love, whether Mrs Woods has written to you, or you to her. Tomorrow, I intend to write a note to the Doctor, and tell him the news.

I was wide of the mark in my calculations just ten days. I will send Mrs Creaths letter to Miss Tene or to Sister Virilla.

In all truth thy devoted husband. Kiss all, double kisses.

Adieu
Houston

[1]This letter has not been located.
[2]Daniel Graham, former Tennessee Secretary of State, who was now serving as Register of the U. S. Treasury. *Writings*, vol. 1, 18n.
[3]Maria McIver Graham. Lucas, 39.
[4]A Houston slave.

Senate Chamber
8th May 1848

My Dearest,

This day eight years ago, you became Mrs Houston, and my beloved wife (or was it on the 9th?)[1] and I have loved you ever since, and to day more than ever. Another link has been added, to the chain of affection! I yet feel anxious, about your situation. I am fearful that you may not have been careful. You were so *[blurred]*. After our little Nannies birth, you know my Love, you caught cold by slight exposure! I will hope that you are entirely free from all risk, and restored to health.

To day I made a speech in the Senate,[2] and I am now resting, at my desk. It was on the subject of Yucatan, who wants aid against the Indians—It was a fair solid and sensible speech. It did no harm to my reputation. If it should be printed, I will send you a copy.

The Baltimore Convention will take place, on the 22nd Inst, and then we will know, who is to be the candidate of the Democratic Party.[3] There is no telling, who it will be. I have this to say,—if I am not nominated, the whigs will take up Taylor, and in all human probability, they will beat. Unless a drum & fife, can be brot in as auxiliary, to the claims of a candidate, of the Democratic party, I fear the acting over, of the scenes of 1840, between Harrison & Van Buren. Worse than Coon-skins, will be rung upon the Democrats.

The Senate has adjourned. My Love to all.

Adieu Dearest
Thine ever
Houston

I dont look over the letter. H.

[1]They were married on May 9, 1840.
[2]For a copy of this speech see *Writings*, vol. 5, 37–53.
[3]For information about this convention see Philip Shriver Klein, *President James Buchanan: A Biography* (University Park: The Pennsylvania State University Press, 1989): 204–205.

☯

On May 8, 1848, Margaret wrote a letter to Houston describing the new baby. The original has not been located, but the following excerpts from it can be found on page 368 of Marquis James's The Raven.

. . . our precious baby enjoys fine health and is beginning to look like her father. . . . She can stand on her feet, with as much strength, as most children three months old. She has the prettiest little hands and feet . . . and from the descriptions you have given me of your mother's I think they must be like hers. . . . She is becoming quite a young lady, to have no name. . . . My dear Love, I fear that you are suffering your mind to be drawn off from the subject of religion, by the political excitement of the day. . . . Oh when I think of the allurements that surround you, I tremble, lest they should steal your heart from God. . . . There is something so bewitching in the voice of fame. . . . I . . . pray with all my heart that you may be kept from the evil of this world and fitted for the joys of the next.

☯

Senate Chamber
10th May 1848

My Beloved,
I do not know how long this letter will be, as we are going into Secrite [sic] Session, and I will close, by the time it is over.

I have no news to tell you, for I have told you how much I love you, that if I were to renew the assurance, I fear you would believe me almost crazy. Well my Love, I am nearly so, but it is my anxiety, to see home—to see you—to see the stranger Miss Maggy Lea, and indeed to see all, that is dear to me. The excitements, of this place, and all its gayeties, can not estrange me, or my affections from you, and from home. The first I do not enter into, and the second, I do not participate in. I go to the Presidents, at receptions, only because, it relieves me from many calls, at my room.

Do not my Love be affected, by the action of the Baltimore Convention. It is utterly uncertain, who will be the nominee. My chances are equal to any one, and by many, they are thought the best. I would rather take my chance. Go as it may, it will not distress me, if an honest man is selected as a candidate.

I will let you know the result, so soon as it is over. I will be there as a delegate from Texas. I will be, if I live, very sedate, and genteel.

My love to Mother, and kiss our dear little flock. You have quite a troop, I suppose you think? I wish you would be so good my dear, as to let me know all about Maggy Lea, and how our Mother, and friends are pleased, with her advent. Every thing from you, my Love, will give me happiness. I even love to look upon any thing which you have seen, and like Sam, <u>kiss</u> your letters. I esteem them "<u>precious little letters</u>." I intend to write to him often, as I can.

Salute the Miss Davis'. My Love, remember me to our friends all, and tell me if you have kissed our excellent friend Mrs Creath.

Thy faithful and devoted husband.

Sam Houston

∽

The following letter is addressed to Revd Doct A. Woods in Providence, Rhode Island, and is from the Alva Woods Papers.

Washington
12th May 1848

My Dear Sir,

As the event imparted the highest pleasure to me, I am not so selfish, as to deny to yourself & Lady all the participation in my joys. Therefore, I will tell you, that on the 13th ult, Mrs Houston, added to our domestic circle, a daughter. In the language of the mother (for she is doing well and wrote to me) "it is one of the prettiest babes, you have ever seen."

It will render me happy at all times, to hear from you, as it conveys much news, that will gratify me, in knowing that Lady, and yourself are well. Furthermore, the first thing done with your letters or notes, is to send them to Mrs Houston. Has Lady Woods written to Mrs Houston lately? Mrs H. has been looking (as she writes me) a long time for letters.

I pray you to present to Lady, Mrs H-s [sic] and my best regards, and affection, and believe us truly, and devotedly your Friends. I have no news. All is hustle here. The Convention excites our Great men, as it approaches. All pulses quicken, but those, who are "lookers on in Vienna."

Thine truly
Sam Houston

Washington
12th May 1848

My Dearest Wife,

I yet feel the happiness which your letter imparted to me. Your own hand, and you my dear One, able to write! The associations consoled me for the painful, and boundless anxieties, which I have felt for months. My Love, I would like to know if you have forgiven me for saying "if you have time" yet? Have you my dear forgiven me for this most careless expression. If you could only know how much

I have regretted that only faulty remark, I am sure you would think if it had ever been intentional, that my suffering ought to be regarded, as penitence for the crime. It would my Love be criminal, to mortify you, without cause. Nay My Love, I hope we will pass through our lives, without any intention to hurt each others feelings. I feel that we have had much happiness, and I regret, that I have not been more sedulous, to make you perfectly happy. Much has been in my power, to do, and I find, that it was left undone. If we are so happy as to meet again, you will find that my disposition, is much changed. I am become almost fat, and you will find me as tame, and quiet as bro. Royston, tho' not so large. On tomorrow our little Maggy Lea, if she lives, will be one month old. You may suppose me very anxious to see the young lady. I am the more so, as Mrs Creath said she was just like you. I do assure you my Love, it was a most delightful assurance.

[*The following was written across the fourth page of the letter:*]
My Love,
From company in my room, that page was overlooked, and not written upon! I have it much oftener here, than if I could have the control of my time.

Adieu,

Houston

[*The letter continues on the fifth page.*]
To you I may say that nothing on this earth, could give me so much pleasure, as to see, and embrace you, and the little flock. Yes, my Love, I would like to chat of the past, and smile upon the <u>present</u>! The contest for preference—Nannies strong will, and Sam's manly self control, rather than quarrel with a sister. Poor little Mag will not feel rivalry, as yet, but for a mothers smiles. How strange it seems, when I compare my feelings now enjoyed, and those I possessed, when I was here some twenty years ago.[1] One thought now, is worth all the feelings of years gone by. My wife, and children, are to me every thing, that can charm or delight my heart. I hope my Love, you will not fail through modesty, to let me know how much little Maggy resembles you! If you intend to gratify me, tell me of the resem-

blance to the full extent. Tell me if she resembles you, as much as Nannie is said to resemble me? Sam is a blended likeness of your brothers, & myself!

Does Nannie walk and act, as much like her dear Grand Ma, as ever? I am curious to know this fact. The time, that Nannie, from instinct, struck poor Sam on the head, satisfied me, that she would be a Lady of impulse, and will require some remonstrance. Nannie [Maggie?] Lea, I hope will partake more of the zephyr than the storm. Tell me of Sam's disposition. Is he generous? Is he humane? Are his affections for you, as great as ever? Is he fond of kindred, and Clan? That he will be brave from principle, I have do doubt! Is he yet a Pharisee, and dependent upon the services of Bernadotte? Oh my Love, I do assure you, that I feel more anxious in my present exile, than I did when in the wilds of Arkansas. I am where it is said the world is, and yet I am far from all that constitutes my world on earth.

Sister Antoinette was kind enough to write me on the 14th of April. It was a pretty, & kind letter. I must pay her soon. To day I wrote to Dr Woods and when I hear from him, I will send you his letter! I told him of Miss Maggy Lea's advent in delicate, and appropriate terms. I did not say she was born, but that you had "added to our domestic circle a beautiful daughter, as you said." My love to Mother and the family. Kisses to our little ones. Say to Sam, I will soon write to him.

Thy faithful & devoted
Houston

[1]Houston is referring to the time when he served as a Congressman from Tennessee.

14th May 1848

My Dearest,

I am just from church. I have been there thrice to day. I heard two interesting sermons. I always try to keep sunday, however much

I may fail in the object. I also feel, and know if I were to regard every day, as the sabbath, I should then fail in my duty. I will not cease to try, and so far as I can, to perform my duty, in life, and prepare for death. We know that it is the end of time, and we are placed in the enjoyment of time, to prepare for eternity.

On last night, I wrote a long letter to our Niece Phoebe Jane[1] to let her know, how matters stood with us, and her Fathers family, and my reasons for not bringing Isabella to see her. I was as delicate as I could be to tell the truth, and I doubt not, but she will be satisfied. She must know her relations. I told her, from my knowledge of her character, I was assured if you and she could meet, that you would love each other! I believe it to be true. I told her of our continued attachment to Betty, Mary, & Houston. She being so well acquainted with her Mother, & Isabella, it was needless, as I apprehend, to offer any explanation, as to our disagreement.

I told her a part of what I had done for the family. I also told her of your feelings, toward the family, and our wishes, that Betty, & Mary should live with us.

You may not approve of my course, but when you reflect you will sanction it, I hope! I have written to her the state of you and the children—number, etc, and requested her to write to me, all about her family, and husband. Should I receive a letter from her, I will enclose it to you.

It is near time, when I begin to look for a letter from our Son, and I hope he will tell me, some of our dear little Nannies prattle, and something pretty about Maggy Lea. I was happy to hear of the joy of Sam, & Nannie at the advent of their little sister. They have none of the <u>cares</u> of their dear Grand ma, about the sub division of property, so that they will not sympathize with her. I wish you would tell me what Ma has to say on the subject. However, I can I can [sic] guess as I believe she said to you—"I love the child, and I am glad that you have a namesake, but I hope you will stop now." Am I right? I think I am!

My fancy about home, is almost wild, to see my home again. To see, to meet, to embrace you, is the most ardent desire of my heart. If

I could, I would, with pleasure leave my seat here, in exchange, for one at my own fire side, if I even had some <u>person to nurse!!!</u> Would you my Love, have any objections to this situation? My Love, commend me to our mother. Kiss the children, and salute friends.

Ever thine,
Houston

[1]Phoebe Jane (Mrs. N. A.) Penland.

∞

Washington
16th May 1848

My Dearest,

I have only time to say that nothing important has transpired, since I last wrote last night. I learn, that all the candidates, are on their feet. Some of them must be <u>disappointed</u>! For my part, so far as my name has been used in connexion [sic], with the high office of the Executive chief of the nation, I have not, nor will I ever set my heart upon it. So let the result be what it may. I pray you to believe, that it will not diminish my happiness, but if it were possible, it would give new charms to home.

I have seen young Mr King,[1] the son of Genl King[2] of Perry, and his mother[3] loves you as much as ever. He informs me that all were well at home, and in the country. He says farther, that Young Royston was on his way to Texas, or would set out soon to see his kindred. So I hope he will call at the house with <u>Brick chimneys</u> & <u>Glass windows</u>. I am only sorry that I can not be there, to meet him. I have seen several Alabamians, and the other day, I called upon Miss Mary Cobb, to let her know that you had presented me with another fine daughter, and that [her] name was Maggy Lea. In all this, I was properly delicate, and modest. She is crazy to see our son, of whom Lucy Ann [Lea] told them so much. In proper circles, I amuse people, about Texas life, by telling the anecdote of the "brick chimneys" etc, and it is the more agreeable to me, because you are embraced in subject. Oh my dear Love, if I could, I would fly to you this very night, altho I should be drenched, well, for it is now raining, and has been for hours past. Miss Cobb bade me, to present you, her devoted affection. I do so with pleasure, as I think her a genteel, and amiable young Lady. I have promised her Houston Moore, and if he were to get her I have no doubt, but what she would make him a splendid wife, or I should rather say, a good, and discreet one.

Present me to mother, [and] the Misses Davis. Kiss the wee ones, and salute all friends. I am thy faithful and devoted

Houston

[1]Porter King. Owen, vol. 3, 982.
[2]Edwin King. Ibid.
[3]Ann Alston Hunter King. Ibid.

∽

Washington
17th May 1848

My Dearest,

Since I wrote to you last night, I have again seen Mr [Porter] King. From him I learned that Brother Henry has kept his pledge, has assumed his position in society, resumed his practice at the bar, with fine success, and has been unanimously elected Mayor of Marion. His family too as said by Mr King, have assumed their place, and it is now a happy family, to use the language of Mr King. Knowing how happy this intelligence would make you, and Mother, I hastened to convey it to you. The confusion of the Delegates, increases, as their numbers increase, in the City. For my own part my Love, I have nothing to say in the matter. If it comes it is well, and I will be prepared to meet the occasion, but I declare to you, I will not truckle, nor degrade my feelings for any station on this earth! I will be at the Convention as a delegate from Texas, but will only stay a short time. So soon as the result is known, I will write to you. In the meantime, be assured my Dearest, I will feel, and think more about you, and the children, than I will about office.

My love to all, and kisses to the children.

> Thy faithful and devoted husband
> Sam Houston

⬤

> Senate Chambers
> 18th May 1848

My Dearest,

I write this morning, because I have to prepare my speech on Yucatan, for the press.[1] I intend to have it out by the time of Convention. It is the wish of my friends. You will suppose that I was not very anxious on my own part, or I would have done it before to day. I have no news to tell you of. Every thing is new, to those here. I can see them, as St Paul found them in Athens. It would not interest you to tell to you any of the subjects, or matters adgitated [sic]. The merits, and claims of parties, and the demerits of others. The affairs are confined to local or personal.

The adherents are all in a <u>bother</u>. They are in trouble, and a reconciliation of their conflicting claims, I imagine will be difficult to reconcile.

Their motto is not that of the acord [sic] "I bide my time."

My love to all, & kisses to the children.

> Thy Devoted
> Houston

[1]For a copy of this speech see *Writings*, vol. 5, 37–53.

⬤

> Huntsville May 24 1848

My ever dear Love,

On last night, I recd your favours of the 1st, 2nd and 3rd inst. The mail came in so late, that I had to send for my letters, after supper, but you may be sure that I did not think much of sleep, until I had read and reflected for hours upon the contents of your truly welcome epistles. I perceive in your feelings, an increasing seriousness and a greater concern than ever for the salvation of your soul. At this I rejoice greatly, for I believe that you "are not far from the kingdom of Heaven," and that the Lord will soon reveal the blessed Jesus unto your soul. Another thing encourages me greatly. It is the feelings with which I pray for you of late. Never have I prayed for any thing, with such strong faith, as the conversion of your soul. I "ask," realy "believing that I shall receive." And yet can it be, that such happiness is in reserve for a poor worm like myself! To see my husband enjoying the comforts of religion, and to have his aid in bringing up our children for the Lord would be greater blessings than I can ever deserve, but the Lord doth not measure his mercies by our worth.

Sam was asleep, when his little letter[1] came, but this morning it gave him an agreeable surprise, and he designs answering it, so soon as mamma can assist him. He was delighted with the picture, which you drew in my letter of Nannie and himself contending for your knee. His first exclamation was "Yes ma, and you must tell pa, that I will take little sissy in my arms." I could fill a letter with his pretty little sayings, but we have so many to write about now, that master Sammy must leave a little room. But I must tell you a question he asked, the first time he saw the baby, as it will give you an insight into some of his little perplexities. After gazing with fondness and admiration for a minute or two, upon her sweet face, a shade of seriousness stole across his brow, and looking up at me he inquired, "Ma will she knock down my houses, when she gets big?" Ah that cruel Nannie of ours, but she is becoming a sort of house builder herself, and I trust that poor Sam will hereafter be suffered to follow his occupation in peace. The baby has taken up a great deal of Nannie's time. I wish you could hear her singing her to sleep. It is the finest melody I have ever heard in my life. It is difficult to decide whether Sam or Nannie is more like you. They are both remarkably like you, and yet they differ from each other. Your features and traits of character seem to be divided between them. The baby's head is as much like yours, as Sam's was at his birth, but her features are said to be all like mine. I feel greatly distrest lest you should have misunderstood me about the names of the children. If you will refer to the letter, you will perceive, that I proposed calling the baby Elizabeth Paxton. My object was, that your mother's name might be as conspicuous in our family, as that of my own mother. But as you are superstitious about changing names, I will say no more about it. It never occurred to me for a moment, that our relations could make any thing out of it, but perhaps they might do so.

Before you get this letter, I expect Mary Moore will be married to John Lehr.[2] They are preparing for the wedding. I am rejoiced at it, for I do not believe she could have made a better selection. The course he has pursued towards his brothers and sisters has raised him higher than ever, in the estimation of people. There are 20 negroes belonging to him and his mother, and John has about seven thousand dollars in cash himself. All this I have learned from Mrs Birdwell. She certainly never could have done so well in Tenn. Mr Moore has paid Dr. [John] Branch in corn for the hire of his negro man, and he still has corn for sale. As it is scarce, I suppose he will get a good price for it. Joshua and Ann have a daughter,[3] and I believe that is all the news I have of them, but you will have perceived that they are prospering, and I am sure you can not rejoice more at it, than I do.

I would have told you before about the pigs, but we have been so unfortunate with them, that I did not like to distress you about them. Your Stubblefield sows have been eating up all the young ones but 11 or 12, and I am at a loss to know what to do with them. I will have them watched as carefully as possible, but they eat them after they are large pigs and are such ravenous creatures, that I do not think you need to calculate on raising a stock with them. Our corn looks beautiful indeed. Sam was walking through it a few evenings ago, with Mrs Creath, and remarked to her as the wind passed over it, that it looked like green water. Mrs C. spends the most of her time with me and is an invaluable friend to me. In my feeble health, she assists me very much in taking care of my little girl. Mother's time is very nearly taken up with Nannie and the household cares. I have not yet recovered from the cold taken after my confinement, and I sometimes fear I never shall be strong again. But I feel better today, than for many days past, and perhaps I may soon be well. I recd a letter last night from Charles Power and Ann. He says it will be out of thier power to come up this summer. It is a great disappointment to us, but can not be helped. He has a barrel of sugar and one of syrup for us, and I hope we will get them soon. The children grow finely and seem to enjoy perfect health. When you come, I wish you would bring locks for our corn-crib, storeroom and potatoe [sic] house. Those we get here are no protection. There are so many just alike. It will require all our vigilance to take care of the little that we make. Do you still think congress will adjourn in July? I trust so indeed, for the hours are long and dreary without you. If you can without troubling yourself procure a copy of "Drellingcourt" for Mrs Birdwell, I would be very glad. She is greatly in love with it, and I am too selfish to part with mine, particularly as it is a present. I wonder what has become of Mrs Allen's journal. I never get it now.

Farewell
Thy devoted wife
M. L. Houston

[1]This letter has not been located.
[2]They were married on August 31, 1848. Mary E. Vick-Rainey, *Marriage Records of Walker County* (Huntsville, Tex.: Walker County Genealogical Society, 1978), 4.
[3]Julie, who was born to Ann Eliza in Crockett, Texas. Patrica Smith Prather and Jane Clements Monday, *From Slave to Statesman* (Denton: University of North Texas Press, 1993), 38.

∽

Huntsville June 2nd 1848

My dear Husband,

More than a week has past since I wrote to you, for the reason that I have not been able to hold my pen long enough to write a letter. My feebleness is truly distressing and unfits me entirely for my household duties, so that I fear when you return, you will think I am a poorer housekeeper than ever. My cough is so bad, that I rarely go out of my room, but my friends think that so soon as I get over the effects of my confinement, it will leave me again, and I think when you come home, I will get right well. I recd your letter in acknowledgement [sic] of sister Creath's, and I gave her your kiss. She and bro. Creath are gone to Gen'l Davis's. He was expected on last night to marry our young friend Carry to Mr McCardell[1] of Swartout, and on sunday I expect he will baptize her and Mrs. Davis.[2] Carry wrote me a very affectionate letter, begging me to go down and witness her nuptials, and I would have been glad to do so, if it had been in my power, as I am told she is making a fine choice. Another peice [sic] of good news for you, is the entire reformation of your friend Wade[3] of this place. They are forming a society of "The sons of temperance," and he is to be one of the members. Truly I do rejoice with his wife.[4] It is expected that she will join our church shortly. Frank Hatch has also repented of his evil doings and made acknowledgements to the church. He is actively engaged in getting up the society. Oh how I wish you were here to put your hand to the blessed work! It is a dear cause to me, and surely it ought to be. My precious brother [Henry], so long a wanderer, hath been drawn within its sacred fold and restored to usefulness.

You were correct about Albert. He was so cunning, that he was very near getting into the church, but fortunately his hypocrisy was discovered, and I fear he is planning some great act of villainy. Our children enjoy fine health and grow very rapidly. Since I commenced writing, the baby laughed aloud for the first time. She takes more notice, than any child of her age, I ever saw. She is getting to be a great big girl. Sam and Nannie are still excessively fond of her. Sam receives one of her little smiles, as if he were the most honoured of human beings, and Nannie thinks all the care of her, devolves upon herself. Sam was delighted with his "New England primer." I have not yet given you a list of the presents that you sent us. We were all delighted I assure you. One dress pattern (silk) for myself and three pairs of gloves, one dress and pair of shoes for Nannie, one plaid suit for Sam, (rather too large, but an excellent fault). Two flannel wrappers for baby, for which she will kiss you when you come home. Three kisses from the children. Nannie could not get her shoes on, but <u>luckily</u> I can put them away for baby. If I think of it, when I write again, I will send you the measure of Sam's boots, and <u>also</u> of his foot. Do not get them too small. Remember you are <u>short-sighted</u> in these matters. Our friends are all very anxious for your return. We expect you early in august. Do not tarry one hour I beg you, for I can never be happy until I see you again. My hand is so weak, that I can not write more.

Thy affectionate wife
M. L. Houston

[1]Caroline Davis married Thomas M. McCardell. Daughters of the Republic of Texas, *Founders and Patriots of Texas: The Lineages of the Members of the Daughters of the Republic of Texas* (Published Privately, 1963), vol. 1, 262.
[2]Ann Eliza Hill Davis.
[3]John H. Wade. Identified in *1850 Census*, vol. 4, 2011.
[4]Virginia Wade. Ibid.

∞

New York
11th June 1848

My Dearest Margaret,

A week has now passed, and I am here. As I told you in my last letter, that I proposed coming here, so I did. Genl Cass, and others would have me to come along, and so soon as I got here, why I must not leave until tomorrow. On this evening, that great "<u>ratification</u>" meeting is to take place in the this [sic] city. It is supposed that at least fifty thousand persons will be present. There is the very greatest excitement here that I have ever seen. The Democracy will succeed in this state, and I think through out the union. Howell Cobb is with me, and will return with me to Washington on tomorrow morning at 8 oclock tomorrow. On tomorrow evening, I am to address at [sic] great meeting at Wilmington, Delaware. I will be on my way to Washington, and happy to be able to devote my self to business, and to writing you.

I will send you my Love, the news papers. In the meantime my Love, and ever be assured, that I can not be for one moment happy, until I can embrace you, and our dear children.

Commend me to Mother, and the family. Also to all our good friends.

Kiss the children for me. I must write every day, or I am miserable.

Thy Devoted & faithful Husband
Sam Houston

∽

Huntsville June 12th 1848

My Love,

Owing to some new arrangement of the mails, I have not recd your letters regularly of late, and I fear that mine to you have been detained likewise. I rejoice sincerely that the period of your absence, the gloomy period of anxiety and suspense, is drawing to a close. I do not feel as if I could bear it much longer. My fortitude is almost exhausted.

We have heard here, that Cass was the nominee for the presidency, and I think from what I can hear, that there is great dissappointment [sic] amongst the democrats. My first thought was that your family would have more of your society than if you had been nominated, and therefore I felt gratified. My health is still very bad. I have used great efforts to get to the sour lake in Liberty co, as I am told that its waters have made some wonderful cures of diseases of every kind, even the consumption in an advanced state, but thus far it has been out of my power, and now I am postponing the journey, until you get home. If you think well of it then, we will try its virtues. Our dear little Nannie still suffers from the effect of neumonia, and I was anxious to try the springs, on her account, as well as my own. It is impossible to get her to take medicine enough to effect a permanent cure.

I mentioned to you in my last that Mr and Mrs Creath were gone to Gen'l Davis's to hold a meeting. They had a very large meeting, and there seemed to be a great deal of feeling amongst the people. Carry was married on the 1st inst, and she and Mrs Davis were baptized on the 4th. Gen'l Davis seems to be under deep conviction, and I hope before long to hear of his conversion. Bro. Vernal and sister Katherine were at the meeting, and started up to see us, but Bro. V. was taken sick, and they were compelled to go back. He sent me word, by the Messrs Ellis[1] who came up, that if I would get down to his house, they would go with me to the sour lake. My friends here are very anxious for me to try its virtues, and Mrs Birdwell has offered to go with me and take care of me, but I think I will put it off until you get home, and then I should not be at all surprised, if my health began to improve immediately, for I am satisfied that my depression of spirits has a great deal to do with it.

Tomorrow our precious babe will be two months old. Oh my love, while I write of her my eyes are blinded with tears. Oh shall I ever place the little cherub in your arms! The charms of early infancy are passing away, and you will never see them. That sweet expression which seems to see more of Heaven than earth is almost gone, and her bright eyes now gaze with delight on earthly things. Our Nannie is still very beautiful, and although her cough is distressing, she has a healthy robust appearance, and is the merriest little creature I ever saw. When asked, "what must papa bring her when he comes home," she answers "doll baby," "and what else," "canny" (candy). Our son Sam at this time is busily engaged in erecting mills on our spring branch. He has some rare inventions in the way of mills, and takes great pain to explain the machinery to me. He enjoys fine health, and I think he is a remarkably handsome boy. I send you the measure of Sam's boots, including the heel. The slip looks so long, that I fear you will measure from the heel mark, but it is the exact length. I told you I would send the measure of his foot also, but I find that the boot is not too short for him, and only needs greater width. Farewell my beloved. My heart is sad without you.

Thy fond and devoted wife
M. L. Houston

P.S. I presume Col. Yokum has written to you that he could do nothing with the lawsuit. Palmer seems to have thrown a Lethean influence over all the witnesses, and they can remember nothing. Well
our children will lose something by it, but I trust they will never
suffer for food or raiment. Col Yokum requested me some weeks
ago, to tell you that you are likely to lose your land-suit in the red-
lands, from want of attention. He says the lawyer who was employed
with Cage,[2] has been made Judge, and he does not think Cage will be
able to manage it alone. I have <u>memorialized</u> to you so often on the
subject of <u>land</u>, that I was inclined to say nothing about it, but a sense
of duty impelled me. I am writing with the baby on my lap, and that
will account for my apparently careless style. I am compelled to act
as nurse for your daughter <u>Maggy</u>, as you call her, for the reasons
that Charlotte was so ungovernable that I hired her out, and Eliza has
the scrofula very badly, and I fear incurably. She still assists about
the house, but I do not know how long she will be able to do so. Mary
has recovered her health, and is a valuable servant. Do not, let me
entreat you, do not buy any more slaves. Mother is well and sends
her love to you.

[1]Joseph and Benjamin Ellis.
[2]Rufus K. Cage. Identified in *Poll Lists*, 24.

Washington
19th June 1848

My Beloved,

I thank [you] for yours of the 17th[1] & 24th ult. The mail will
close in a few minutes and I write before it closes merely to tell you
that I will write you a long letter, this evening. I am distressed at your
bad health, and you see ire this that I feared it would be the case. I am

truly glad to hear of the welfare, of Mother, & the children.

If this letter reaches you a week or more before the one which I intend to write this evening, it is what I expect. I will write to Sam also, and send word to Nannie, & kisses to Maggy Lea.

I know you will excuse this short letter. I see you were a little jealous of my attractions to the Ladies. For instance "very short letters." & that in connexion [sic] with Miss [Mary] Cobb, whom I have seen but three, or four times this season. My Love, the sun will change his place, so soon as I find in this world, a being to supply your place in my affections. I could not love, any one on earth, but my dear Margaret, nor little ones, but, my Margarets, & my own.

Thy devoted Husband
Houston

P.S. Love & kisses to all!

H

¹This letter has not been located.

Senate Chamber
20th June 1848

My Beloved,

It was my promise to write to you, and our Boy, on last night. I found on my return so much to do, that my time has not been my own. Nothing cou'd be so agreeable to me as to employ my time in communing with you by letter. It affords me the only consolation which I can derive, while I am absent from you, and our dear children. You can have but little idea of my anxiety to see our little rosebud, Maggy Lea. The fact that she resembles you so much, is to me a cause of true pleasure. First because I wish it to be so, and again because Sam will be more gratified, than if she resembled me. But from what you say, [of] his increasing in likeness to me, he will cease to be jealous of Miss Nannie. I think I can tell you the reason, that

Sam wants "six little brothers." He thinks there will be a preponderance in power, and influence against him, as the family now stands. It is very unequal, for it is much more easy, to "spoil" than it is to build houses. Sam is a curious Boy. I hope our Nannie will be a fair musician, and I can fancy her gravity, and composure when singing her little sissy to sleep. I hope Sam is a good nurse, tho' I am fearful, that he will not be very graceful, or easy, in handling the little one. No doubt he has fancied my agreeable surprise (if I live to return) on seeing Maggy Lea. I have a fancy, that Sam supposes he is now the richest Boy in Texas, & would be entirely happy, if it were not for spoiling houses.

On yesterday, I sent you many scraps, of News papers to show you how things went to the North, on the town, in which I was associated. I went at the proposing request, of Genl Cass, and my friends. At first I refused to go, but I could not get off. I was absent two weeks, and my expenses were met by the several committees where we went. Indeed, it was with much difficulty that I could return, as the party wished me to go to all the important cities & towns in New York. Would you believe it possible for men to desire me, to pass the whole summer in the North, & speak to the people, on political topics. Yes, My Dearest, and not to see you, nor our dear little ones. It is all that I can do to keep my temper, at such suggestions. I assure that not [sic] station on earth, could induce me to forego, my instant return to my home, so soon as Congress adjourns! It is true that I have been very much caressed, by the people, wherever I have been. I have but one more appointment to meet, and that is on the 4th of July, at Carlyle Penna. This is the place of my ancestors. I have been invited to go, and to the most remote parts of Maine. Virginia, too, and most of the middle states, and the Western. Well my Love, I declare to you, that such things here cause me but little pleasure. And that I was not the nominee of the convention, is truly gratifying to me. You had a dream which I thought of, and I was unhappy, until the selection was made. Then I was cheerful, & happy. Had I been selected, it would not have increased my reputation. As it is, my name is used with good effect, and there will not be the same cause, or reason to assail me. I defy all assaults, of every character, but things are, my name will insinuate its self, among the people, & will there settle down, to a decided bias in my favor, and should I at some future day be brought before the nation, it can be done successfully. The feeling in all parts, even beyond the strength of the Democracy is in favor of my name being used in 1852, if I should live. I had to refuse the Vice Presidency most positively. I hope my Love, that you will no[t] chagrin, at the result of matters.

Now my Love, I hope you will not think this letter too short. It might have been much shorter, and more interesting. I tell you dearest, I do assure you that I would rather talk to you twenty years, than write two letters from this city. While talking, I could see your dear face, and hear your voice. I hope you are again restored to health. I will be miserable until I know that you are well.

Thine ever truly
Houston

∞

Senate Chambers
22nd June 1848

My Dearest,

I will write to you, altho' I do not promise to write you a "long letter." Now my Love, if I were only to write to you, occasionally, I might then write you a long letter, and have a mass of news, but really my Love, I write so often, that I have at times, been fearful, that my letters would appear insipid to you. Now I have little else to tell you, than that I love you, and the children, & that I am almost crazy to see you, and be with you, and never again, to be seperated in life. I sent your letters to Miss Cobb for her perusal, as you alluded to her. She thought you a little jealous, as you associated "short letters" with the reference to her. She said that she truly forgave you. I told her that you told me (before marriage,) "that it was an infirmity of yours." Now my Love, if you could only look into my heart, I feel assured, (as my brightest hope is in Heaven,) you woud never believe, for one moment that my <u>affections</u>, or my <u>passions</u>, could attach to any earthly object but your dear self. My Love, I am not irritated, nor provoked, but I do really regret, that my dear wife should fancy for one moment, that my whole heart is not devoted to her. It is an evidence of your affection, and however gratifying it is to me, that you should love me, I feel, that the expression is prompted by painful doubts entertained by you. My Love, so long as I hope, to be with you again, on earth, and to unite with you, in preparing ourselves, and our children for a happy eternity, so long may you rely upon my <u>constancy</u>, and my affection.

I have thus given you assurances, my Dearest, for the reason, that your health is delicate, and I will never with-hold any means, in my power, which can minister to your happiness & contentment! For my self, I can never be happy, until I can again embrace you, and our babes. At times, I really envy you a portion, of your enjoyments, such as the prattle of our little ones. I wish to hear Miss Nannie singing her Lullaby to Miss Maggy Lea. The most beautiful trait in the character, of our son, is his devotion to you. I feel assured, that he will be noble, intellectual, and brave!! He will be moral as I hope. His love of approbation, will be a guarantee for his rectitude, and delicate propriety of conduct. Each day, I am more anxious to see our little Rose-bud. I hope to find her your miniature likeness. If she has yours, I do not care that she should have one feature of me, farther than our resemblance to each other.

As for our Nannie, I regard her as Lady Bunch, stumping about,— a being of her own <u>will</u>, and own head. But the Babe! my fancy can not embrace the little miniature, of my dear wife, who is always present to my heart, and my mind.

I discover my Love, a thing, that you have not, & will not admit. Sam is truly your favorite! You do not know it, nor is it necessary that you should. Now my dearest, I hope you will not, by any means suppose, that I could intend to rebuke, or mortify you by anything, which I have written, or can ever write, or say to you! I do not regard any one thing as unamiable, which I have alluded to. No my Love, I have been in the habit, and never expect to change, of regarding you, and loving you, as the best, and to me the loveliest of mortals. Because, you are diffident of your attractions, you suppose, that I concur with you. My Love! In this my Love you are in error, I can assure you! When you were Miss Lea, you believed me, and now Dearest, when I am a better man, and you have higher claims, and I love you much more, I am satisfied you will be at rest, on all matters, touching my love, and devotion to you.

Give my love to Mother, and Kisses to the little ones, and a "squeeze" to Sam, if he does not object to it. Salute our friends, and tell the Blacks howda, & say that I expect them to do their duty!

Thy devoted & faithful Husband

Sam Houston

Washington
24th June 1848

My Beloved,

Yesterday I did not write to you, for the reason that I had nothing to write, but what you must by this time be tired of. I mean my prosing, about you, and the weans. Well to tell you the truth, my writing takes complexion from my thoughts, and they are prompted by my feelings. Now I will tell you of my troubles in part. For a few days past, I have received no less, than four invitations to various sections of the country, to attend on the 4th of July, and address large meetings.[1] One was from Maine, one from Ohio, two from Pennsylvania, and another from North Carolina. These I was compelled to decline, as I intend to be at Carlile in Penna, on the 4th. I can not, and will not worry myself. I will do for the Democracy, all and every thing, which as a true Democrat I ought to do for the party, but I will not expend my private means, or funds. I must husband them for home, and take care to them, until we come to some understanding about the number, which have to be provided for. If I live to reach home, this of course will have to be the first thing arranged, so that no more mistakes may be made, in family matters. I am willing, that you should refer the subject to our friends, Mrs Birdwell, & Mrs Evans for their <u>advice</u>, and if you insist upon it, even for their <u>decision</u>. They will be the proper persons, for they have "been lookers on in Vienna." You see my Love, how rational I am becoming, since Mother was thrown into so much trouble, and displeasure. I sincerely hope my Dearest, that we will never have any bickering, nor heart burnings, on this subject, nor any other. These are matters which will bear, wide reflection, and while we are distant from each other, we can philosophize [sic] upon such matters, and can resolve upon our future action. With such notions as these, I refer you to the Ladies spoken of. My Love, I wrote to you since your last letter arrived, and I did not express what I have continually thought of. I mean your cough, and bad health. This wrings my heart, and makes me very unhappy. I think, had I been at home, it might have been otherwise. My heart was touched by the delicate attention, & sympathy, of our dear Boy. Poor little fellow. I only wish that I cou'd be with him, and unite in the ministrations of kindness, and affection. Our Nannie is too young to know, or feel, what is kindness to a parent. You tell me the Miss Maggy Lea is a "fine babe," but is she fat, and plump as Nannie was at her age? My Dearest, I will not say how anxious I am to see you all, and bestowing a kiss of welcome upon Maggy. I would, it seems to me, be more happy than I have ever been to witness the contest for kisses. I see it now, in my minds eye. Nannie will stand aloof in a kind of doubt, & bewilderment, until she is assured that all is right, and that it is really her Pa. Sams first effort would be to get the kiss, and then to introduce me to Sissy—and Ma!!! These my Love, are painfully pleasant anticipations to me. If they were near fruition, I would be almost delirious, with hope, and joy, but as matters now stand and the delay in business, I am fearful, that we will not get off before the 20th of July, or the 1st of August. I am worried out of all patience. The truth is, that some here to my fancy would just as soon be here as at home. I am not one of the number, I assure you my Love. I have just lost, no less than three precious hours, by "Coaters" calling in my room and interrupting me, since I commenced this letter. I will try, and write you a letter every other day, if possible. I am now getting up my business, so that at the adjournment I may be ready to be off at once.

My Love to all, & kisses to the children

Thy ever devoted Husband
Sam Houston

[1]On July 2, 1848, Houston wrote to the Washington Monument Society expressing his regrets that he would not be able to attend the July 4th celebration. *Writings*, vol. 5, 56.

Washington
26th June (48)

My Dearest,

I write to you this morning, lest I may not have time to write this evening. On yesterday I attended as usual, the Baptist church. I heard as I always do there an excellent sermon. In the evening, I read, and took an airing in a carriage, as I did not feel quite well. The season is not "<u>mighty</u> <u>hot</u>," tho Sam objects, you know, to this expression. Poor fellow, while I was riding over the hights [sic] of Georgetown, I sighed for his presence with that of his dear mother, and his little sisters. Do you my dear, recollect Sam's quarrel with me about "striking" his horses, when we made the trip in 1845?[1] Does he surrender the palm of music to Nannie? I do wish he could sing! Tell me my Love. all about their little eccentricities. You need not think, my Dear, that I will become weary, in reading any thing that you may write.

You have told me about the wedding of our [niece, Mary Moore][2] that was to be. I hope it is so. She will have done very well. Lehr is a clever young man, and I doubt not will make her a good husband. One thing he will have to look to, and that is the influence of her mother, or he will get rid of his own mothers[3] society. I hope, nay I pray, that they may do well, and be happy. It is a source of pleasure to me that our Cally,[4] is about, or has formed a happy union. She deserves it richly. I always regarded her in the light of a relation, even before the famalies [sic] were connected by marriage.[5]

She will make an affectionate, and excellent wife. I do not know, or at this moment recall, the gentleman to memory. But I suppose he is a clever fellow, or Cally would [not] have accepted him, as her Lord, earthly!

Will this letter do my dear as to its length? If I were to write, in the proportion which I love, I would write Books, and now, and then, a dash of Poetry. I do not know my dear, what has become of Mrs Allen, as she has ceased to send her periodical to you. Had I known, the fact, when I was in New York. [sic]

I think I will try, and find her, by enquiry. I do not know my dearest, that I have any thing of importance, further to write at this time.

Have you my dear written to Mrs Woods. I fear you have forgotten her, and the Doctor. You ought to write to Mrs Graham, & Miss Cobb if you have time. I will not go to see Miss Cobb, until you write to her. So you have my visits in your control. You would not if you were to see her, suppose, that she cou'd ever supplant you, in my affections. I can not tell you anything about the fashions of the city, either of the males, or females. For myself, I wear a broad brim white hat, with a small crown, and I learn, that there is one, at the shop for Sam, of the same fashion. Do you my dear, wish a fine bonnet, or does Nannie, or does Maggy Lea? Send me measures of their little heads. Send me measures of their feet, and let me know again your No. I think it is 5. You can tell me. My Dearest, do not be fearful, of writing me too long letters. I will read them again, and again, no matter how long they may be. Every word of yours, or our children, I cherish, and treasure in my heart. Does Nannie assume, that she belongs to you, or her Grand ma? I guess, she thinks you a Mistress of authority. I have not said any thing, about adjournment because, I wish to disappoint you, in nothing. So soon as we can, rely upon it, I will be in favor of getting home.

My love to Mother, and kisses to Babies. Thy ever faithful, &
devoted husband.

Houston

[1]Houston is referring to the family's trip to Tennessee and Alabama.
[2]Houston ends one page with the word "our" and begins the next page with the word "that."
[3]Trecilla Lehr. Identified in Stewart, Banes, and Banes, 144.
[4]Caroline Davis.
[5]Houston is referring to the marriage of Vernal Lea to Caroline Davis's sister, Katherine
Davis Goodall Lea.

Senate Chambers

28th June 1848

Dearest,

While I can command time, I will write again. It is not that I
have any thing to interest you, but because I hope you may derive
some satisfaction. If you are, as I am, you must be lonesome. I assure
you that nothing can afford me half the pleasure, of finding in my
mail, your letters. I tear them open, and when they are read like Sam,
I take time to kiss them. A few nights since, I had a dream, and regret
that I can not impart it to you, or rather I regret that I can not tell it in
person. It is too long, but was not disagreeable if I could see you. I
hope ire long, to have the pleasure. I sit down at times to listen to
speeches, in the Senate, intending not to lose a word. The first thing
I know, is, that I have lost all note of it, and find that my mind has
wandered to my woodland home, and I fancy my self, enjoying some
scenes, which you have so prettily described. Sam, watching and
Nannie rocking the crib, with Sissy, and tuning her melodious notes.
Oh my Dear! It is a painful tribute, that I pay, for the little Fame,
which will attach to my name, to be absent from my home. You have
with you, our treasures, and our troubles, or rather, our cares, for we
are careful of our treasures. Day, after day, brings no agreeable variety to me. My meditation, with all matters of public concern, is almost extinct.

One subject my Love, I will speak of to you. I am now engaged in reading the Testament a second time, since we parted. Each night ire I retire to rest, I read a Chapter, and present my prayer to our Heavenly Father, for our safety, and happiness, and that our "children may be reared in the nurture, and admonition of the Lord." If I have labored until 2 oclock, it makes no difference in my duties. I perform them strictly, but I fear it is only a work of formality. It is true that it is not altogether Pharisaical, for it is in secrite that my offerings are made, nor is it that the world may bear witness [to] my actions. What I do arises from a sense of duty, to my God, and conscience, and my conscience, is so far acquitted that there was an implied assurance to you, that such would be my conduct. By bringing my Testament with me, it imparted that I would, while absent, act in my relations to you, and our family, as tho' I was at home! With such principles, and such feelings, my Love, I can have but little here, to fascinate, or charm me. Fascinated, I will not be. Charmed, I can not my Love, while absent from <u>you</u>, and our <u>little charmers</u>.

The first time for several weeks, last night I went to the Presidents reception, and there saw Miss Cobb, who mentioned to me some Poetry, which she sent me yesterday for you. She said she was sure it would gratify you to see it. She sent much love to you, and the children. I also saw Mrs Genl Pillow[1] who is a cousin of ours. She is the Niece of Cousin Hetty McEwen. She is a fine woman. I have not seen her before, for the last sixteen years. The Genl will come out with honor, and credit. He is a brave honorable man. He is smarter than all his persecutors. He has double the talent of Genl [Winfield] Scott. I am fearful my dear, that you will think, it a task for me to write you any but a "short letter." I am fearful my dearest, that I will have to write more to Sam, and less to you. He would prefer "short letters," I think, and you will not be satisfied, only with long ones. My Love, I have not less, than one hundred letters on my table unanswered. What think you of this?

Present my love to Mother, and friends. Kiss our dear, dear children.

Thy devoted Husband

Houston

[1]Sarah White (Mrs. Gideon) Pillow. Byron Sistler and Barbara Sistler, *Early Middle Tennessee Marriages* (Nashville: B. S. and Associates, 1988), vol. 1, 431.

∞

Huntsville Texas June 28th 1848

My Beloved,

Yesterday, I received quite a package from you. My joy was indescribable. I had been so often dissappointed [sic], that I had hardly courage to send to the post office, but while I was deliberating upon it, your letters were sent to me. Each day, I grow more impatient to see you. And must I endure this increasing anxiety for weeks to come! Well I will try to bow in meeknesss, to the will of him, who knoweth what is best for me. The chastening is sore, but I do not believe any affliction can come upon us, without his direction.

My love, I can not describe to you my feelings, while I read your account of our dear sister Wallace. My heart is cheered by the least hope of returning reason, and I humbly trust that the Lord will banish her night of gloom and darkness. I determined once to write to her today, but on reflection concluded as you would be at home so soon, it would be better to wait until we could consult about the language, and determine what would be the most suitable things to say to her. When you write to her again, you must tell her that I say Nannie is the very picture of her. Her eyes have the same color and expression, and she is so much like her, that I know she could not help loving her. She is the most amusing little creature I ever saw. She has none of Sam's gravity, but evidently a great deal of genius. She calls Sam "Sam Hooten," herself "Nannie Hooten" and the little one "Baby Hooten." The latter was a fancy of her own, and she seems determined to adhere to it. The baby enjoys fine health, but is not a large child. I could say a great deal about her beauty, but as she is said to be so much like me, I will leave that for you to do.

On the night before last, Col Grant[1] lost his only child, a little boy eight years old.[2] The little fellow marched with the masons on the 24th, a very warm day, took the congestive fever, and died on the night of the 26th. As the breath left him, his father exclaimed "My Last hope is gone!" His mother[3] seems to have sunk into a quiet but hopeless grief. Oh my love, how forcibly was I reminded, that we too had treasures in earthen vessels. Oh that the Lord may enable us to look upon them as loans, which we may be required to return at any time.

Our family are all in fine health, except poor Eliza,[4] and she is a pitiable object indeed. She is so disfigured with the scrofula, that you would not recognize her. I have sent her to Dr Evans, and he seems to have some hopes of curing her.

Our farming is doing well, in spite of all the disadvantages it has had. Our corn is fine, and the potatoe [sic] vines look flourishing. We had fine watermelons on the fifteenth inst. before any one in the neighborhood except Dr Evans.

My health is improving every day. I do not nurse with my right breast, but could have done so, but for my timidity, as it discharges milk freely. I was delighted with the letter from your New York friend. I admire his views on family matters. I have not yet recd a letter from our friend Mrs Woods. Have you heard from them lately? I send you the measures of the children's heads, but do not wish you to set off with any thing that may encumber you on the way. I believe I never told you yet, what an agreeable neighbor I have found in our friend Mrs Branch.[5] They moved near us, about the time of your departure, and she has been a pleasant companion for me. Indeed I have so many more friends in this place, that I hardly know which to tell you about. They seem to feel so much for me on account of your absence, that they have endeared themselves to me in a peculiar manner. Mother and Sam send thier love to you.

Thine with fondest affection
M. L. Houston

P.S.

You need not get a bonnet for me, unless you desire it particularly.

[1]George W. Grant. Identified in *1850 Census*, vol. 4, 2029.
[2]William Grant. Identified in Stewart, Banes, and Banes, 140.
[3]Mary Grant. Ibid.
[4]Margaret's slave Eliza.
[5]Mariah (Mrs. John) Branch. Identified in *1850 Census*, vol. 4, 2010.

∞

Senate Chambers
1 July 1848

My Dearest,

I had not the pleasure, as usual on thursday last, to receive a letter from you. I am fearful, that you, or some of the family are ill. I am prepared to fear the worst. My heart is pained, and I arise in the morning, unrefreshed. If it were possible, I would set off today, & fly to my little flock. Business of great importance, is pending now before us, that I can not leave. Otherwise I could obtain leave, and return to my home. I do not anticipate an hours happiness whilst, I am detained at this place. My heart, and indeed my whole mind is with you, and our children. I send you something every day to let you know that you are always present to me. Not only present every day, but many nights, and every hour. The weather here is more disagreeably warm, than in Texas. The grass is sour, and the mire, only seem verdurous and flourishing. I am fearful my Love, that you will not enjoy health, where you are now are [sic]. About a removal, I am free my Dearest, to be influenced by your wishes. I assure you, that my only wish on earth, is to promote your health, and the happiness, & prosperity of the children. To promote these, I would freely jeopard[ize] my own health. If I live to return, I am fearful you will quarrel with me. I now weigh 224 pounds. When I left home, I weighed 205. So you may say to Sam, that I will be able to nurse three <u>children</u>. I will be miserable my Love, until I can hear from you. I send to you a note from our relation.[1] She is a plain, and excellent Lady. The mother of only nine children, and the youngest is older than Sam. Houston is a clever fellow, and he with his grown family are in the Presbyterian Church. They all remind me of the old stock of Houstons. Their youngest daughter is much like our Nannie, as I think she is about the same size.

I must close my dearest, as the mail of today will soon be off, of today. My love to all

Thy devoted Husband
Sam Houston

[1]It is unclear to which relative Houston refers.

∽

Washington
2nd July 1848

My Dearest,

Altho I wrote to you, on yesterday, as I intend to set out tomorrow, at 6 A.M., I will write again, if you will be satisfied, with a short letter. I saw in New York, a "new thing under the Sun," called Gutta Percha.[1] Since my return here I have written for some to send you for Miss Maggy Lea, in place of <u>oil cloth</u>. It will absorb precisely. I send you specimens of the <u>thing</u>, for I do not know what to call it. I suppose cloth, because it will clothe, tho the clothing will be very thin. It is made from the Gum, of some tree in S. America. I will write for some like the sample, on which there is no printing. Until now I did not know, that on the composition printing could be done. If it is cheaper than paper, I presume books, and maps will be printed upon it. It is more impervious to water than India rubber, and I do hope you will find it a very useful, & pleasant, thing for Maggy Lea, for as I am sure you will not wish to rob her of it, for any peculiar fancy of your own. <u>If it were only a Box</u>, I would not say so much!!! Well to day I have sent you by my friend "honest Bob Wilson" of Houston a Box of wedding cake from our friend Auchincloss.[2] You will see all about it when it arrives. I send to you & Nannie each a Reticule, made by the Northern Indians. A likeness of Doct Chalmers,[3] is sent to you by Mr. Auchincloss. In addition to these trifles, I send to Master Sam, a Lithograph of my self.[4] All here say it looks too old for me. I think so indeed. So you see my Love, I have spun out my letter to a pretty good length. It contains many items, tho' some of much importance. This morning I was at church, & found that my favorite from indisposition could not attend, but found his place supplied by a very respectable clergyman. If Mr. Cushman does not soon recover, I intend to go, and visit him, as a friend.

My Dearest I am entirely, and devotedly thy husband. Love to all, & kiss all.

Adieu

Sam Houston

[1] A material made from the juice of a Malaysian sapotaceous tree.
[2] James Auchincloss. Identified in *Writings*, vol. 4, 499.
[3] Dr. Thomas Chalmers, a Scottish theologian and philanthropist. Winthrop S. Hudson, *Religion in America* (New York: Charles Scribner 's Sons, 1981), 312.
[4] A lithograph of Houston was made in 1848 by Davignon. Sam Houston Library and Research Center, Liberty, Texas.

∞

Senate Chambers

9th July 1848

My dearly Beloved,

This morning, at 2 oclock A.M., I arrived from old Pennsylvania, and was near the birth place of my Parents. It is a great country, and in a state of the highest cultivation. I hope, at some point, to visit it again in company with my dear Wife, and some little Houstons. I know in harvest, which is now going on, you wou'd be greatly pleased, with a trip to that delightful region.

For the last two thursdays, I have not had the happiness to receive a letter from you. What the cause is, I can not imagine, but hope my disappointment, and anxiety arises from the irregularity of the mails. If it were not for this reason, I would be most miserable. I feel very confident, that you have written regularly every Wednesday, unless you, or some of the family, were ill. This conviction renders me truly unhappy. I hope now, as the only resource, that by the next mail, that I will receive some two, or three letters, and hear from you, and our dear little ones. I have had a pretty pleasant trip, but it worried me a good deal. Besides riding in Cars, and stages for several hundred miles, I made three speeches, and Col [David] Kaufman made as many. Our speeches were extremely well received. I sustained my self quite as well as usual, & in some instances better. So soon as I can get the papers, I will send them to you. I send you by this mail, letters from our friends, Doct & Mrs Woods. You will see, that my excuses, have not been accepted. They must be accepted. I can not be at the wedding.[1] Business here will detain me, and I can not leave. I send to you your invitation, and Master Sams. I will not even break the seal, reserving for a future time, the pleasure of seeing them. I will write a pretty letter to Madam, as well as the Doctor. If you were here, I would go with you, and be happy in so doing. I hope my Dearest, that you will write a letter to Madam Woods.

Give my love to Mother, and kisses to the little ones.

Thy faithful, and ever devoted husband.

Houston

[1]Houston is referring to the wedding of Marshall Woods, the son of Dr. and Mrs. Woods.

Washington 14th July 1848

My Beloved,

Since I last wrote to you, I have been quite unwell, but now feel restored. My arm was inflamed,[1] and since my return from Carlile, I had an attack of the piles. To day they have left me, but my hand cramps so much, that is painful for me to write. I wish to get away from this place, and will at the first moment in my power. To day, the thermometer was at 82, and in a little while it was down to 73. We have to have fires, almost every day that it rains, & of late, we have frequent showers. My indisposition has been caused by changes, extreme, and sudden, as they have been. The cramp is now so bad in my hand, that I would not write, only that I can not deny myself the pleasure of writing to you. I am distressed too, at not having heard from you, since the 12th of June, and satisfied that you have written to me, unless you were too unwell to write. I have heard that the mail Boats, have been taken out of the line from Galveston to New Orleans, and are now engaged in transporting troops from Vera Cruz to New Orleans, and this I hope will account for my not receiving your letters. I, notwithstanding this hope, am truly miserable, because you and Nannie were not well, when you last wrote. I know too my Love, you were in trouble, in as much as our relations from Matagorda[2] could not come to see you, and the family. Nor could you make a trip, for the benefit of yours and the childrens health. All this is owing to my absence, and painful as it has been to you, I think it has been as distressing to me. I do pray, and hope it is the last time in life, that we will be seperated if only for a few days. I hope that Congress will adjourn by the 31st Inst. You need not write again to me at this place. You may my Love, write to me at Memphis, to the care of bro William. I intend to return by that route. I have procured for our friend Mrs Birdwell, "Drelincourt, on death."

I will write to you as often as I can. I have a young man to frank, and address my Documents. I have ordered some pretty things of dress for you, and the children.

Give my love to our Mother and kisses, to our little ones. I am thy faithful & devoted husband

Houston

[Cross-writing:] Love, on looking over letter, it is so very badly written, that I would employ an amanuensis, only that I feel assured you

would rather see it in my very own hand badly as it is written. If tomorrow is a warm day, I will try, and do better.

Thine ever

Houston

[1]Houston is probably referring to problems with his right arm in which he received a wound at the Battle of Horseshoe Bend.
[2]The Powers.

Washington

16th July 1848

My Dearest,

To day on my return from church, and from hearing one of the most interesting sermons, that I ever heard, I found on my table a large mail. As it was not the day to hear from you, or from the South, I took it up without hope, when to my most truly agreeable surprize, I found that it contained no less than two letters from you of the 22nd[1] and the 28th of June. I read the last first, and perused them both, with indescribable pleasure. I had desponded as you will see, in relation, first as to your health, and lastly as to the mail. I yet have a hope that it will not be long, when counting weeks, that we are to be seperated. Should it be longer, than we anticipated, we must bear it for the sake, of that Providence which sends it as dispensation, and for the sake of each other.

I truly regret, that Houston Moore did not call to see you. There is no possible excuse for him, for he could only have heard reports from his people, and knows well (unless Betty or Mary should do so) that not one of the family, will tell the truth. [The] poor Girls are under duress, and dare only say, what they are bid to say.

I deplore the loss of poor Grant. Him, & his poor wife must be inconsolable, in the bereavement. I hope their treasures may not alone be "contained in earthly vessels," but that their souls may be enriched, by the influence of Divine Grace! I feel grateful truly so, that the destroying Angel has not brought affliction to us, in taking away some of our little family.

I was delighted by your description of the children. I am happy to hear of Sam's gravity, and of Nannies cheerfulness. They, I can fancy something about, but as for Miss Maggy Lea, I am much at a loss. I can fancy a miniature of you, but not in the character of a "Baby Hooton." I admire Nannies taste in names. She evinces the same talent of convertibility, for which Sam, was so distinguished. I am sure you will remember, to what I allude. It was, and is my intention, that you shall have a summer dress. There is a kind of linen here which [I] designed to send by honest Bob Wilson for you, but his trunk was so full that he could only take one or two trifles, which he promised to send, or deliver safely to you, at home. I was able while he was here, to do, (as he thought) much for him. I got him out a <u>Patent</u>, which he thinks very valuable, and I hope it will prove so.

I am truly distressed at the situation of poor Eliza. I hope that she can be cured, and if not otherwise, I have no doubt but the sour lake would cure her, and if needful, or you think well of it, contrive to get some of the <u>oil</u> from the lake, & give it to her. At this distance, all that I can do, is to make suggestions. Has Col [Robert] Williamson[2] heard of the case? If not send him a description. Do Dearest, as you think best. If I find you, and Mother, and the children in health, & happy, I will not quarrel about the corn, or the Potatoes, or much else. You will find, if we live to meet, at least one thing, and that is indeed a change in my disposition, & that for the better. It may be the effect of climate, but I hope it is owing to a change in disposition, that will last as long as my life does! I am very happy dear that you expressed yourself, so <u>properly</u> about Houstons[3] not calling upon you, for I will send an extract from your letter announcing the fact of his not calling. It was all owing to <u>lies</u> (which were of some mean character,) of what you should have said about him. Any thing which would deter him from calling, lest his feelings might be wounded. This is my belief, and that they were written to him, before he went up! Not long since he wrote to me, asking my advice about what he should do, and spoke of hearing from you, and Mother, and the children. He wrote to me that you had drawn on the Torreys and how it was <u>raised</u>. I paid the $100, but I omitted mentioning it to you. It was all right, & proper. Do not let them harrass [sic] you, I pray you my Love. Their conduct, I mean that of Eliza [Moore], accounts to me, for something which took place, while my sainted Mother was on her death bed. One was, her bestowing her blessing upon me. I am fearful since Eliza treated my poor sister [Mary] as she has done, & caused me to do her injustice that poor Mother, in her last days, and hours, wished to remain no longer on earth. I pray, and beseech you, not to let them occupy your thoughts, nor add to your cares.

I will write as often as I can my Love, until we meet. I will not appoint a time, for business is not yet through, nor have we yet fixed a day for adjournment as I have before stated my Love! Give my love to mother, and to our friends. Kisses & hugs to the children.

Truly thy husband
Houston

[Cross-writing across one page:] Dearest please tell the servants that I yet hope they will all behave well. I trust pride of character will make them do right. They know how, and they ought to be ashamed, not to do well! Give them all howda.

[Cross-writing across another page:] The head measures are all safe and will be attended to and your <u>bonnet</u> certainly.

[1]This letter has not been located.
[2]Houston is referring to the fact that Williamson had been crippled by an illness. *New Handbook of Texas*, vol. 6, 992.
[3]Houston Moore.

Senate Chambers
21st July 1848

My Beloved,

I am overwhelmed with business, so as to be ready to depart, so soon as we adjourn. We meet at 11 oclk, and sometimes sit until 6 oclk P.M. I have often started to write you letters, and because I coud not write long letters, I wou'd not send them. Now I have concluded to write when I can, and as much as I can. I am now in as good health as I ever was in my life. My arm too you will see by my hand writing has recovered. It leaves me able to write at all times, when I have time! If they should be short you must be assured, that I intend to write just as much as I can. If I were to write, but seldom, the case wou'd be different. Writing as often, as I wish to do, it would be impossible, for want of materials to say any thing of interest to you! To tell you how much I love you, would appear uxorious, and you would laugh at me! I hope, if you should be disposed to rebuke me, it will be in my power to render to you, a personal apology.

My business is now so great, that I have the assistance of two young men. We are all busy, and I never retire until midnight, after having been confined in [a] hot Senate Chamber, from 5 to 7 hours. Then [in] the morning you know I will have a good excuse to rest in the morning.

I have ordered & procured for you, and the young Ladies, each, pretty Bonnets. For yourself, I have ordered a very pretty one. It has some flowers which I hope you [will] be pleased with. With Nannie's and Maggy Lea's, I am sure you will be pleased. I have ordered [for] Miss Nannie, a pretty little mantilla (very tasty). She will look like "Mother Bunch" I fancy, & I think I can see Sam's Irish face suf-fused, with the glow of pride at his little Sisters [sic] finery. Your dress too, My Love, you must make up your mind to be pleased with. I hope it will suit you. It is a kind of silk, I grant you, but it is a kind which you have not seen. It is a China blue, with a small white stripe in it.

As to the other articles, I hope to have the pleasure of exhibiting them in person. I do not wish to deceive you my Love! I must tell you that I am fearful, that we will not be able to adjourn before the 10th of August. If then, I will be most happy. You will see some difference in my hand writing, since this letter was commenced. The reason is I had to make a short speech, and my pulse has become excited.

I am pained. I am sorrowful, that I can not leave here at once, and relieve you from the cares of the farm. My Love, I want you to arouse the pride of the servants, if possible, so that they will behave, and will take care of things, until I can get home. I want them to have the fodder taken, when it is proper time. Consult with Col Birdwell and Mrs Birdwell, if Mothers advice should fail you. I did hope, when I left home, that they (the servants) would act so that I could look on them with pleasure, and treat them as a master should do! Tell them my Dearest, that I will look for all things to be in good order. Give Joshua money, to go to the Tanners, and get Dubbin, to use upon Buggy harness, and tell him to attend to the Buggy, and not let it be injured. Now pray, My Love, don't be disturbed about any thing, if you are well, & happy. You need not think that I will stay one moment longer than I can make my way home. No my Love, if I could, I would fly to embrace you this moment. I must cease, as the mail will leave the Capitol any minute. I will write soon. My love to all, and kisses to the children.

Thy ever devoted & faithful husband
Sam Houston

[In margin:] I have not had time to read over this letter.

∞

21st July 1848

My Dearest,

About three hours since I wrote you a letter, & and as I will be kept here for sometime yet, waiting upon a call of the Senate for absent members, I have by way of being agreeable to my self commenced a second letter to day. It is nearly six oclock P.M. and we may as things now seem be detained until night. If members would only attend to their duties, we could soon adjourn, and get home to our families. Well my very Dearest Love, I am doomed to endure all that absence can impose upon us. I hope my own one, that you will bring your mind to bear the delay, which is no fault of mine. Indeed if it were not that Bills are yet before the Senate, in which Texas is greatly interested, I wou'd leave here, and fly to my Dear Margaret, & the <u>children</u>. In all purpose of heart, never again to be seperated from them all at once, while we live. I am sure there is not one man in the Senate who thinks about home, as I do, or is so anxious to see his family as myself, ergo, there is no man who loves his wife & children, as much as I do!

Love to all. Hug the children for me.

Thy faithful
Sam Houston

P.S.
6 oclk
Senate adjourned for to day

Senate Chamber
22nd July 1848

My Dearest,

Altho' I wrote you two letters yesterday, I find that I have just 15 minutes to write before the mail starts. I can only say that I received from Thomas Parmer a letter, telling that <u>you</u> were all well.

This was some, nay much pleasure! I can not think, or hear of home, but what it is a pleasure to me. No one can be so purely, and devotedly feel the love of home, as I do. My first thought of morning, is my home, blended with gratitude, to my Creator, for my preservation. At noon, and at night, my heart, and my thoughts, are with <u>you</u>, & home.

My Love to Mother, and all! Kisses to the Babes. The mail is waiting. My arm, as you will see by my writing, is better than it has been for years.

Thy faithful, and devoted husband
Sam Houston

Senate Chambers
26th July 1848

My ever Dearest,

This morning I had the pleasure to hear from Charles Power in New York. He is well, and left all well at home. He wrote that he wou'd be here in a few days, to see me. Not on business I presume, that we may have the pleasure of meeting, & talking about our families. This we always do much of when we are together!

Dearest, I have sent your Bonnet, Nannie's and Maggy Lea's. They are all beautiful. Yours is of dark French lace, and the prettiest wreath around it that I have seen, and the flowers inside are superb. Nannies is a tasty blue, & Maggy Lea's is white, with a white silk rose, and is the sweetest little thing that I have ever seen. Nannies little black Jenny Lynn is black silk, or sattin [sic]. It is pretty, and will look like a Dutch womans bed gown, (as they used to be called.) Your dress I think you will like. It is pretty! There is one pair of shoes for each of the children, and red morocco boots, are ordered from [sic] Master Sam. So my Love you will see, that I can attend to these matters occasionally.

You will see that my arm has become perfectly well. I write in haste, for a speech is now making in my hearing. I have not written for two or three days, in hopes that I could write, when we wou'd adjourn. My Love, painful as it is for me to say so, I have no hopes, of getting off before the 10th of August. If it is proper, I would be willing that the servants should expect me constantly, and soon. It will make them more careful, and industrious. I only write to you my Love, because it [is my] duty to let you know it. It is to face <u>abolition</u>, that we are to stay here. You may rely, upon my hastening home without a moments delay. My love to all. Kisses to the children.

Thy ever devoted Husband
Houston

Senate Chamber
2 oclock A.M. 27th July [1848]

My Dearest,

On yesterday we met at eleven o'clock A.M., & have not since adjourned. It is the determination of the Senate not to adjourn, until the question is taken on the compromise Bill, in relation, to the organization, of the Territories of Oregon, New Mexico, and California. We have now been in session, for fifteen hours, and I would not be astonished if we sit, for three hours more. It is owing to a disposition of persons, or members to speak, out of all reason, and temper. There was an amusing scene here, a short time since. One member was speaking. The Vice President[1] was in his chair, & there was but one member in the chamber.—Well, the Senator spoke for two hours. Of course there were none present in the galleries. All the members had retired to the <u>reception</u> room of the Senate. We have had nothing to eat to day, or since breakfast. We have pure and cold ice water plenty. I write, because I hope you will be gratified to know, that I would rather write to you, than to hear Senatorial Speeches. Yes my Love, my heart is always with you. On last night, I mean the 26th, I never closed my eyes, until day was bright in my room, and not one moment passed of the night, but what you were present to my mind, & often the little "Hootons." So you see my Love, where my affections are. I need not tell you that you are their earthly Idol. I hope you will not think this declaration <u>idle</u>! I am not, my Love, trying to write love letters. No I retain all my pretty things to say in person. I can talk better, than I can write, and I am sure, I feel more, than I can ever say!

I want you to bear with my absence. I have counted, and endured every day. It is a long, sad, & painful absence. I have never seen <u>Maggy Lea</u>! You have! I pray Heaven, to grant me that joy, with you. I hope she is, your image. My love to all, & kisses to the little Hootons.

Thine ever truly
Houston

[In the margin:] I do not read this over! Excuse errors.

[1]George M. Dallas, of Pennsylvania. Identified in *Biographical Directory*, 16.

Washington
30th July 1848

My Dearest Wife,

Yesterday I wrote you a short note, with some of Sam's news papers. The last letter I wrote was at 2 oclock A.M., on the 28th. At 8 on that morning after adjourning, until the 29th we adjourned, until yesterday. You can imagine the press of business which is upon us. In the midst of these matters, I was most agreeably surprised this morning (sunday) by the arrival of my mail, before I had risen. I did not expect any letters from you until I would reach Memphis, on my way home. I ran over the address of my letters, and to my inexpressible surprise, I saw one from you. Of course it was devoured, or at least its contents.

I was rejoiced to hear of your improvement, in health, but at the same time, my heart was wrung by "the narrative," which you gave of our dear Nannies sufferings, and the danger thro which she has passed. Poor, dear little thing, I would that I could have been with her. I might have taken a share of the burden, from you! I am sorry to hear the dear, sweet babe is not well. It is some consolation, that Mother, Sam, and yourself are well. Why have you not hired a nurse? I do not my Love, care what price you give. Have one, and do not my dearest, permit yourself to be worried. I wish you to be happy, and comfortable, if earth has means, within my command, to make you so! I send Sam, at various times pictures etc. I hope he will be pleased with them, and for your dear self, I have some Books, which, I hope will please you.

Our brother Charles was here, and spent two nights, and one day with me. He left all well on the 10th, and says, our Sister, & the boy are very well. Tom's nose is very bad, and Sarah is *[blurred]*, as well as the Babe. She has weaned it, but I did not ask the cause. It may be so? To attempt to tell you of my anxiety to be with you, would be ridiculous. You can form some idea of my boundless devotion to my dear, and beloved family. I have made some arrangements to make some money, if I live to get home. Understand me my dearest, that I will not pay out <u>any</u> <u>money</u>, to secure the speculation! I will not tell you, until we meet.

I have sent for a book for you which was recommended by brother Cushman. It is entitled "A pure Christianity, the Worlds last hope!" I[t] will be here soon, and I may forward it by mail. It is now late in the evening, and at 8 P.M., I will attend Church. I am sure it is the best manner in which, I can pass the evening, of the Lords day.

If spared until Congress adjourns, my labours will be incessant. Day, and night we will be engaged. Already, I have begun to arrange my papers, and pack up! I do not desire to remain for one moment after Adjournment, but, if possible, to get off before it takes place. In the while, I will write often. I have not for a time, seen any of your friends, of the females. I told you, I think, that I had seen Miss Gayle[1] of Alabama. She is not pretty, but very genteel, & seems intelligent. She recollects you, when she was a little Girl, and is attached to you. I told her of you fondness for her mother![2] She was invited by Mrs Woods, to Marshalls[3] wedding, but did not attend, for want of a Beau. What will Sam say about Marshalls marriage? It will cause Sam some troublesome arrangements. I will write as often as I can. My love to Mother, and kisses to the children.

Thine ever devotedly
Houston

[1]Amelia Ross Gayle. For a biography see *Dictionary of American Biography*, v. 4, Part I, p. 198.
[2]Sarah Ann Haynsworth. Ibid.
[3]Marshall Woods, the son of Alva and Elvira Woods.

My Dear Wife,

There has been, and yet is, great complaint, of warm weather here. For my own part, I suffer none, and I think it is owing my excellent health at this time. I am not yet, as large, as Dixon H. Lewis, but I am fearful you will think that I am (almost) inelegant, in my personal appearance.[1] It is certainly true, that I am much larger, than you have ever seen me! You say our friend Mrs B[irdwell] is anxious that you should be quite fleshy, on my return. I assure you my Dearest, that it will be a most agreeable incident. So much so that if you shou'd weigh at least 140 lbs, or a little over that, will gratify me. If this should be the case, I have had your dress so made that it will be easily made to fit you! I intend to take a trunk with me, and one that will contain the few presents which I have for home! You need not my Love, suppose that I will encumber myself. No Dearest, I have often said, if it were possible, I [would] send myself home, by the electric Telegraph, or by an air Balloon. But this can not be done. I must take advantage, of every chance, which may be presented, to expedite my homeward trip.

I am fearful that I will not have it in my power, to reach home, earlier than I did in 1846. I hope to be home in less time, but will do my best. I will neither eat, nor sleep much, until we meet. If ever a heart glowed, with love, and hope, on earth, my own seems to realise, a double portion. I feel at times, that I must be an unpleasant companion, to those, with whom I am associated, on account of my absence of mind. Upon this subject, you have some experience, from the times of 1842 & 3, in Washington Texas. One thing is certain, if we are spared, I intend never again to visit this place without you, as my companion, & friend. I am too solitary, and my anxiety, is so boundless to see you, and the little Brood. Our little Maggy Lea, I am prepared to love exceedingly. I wish to see a baby, just like you my Love, and I fancy she does. She will be about the right age, to converse with me that Nannie was when we used to hold our little

<u>talks</u>. I am sensible, that if we live, we will have little time to prepare for our trip to this place.

I presume all the family will not come! You will want Sam, & Maggy Lea, & Mother will be for keeping Nannie. If Sam comes, he will think, that he is a member of the Senate. He thinks, whatever is his Pa's, also belongs to him. Sam wou'd cut a rare show here. He wou'd tell, I have no doubt, that "we have got Possums, in Texas." I fear my Love, Sam will be quite as great [a] braggart, as I ever was. I assure you my Dear, in this respect, I have changed more, than any one, that I have known. You will be gratified, at this statement, and that is my only reason, for alluding to the subject. This will be enough for you to read at one time!

Present my love to Mother, and kisses to Babies.

Thy devoted husband
Houston

P.S. The Senate has just risen for today, so I will seal this without reading.

---

[1]An Alabama congressman who weighed over 425 pounds. For a biography see *Dictionary of American Biography*, v. 4, Part I, p. 209–10.

☙

Senate Chamber
5th Aug 1848

My Dearest,

It is now after nine oclock at night, and we are still in session. As our time draws to a close in the session, our duties are more pressing. My anxiety increases as well as my duties. If I could but once get started, it seems to me the distance would be but short, for I feel that I would travel day, and night, until I would reach home if preserved by Providence. Oh my Love, I am indeed very miserable. Every day, I am more, and more, weary, and anxious, to see all my little flock. As one evidence of the fact, I have now some 15 or 20 invitations, to go, and speak in different places, after Congress adjourns. I either have refused, positively to attend, or have sent no answer. It does seem to me as an insult, to suppose, for one moment that I would stay [from] my family, for any earthly consideration, connected with politics. It is mortifying to me, that people do not think, that I have feelings such as I could possess, being a husband and father! I am sick, heart sick of absence, from home! My dearest Love, I am sure you will sympathize with me, and I do suppose our dear Boy will also. Little Nannie is curious to see who Pa is, for she must have forgotten me, or it is to her a dizzy dream. She thinks she remembers me well, and is, by fits anxious to see me. But the two Maggy Leas I am, if possible, most anxious to see. If I live to reach home, and you will show me this letter, I will tell you something rather funny! It is 10 oclk and we are yet in session

My love to mother, & kisses to the children!

Thy husband
Sam Houston

∞

Senate Chamber
8th Aug 1848

My Dearest

It is now past 8 oclock P.M. and we are yet in session, with a prospect of remaining for hours. Last night it was near midnight, when [we] adjourned, and all pretty much fatigued. Our duties keep pace with our anxiety, to get off, to our families! I feel that mine are very dear to me, and I find some others to some extent are like me.

After our brother Charles Power left here, he was taken sick, at Baltimore, with chills and fever. I did not know of it until he had started North, or I would have gone over to see him. Dawson told me that he had been quite ill, but when he left, he thought him recovered. I am in all our little fixings, in the way of dress, ready to set out so soon as they adjourn. Sams red boots are made, but I have [not]

seen them. The Senate has adjourned until morning. I must close
Love to all.

Thy devoted husband
Sam Houston

∞

Senate Chambers
10th Aug 1848

My Dearest,

I had to cut my last letter short, for want of time. In the hustle of business, it is not possible that I can write you any thing interesting, only that I become more, & more anxious, to get off. My labor will be intense until I can leave here. Genl Rusk has been unwell, but is at this time, on the recovery, and I hope will be able to travel by the time Congress adjourns. Each day, only brings to me, more, and more invitations to visit various parts, of the various states of the Union. I have but one answer, and that is laconic "I will not go." I would be irritated if it would do any good, or prevent invitations. I feel as tho the people intended to insult me, if it were not, that they all express, what they say, is the <u>wish</u> of the <u>people</u>, for whom they act. I tell them that I wish to see my family, as my first earthly desire of heart. I have been assured, that if I would only return thro Tennessee, they wou'd afford me, private, and most comfortable conveyance thro the state. No one can be so anxious, I fancy, as I am to see my woodland home, and my dear, dear family. I hope my dear, if this letter travels as slow, as others have done heretofore, that I will have the pleasure, to read it to you, and the urchins. I will try, and take you some Books, with which I hope you will be gratified. I will write to you every day if possible while I am here. Tell Sam that I have some pictures for him. I send him one to show him how to look, into an Egg. He will be amused, if you will explain to him, as I am sure you do every thing.

Dearest, believe me, my only one, that my heart pants to know, who will get the first kiss, and to embrace you, and our dear children. My love to all, & commend me to our dear friends.

Thy devoted & faithful husband
Sam Houston

Office of the N. York Recorder
August 10, 1848

Gen. S. Houston
Dear Sir,

In this we inclose [sic] your bill for the New York Recorder. Will you have the goodness to give it your immediate attention & forward us the amount by mail 122 Nassau St. N. Y. & oblige your *[blurred]*.

Colley & Ballave *[?]*

11th August 1848

Dearest,

I have answered this, and told them, that it was paid to Mr [James] Huckins, and the paper ordered to be stopped.

I have only time to send this scrawl. We are now engaged day, and night in this hot Chamber. From 10 A.M. to 10 P.M. with a recess of one hour and a half. My love to all.

Thine Ever
Houston

P.S. They charged from 1844 to 48 $10.00.

Senate Chamber
11th Aug 1848

My Dearest,

We are again sitting at night, and I expect we will, from appearances be found here, at midnight. You will suppose that it is some what fatigueing [sic]. If so, you will be right. If we had wasted less time, to silly declamation during the session, we might have been with our families, and more happy than any one can be here.

The evening sessions bring large audiences, and hard as we are pressed for time, there are members who wish to make display, before a wondering crowd. My Love, I am not among the number! It is scandalous to see grave Senators, thus play the fool.

Another thing is the recess at 4 ocl P.M. When they meet at half past five, after dinner, they are in some instances pretty well <u>Wined</u> and some <u>otherwise</u>, wise think that they are so smart, that they must let others know, how smart they are. Your husband is not one of <u>these</u>!

You will think, I am hard run for something to write, as I fear! I woud try, and write a love letter, were it not, that I am reserving all my fine sayings to present to your ears in person, and "suiting the action to the word," <u>squeeze</u> you most heartily.

I need not assure you, of the feverish, and settled anxiety which I feel to see all my dear Treasures! Yes, my Love, I say <u>treasures</u>, for I have none save in my woodland home.

Do you not call the Babe, "Maggy Lea" in full? I suppose you do, unless you have adopted Miss Nannie's fancy, to call her "baby Hooton." I am always fancying the contest between Sam and Nannie for my knee! Is it possible (I ask myself at times) ever to be so happy, as to be with my family, again at home, as I have been? I trust Heaven, that has been so kind to me, in times past, will grant me this dear boon. My love to all. Thy ever devoted, and faithful husband.

Houston

Congress adjourned on August 14, 1848. For a copy of the speech Houston made on that day see Writings, *vol. 5, 58–61.*

∽

Bibliography

for Volume II

Manuscript Collections:

Atascosito Historical Society Collection. Sam Houston Library and Research Center, Liberty, Texas.

Burch-Remick-Roberts Collection. Family papers of 1849 in the possession of Madge Thornall Roberts, San Antonio, Texas, but jointly owned by her, and her two sisters.

Gott-Thorne collection of papers in the possession of Tom Weldon Sneed, San Antonio, Texas.

Hearne, Madge W. Family Papers. Center for American History (formerly the Barker History Center), University of Texas, Austin, Texas.

Hearne, M. W. Madge W. Hearne Collection of family papers in the possession of Madge Thornall Roberts, San Antonio, Texas.

Hearne, Sam Houston. Collection. Center for American History (formerly the Barker History Center), University of Texas, Austin, Texas.

Houston, Margaret. Papers. Center for American History (formerly the Barker History Center), University of Texas, Austin, Texas.

Houston, Sam. Collection. Texas State Archives, Austin, Texas.

McDonald, Alexander. Papers, Verticle Files. Sam Houston Memorial Museum, Huntsville, Texas.

Woods, Alva. Papers (Mss 816). Manuscript collection of the Rhode Island Historical Society Library, Providence, Rhode Island.

Printed Sources:

1850 Census of Texas. Transcribed by V. K. Carpenter. 4 vols. Huntsville, Ark.: Century Enterprises, 1969.

Baker, De Witt Clinton. *Texas Scrapbook*. New York: A. S. Barnes. 1875. Reprint. Austin: Texas State Historical Association, 1991.

Bartlett, Irving H. *John C. Calhoun: A Biography*. New York: W. W. Norton, 1993.

[Benton, Thomas Hart.] *Thirty Years' View; or, A History of the Working of the American Government for Thirty Years, from 1820 to 1850. . . .* 2 vols. New York: D. Appleton and Company, 1854–1856. Reprint. New York: Greenwood Press, 1968.

Bergeron, Paul H. *The Presidency of James K. Polk*. Lawrence: University Press of Kansas, 1987.

Best, Hugh. *Debrett's Texas Peerage*. New York: Coward-McCann, 1983.

Bill, Alfred Hoyt. *Rehearsal for Conflict: The War with Mexico 1846–1848*. New York: Knopf, 1947. Reprint. New York: Cooper Square Publishers, 1969.

Biographical Directory of the United States Congress, 1774–1989. Washington, D. C.: United States Government Printing Office, 1989.

Bollaert, William. *William Bollaert's Texas*. Edited by W. Eugene Hollon and Ruth Lapham Butler. Norman: University of Oklahoma Press in cooperation with The Newberry Library (Chicago), 1956.

Brewer, Willis. *Alabama: Her History, Resources, War Record and Public Men, from 1540 to 1872*. Montgomery, Alabama: Barrett & Brown, 1872. Reprint. Spartanburg, S. C.: Reprint Company, 1975.

Brooks, Elizabeth. *Prominent Women of Texas*. Akron, Ohio: The Werner Company, 1896.

Christman, Margaret C. S. *1846 Portrait of the Nation*. Washington, D.C.: Smithsonian Institution Press, 1996.

Clarke, Mary Whatley. *Thomas J. Rusk: Soldier, Statesman, and Jurist*. Austin, Tex.: Jenkins Publishing Company, 1971.

Coulter, E. Merton. *Georgia: A Short History*. Rev. and enl. Chapel Hill: University of North Carolina Press, 1960.

Daughters of the Republic of Texas. *Founders and Patriots of Texas: The Lineages of the Members of the Daughters of the Republic of Texas*. 3 vols. 1963–1985

Dictionary of American Biography. Edited by Allen Johnson and Dumas Malone. 11 vols. New York: Charles Scribners & Sons, 1964.

District of Columbia Marriage Licenses Register. Compiled by Wesley Peppenger. Westminster, Md.: Family Line Publishers, 1994.

Dufour, Charles L. *The Mexican War: A Compact History, 1846–1848*. New York: Hawthorn Books, 1969.

Eisenhower, John S. D. *So Far From God: The U. S. War with Mexico 1846–1848*. New York: Random House, 1989.

Ellis, J. H. H. *Sam Houston and Related Spiritual Forces*. Houston, Tex.: Concord Press, 1945.

England, Flora D., comp. *Alabama Notes*. 4 vols. Baltimore: Genealogical Publishing, 1978.

Faulk, Odie B., and Joseph A. Stout, Jr., eds. *The Mexican War: Changing Interpretations*. Chicago: The Swallow Press, 1973.

Foreman, Grant. *The Five Civilized Tribes: Cherokee, Chickasaw, Choctaw, Creek, Seminole*. Norman: University of Oklahoma Press, 1970.

Freehling, William W. *The Road to Disunion*. Vol. 1, *Secessionists at Bay, 1776–1854*. New York: Oxford University Press, 1990.

Friend, Llerena. *Sam Houston: The Great Designer*. Austin: University of Texas Press, 1954.

Ganrud, Pauline Jones. *Marriage, Death and Legal Notices from Early Alabama Newspapers 1819–1893*. Easley, S. C.: Southern Historical Press, 1981.

Graham, Philip. *The Life and Poems of Mirabeau Bonaparte Lamar*. Chapel Hill: University of North Carolina Press, 1938.

Grammer, Norma Ruthledge. *Marriage Records of Early Texas 1824–1846*. Fort Worth: Fort Worth Genealogical Society, 1971.

Gregory, Jack and Rennard Strickland. *Sam Houston with the Cherokees, 1829–1833*. Norman: University of Oklahoma Press, 1996.

The Handbook of Texas. Edited by Walter Prescott Web, et al. 3 vols. Austin: Texas State Historical Association, 1952.

Haynes, Emma. "A History of Polk County." 1937 bound manuscript in the Daughters of the Republic of Texas Library, San Antonio, Texas.

Healy, George P. A. *Reminiscences of a Portrait Painter.* Chicago: A. C. McClurg and Company, 1894.

Hearne, William T. *A History and Genealogy of the Hearne Family*. Independence, Mo.: Examiner Printing Company, 1907.

Hogan, William Ransom. *The Texas Republic: A Social and Economic History.* Norman: University of Oklahoma Press, 1946. Reprint. Austin: University of Texas Press, 1969.

Houston, Dr. Samuel Rutherford. *Brief Biographical Accounts of Many Members of the Houston Family*. Cincinnati, Ohio: Elm Street Printing Company, 1882.

Houston, Sam Houston. *The Writings of Sam Houston, 1813–1863.* Edited by Amelia W. Williams and Eugene C. Barker. 8 vols. Austin: University of Texas Press, 1938–43.

Hudson, Winthrop S. *Religion in America: An Historical Account of the Development of American Religious Life*. 3rd ed. New York: Charles Scribner's Sons, 1981.

James, Marquis. *The Life of Andrew Jackson.* 2 vols. 1933, 1937. Reprint (2 vols. in 1). New York: Bobbs & Merrill, 1938.

_____. *The Raven: A Biography of Sam Houston.* Indianapolis: Bobbs-Merrill Company, 1929.

Klein, Philip Shriver. *President James Buchanan: A Biography*. University Park, Penn.: Pennsylvania State University Press, 1989.

Lee, Rebecca Smith. *Mary Austin Holley*. Elma Dill Russell Spencer Foundation Series, no. 2. Austin: University of Texas Press, 1962.

Lucas, Silas Emmet, Jr., ed. *Obituaries from Early Tennessee Newspapers, 1794–1851*. Easley, S.C.: Southern Historical Press, 1978.

McLaughlin, Andrew C. *Lewis Cass*. New York: Houghton, Mifflin, 1898.

Montgomery, Robin. *The History of Montgomery County*. Austin, Tex.: Jenkins Publishing Company, 1975.

Morrison, Chaplain W. *Democratic Politics and Sectionalism: The Wilmot Proviso Controversy*. Chapel Hill: University of North Carolina Press, 1967.

Murrie, Pauline. *Early Records of Nacogdoches County, Texas*. Waco, 1965.

Nevin, David. *The Mexican War*. Alexandria, Virg.: Time-Life Books, 1978.

The New Handbook of Texas. Edited by Ron Tyler, et al. 6 vols. Austin: The Texas State Historical Association, 1996.

Nixon, Pat Ireland. *The Medical Story of Early Texas, 1528–1853*. San Antonio, Tex.: Mollie Bennett Lupe Memorial Fund, 1946.

O'Brien, Robert and Harold H. Martin, eds. *The Encyclopedia of the South*. New York: Facts on File, 1985.

Owen, Thomas McAdory. *History of Alabama and Dictionary of Alabama Biography*. 4 vols. Chicago: The S. J. Clarke Publishing Company, 1921.

Partlow, Miriam. *Liberty County and the Atascocito District*. Austin: Jenkins Publishing Company, 1974.

Paxton, W. M. *The Paxtons: We Are One!* Platte City, Mo.: Landmark Print, 1903.

Pickrell, Annie Doom. *Pioneer Women in Texas*. Austin: E. L. Steck, 1929. Reprint. Austin, Tx.: State House Press, 1991.

Polk, James K. *The Diary of James K. Polk during His Presidency, 1845–1849*. Edited by M. M. Quaife. Chicago: A. C. McClurg, 1910.

_____. *Polk: The Diary of a President 1845–1849, Covering the Mexican War, the Acquisition of Oregon, and the Conquest of Caifornia and the Southwest*. Edited by Allan Nevins. New York: Longmans, Green and Company, 1929.

Prather, Patricia Smith and Jane Clements Monday. *From Slave to Statesman*. Denton: University of North Texas Press, 1993.

Ray, Worth. *Tennessee Cousins*. Baltimore: Genealogical Publishing Company, 1994.

Remini, Robert V. *Andrew Jackson and the Course of American Freedom, 1822–1832*. New York: Harper & Row Publishers, 1977.

Republic of Texas Poll Lists for 1846. Compiled by Marion Day Mullins. Baltimore: Genealogical Publishing Company, 1982.

Roberts, Madge Thornall. *Star of Destiny: The Private Life of Sam and Margaret Houston*. Denton: University of North Texas Press, 1993.

Rose, Ben L. & Margaret M. Marty. *The Lea Ancestry of Margaret Lea, Wife of Gen. Sam Houston*. Richmond, Virg.: Printing Services, 1986.

Scharf, J. Thomas. *History of Baltimore City and County*. Philadelphia: Louis H. Everts, 1881.

Seale, William. *Sam Houston's Wife: A Biography of Margaret Lea Houston*. Norman: University of Oklahoma Press, 1970.

Shinn, Josiah H. *Pioneers and Makers of Arkansas*. Little Rock, 1908. Reprint. Baltimore: Genealogical Publishing Company, 1967.

Silverthorne, Elizabeth. *Ashbel Smith of Texas: Pioneer, Patriot, Statesman, 1805–1886*. College Station: Texas A&M University Press, 1982.

Sistler, Byron, and Barbara Sistler. *Early Middle Tennessee Marriages*. 2 vols. Nashville, Tenn.: B. S. & Associates, 1988.

Spurlin, Charles D., comp. *Texas Veterans in the Mexican War: Muster Rolls of Texas Military Units*. St. Louis: Ingmire Publications, 1984.

Stewart, Lucy Alice Bruce, Verna Baker Banes, and Anthony V. Banes, comps. *Walker County Cemetery Records*. Huntsville, Tex.: Walker County, Texas, Genealogical Society, 1992.

Swenson, Helen Smothers. *8800 Texas Marriages, 1823–1850*. 2 vols. St. Louis, Mo.: Frances Terry Ingmire, 1981.

Thompson, Karen, ed. *Defenders of the Republic of Texas*. Austin, Tx.: Laurel House Press, 1989.

Tolbert, Frank X. *An Informal History of Texas from Cabeza de Vaca to Temple Houston.* New York: Harper & Brothers Publishers, 1961.

Vick-Rainey, Mary E. *Marriage Records of Walker County.* Huntsville, Tex.: Walker County Genealogical Society, 1978.

Walker County Genealogical Society. *Walker County History.* Dallas: Curtis Media Corporation, 1986.

Wallis, Johnnie Lockhart. *Sixty Years on the Brazos.* Austin, Tx.: Texian Press, 1967.

White, Gifford. *The First Settlers of Galveston County, Texas.* Nacogdoches, Tex.: Ericsons Books, 1985.

Wilson, Mabel Ponder, Dorothy Youngblood Woodyerd, and Rosa Lee Busby, comps. *Some Early Alabama Churches (Established before 1870).* Birmingham: Alabama Society of the Daughter of the American Revolution, 1973.

Wisehart, Marion K. *Sam Houston: American Giant.* Washington, D. C.: Robert B. Luce, 1962.

Index
to Volume II

finance bill, 212, 216, 217, 218

Fisher, John D., 18, 19

Fitzpatrick, Benjamin, 136

Fosgate, Walter, 79

Fremont, John Charles, 30

Gaines, Edmund P., 98–99, 108, 199, 248

Gaines, James, 237–38

Gaines, Myra Whitney (Mrs. E. P.), 174, 199, 248

Galveston, Texas, 52, 132, 159, 286

Gantier (Peter) family, 167

Gayle, Amelia, 366

Gelespey, Elizabeth, 251

Gibbs, Sanford and Thomas, 39n

Goodall, Ann Eliza (Missy), 169, 192

Goree, Miss, 135

Graham, Daniel, 320, and Maria (McIver), 320

Graham, Jane L. Watson, 170, 174, 192, 216, 255, 256, 278, 347

Grant, George W., 351, 357

Grant, Mary, 351, 352n

Grant, William, 351, 352n

Gray, Pleasant, 255, 257

Green, Thomas Jefferson, 47, 48n

Grosbeck, John D., 93

Hadley, Joyce V. McGuffin (Mrs. Joshua), 255

Hadley, Piety Smith, 256n

Hamilton, Narcissa B., 255, 256n

Hannay, Robert, 65

Hannegan, Edward A., 205n

Hatch, Frank, 335

Hatch, Katherine, 273

Hatfield, B. F., 293

Haywood, William H. Jr., 151

Healey, George P. H., 54, 57

Hearne, Ebenezer, 243n

Hearne, William C., 242, 243n

Hemphill, Judge, 131

Henderson, James Pinckney, 52, 117

Hoffman, Kitty, 17, 252; education of, 21, 32, 49, 56, 66, 107

Holliman, Howell, 159, 163, 171

Hopkins, John, 296

Hotchkiss, Mrs. R., 161

Houston, Claude, 18, 20n

Houston, Eugene, 18, 20n

Houston, George S., 214

Houston, John (Jack), 87, 88n, 245, 269, 283

Houston, Margaret,
   descriptions of home & plantation
   life, 16, 61, 83, 106, 250, 274, 280,
   284, 298, 319, 334, 341; estrangement from Moores, 164, 228, 252,
   284; health, 26, 83, 163–64, 186,
   191, 250–51, 259, 262, 272, 279,
   318, 334–35, 337; loneliness, 16–17,
   61, 192, 298, 350; on religion, 81,
   116, 191–92, 194–95, 323, 332; on
   Sam's possible army commission,
   118–19, 129–30, 210; operation for
   tumor, 163–64, 210, 222; pregnan-
   cies, 13, 43, 68, 106, 242, 264, 276,
   302, 305, 308; relationship with